50th Annual Meeting of the Association for Computational Linguistics 2012 (ACL 2012)

System Demonstrations

Jeju Island, Korea
8-14 July 2012

ISBN: 978-1-62276-275-0

Printed from e-media with permission by:

Curran Associates, Inc.
57 Morehouse Lane
Red Hook, NY 12571

Some format issues inherent in the e-media version may also appear in this print version.

Printed by Curran Associates, Inc. (2012)

For permission requests, please contact the Association for Computational Linguistics at the address below.

Association for Computational Linguistics
209 N. Eighth Street
Stroudsburg, Pennsylvania 18360

Phone: 1-570-476-8006
Fax: 1-570-476-0860

acl@aclweb.org

Additional copies of this publication are available from:

Curran Associates, Inc.
57 Morehouse Lane
Red Hook, NY 12571 USA
Phone: 845-758-0400
Fax: 845-758-2634
Email: curran@proceedings.com
Web: www.proceedings.com

Preface

Welcome to the proceedings of the system demonstration session. This volume contains the papers of the system demonstrations presented at the 50th Annual Meeting of the Association for Computational Linguistics, held in Jeju, Republic of Korea, on July 10, 2012.

The system demonstrations program offers the presentation of early research prototypes as well as interesting mature systems. The system demonstration chair and the members of the program committee received 49 submissions, 29 of which were selected for inclusion in the program after review by three members of the program committee.

I would like to thank the members of the program committee for their excellent job in reviewing the submissions and providing their support for the final decision.

Chair:

Min Zhang (Institute for Infocomm Research, Singapore)

Program Committee:

Ai Ti Aw (Institute for Infocomm Research, Singapore)
Kalika Bali (Microsoft Research India, India)
Rafael Banchs (Institute for Infocomm Research, Singapore)
Sivaji Bandyopadhyay (Jadavpur University, India)
Francis Bond (NTU, Singapore)
Monojit Choudhury (Microsoft Research India, India)
Eng Siong Chng (NTU, Singapore)
Ido Dagan (Bar Ilan University, Israel)
Xiangyu Duan (Institute for Infocomm Research, Singapore)
George Foster (IIT, NRC, Canada)
Guohong Fu (Heilongjiang University, China)
Sarvnaz Karimi (The University of Melbourne, Australia)
Mitesh Khapra (Indian Institute of Technology Bombay, India)
Su Nam Kim (Monash University, Australia)
A Kumaran (Microsoft Research India, India)
Sadao Kurohashi (Kyoto University, Japan)
Olivia Kwong (City University of Hong Kong, China)
Mu Li (Microsoft Research Asia, China)
Ziheng Lin (NUS, Singapore)
Qun Liu (ICT, CAS, China)
R. Costa-jussà Marta (Barcelona Media, Spain)
Alessandro Moschitti (Trento University, Italy)
Jong-Hoon Oh (NICT, Japan)
Long Qiu (Institute for Infocomm Research, Singapore)
Yan Qu (ShareThis Inc., USA)
Xiaodong Shi (Xiamen University, China)
Maosong Sun (Tsinghua University, China)
Jun Sun (NUS, Singapore)
Le Sun (IS, CAS, China)
Chew Lim Tan (NUS, Singapore)
Raghavendra Udupa (Microsoft Research India, India)
yunqing xia (Tsinghua University, China)
Deyi Xiong (Institute for Infocomm Research, Singapore)
Myun Yang (Harbin Institute of Technology, China)
Tiejun Zhao (Harbin Institute of Technology, China)
Changle Zhou (Xiamen University, China)
GuoDong Zhou (Suzhou University, China)

Chengqing Zong (IA, CAS, China)

Table of Contents

This page intentionally left blank.

Conference Program

July 10, 2012

10:30-16:00 Session 1

Applications of GPC Rules and Character Structures in Games for Learning Chinese Characters
Wei-Jie Huang, Chia-Ru Chou, Yu-Lin Tzeng, Chia-Ying Lee and Chao-Lin Liu

Specifying Viewpoint and Information Need with Affective Metaphors: A System Demonstration of the Metaphor-Magnet Web App/Service
Tony Veale and Guofu Li

QuickView: NLP-based Tweet Search
Xiaohua LIU, Furu WEI, Ming ZHOU and QuickView Team Microsoft

NiuTrans: An Open Source Toolkit for Phrase-based and Syntax-based Machine Translation
Tong Xiao, Jingbo Zhu, Hao Zhang and Qiang Li

langid.py: An Off-the-shelf Language Identification Tool
Marco Lui and Timothy Baldwin

Personalized Normalization for a Multilingual Chat System
Ai Ti Aw and Lian Hau Lee

IRIS: a Chat-oriented Dialogue System based on the Vector Space Model
Rafael E. Banchs and Haizhou Li

LetsMT!: Cloud-Based Platform for Do-It-Yourself Machine Translation
Andrejs Vasiļjevs, Raivis Skadiņš and Jörg Tiedemann

A Web-based Evaluation Framework for Spatial Instruction-Giving Systems
Srinivasan Janarthanam, Oliver Lemon and Xingkun Liu

DOMCAT: A Bilingual Concordancer for Domain-Specific Computer Assisted Translation
Ming-Hong Bai, Yu-Ming Hsieh, Keh-Jiann Chen and Jason S. Chang

The OpenGrm open-source finite-state grammar software libraries
Brian Roark, Richard Sproat, Cyril Allauzen, Michael Riley, Jeffrey Sorensen and Terry Tai

Multilingual WSD with Just a Few Lines of Code: the BabelNet API
Roberto Navigli and Simone Paolo Ponzetto

July 10, 2012 (continued)

July 10, 2012 (continued)

10:30-16:00 Session 1

Applications of GPC Rules and Character Structures in Games for Learning Chinese Characters

[§]Wei-Jie Huang [†]Chia-Ru Chou [‡]Yu-Lin Tzeng [‡]Chia-Ying Lee [†]Chao-Lin Liu
[†§]National Chengchi University, Taiwan [‡†‡]Academia Sinica, Taiwan
[†]chaolin@nccu.edu.tw, [‡]chiaying@gate.sinica.edu.tw

Abstract

We demonstrate applications of psycholinguistic and sublexical information for learning Chinese characters. The knowledge about the grapheme-phoneme conversion (GPC) rules of languages has been shown to be highly correlated to the ability of reading alphabetic languages and Chinese. We build and will demo a game platform for strengthening the association of phonological components in Chinese characters with the pronunciations of the characters. Results of a preliminary evaluation of our games indicated significant improvement in learners' response times in Chinese naming tasks. In addition, we construct a Web-based open system for teachers to prepare their own games to best meet their teaching goals. Techniques for decomposing Chinese characters and for comparing the similarity between Chinese characters were employed to recommend lists of Chinese characters for authoring the games. Evaluation of the authoring environment with 20 subjects showed that our system made the authoring of games more effective and efficient.

1 Introduction

Learning to read and write Chinese characters is a challenging task for learners of Chinese. To read everyday news articles, one needs to learn thousands of Chinese characters. The official agents in Taiwan and China, respectively, chose 5401 and 3755 characters as important basic characters in national standards. Consequently, the general public has gained the impression that it is not easy to read Chinese articles, because each of these thousands of characters is written in different ways.

Teachers adopt various strategies to help learners to memorize Chinese characters. An instructor at the University of Michigan made up stories based on decomposed characters to help students remember their formations (Tao, 2007). Some take linguistics-based approaches. Pictogram is a major formation of Chinese characters, and radicals carry partial semantic information about Chinese characters. Hence, one may use radicals as hints to link the meanings and writings of Chinese characters. For instance, "河"(he2, river) [Note: Chinese characters will be followed by their pronunciations, denoted in Hanyu pinyin, and, when necessary, an English translation.], "海"(hai3, sea), and "洋"(yang2, ocean) are related to huge water systems, so they share the semantic radical, 氵, which is a pictogram for "water" in Chinese. Applying the concepts of pictograms, researchers designed games, e.g., (Lan et al., 2009) and animations, e.g., (Lu, 2011) for learning Chinese characters.

The aforementioned approaches and designs mainly employ visual stimuli in activities. We report exploration of using the combination of audio and visual stimuli. In addition to pictograms, more than 80% of Chinese characters are phono-semantic characters (**PSCs**, henceforth) (Ho and Bryant, 1997). A PSC consists of a phonological component (**PC**, henceforth) and a semantic component. Typically, the semantic components are the radicals of PSCs. For instance, "讀"(du2), "瀆"(du2), "犢" (du2), "牘"(du2) contain different radicals, but they share the same phonological components, "賣"(mai4), on their right sides. Due to the shared PC, these four characters are pronounced in exactly the same way. If a learner can learn and apply this rule, one may guess and read "黷"(du2) correctly easily.

In the above example, "賣" is a normal Chinese character, but not all Chinese PCs are standalone characters. The characters "檢"(jian3), "撿" (jian3), and "儉"(jian3) share their PCs on their right sides, but that PC is not a standalone Chinese character. In addition, when a PC is a standalone character, it might not indicate its own or similar pronunciation when it serves as a PC in the hosting character, e.g., "賣" and "讀" are pronounced as /mai4/ and /du2/, respectively. In contrast, the pronunciations of "匋", "淘", "陶", and "啕" are /tao2/.

Pronunciations of specific substrings in words of alphabetic languages are governed by grapheme-phoneme conversion (GPC) rules, though not all languages have very strict GPC rules. The GPC rules in English are not as strict as those in Finish

Proceedings of the 50th Annual Meeting of the Association for Computational Linguistics, pages 1–6,
Jeju, Republic of Korea, 8-14 July 2012. ©2012 Association for Computational Linguistics

(Ziegler and Goswami, 2005), for instance. The substring "ean" are pronounced consistently in "bean", "clean", and "dean," but the substring "ch" does not have a consistent pronunciation in "school", "chase", and "machine." PCs in Chinese do not follow strict GPC rules either, but they remain to be good agents for learning to read.

Despite the differences among phoneme systems and among the degrees of strictness of the GPC rules in different languages, ample psycholinguistic evidences have shown that phonological awareness is a crucial factor in predicting students' reading ability, e.g., (Siok and Fletcher, 2001). Moreover, the ability to detect and apply phonological consistency in GPCs, including the roles of PCs in PSCs in Chinese, plays an instrumental role in learners' competence in reading Chinese. Phonological consistency is an important concept for learners of various alphabetic languages (Jared et al., 1990; Ziegler and Goswami, 2005) and of Chinese, e.g., (Lee et al., 2005), and is important for both young readers (Ho and Bryant, 1997; Lee, 2009) and adult readers (Lin and Collins, 2012).

This demonstration is unique on two aspects: (1) students play games that are designed to strengthen the association between Chinese PCs and the pronunciations of hosting characters and (2) teachers compile the games with tools that are supported by sublexical information in Chinese. The games aim at implicitly informing players of the Chinese GPC rules, mimicking the process of how infants would apply statistical learning (Saffran et al., 1996). We evaluated the effectiveness of the game platform with 116 students between grade 1 and grade 6 in Taiwan, and found that the students made progress in the Chinese naming tasks.

As we will show, it is not trivial to author games for learning a GPC rule to meet individualized teaching goals. For this reason, techniques reported in a previous ACL conference for decomposing and comparing Chinese characters were employed to assist the preparation of games (Liu et al., 2011). Results of our evaluation showed that the authoring tool facilitates the authoring process, improving both efficiency and effectiveness.

We describe the learning games in Section 2, and report the evaluation results of the games in Section 3. The authoring tool is presented in Section 4, and its evaluation is discussed in Section 5. We provide some concluding remarks in Section 6.

2 The Learning Games

A game platform should include several functional components such as the management of players' accounts and the maintenance of players' learning profiles. Yet, due to the page limits, we focus on the parts that are most relevant to the demonstration.

Figure 1. The learning game

Figure 1 shows a screenshot when a player is playing the game. This is a game of "whac-a-mole" style. The ***target PC*** appears in the upper middle of the window ("里"(li3) in this example), and a character and an accompanying monster (one at a time) will pop up randomly from any of the six holes on the ground. The player will hear the pronunciation of the character (i.e., "裡"(li3)), such that the player receives both audio and visual stimuli during a game. Players' task is to hit the monsters for the characters that contain the shown PC. The box at the upper left corner shows the current credit (i.e., 3120) of the player. The player's credit will be increased or decreased if s/he hits a correct or an incorrect character, respectively. If the player does not hit, the credit will remain the same. Players are ranked, in the Hall of Fame, according to their total credits to provide an incentive for them to play the game after school.

In Figure 1, the player has to hit the monster before the monster disappears to get the credit. If the player does not act in time, the credit will not change.

On ordinary computers, the player manipulates the mouse to hit the monster. On multi-touch tablet computers, the play can just touch the monsters with fingers. Both systems will be demoed.

2.1 Challenging Levels

At the time of logging into the game, players can choose two parameters: (1) class level: lower class (i.e., grades 1 and 2), middle class (i.e., grades 3 and 4), or upper class (i.e., grades 5 and 6) and (2) speed level: the duration between the monsters' popping up and going down. The characters for lower, middle, and upper classes vary in terms of frequency and complexity of the characters. A student can choose the upper class only if s/he is in the upper class or if s/he has gathered sufficient credits. There are three different speeds for the monsters to appear and hide: 2, 3, and 5 seconds. Choosing different combinations of these two pa-

	Lower	Middle	Upper
5	10	20	30
3	15	25	35
2	20	30	40

Table 1.Credits for challenging levels

rameters affect how the credits are added or deducted when the players hit the monsters correctly or incorrectly, respectively. Table 1 shows the increments of credits for different settings. The numbers on the leftmost column are speed levels.

2.2 Feedback Information

After finishing a game, the player receives feedback about the correct and incorrect actions that were taken during the game. Figure 2 shows such an example.

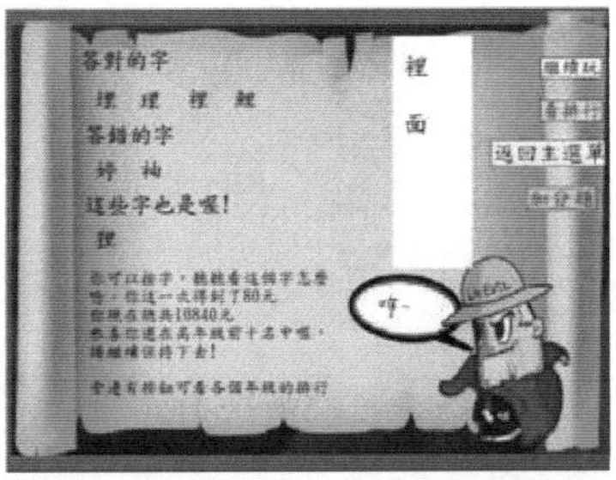

Figure 2. Feedback information

The feedback informs the players what characters were correctly hit ("埋"(mai2), "理"(li3), "裡"(li3), and "鯉"(li3)), incorrectly hit ("婷"(ting2) and "袖"(show4)), and should have been hit ("狸"(li2)). When the player moves mouse over these characters, a sample Chinese word that shows how the character is used in daily lives will show up in a vertical box near the middle (i.e., "裡面"(li3 mian4)).

The main purpose of providing the feedback information is to allow players a chance to reflect on what s/he had done during the game, thereby strengthening the learning effects.

On the upper right hand side of Figure 2 are four tabs for more functions. Clicking on the top tab (繼續玩) will take the player to the next game. In the next game, the focus will switch to a different PC. The selection of the next PC is random in the current system, but we plan to make the switching from a game to another adaptive to the students' performance in future systems. Clicking on the second tab (看排行) will see the player list in the Hall of Fame, clicking on the third tab (返回主選單) will return to the main menu, and clicking on the fourth (加分題) will lead to games for extra credits. We have extended our games to lead students to learning Chinese words from characters, and details will be illustrated during the demo.

2.3 Behind the Scene

	Lower	Middle	Upper
Experimental	11	23	24
Control	11	23	24

Table 2. Number of participants

The data structure of a game is simple. When compiling a game, a teacher selects the PC for the game, and prepares six characters that contain the PC (to be referred as an **In-list** henceforth) and four characters as distracter characters that do not contain the PC (to be referred as an **Out-list** henceforth). The simplest internal form of a game looks like {target PC= "里", In-list= "裡理鯉浬哩鋰", Out-list= "塊鰓嘿鉀" }. We can convert this structure into a game easily. Through this simple structure, teachers choose the PCs to teach with character combinations of different challenging levels.

During the process of playing, our system randomly selects one character from the list of 10 characters. In a game, 10 characters will be presented to the player.

3 Preliminary Evaluation and Analysis

The game platform was evaluated with 116 students, and was found to shorten students' response times in Chinese naming tasks.

3.1 Procedure and Participants

The evaluation was conducted at an elementary school in Taipei, Taiwan, during the winter break between late January and the end of February 2011. The lunar new year of 2011 happened to be within this period.

Students were divided into an experimental group and a control group. We taught students of the experimental group and showed them how to play the games in class hours before the break began. The experimental group had one month of time to play the games, but there were no rules asking the participants how much time they must spend on the games. Instead, they were told that they would be rewarded if they were ranked high in the Hall of Fame. Table 2 shows the numbers of participants and their actual class levels.

As we explained in Section 2.1, a player could choose the class level before the game begins. Hence, for example, it is possible for a lower class player to play the games designed for middle or even upper class levels to increase their credits faster. However, if the player is not competent, the credits may be deducted faster as well. In the evaluation, 20 PCs were used in the games for each class level in Table 1.

Pretests and posttests were administered with the standardized (1) Chinese Character Recognition

Control Group				
	Class	Pretests	Posttests	p-value
CCRT (charac-ters)	Lower	59	61	.292
	Middle	80	83	.186
	Upper	117	120	.268
RAN Correct Rate	Lower	83%	79%	.341
	Middle	59%	64%	.107
	Upper	89%	89%	1.00
RAN Speed (second)	Lower	23.1	20.6	.149
	Middle	24.3	20.2	.131
	Upper	15.7	14.1	**.026**

Table 3. Results for control group

Experimental Group				
	Class	Pretests	Posttests	p-value
CCRT (charac-ters)	Lower	64	61	.226
	Middle	91	104	**.001**
	Upper	122	124	.52
RAN Correct Rate	Lower	73%	76%	.574
	Middle	70%	75%	.171
	Upper	89%	91%	.279
RAN Speed (second)	Lower	21.5	16.9	**.012**
	Middle	24.6	19.0	**.001**
	Upper	16.9	14.7	**<0.001**

Table 4. Results for experimental group

Test (CCRT) and (2) Rapid Automatized Naming Task (RAN). In CCRT, participants needed to write the pronunciations in Jhuyin, which is a phonetic system used in Taiwan, for 200 Chinese characters. The number of correctly written Jhuyins for the characters was recorded. In RAN, participants read 20 Chinese characters as fast as they could, and their speeds and accuracies were recorded.

3.2 Results and Analysis

Table 3 shows the statistics for the control group. After the one month evaluation period, the performance of the control group did not change significantly, except participants in the upper class. This subgroup improved their speeds in RAN. (Statistically significant numbers are highlighted.)

Table 4 shows the statistics for the experimental group. After the evaluation period, the speeds in RAN of all class levels improved significantly.

The correct rates in RAN of the control group did not improve or fall, though not statistically significant. In contrast, the correct rates in RAN of the experimental group improved, but the improvement was not statistically significant either.

The statistics for the CCRT tests were not statistically significant. The only exception is that the middle class in the experimental group achieved better CCRT results. We were disappointed in the falling of the performance in CCRT of the lower class, though the change was not significant. The lower class students were very young, so we conjectured that it was harder for them to remember the writing of Jhuyin symbols after the winter break. Hence, after the evaluation, we strengthened the feedback by adding Jhuyin information. In Figure 2, the Jhuyin information is now added beside the sample Chinese words, i.e., "裡面" (li3 mian4).

4 An Open Authoring Tool for the Games

Our game platform has attracted the attention of teachers of several elementary schools. To meet the teaching goals of teacher in different areas, we have to allow the teachers to compile their own games for their needs.

The data structure for a game, as we explained in Section 2.3, is not complex. A teacher needs to determine the PC to be taught first, then s/he must choose an In-list and an Out-list. In the current implementation, we choose to have six characters in the In-list and four characters in the Out-list. We allow repeated characters when the qualified characters are not enough.

This authoring process is far less trivial as it might seem to be. In a previous evaluation, even native speakers of Chinese found it challenging to list many qualified characters out of the sky. Because PCs are not radicals, ordinary dictionaries would not help very much. For instance, "埋" (mai2), "狸"(li2), "裡"(li3), and "鯉"(li3) belong to different radicals and have different pronunciations, so there is no simple way to find them at just one place.

Identifying characters for the In-list of a PC is not easy, and finding the characters for the Out-list is even more challenging. In Figure 1, "里" (li3) is the PC to teach in the game. Without considering the characters in In-list for the game, we might believe that "甲" (jia3) and "呈" (cheng2) look equally similar to "里", so both are good distracters. If, assuming that "理"(li3) is in the In-list, "玾" (jia3) will be a better distracter than "埕" (cheng2) for the Out-list, because "玾" and "理" are more similar in appearance. By contrast, if we have "裡" in the In-list, we may prefer to having "程" (cheng2) than having "玾" in the Out-list.

Namely, given a PC to teach and a selected In-list, the "quality" of the Out-list is dependent on the characters in In-list. Out-lists of high quality influence the challenging levels of the games, and will become a crucial ingredient when we make the games adaptive to players' competence.

4.1 PC Selection

In a realistic teaching situation, a teacher will be teaching new characters and would like to provide students games that are related to the structures of the new characters. Hence, it is most convenient for the teachers that our tool decomposes a given character and recommends the PC in the character. For instance, given "理", we show the teacher that we could compile a game for "里". This is achievable using the techniques that we illustrate in the next subsection.

4.2 Character Recommendation

Given a selected PC, a teacher has to prepare the In-list and Out-list for the game. Extending the techniques we reported in (Liu et al., 2011), we decompose every Chinese character into a sequence of detailed Cangjie codes, which allows us to infer the PC contained in a character and to infer the similarity between two Chinese characters.

For instance, the internal codes for "里", "理", "裡", and "玾" are, respectively, "WG", "MGWG", "LWG", and "MGWL". The English letters denote the basic elements of Chinese characters. For instance, "WG" stands for "田土", which are the upper and the lower parts of "里", "WL" stands for "田中", which could be used to rebuild "甲" in a sense. By comparing the internal codes of Chinese characters, it is possible to find that (1) "理" and "裡" include "里" and that (2) "理" and "玾" are visually similar based on the overlapping codes.

For the example problem that we showed in Figures 1 and 2, we may apply an extended procedure of (Liu et al., 2011) to find an In-list for "里": "鋰裡浬狸埋理娌哩俚". This list includes more characters than most native speakers can produce for "里" within a short period. Similar to what we reported previously, it is not easy to find a perfect list of characters. More specifically, it was relatively easy to achieve high recall rates, but the precision rates varied among different PCs. However, with a good scoring function to rank the characters, it is not hard to achieve quality recommendations by placing the characters that actually contain the target PCs on top of the recommendation.

Given that "里" is the target PC and the above In-list, we can recommend characters that look like the correct characters, e.g., "鈿鉀鍾" for "鋰", "裸袖嘿" for "裡", "湮潼渭" for "浬", "狎猥狠狙" for "狸", and "黑墨" for "里".

We employed similar techniques to recommend characters for In-lists and Out-lists. The database that contains information about the decomposed Chinese characters was the same, but we utilized different object functions in selecting and ranking the characters. We considered all elements in a character to recommend characters for In-lists, but focused on the inclusion of target PCs in the decomposed characters to recommend characters for Out-lists. Again our recommendations for the Out-lists were not perfect, and different ranking functions affect the perceived usefulness of the authoring tools.

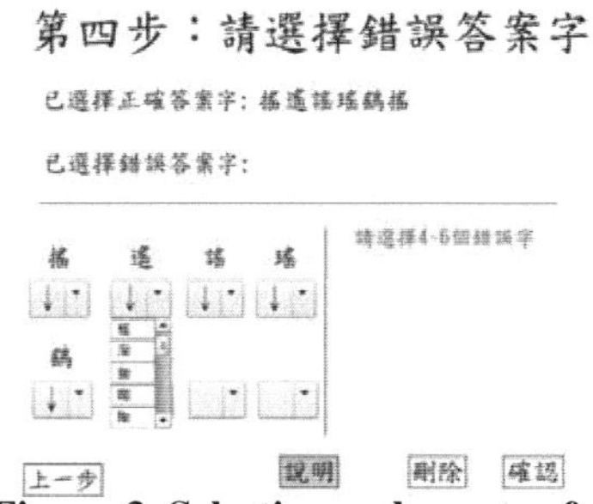

Figure 3. Selecting a character for an Out-list

Figure 3 shows the step to choose characters in the Out-list for characters in the In-list. In this example, six characters for the In-list for the PC "䍃" had been chosen, and were listed near the top: "搖遙謠瑤鷂搖". Teachers can find characters that are similar to these six correct characters in separate pull-down lists. The screenshot shows the operation to choose a character that is similar to "遙" (yao2) from the pull-down list. The selected character would be added into the Out-list.

4.3 Game Management

We allow teachers to apply for accounts and prepare the games based on their own teaching goals. However, we cannot describe this management subsystem for page limits.

5 Evaluation of the Authoring Tool

We evaluated how well our tools can help teachers with 20 native speakers.

5.1 Participants and Procedure

We recruited 20 native speakers of Chinese: nine of them are undergraduates, and the rest are graduate students. Eight are studying some engineering fields, and the rest are in liberal arts or business.

The subjects were equally split into two groups. The control group used only paper and pens to author the games, and the experimental group would use our authoring tools. We informed and showed the experimental group how to use our tool, and members of the experimental group must follow an illustration to create a sample game before the evaluation began.

Every subject must author 5 games, each for a

	Avg. scores (In-list and Out-list)	Avg. time
Control	16.8	15 min
Experimental	52.8	7.1 min
p-value	< 0.0001	< 0.0001

Table 5. Improved effectiveness and efficiency

	Avg. scores	
	In-list	Out-list
Control	15.9	1
Experimental	29.9	22.9

Table 6. Detailed scores for the average scores

different PC. A game needed 6 characters in the In-list and 4 characters in the Out-list. Every evaluator had up to 15 minutes to finish all tasks.

The games authored by the evaluators were judged by psycholinguists who have experience in teaching. The highest possible scores for the In-list and the Out-list were both 30 for a game.

5.2 Gains in Efficiency and Effectiveness

Table 5 shows the results of the evaluation. The experimental group outperformed the control group in both the quality of the games and in the time spent on the authoring task. The differences are clearly statistically significant.

Table 6 shows the scores for the In-list and Out-list achieved by the control and the experimental groups. Using the authoring tools helped the evaluators to achieved significantly higher scores for the Out-list. Indeed, it is not easy to find characters that (1) are similar to the characters in the In-list and (2) cannot contain the target PC.

Due to the page limits, we could not present the complete authoring system, but hope to have the chance to show it during the demonstration.

6 Concluding Remarks

We reported a game for strengthening the association of the phonetic components and the pronunciations of Chinese characters. Experimental results indicated that playing the games helped students shorten the response times in naming tasks. To make our platform more useable, we built an authoring tool so that teachers could prepare games that meet specific teaching goals. Evaluation of the tool with college and graduate students showed that our system offered an efficient and effective environment for this authoring task.

Currently, players of our games still have to choose challenge levels. In the near future, we wish to make the game adaptive to players' competence by adopting more advanced techniques, including the introduction of "consistency values" (Jared et al., 1990). Evidence shows that foreign students did not take advantage of the GPC rules in Chinese to learn Chinese characters (Shen, 2005). Hence, it should be interesting to evaluate our system with foreign students to see whether our approach remains effective.

Acknowledgement

We thank the partial support of NSC-100-2221-E-004-014 and NSC-98-2517-S-004-001-MY3 projects of the National Science Council, Taiwan. We appreciate reviewers' invaluable comments, which we will respond in an extended version of this paper.

References

C. S.-H. Ho and P. Bryant. 1997. Phonological skills are important in learning to read Chinese, *Developmental Psychology*, 33(6), 946–951.

D. Jared, K. McRae, and M. S. Seidenberg. 1990. The basis of consistency effects in word naming, *J. of Memory & Language*, 29(6), 687–715.

Y.-J. Lan, Y.-T. Sung, C.-Y. Wu, R.-L. Wang, and K.-E. Chang. 2009. A cognitive interactive approach to Chinese characters learning: System design and development, *Proc. of the Int'l Conf. on Edutainment*, 559–564.

C.-Y. Lee. 2009. The cognitive and neural basis for learning to reading Chinese, *J. of Basic Education*, 18(2), 63–85.

C.-Y. Lee, J.-L. Tsai, E. C.-I Su, O. J.-L. Tzeng, and D.-L. Hung. 2005. Consistency, regularity, and frequency effects in naming Chinese characters, *Language and Linguistics*, 6(1), 75–107.

C.-H. Lin and P. Collins. 2012. The effects of L1 and orthographic regularity and consistency in naming Chinese characters. *Reading and Writing*.

C.-L. Liu, M.-H. Lai, K.-W. Tien, Y.-H. Chuang, S.-H. Wu, and C.-Y. Lee. 2011. Visually and phonologically similar characters in incorrect Chinese words: Analyses, identification, and applications, *ACM Trans. on Asian Language Information Processing*, 10(2), 10:1–39.

M.-T. P. Lu. 2011. *The Effect of Instructional Embodiment Designs on Chinese Language Learning: The Use of Embodied Animation for Beginning Learners of Chinese Characters*, Ph.D. Diss., Columbia University, USA.

J. R. Saffran, R. N. Aslin, and E. L. Newport. 1996. Statistical learning by 8-month-old infants, *Science*, 274(5294), 1926–1928.

H. H. Shen. 2005. An investigation of Chinese-character learning strategies among non-native speakers of Chinese, *System*, 33, 49–68.

W.T. Siok and P. Fletcher. 2001. The role of phonological awareness and visual-orthographic skills in Chinese reading acquisition, *Developmental Psychology*, 37(6), 886–899.

H. Tao. 2007. *Stories for 130 Chinese characters*, textbook used at the University of Michigan, USA.

J. C. Ziegler and U. Goswami. 2005. Reading acquisition, developmental dyslexia, and skilled reading across languages: A psycholinguistic grain size theory, *Psychological Bulletin*, 131(1), 3–29.

Specifying Viewpoint and Information Need with Affective Metaphors

A System Demonstration of the *Metaphor Magnet* Web App/Service

Tony Veale
Web Science and Technology Division,
KAIST, Daejeon,
South Korea.
Tony.Veale@gmail.com

Guofu Li
School of Computer Science & Informatics,
University College Dublin,
Belfield, Dublin D4, Ireland.
Yanfen.Hao@UCD.ie

Abstract

Metaphors pervade our language because they are elastic enough to allow a speaker to express an affective viewpoint on a topic without committing to a specific meaning. This balance of expressiveness and indeterminism means that metaphors are just as useful for eliciting information as they are for conveying information. We explore here, via a demonstration of a system for metaphor interpretation and generation called *Metaphor Magnet*, the practical uses of metaphor as a basis for formulating affective information queries. We also consider the kinds of deep and shallow stereotypical knowledge that are needed for such a system, and demonstrate how they can be acquired from corpora and the web.

1 Introduction

Metaphor is perhaps the most flexible and adaptive tool in the human communication toolbox. It is suited to any domain of discourse, to any register, and to the description of any concept we desire. Speakers use metaphor to communicate not just meanings, but their feelings about those meanings. The open-ended nature of metaphor interpretation means that we can use metaphor to simultaneously express and elicit opinions about a given topic. Metaphors are flexible conceits that allow us to express a position while seeking elaboration or refutation of this position from others. A metaphor is neither true or false, but a conceptual model that allow speakers to negotiate a common viewpoint.

Computational models for the interpretation and elaboration of metaphors should allow speakers to exploit the same flexibility of expression with machines as they enjoy with other humans. Such a goal clearly requires a great deal of knowledge, since metaphor is a knowledge-hungry mechanism *par excellance* (see Fass, 1997). However, much of the knowledge required for metaphor interpretation is already implicit in the large body of metaphors that are active in a community (see Martin, 1990; Mason, 2004). Existing metaphors are themselves a valuable source of knowledge for the production of new metaphors, so much so that a system can mine the relevant knowledge from corpora of figurative text (e.g. see Veale, 2011; Shutova, 2010).

One area of human-machine interaction that can clearly benefit from a competence in metaphor is that of information retrieval (IR). Speakers use metaphors with ease when eliciting information from each other, as e.g. when one suggests that a certain CEO is a tyrant or a god, or that a certain company is a dinosaur while another is a cult. Those that agree might respond by elaborating the metaphor and providing substantiating evidence, while those that disagree might refute the metaphor and switch to another of their own choosing. A well-chosen metaphor can provide the talking points for an informed conversation, allowing a speaker to elicit the desired knowledge as a combination of objective and subjective elements.

In IR, such a capability should allow searchers to express their information needs subjectively, via affective metaphors like “X is a cult”. The goal, of course, is not just to retrieve documents that make explicit use of the same metaphor – a literal matching of non-literal texts is of limited use – but to

Proceedings of the 50th Annual Meeting of the Association for Computational Linguistics, pages 7–12,
Jeju, Republic of Korea, 8-14 July 2012.

retrieve texts whose own metaphors are consonant with those of the searcher, and which elaborate upon the same talking points. This requires a computer to understand the user's metaphor, to appreciate how other metaphors might convey the same affective viewpoint, and to understand the different guises these metaphors might assume in a text.

IR extends the reach of its retrieval efforts by expanding the query it is given, in an attempt to make explicit what the user has left implicit. Metaphors, like under-specified queries, have rich meanings that are, for the most part, implicit: they imply and suggest much more than they specify. An expansionist approach to metaphor meaning, in which an affective metaphor is interpreted by generating the space of related metaphors and talking points that it implies, is thus very much suited to a more creative vision of IR, as e.g. suggested by Veale (2011). To expand a metaphorical query (like "company-X is a cult" or "company-Y is a dinosaur" or "Z was a tyrant"), a system must first expand the metaphor itself, into a set of plausible construals of the metaphor (e.g. a company that is viewed as a *dinosaur* will likely be *powerful*, but also *bloated*, *lumbering* and *slow*).

The system described in this paper, *Metaphor Magnet*, demonstrates this expansionist approach to metaphorical inference. Users express queries in the form of affective metaphors or similes, perhaps using explicit + or – tags to denote a positive or negative spin on a given concept. For instance, "*Google is as –powerful as Microsoft*" does not look for documents that literally contain this simile, but documents that express viewpoints that are implied by this simile, that is, documents that discuss the negative implications of Google's power, where these implications are first understood in relation to Microsoft. The system does this by first considering the metaphors that are conventionally used to describe Microsoft, focusing only on those metaphors that evoke the property *powerful*, and which cast a negative light on Microsoft. The implications of these metaphors (e.g., *dinosaur*, *bully*, *monopoly*, etc.) are then examined in the context of Google, using the metaphors that are typically used to describe Google as a guide to what is most apt. Thus, since Google is often described as a *giant* in web texts, the negative properties and behaviors of a stereotypical giant – like *lumbering* and *sprawling* – will be considered apt and highlighted.

To perform this kind of analysis reliably, for a wide range of metaphors and an even wider range of topics, requires a robustly shallow approach. We exploit the fact that the Google n-grams (Brants and Franz, 2006) contains a great many copula metaphors of the form "X is a Y" to understand how X is typically viewed on the web. We further exploit a large dictionary of affective stereotypes to provide an understanding of the +/- properties and behaviors of each source concept Y. Combining these resources allows the *Metaphor Magnet* system to understand the implications of a metaphorical query "X as Z" in terms of the qualities that are typically considered salient for Z and which have been corpus-attested as apt for X.

We describe the construction of our lexicon of affective stereotypes in section 2. Each stereotype is associated with a set of typical properties and behaviors (like *sprawling* for *giant,* or *inspiring* for *guru*), where the overall affect of each stereotype depends on which subset of qualities is activated in a given context (e.g., *giant* can be construed positively or negatively, as can *baby*, *soldier*, etc.). We describe how *Metaphor Magnet* exploits these stereotypes in section 3, before providing a worked example in section 4 and screenshots in section 5.

2 An Affective Lexicon of Stereotypes

We construct the lexicon in two stages. In the first stage, a large collection of stereotypical descriptions is harvested from the Web. As in Liu *et al.* (2003), our goal is to acquire a lightweight common-sense representation of many everyday concepts. In the second stage, we link these common-sense qualities in a *support graph* that captures how they mutually support each other in their co-description of a stereotypical idea. From this graph we can estimate positive and negative valence scores for each property and behavior, and default averages for the stereotypes that exhibit them.

Similes and stereotypes share a symbiotic relationship: the former exploit the latter as reference points for an evocative description, while the latter are perpetuated by their constant re-use in similes. Expanding on the approach in Veale (2011), we use two kinds of query for harvesting stereotypes from the web. The first, "as ADJ as a NOUN", acquires typical adjectival properties for noun concepts; the second, "VERB+*ing* like a NOUN" and "VERB+*ed* like a NOUN", acquires typical verb behaviors. Rather than use a wildcard * in both positions (ADJ and NOUN, or VERB and NOUN), which yields limited results with a search engine like Google, we generate fully instantiated similes from hypotheses generated via the Google n-grams. Thus, from the 3-gram "a drooling zombie" we generate the query "drooling like a zombie", and from the 3-gram "a mindless zombie" we generate "as mindless as a zombie".

Only those similes whose queries retrieve one or more web documents via Google are considered to contain promising associations. But this still gives us over 250,000 web-validated simile associations for our stereotypical model. We quickly filter these candidates manually, to ensure that the contents of the lexicon are of the highest quality. As a result, we obtain rich descriptions for many stereotypical ideas, such as *Baby*, which is described via 163 typical properties and behaviors like *crying*, *drooling* and *guileless*. After this filtering phase, the stereotype lexicon maps 9,479 stereotypes to a set of 7,898 properties and behaviors, to yield more than 75,000 pairings.

We construct the second level of the lexicon by automatically linking these properties and behaviors to each other in a support graph. The intuition here is that properties which reinforce each other in a single description (e.g. "as *lush and green* as a jungle" or "as *hot and humid* as a sauna") are more likely to have a similar affect than properties which do not support each other. We first gather all Google 3-grams in which a pair of stereotypical properties or behaviors X and Y are linked via coordination, as in "*hot and humid*" or "*kicking and screaming*". A bidirectional link between X and Y is added to the support graph if one or more stereotypes in the lexicon contain both X and Y. If this is not so, we consider whether both descriptors ever reinforce each other in web similes, by posing the web query "*as X and Y as*". If this query has non-zero hits, we also add a link between X and Y.

Let **N** denote this support graph, and N(p) denote the set of neighboring terms to p, that is, the set of properties and behaviors that can mutually support p. Since every edge in **N** represents an affective context, we can estimate the likelihood that a property p is ever used in a positive or negative context if we know the positive or negative affect of enough members of N(p). So if we label enough vertices of **N** as + or -, we can interpolate a positive/negative valence score for all vertices p in **N**.

To do this, we build a reference set **-R** of typically negative words, and a set **+R** of typically positive words. Given a few seed members of **-R** (such as *sad*, *disgusting*, *evil*, etc.) and a few seed members of **+R** (such as *happy*, *wonderful*, etc.), we find many other candidates to add to **+R** and **-R** by considering neighbors of these seeds in **N**. After three iterations in this fashion, we populate **+R** and **-R** with approx. 2000 words each.

For a property p we can now define $N^{+}(p)$ and $N^{-}(p)$ as follows:

$$(1) \quad N^{+}(p) = N(p) \cap +\mathbf{R}$$

$$(2) \quad N^{-}(p) = N(p) \cap -\mathbf{R}$$

We can now assign positive and negative valence scores to each vertex p by interpolating from reference values to their neighbors in **N**:

$$(3) \quad \mathrm{pos}(p) = \frac{|N^{+}(p)|}{|N^{+}(p) \cup N^{-}(p)|}$$

$$(4) \quad \mathrm{neg}(p) = 1 - \mathrm{pos}(p)$$

If a term S denotes a stereotypical idea and is described via a set of typical properties and behaviors *typical(S)* in the lexicon, then:

$$(5) \quad \mathrm{pos}(S) = \frac{\sum_{p \in \mathrm{typical}(S)} \mathrm{pos}(p)}{|\mathrm{typical}(S)|}$$

$$(6) \quad \mathrm{neg}(S) = 1 - \mathrm{pos}(S)$$

Thus, (5) and (6) calculate the mean affect of the properties and behaviors of S, as represented via *typical(S)*. We can now use (3) and (4) to separate *typical(S)* into those elements that are more negative than positive (putting a negative spin on S) and into those that are more positive than negative (putting a positive spin on S):

$$(7) \quad \mathrm{posTypical}(S) = \{p \mid p \in \mathrm{typical}(S) \wedge \mathrm{pos}(p) > 0.5\}$$

$$(8) \quad \mathrm{negTypical}(S) = \{p \mid p \in \mathrm{typical}(S) \wedge \mathrm{neg}(p) > 0.5\}$$

2.1 Evaluation of Stereotypical Affect

In the process of populating **+R** and **-R**, we identify a reference set of 478 positive stereotypes (such as *saint* and *hero*) and 677 negative stereotypes (such as *tyrant* and *monster*). When we use these reference points to test the effectiveness of (5) and (6) – and thus, indirectly, of (3) and (4) and of the stereotype lexicon itself – we find that **96.7%** of the positive stereotypes in **+R** are correctly assigned a positivity score greater than 0.5 (*pos(S) > neg(S)*) by (5), while **96.2%** of the negative stereotypes in **-R** are correctly assigned a negativity score greater than 0.5 (*neg(S) > pos(S)*) by (6).

3 Expansion/Interpretation of Metaphors

The Google n-grams are a rich source of affective metaphors of the form *Target is Source*, such as "politicians are crooks", "Apple is a cult", "racism is a disease" and "Steve Jobs is a god". Let *src(T)* denote the set of stereotypes that are commonly used to describe T, where commonality is defined as the presence of the corresponding copula metaphor in the Google n-grams. To find metaphors for proper-named entities like "Bill Gates", we also analyze n-grams of the form *stereotype First [Middle] Last*, such as "*tyrant* Adolf Hitler". Thus:

src(racism) = {*problem, disease, joke, sin, poison, crime, ideology, weapon*}

src(Hitler) = {*monster, criminal, tyrant, idiot, madman, vegetarian, racist, ...*}

We do not try to discriminate literal from non-literal assertions, nor do we even try to define literality. We simply assume each putative metaphor offers a potentially useful perspective on a topic T.

Let *srcTypical*(T) denote the aggregation of all properties ascribable to T via metaphors in *src*(T):

$$(9)\quad srcTypical(T) = \bigcup_{M \in src(T)} typical(M)$$

We can also use the *posTypical* and *negTypical* variants in (7) and (8) to focus only on metaphors that project positive or negative qualities onto T.

(9) is especially useful when the source *S* in the metaphor *T is S* is not a known stereotype in the lexicon, as happens when one describes *Apple as Scientology*. When the set *typical*(S) is empty, *srcTypical(S)* may not be, so *srcTypical(S)* can act as a proxy representation for S in these cases.

The properties and behaviors that are salient to the interpretation of *T is S* are given by:

$$(10)\quad salient(T,S) = |srcTypical(T) \cup typical(T)| \cap |srcTypical(S) \cup typical(S)|$$

In the context of *T is S*, the metaphorical stereotype $M \in src(S) \cup src(T) \cup \{S\}$ is an apt vehicle for T if:

$$(11)\quad apt(M, T,S) = |salient(T,S) \cap typical(M)| > 0$$

and the degree to which M is apt for T is given by:

$$(12)\quad aptness(M,T,S) = \frac{|salient(T, S) \cap typical(M)|}{|typical(M)|}$$

We can construct an interpretation for *T is S* by considering not just {S}, but the stereotypes in *src*(T) that are apt for T in the context of *T is S*, as well as the stereotypes that are commonly used to describe S – that is, *src*(S) – that are also apt for T:

$$(13)\quad interpretation(T, S) = \{M | M \in src(T) \cup src(S) \cup \{S\} \wedge apt(M, T, S)\}$$

In effect then, the interpretation of *T is S* is itself a set of apt metaphors for T that expand upon S. The elements $\{M_i\}$ of *interpretation*(T, S) can now be sorted by $aptness(M_i\ T, S)$ to produce a ranked list of interpretations $(M_1, M_2 \ldots M_n)$. For any interpretation M, the salient features of M are thus:

$$(14)\quad salient(M, T,S) = typical(M) \cap salient(T,S)$$

If *T is S* is a creative IR query – to find documents that view T as S – then *interpretation*(T, S) is an expansion of *T is S* that includes the common metaphors that are consistent with T viewed as S. For any viewpoint M_i, $salient(M_i, T, S)$ is an expansion of M_i that includes all of the qualities that T is likely to exhibit when it behaves like M_i.

4 *Metaphor Magnet*: A Worked Example

Consider the query "*Google is Microsoft*", which expresses a need for documents in which Google exhibits qualities typically associated with Microsoft. Now, both *Google* and *Microsoft* are complex concepts, so there are many ways in which they can be considered similar or dissimilar, either in a good or a bad light. However, the most salient aspects of Microsoft will be those that underpin our common metaphors for Microsoft, i.e., stereotypes in *src*(Microsoft). These metaphors will provide the talking points for the interpretation.

The Google n-grams yield up the following metaphors, 57 for Microsoft and 50 for Google:

src(Microsoft) = {*king, master, threat, bully, giant, leader, monopoly, dinosaur ...*}

src(Google) = {*king, engine, threat, brand, giant, leader, celebrity, religion* ...}

So the following qualities are aggregated for each:

srcTypical(Microsoft) = {*trusted, menacing, ruling, threatening, overbearing, admired, commanding,* ...}

srcTypical(Google) = {*trusted, lurking reigning, ruling, crowned, shining, determined, admired* ...}

Now, the salient qualities highlighted by the metaphor, namely *salient*(Google, Microsoft), are:

{*celebrated, menacing, trusted, challenging, established, threatening, admired, respected,* ...}

Thus, *interpretation*(Google, Microsoft) contains:

{*king, criminal, master, leader, bully, threatening, giant, threat, monopoly, pioneer, dinosaur, ...*}

Suppose we focus on the metaphorical expansion "Google is king", since *king* is the most highly ranked element of the interpretation. Now, *salient*(*king*, Google, Microsoft) contains:

{*celebrated, revered, admired, respected, ruling, arrogant, commanding, overbearing, reigning,* ...}

These properties and behaviors are already implicit in our perception of Google, insofar as they are salient aspects of the stereotypes to which Google is frequently compared. The metaphor "Google is Microsoft" – and its expansion "Google is king" – simply crystalizes these qualities, from perhaps different comparisons, into a single act of ideation.

Consider the metaphor "Google is -Microsoft". Since **-Microsoft** is used to impart a negative spin (+ would impart a positive spin), *negTypical* is here used in place of *typical* in (9) and (10). Thus:

srcTypical(**-Microsoft**) =

{*menacing, threatening, twisted, raging, feared, sinister, lurking, domineering, overbearing,* ...}

salient(Google, **-Microsoft**) =

{*menacing, bullying, roaring, dreaded*...}

Now *interpretation*(Google, **-Microsoft**) becomes:

{*criminal, giant, threat, bully, victim, devil, ...*}

In contrast, *interpretation*(Google, **+Microsoft**) is:

{*king, master, leader, pioneer, partner, ...*}

More focus is achieved with the simile query "Google is as **–powerful** as Microsoft". In explicit similes, we need to focus on just a subset of the salient properties, using e.g. this variant of (10):

$\{p \mid p \in salient(\text{Google, Microsoft}) \cap \text{N}(powerful) \wedge neg(p) > pos(p)\}$

In this **-powerful** case, the interpretation becomes:

{*bully, giant, devil, monopoly, dinosaur, ...*}

5 The *Metaphor Magnet* Web App

Metaphor Magnet is designed to be a lightweight web application that provides both HTML output (for humans) and XML (for client applications). The system allows users to enter queries such as *Google is –Microsoft*, *life is a +game*, *Steve Jobs is Tony Stark,* or even *Rasputin is Karl Rove* (queries are case-sensitive). Each query is expanded into a set of apt metaphors via mappings in the Google n-grams, and each metaphor is expanded into a set of contextually apt qualities. In turn, each quality is then expanded into an IR query that is used to retrieve relevant hits from Google. In effect, the system allows users to interface with a search engine like Google using metaphor and other affective language forms. The demonstration system can be accessed using a standard browser at this URL:

http://boundinanutshell.com/metaphor-magnet

Metaphor Magnet can exploit the properties and behaviors of its stock of almost 10,000 stereotypes, and can infer salient qualities for many proper-named entities like *Karl Rove* and *Steve Jobs* using a combination of copula statements from the Google n-grams (e.g., "*Steve Jobs is a visionary*") and category assignments from Wikipedia.

The interpretation of the simile/query "*Google is as -powerful as Microsoft*" thus highlights a selection of affective viewpoints on the source concept, *Microsoft*, and picks out an apt selection of viewpoints on the target *Google*. *Metaphor Magnet* displays both selections as phrase clouds in which each hyperlinked phrase – a combination of an apt stereotype and a salient quality – is clickable, to yield linguistic evidence for the selection and corresponding web-search results (via a Google gadget). The phrase cloud representing *Microsoft* in this simile is shown in the screenshot of Figure 1, while the phrase cloud for *Google* is shown in Figure 2.

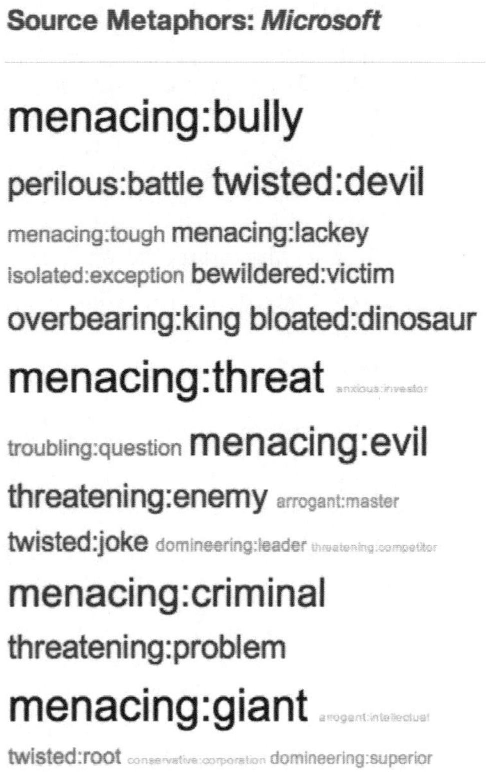

Figure 1. A screenshot of a phrase cloud for the perspective cast upon the source "Microsoft" by the simile "*Google is as –powerful as Microsoft*".

Figure 2. A screenshot of a phrase cloud for the perspective cast upon the target term "Google" by the simile "*Google is as –powerful as Microsoft*".

Metaphor Magnet demonstrates the potential utility of affective metaphors in human-computer linguistic interaction, and acts as a web service from which other NL applications can derive a measure of metaphorical competence. When accessed as a service, *Metaphor Magnet* returns either HTML or XML data, via simple *get* requests. For illustrative purposes, each HTML page also provides the URL for the corresponding XML-structured data set.

Acknowledgements

This research was partly supported by the WCU (World Class University) program under the National Research Foundation of Korea (Ministry of Education, Science and Technology of Korea, Project No: R31-30007), and partly funded by Science Foundation Ireland via the Centre for Next Generation Localization (CNGL).

References

Thorsten Brants and Alex Franz. 2006. *Web 1T 5-gram Version 1*. Linguistic Data Consortium.

Dan Fass. 1997. Processing Metonymy and Metaphor. *Contemporary Studies in Cognitive Science & Technology*. New York: Ablex.

Hugo Liu, Henry Lieberman and Ted Selker. 2003. A Model of Textual Affect Sensing Using Real-World Knowledge. *Proc. of the 8th international conference on Intelligent user interfaces*, 125-132.

James H. Martin. 1990. A Computational Model of Metaphor Interpretation. NY: Academic Press.

Zachary J. Mason. 2004. CorMet: A Computational, Corpus-Based Conventional Metaphor Extraction System, Computational Linguistics, 30(1):23-44.

Ekaterina Shutova. 2010. Metaphor Identification Using Verb and Noun Clustering. In Proc. of the 23rd International Conference on Computational Linguistics, 1001-1010

Tony Veale. 2011. Creative Language Retrieval. Creative Language Retrieval: A Robust Hybrid of Information Retrieval and Linguistic Creativity. In Proc. of ACL'2011, the 49th Annual Meeting of the Association for Computational Linguistics.

QuickView: NLP-based Tweet Search

Xiaohua Liu [‡] [†], Furu Wei [†], Ming Zhou [†], Microsoft QuickView Team [†]
[‡]School of Computer Science and Technology
Harbin Institute of Technology, Harbin, 150001, China
[†]Microsoft Research Asia
Beijing, 100190, China
[†]{xiaoliu, fuwei, mingzhou,qv}@microsoft.com

Abstract

Tweets have become a comprehensive repository for real-time information. However, it is often hard for users to quickly get information they are interested in from tweets, owing to the sheer volume of tweets as well as their noisy and informal nature. We present *QuickView*, an NLP-based tweet search platform to tackle this issue. Specifically, it exploits a series of natural language processing technologies, such as tweet normalization, named entity recognition, semantic role labeling, sentiment analysis, tweet classification, to extract useful information, i.e., named entities, events, opinions, etc., from a large volume of tweets. Then, non-noisy tweets, together with the mined information, are indexed, on top of which two brand new scenarios are enabled, i.e., categorized browsing and advanced search, allowing users to effectively access either the tweets or fine-grained information they are interested in.

1 Introduction

Tweets represent a comprehensive fresh information repository. However, users often have difficulty finding information they are interested in from tweets, because of the huge number of tweets as well as their noisy and informal nature. Tweet search, e.g., Twitter [1], is a kind of service aiming to tackle this issue. Nevertheless, existing tweet search services provide limited functionality. For example, in Twitter, only a simple keyword-based search is supported, and the returned list often contains meaningless results.

This demonstration introduces *QuickView*, which employs a series of NLP technologies to extract useful information from a large volume of tweets. Specifically, for each tweet, it first conducts normalization, followed by named entity recognition (NER). Then it conducts semantic role labeling (SRL) to get predicate-argument structures, which are further converted into events, i.e., triples of who did what. After that, it performs sentiment analysis (SA), i.e., extracting positive or negative comments about something/somebody. Next, tweets are classified into predefined categories. Finally, non-noisy tweets together with the mined information are indexed.

On top of the index, *QuickView* enables two brand new scenarios, allowing users to effectively access the tweets or fine-grained information mined from tweets.

Categorized Browsing. As illustrated in Figure 1(a), *QuickView* shows recent popular tweets, entities, events, opinions and so on, which are organized by categories. It also extracts and classifies URL links in tweets and allows users to check out popular links in a categorized way.

Advanced Search. As shown in Figure 1(b), *QuickView* provides four advanced search functions: 1) search results are clustered so that tweets about the same/similar topic are grouped together, and for each cluster only the informative tweets are kept; 2) when the query refers to a person or a company, two bars are presented followed by the words that strongly suggest opinion polarity. The bar's width

[1]http://twitter.com/

Proceedings of the 50th Annual Meeting of the Association for Computational Linguistics, pages 13–18,
Jeju, Republic of Korea, 8-14 July 2012.

is proportional to the number of associated opinions; 3) similarly, the top six most frequent words that most clearly express event occurrences are presented; 4) users can search tweets with opinions or events, e.g., search tweets containing any positive/negative opinion about "Obama" or any event involving "Obama".

The implementation of *QuickView* requires adapting existing NLP components trained on formal texts, which often performs poorly on tweets. For example, the average F1 of the Stanford NER (Finkel et al., 2005) drops from 90.8% (Ratinov and Roth, 2009) to 45.8% on tweets, while Liu et al. (2010) report that the F1 score of a state-of-the-art SRL system (Meza-Ruiz and Riedel, 2009) falls to 42.5% on tweets as apposed to 75.5% on news. However, the adaptation of those components is challenging, owing to the lack of annotated tweets and the inadequate signals provided by a noisy and short tweet. Our general strategy is to leverage existing resources as well as unsupervised or semi-supervised learning methods to reduce the labeling efforts, and to aggregate as much evidence as possible from a broader context to compensate for the lack of information in a tweet.

This strategy is embodied by various components we have developed. For example, our NER component combines a k-nearest neighbors (KNN) classifier, which collects global information across recently labeled tweets with a Conditional Random Fields (CRF) labeler, which exploits information from a single tweet and the gazetteers. Both the KNN classifier and the CRF labeler are repeatedly retrained using the results that they have confidently labeled. The SRL component caches and clusters recent labeled tweets, and aggregates information from the cluster containing the tweet. Similarly, the classifier considers not only the current tweet but also its neighbors in a tweet graph, where two tweets are connected if they are similar in content or have a tweet/retweet relationship.

QuickView has been internally deployed, and received extremely positive feedback. Experimental results on a human annotated dataset also indicate the effectiveness of our adaptation strategy.

Our contributions are summarized as follows.

1. We demonstrate *QuickView*, an NLP-based tweet search. Different from existing methods, it exploits a series of NLP technologies to extract useful information from a large volume of tweets, and enables categorized browsing and advanced search scenarios, allowing users to efficiently access information they are interested in from tweets.

2. We present core components of *QuickView*, focusing on how to leverage existing resources and technologies as well as how to make up for the limited information in a short and often noisy tweet by aggregating information from a broader context.

The rest of this paper is organized as follows. In the next section, we introduce related work. In Section 3, we describe our system. In Section 4, we evaluate our system. Finally, Section 5 concludes and presents future work.

2 Related Work

Information Extraction Systems. Essentially, *QuickView* is an information extraction (IE) system. However, unlike existing IE systems, such as Evita (Saurí et al., 2005), a robust event recognizer for QA system, and SRES (Rozenfeld and Feldman, 2008), a self-supervised relation extractor for the web, it targets tweets, a new genre of text, which are short and informal, and its focus is on adapting existing IE components to tweets.

Tweet Search Services. A couple of tweet search services exist, including Twitter, Bing social search [2] and Google social search [3]. Most of them provide only keyword-based search interfaces, i.e., returning a list of tweets related to a given word/phrase. In contrast, our system extracts fine-grained information from tweets and allows a new end-to-end search experience beyond keyword search, such as clustering of search results, and search with events/opinions.

NLP Components. The NLP technologies adopted in our system , e.g., NER, SRL and classification, have been extensively studied on formal text but rarely on tweets. At the heart of our system is the re-use of existing resources, methodologies as

[2] http://www.bing.com/social

[3] http://www.google.com/realtime

(a) A screenshot of the categorized browsing scenario.

(b) A screenshot of the advanced search scenario.

Figure 1: Two scenarios of *QuickView*.

well as components, and the the adaptation of them to tweets. The adaptation process, though varying across components, consists of three common steps: 1) annotating tweets; 2) defining the decision context that usually involves more than one tweet, such as a cluster of similar tweets; and 3) re-training models (often incrementally) with both conventional features and features derived from the context defined in step 2.

3 System Description

We first give an overview of our system, then present more details about NER and SRL, as two representative core components, to illustrate the adaptation process.

3.1 Overview

Architecture. *QuickView* can be divided into four parts, as illustrated in Figure 2. The first part includes a crawler and a buffer of raw tweets. The crawler repeatedly downloads tweets using the Twitter APIs, and then pre-filters noisy tweets using some heuristic rules, e.g., removing a tweet if it is too short, say, less than 3 words, or if it contains any predefined banned word. At the moment, we focus on English tweets, so non-English tweets are filtered as well. Finally, the un-filtered are put into the buffer.

The second part consists of several tweet extraction pipelines. Each pipeline has the same configuration, constantly fetching a tweet from the raw tweet buffer, and conducting the following processes se-

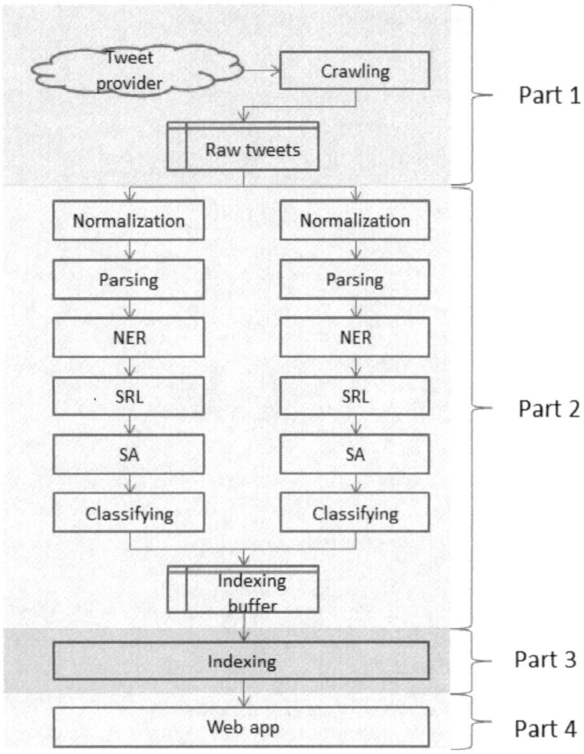

Figure 2: System architecture of *QuickView*.

quentially: 1) normalization; 2) parsing including part-of-speech (POS), chunking, and dependency parsing; 3) NER; 4) SRL; 5) SA and 6) classification. The normalization model identifies and corrects ill-formed words. For example, after normalization, "loooove" in "··· I loooove my icon···" will be transformed to "love". A phrase-based translation system without re-ordering is used to implement this model. The translation table includes manually compiled ill/good form pairs, and the language model is a trigram trained on LDC data [4] using SRILM (Stolcke, 2002). The OpenNLP [5] toolkit is directly used to implement the parsing model. In future, the parsing model will be re-trained using annotated tweets. The SA component is implemented according to Jiang et al. (2011), which incorporates target-dependent features and considers related tweets by utilizing a graph-based optimization. The classification model is a KNN-based classifier that caches confidently labeled results to re-train itself, which also recognizes and drops noisy tweets. Each processed tweet, if not identified as noise, is put into a shared buffer for indexing.

The third part is responsible for indexing and querying. It constantly takes from the indexing buffer a processed tweet, which is then indexed with various entries including words, phrases, metadata (e.g., source, publish time, and account), named entities, events, and opinions. On top of this, it answers any search request, and returns a list of matched results, each of which contains both the original tweet and the extracted information from that tweet. We implement an indexing/querying engine similar to Lucene [6] in C#. This part also maintains a cache of recent processed tweets, from which the following information is extracted and indexed: 1) top tweets; 2) top entities/events/opinions in tweets; and 3) top accounts. Whether a tweet/entity/event/opinion ranks top depends on their re-tweeted/mentioned times as well as its publisher, while whether an account is top relies on the number of his/her followers and tweets.

The fourth part is a web application that returns related information to end users according to their browsing or search request. The implementation of the web application is organized with the model-view-control pattern so that other kinds of user interfaces, e.g., a mobile application, can be easily implemented.

Deployment. *QuickView* is deployed into 5 workstations [7] including 2 processing pipelines, as illustrated in Table 1. The communication between components is through TCP/IP. On average, it takes 0.01 seconds to process each tweet, and in total about 10 million tweets are indexed every day. Note that *QuickView*'s processing capability can be enhanced in a straightforward manner by deploying additional pipelines.

3.2 Core Components

Because of limited space, we only discuss two core components of *QuickView*: NER and SRL.

NER. NER is the task of identifying mentions of rigid designators from text belonging to named-entity types such as persons, organizations and locations. Existing solutions fall into three categories: 1)

[4]http://www.ldc.upenn.edu/Catalog/CatalogEntry.jsp ?catalogId=LDC2005T12

[5]http://sourceforge.net/projects/opennlp/

[6]http://lucene.apache.org/java/docs/index.html

[7]Intel® Xeon® 2.33 CPU 5140 @2.33GHz, 4G of RAM, OS of Windows Server 2003 Enterprise $X64$ version

Table 1: Current deployment of *QuickView*.

Workstation	Hosted components
$\#1$	Crawler,Raw tweet buffer
$\#2, 3$	Process pipeline
$\#4$	Indexing Buffer, Indexer/Querier
$\#5$	Web application

the rule-based (Krupka and Hausman, 1998); 2) the machine learning based (Finkel and Manning, 2009; Singh et al., 2010); and 3) hybrid methods (Jansche and Abney, 2002). With the availability of annotated corpora, such as ACE05, Enron and CoNLL03, the data-driven methods become the dominating methods. However, because of domain mismatch, current systems trained on non-tweets perform poorly on tweets.

Our NER system takes three steps to address this problem. Firstly, it defines those recently labeled tweets that are similar to the current tweet as its recognition context, under which a KNN-based classifier is used to conduct word level classification. Following the two-stage prediction aggregation methods (Krishnan and Manning, 2006), such pre-labeled results, together with other conventional features used by the state-of-the-art NER systems, are fed into a linear CRF models, which conducts fine-grained tweet level NER. Secondly, the KNN and CRF model are repeatedly retrained with an incrementally augmented training set, into which highly confidently labeled tweets are added. Finally, following Lev Ratinov and Dan Roth (2009), 30 gazetteers are used, which cover common names, countries, locations, temporal expressions, etc. These gazetteers represent general knowledge across domains, and help to make up for the lack of training data.

SRL. Given a sentence, the SRL component identifies every predicate, and for each predicate further identifies its arguments. This task has been extensively studied on well-written corpora like news, and a couple of solutions exist. Examples include: 1) the pipelined approach, i.e., dividing the task into several successive components such as argument identification, argument classification, global inference, etc., and conquering them individually (Xue, 2004; Koomen et al., 2005); 2) sequentially labeling based approach (Màrquez et al., 2005), i.e., labeling the words according to their positions relative to an argument (i.e., inside, outside, or at the beginning); and 3) Markov Logic Networks (MLN) based approach (Meza-Ruiz and Riedel, 2009), i.e., simultaneously resolving all the sub-tasks using learnt weighted formulas. Unsurprisingly, the performance of the state-of-the-art SRL system (Meza-Ruiz and Riedel, 2009) drops sharply when applied to tweets.

The SRL component of *QuickView* is based on CRF, and uses the recently labeled tweets that are similar to the current tweet as the broader context. Algorithm 1 outlines its implementation, where: $train$ denotes a machine learning process to get a labeler l, which in our work is a linear CRF model; the $cluster$ function puts the new tweet into a cluster; the $label$ function generates predicate-argument structures for the input tweet with the help of the trained model and the cluster; p, s and cf denote a predicate, a set of argument and role pairs related to the predicate and the predicted confidence, respectively. To prepare the initial clusters required by the SRL component as its input, we adopt the predicate-argument mapping method (Liu et al., 2010) to get some automatically labeled tweets, which (plus the manually labeled tweets) are then organized into groups using a bottom-up clustering procedure.

It is worth noting that: 1) our SRL component uses the general role schema defined by PropBank, which includes core roles such as A0, A1 (usually indicating the agent and patient of the predicate, respectively), and auxiliary roles such as AM-TMP and AM-LOC (representing the temporal and location information of the predicate, respectively); 2) only verbal predicates are considered, which is consistent with most existing SRL systems; and 3) following Màrquez et al. (2005), it conducts word level labeling.

4 Evaluation

Overall Performance. We provide a textbox in the home page of *QuickView* to collect feedback. We have got 165 feedbacks, of which 85.5% are positive. The main complaint is related to the quality of the extracted information.

Core Components. We manually labeled the POS,

Algorithm 1 SRL of *QuickView*.

Require: Tweet stream i;clusters cl;output stream o.

Initialize l, the CRF labeler: $l = train(cl)$.
while Pop a tweet t from i and $t \neq null$ **do**
  Put t to a cluster c: $c = cluster(cl, t)$.
  Label t with l:$(t, \{(p, s, cf)\}) = label(l, c, t)$.
  Update cluster c with labeled results $(t, \{(p, s, cf)\})$.
  Output labeled results $(t, \{(p, s, cf)\})$ to o.
end while
return o.

NER, SRL and SA information for about 10,000 tweets, based on which the NER and SRL components are evaluated. Experimental results show that: 1) our NER component achieves an average F1 of 80.2%, as opposed to 75.4% of the baseline, which is a CRF-based system similar to Ratinov and Roth's (2009) but re-trained on annotated tweets; and 2) our SRL component gets an F1 of 59.7%, outperforming both the state-of-the-art system (Meza-Ruiz and Riedel, 2009) (42.5%) and the system of Liu et al. (2010) (42.3%), which is trained on automatically annotated news tweets (tweets reporting news).

5 Conclusions and Future work

We have described the motivation, scenarios, architecture, deployment and implementation of *QuickView*, an NLP-based tweet search. At the heart of *QuickView* is the adaptation of existing NLP technologies, e.g., NER, SRL and SA, to tweets, a new genre of text, which are short and informal. We have illustrated our strategy to tackle this challenging task, i.e., leveraging existing resources and aggregating as much information as possible from a broader context, using NER and SRL as case studies. Preliminary positive feedback suggests the usefulness of *QuickView* and its advantages over existing tweet search services. Experimental results on a human annotated dataset indicate the effectiveness of our adaptation strategy.

We are improving the quality of the core components of *QuickView* by labeling more tweets and exploring alternative models. We are also customizing *QuickView* for non-English tweets. As it progresses, we will release *QuickView* to the public.

References

Jenny Rose Finkel and Christopher D. Manning. 2009. Nested named entity recognition. In *EMNLP*, pages 141–150.

Jenny Rose Finkel, Trond Grenager, and Christopher Manning. 2005. Incorporating non-local information into information extraction systems by gibbs sampling. In *ACL*, pages 363–370.

Martin Jansche and Steven P. Abney. 2002. Information extraction from voicemail transcripts. In *EMNLP*, pages 320–327.

Long Jiang, Mo Yu, Ming Zhou, and Xiaohua Liu. 2011. Target-dependent twitter sentiment classification. In *ACL*.

Peter Koomen, Vasin Punyakanok, Dan Roth, and Wen-tau Yih. 2005. Generalized inference with multiple semantic role labeling systems. In *CONLL*, pages 181–184.

Vijay Krishnan and Christopher D. Manning. 2006. An effective two-stage model for exploiting non-local dependencies in named entity recognition. In *ACL*, pages 1121–1128.

George R. Krupka and Kevin Hausman. 1998. Isoquest: Description of the netowl^{TM} extractor system as used in muc-7. In *MUC-7*.

Xiaohua Liu, Kuan Li, Bo Han, Ming Zhou, Long Jiang, Zhongyang Xiong, and Changning Huang. 2010. Semantic role labeling for news tweets. In *Coling*, pages 698–706.

Lluís Màrquez, Pere Comas, Jesús Giménez, and Neus Català. 2005. Semantic role labeling as sequential tagging. In *CONLL*, pages 193–196.

Ivan Meza-Ruiz and Sebastian Riedel. 2009. Jointly identifying predicates, arguments and senses using markov logic. In *NAACL*, pages 155–163.

Lev Ratinov and Dan Roth. 2009. Design challenges and misconceptions in named entity recognition. In *CoNLL*, pages 147–155.

Benjamin Rozenfeld and Ronen Feldman. 2008. Self-supervised relation extraction from the web. *Knowl. Inf. Syst.*, 17:17–33, October.

Roser Saurí, Robert Knippen, Marc Verhagen, and James Pustejovsky. 2005. Evita: A robust event recognizer for qa systems. In *EMNLP*, pages 700–707.

Sameer Singh, Dustin Hillard, and Chris Leggetter. 2010. Minimally-supervised extraction of entities from text advertisements. In *HLT-NAACL*, pages 73–81.

Andreas Stolcke. 2002. SRILM – an extensible language modeling toolkit. In *ICSLP*, volume 2, pages 901–904.

Nianwen Xue. 2004. Calibrating features for semantic role labeling. In *In Proceedings of EMNLP 2004*, pages 88–94.

NiuTrans: An Open Source Toolkit for Phrase-based and Syntax-based Machine Translation

Tong Xiao[†‡], Jingbo Zhu[†‡], Hao Zhang[†] and Qiang Li[†]

[†]Natural Language Processing Lab, Northeastern University

[‡]Key Laboratory of Medical Image Computing, Ministry of Education

{xiaotong,zhujingbo}@mail.neu.edu.cn

{zhanghao1216,liqiangneu}@gmail.com

Abstract

We present a new open source toolkit for phrase-based and syntax-based machine translation. The toolkit supports several state-of-the-art models developed in statistical machine translation, including the phrase-based model, the hierachical phrase-based model, and various syntax-based models. The key innovation provided by the toolkit is that the decoder can work with various grammars and offers different choices of decoding algrithms, such as phrase-based decoding, decoding as parsing/tree-parsing and forest-based decoding. Moreover, several useful utilities were distributed with the toolkit, including a discriminative reordering model, a simple and fast language model, and an implementation of minimum error rate training for weight tuning.

1 Introduction

We present NiuTrans, a new open source machine translation toolkit, which was developed for constructing high quality machine translation systems. The NiuTrans toolkit supports most statistical machine translation (SMT) paradigms developed over the past decade, and allows for training and decoding with several state-of-the-art models, including: the phrase-based model (Koehn et al., 2003), the hierarchical phrase-based model (Chiang, 2007), and various syntax-based models (Galley et al., 2004; Liu et al., 2006). In particular, a unified framework was adopted to decode with different models and ease the implementation of decoding algorithms. Moreover, some useful utilities were distributed with the toolkit, such as: a discriminative reordering model, a simple and fast language model, and an implementation of minimum error rate training that allows for various evaluation metrics for tuning the system. In addition, the toolkit provides easy-to-use APIs for the development of new features. The toolkit has been used to build translation systems that have placed well at recent MT evaluations, such as the NTCIR-9 Chinese-to-English PatentMT task (Goto et al., 2011).

We implemented the toolkit in C++ language, with special consideration of extensibility and efficiency. C++ enables us to develop efficient translation engines which have high running speed for both training and decoding stages. This property is especially important when the programs are used for large scale translation. While the development of C++ program is slower than that of the similar programs written in other popular languages such as Java, the modern compliers generally result in C++ programs being consistently faster than the Java-based counterparts.

The toolkit is available under the GNU general public license [1]. The website of NiuTrans is http://www.nlplab.com/NiuPlan/NiuTrans.html.

2 Motivation

As in current approaches to statistical machine translation, NiuTrans is based on a log-linear

[1] http://www.gnu.org/licenses/gpl-2.0.html

Proceedings of the 50th Annual Meeting of the Association for Computational Linguistics, pages 19–24, Jeju, Republic of Korea, 8-14 July 2012.

model where a number of features are defined to model the translation process. Actually NiuTrans is not the first system of this kind. To date, several open-source SMT systems (based on either phrase-based models or syntax-based models) have been developed, such as Moses (Koehn et al., 2007), Joshua (Li et al., 2009), SAMT (Zollmann and Venugopal, 2006), Phrasal (Cer et al., 2010), cdec (Dyer et al., 2010), Jane (Vilar et al., 2010) and SilkRoad [2], and offer good references for the development of the NiuTrans toolkit. While our toolkit includes all necessary components as provided within the above systems, we have additional goals for this project, as follows:

- *It fully supports most state-of-the-art SMT models*. Among these are: the phrase-based model, the hierarchical phrase-based model, and the syntax-based models that explicitly use syntactic information on either (both) source and (or) target language side(s).
- *It offers a wide choice of decoding algorithms*. For example, the toolkit has several useful decoding options, including: standard phrase-based decoding, decoding as parsing, decoding as tree-parsing, and forest-based decoding.
- *It is easy-to-use and fast*. A new system can be built using only a few commands. To control the system, users only need to modify a configuration file. In addition to the special attention to usability, the running speed of the system is also improved in several ways. For example, we used several pruning and multithreading techniques to speed-up the system.

3 Toolkit

The toolkit serves as an end-to-end platform for training and evaluating statistical machine translation models. To build new translation systems, all you need is a collection of word-aligned sentences [3], and a set of additional sentences with one or more reference translations for weight tuning and test. Once the data is prepared, the MT system can be created using a sequence of commands. Given a number of sentence-pairs and the word alignments between them, the toolkit first extracts a phrase table and two reordering models for the phrase-based system, or a Synchronous Context-free/Tree-substitution Grammar (SCFG/STSG) for the hierarchical phrase-based and syntax-based systems. Then, an n-gram language model is built on the target-language corpus. Finally, the resulting models are incorporated into the decoder which can automatically tune feature weights on the development set using minimum error rate training (Och, 2003) and translate new sentences with the optimized weights.

In the following, we will give a brief review of the above components and the main features provided by the toolkit.

3.1 Phrase Extraction and Reordering Model

We use a standard way to implement the phrase extraction module for the phrase-based model. That is, we extract all phrase-pairs that are consistent with word alignments. Five features are associated with each phrase-pair. They are two phrase translation probabilities, two lexical weights, and a feature of phrase penalty. We follow the method proposed in (Koehn et al., 2003) to estimate the values of these features.

Unlike previous systems that adopt only one reordering model, our toolkit supports two different reordering models which are trained independently but jointly used during decoding.

- The first of these is a *discriminative reordering model*. This model is based on the standard framework of maximum entropy. Thus the reordering problem is modeled as a classification problem, and the reordering probability can be efficiently computed using a (log-)linear combination of features. In our implementation, we use all boundary words as features which are similar to those used in (Xiong et al., 2006).
- The second model is the *MSD reordering model*[4] which has been successfully used in the Moses system. Unlike Moses, our toolkit supports both the word-based and phrase-based methods for estimating the

[2] http://www.nlp.org.cn/project/project.php?proj_id=14

[3] To obtain word-to-word alignments, several easy-to-use toolkits are available, such as GIZA++ and Berkeley Aligner.

[4] Term MSD refers to the three orientations (reordering types), including Monotone (M), Swap (S), and Discontinuous (D).

probabilities of the three orientations (Galley and Manning, 2008).

3.2 Translation Rule Extraction

For the hierarchical phrase-based model, we follow the general framework of SCFG where a grammar rule has three parts – a source-side, a target-side and alignments between source and target non-terminals. To learn SCFG rules from word-aligned sentences, we choose the algorithm proposed in (Chiang, 2007) and estimate the associated feature values as in the phrase-based system.

For the syntax-based models, all non-terminals in translation rules are annotated with syntactic labels. We use the GHKM algorithm to extract (minimal) translation rules from bilingual sentences with parse trees on source-language side and/or target-language side[5]. Also, two or more minimal rules can be composed together to obtain larger rules and involve more contextual information. For unaligned words, we attach them to all nearby rules, instead of using the most likely attachment as in (Galley et al., 2006).

3.3 *N*-gram Language Modeling

The toolkit includes a simple but effective *n*-gram language model (LM). The LM builder is basically a "sorted" trie structure (Pauls and Klein, 2011), where a map is developed to implement an array of key/value pairs, guaranteeing that the keys can be accessed in sorted order. To reduce the size of resulting language model, low-frequency *n*-grams are filtered out by some thresholds. Moreover, an *n*-gram cache is implemented to speed up *n*-gram probability requests for decoding.

3.4 Weight Tuning

We implement the weight tuning component according to the minimum error rate training (MERT) method (Och, 2003). As MERT suffers from local optimums, we added a small program into the MERT system to let it jump out from the coverage area. When MERT converges to a (local) optimum, our program automatically conducts the MERT run again from a random starting point near the newly-obtained optimal point. This procedure is repeated for several times until no better weights (i.e., weights with a higher BLEU score) are found. In this way, our program can introduce some randomness into weight training. Hence users do not need to repeat MERT for obtaining stable and optimized weights using different starting points.

3.5 Decoding

Chart-parsing is employed to decode sentences in development and test sets. Given a source sentence, the decoder generates 1-best or *k*-best translations in a bottom-up fashion using a CKY-style parsing algorithm. The basic data structure used in the decoder is a *chart*, where an array of *cells* is organized in topological order. Each cell maintains a list of hypotheses (or *items*). The decoding process starts with the minimal cells, and proceeds by repeatedly applying translation rules or composing items in adjunct cells to obtain new items. Once a new item is created, the associated scores are computed (with an integrated *n*-gram language model). Then, the item is added into the list of the corresponding cell. This procedure stops when we reach the final state (i.e., the cell associates with the entire source span).

The decoder can work with all (hierarchical) phrase-based and syntax-based models. In particular, our toolkit provides the following decoding modes.

- *Phrase-based decoding*. To fit the phrase-based model into the CKY paring framework, we restrict the phrase-based decoding with the ITG constraint (Wu, 1996). In this way, each pair of items in adjunct cells can be composed in either monotone order or inverted order. Hence the decoding can be trivially implemented by a three-loop structure as in standard CKY parsing. This algorithm is actually the same as that used in parsing with bracketing transduction grammars.
- *Decoding as parsing (or string-based decoding)*. This mode is designed for decoding with SCFGs/STSGs which are used in the hierarchical phrase-based and syntax-based systems. In the general framework of synchronous grammars and tree transducers, decoding can be regarded as a parsing problem. Therefore, the above chart-based decoder is directly applicable to

[5] For tree-to-tree models, we use a natural extension of the GHKM algorithm which defines admissible nodes on tree-pairs and obtains tree-to-tree rules on all pairs of source and target tree-fragments.

the hierarchical phrase-based and syntax-based models. For efficient integration of n-gram language model into decoding, rules containing more than two variables are binarized into binary rules. In addition to the rules learned from bilingual data, glue rules are employed to glue the translations of a sequence of chunks.

- *Decoding as tree-parsing (or tree-based decoding).* If the parse tree of source sentence is provided, decoding (for tree-to-string and tree-to-tree models) can also be cast as a tree-parsing problem (Eisner, 2003). In tree-parsing, translation rules are first mapped onto the nodes of input parse tree. This results in a translation tree/forest (or a hypergraph) where each edge represents a rule application. Then decoding can proceed on the hypergraph as usual. That is, we visit in bottom-up order each node in the parse tree, and calculate the model score for each edge rooting at the node. The final output is the 1-best/k-best translations maintained by the root node of the parse tree. Since tree-parsing restricts its search space to the derivations that exactly match with the input parse tree, it in general has a much higher decoding speed than a normal parsing procedure. But it in turn results in lower translation quality due to more search errors.
- *Forest-based decoding.* Forest-based decoding (Mi et al., 2008) is a natural extension of tree-based decoding. In principle, forest is a data structure that can encode exponential number of trees efficiently. This structure has been proved to be helpful in reducing the effects caused by parser errors. Since our internal representation is already in a hypergraph structure, it is easy to extend the decoder to handle the input forest, with little modification of the code.

4 Other Features

In addition to the basic components described above, several additional features are introduced to ease the use of the toolkit.

4.1 Multithreading

The decoder supports multithreading to make full advantage of the modern computers where more than one CPUs (or cores) are provided. In general, the decoding speed can be improved when multiple threads are involved. However, modern MT decoders do not run faster when too many threads are used (Cer et al., 2010).

4.2 Pruning

To make decoding computational feasible, *beam pruning* is used to aggressively prune the search space. In our implementation, we maintain a beam for each cell. Once all the items of the cell are proved, only the top-k best items according to model score are kept and the rest are discarded. Also, we re-implemented the *cube pruning* method described in (Chiang, 2007) to further speed-up the system.

In addition, we develop another method that prunes the search space using punctuations. The idea is to divide the input sentence into a sequence of segments according to punctuations. Then, each segment is translated individually. The MT outputs are finally generated by composing the translations of those segments.

4.3 APIs for Feature Engineering

To ease the implementation and test of new features, the toolkit offers APIs for experimenting with the features developed by users. For example, users can develop new features that are associated with each phrase-pair. The system can automatically recognize them and incorporate them into decoding. Also, more complex features can be activated during decoding. When an item is created during decoding, new features can be introduced into an internal object which returns feature values for computing the model score.

5 Experiments

5.1 Experimental Setup

We evaluated our systems on NIST Chinese-English MT tasks. Our training corpus consists of 1.9M bilingual sentences. We used GIZA++ and the "grow-diag-final-and" heuristics to generate word alignment for the bilingual data. The parse trees on both the Chinese and English sides were

Entry			BLEU4[%]	
			Dev	Test
Moses: phrase			36.51	34.93
Moses: hierarchical phrase			36.65	34.79
NiuTrans	phrase		36.99	35.29
	hierarchical phrase		37.41	35.35
	t2s	parsing	36.48	34.71
		tree-parsing	35.54	33.99
		forest-based	36.14	34.25
	t2t	parsing	35.99	34.01
		tree-parsing	35.04	33.21
		forest-based	35.56	33.45
	s2t	parsing	37.63	35.65

Table 1: BLEU scores of various systems. t2s, t2t, and s2t represent the tree-to-string, tree-to-tree, and string-to-tree systems, respectively.

generated using the Berkeley Parser, which were then binarized in a head-out fashion [6]. A 5-gram language model was trained on the Xinhua portion of the Gigaword corpus in addition to the English part of the LDC bilingual training data. We used the NIST 2003 MT evaluation set as our development set (919 sentences) and the NIST 2005 MT evaluation set as our test set (1,082 sentences). The translation quality was evaluated with the case-insensitive IBM-version BLEU4.

For the phrase-based system, phrases are of at most 7 words on either source or target-side. For the hierarchical phrase-based system, all SCFG rules have at most two variables. For the syntax-based systems, minimal rules were extracted from the binarized trees on both (either) language-side(s). Larger rules were then generated by composing two or three minimal rules. By default, all these systems used a beam of size 30 for decoding.

5.2 Evaluation of Translations

Table 1 shows the BLEU scores of different MT systems built using our toolkit. For comparison, the result of the Moses system is also reported. We see, first of all, that our phrase-based and hierarchical phrase-based systems achieve competitive performance, even outperforms the Moses system over 0.3 BLEU points in some cases. Also, the syntax-based systems obtain very promising results. For example, the string-to-tree system significantly outperforms the phrase-based and hierarchical phrase-based counterparts. In addition, Table 1 gives a test of different decoding methods (for syntax-based systems). We see that the parsing-based method achieves the best BLEU score. On the other hand, as expected, it runs slowest due to its large search space. For example, it is 5-8 times slower than the tree-parsing-based method in our experiments. The forest-based decoding further improves the BLEU scores on top of tree-parsing. In most cases, it obtains a +0.6 BLEU improvement but is 2-3 times slower than the tree-parsing-based method.

Entry	BLEU4[%]		Speed (sent/sec)
	Dev	Test	
Moses: phrase	36.69	34.99	0.11
+ cube pruning	36.51	34.93	0.47
NiuTrans: phrase	37.14	35.47	0.14
+ cube pruning	36.98	35.39	0.60
+ cube & punct pruning	36.99	35.29	3.71
+ all pruning & 8 threads	36.99	35.29	21.89
+ all pruning & 16 threads	36.99	35.29	22.36

Table 2: Effects of pruning and multithreading techniques.

5.3 System Speed-up

We also study the effectiveness of pruning and multithreading techniques. Table 2 shows that all the pruning methods implemented in the toolkit is helpful in speeding up the (phrase-based) system, while does not result in significant decrease in BLEU score. On top of a straightforward baseline (only beam pruning is used), cube pruning and pruning with punctuations give a speed improvement of 25 times together[7]. Moreover, the decoding process can be further accelerated by using multithreading technique. However, more than 8 threads do not help in our experiments.

6 Conclusion and Future Work

We have presented a new open-source toolkit for phrase-based and syntax-based machine translation. It is implemented in C++ and runs fast. Moreover, it supports several state-of-the-art models ranging from phrase-based models to syntax-based models,

[6] The parse trees follow the nested bracketing format, as defined in the Penn Treebank. Also, the NiuTrans package includes a tool for tree binarization.

[7] The translation speed is tested on Intel Core Due 2 E8500 processors running at 3.16 GHz.

and provides a wide choice of decoding methods. The experimental results on NIST MT tasks show that the MT systems built with our toolkit achieve state-of-the-art translation performance.

The next version of NiuTrans will support ARPA-format LMs, MIRA for weight tuning and a beam-stack decoder which removes the ITG constraint for phrase decoding. In addition, a Hadoop-based MapReduce-parallelized version is underway and will be released in near future.

Acknowledgments

This research was supported in part by the National Science Foundation of China (61073140), the Specialized Research Fund for the Doctoral Program of Higher Education (20100042110031) and the Fundamental Research Funds for the Central Universities in China.

References

Daniel Cer, Michel Galley, Daniel Jurafsky and Christopher D. Manning. 2010. Phrasal: A Toolkit for Statistical Machine Translation with Facilities for Extraction and Incorporation of Arbitrary Model Features. In *Proc. of* HLT/NAACL 2010 demonstration Session, pages 9-12.

David Chiang. 2007. Hierarchical phrase-based translation. *Computational Linguistics*, 33(2):201–228.

Chris Dyer, Adam Lopez, Juri Ganitkevitch, Jonathan Weese, Ferhan Ture, Phil Blunsom, Hendra Setiawan, Vladimir Eidelman, Philip Resnik. 2010. cdec: A Decoder, Alignment, and Learning Framework for Finite-State and Context-Free Translation Models. In *Proc. of* ACL 2010 System Demonstrations, pages 7-12.

Jason Eisner. 2003. Learning non-isomorphic tree mappings for machine translation. In *Proc. of* ACL 2003, pages 205-208.

Michel Galley, Mark Hopkins, Kevin Knight and Daniel Marcu. 2004. What's in a translation rule? In *Proc. of* HLT-NAACL 2004, pages 273-280.

Michel Galley, Jonathan Graehl, Kevin Knight, Daniel Marcu, Steve DeNeefe, Wei Wang and Ignacio Thayer. 2006. Scalable inferences and training of context-rich syntax translation models. In *Proc. of* COLING/ACL 2006, pages 961-968.

Michel Galley and Christopher D. Manning. 2008. A Simple and Effective Hierarchical Phrase Reordering Model. In *Proc. of* EMNLP2008, pages 848-856.

Isao Goto, Bin Lu, Ka Po Chow, Eiichiro Sumita and Benjamin K. Tsou. 2011. Overview of the Patent Machine Translation Task at the NTCIR-9 Workshop. In *Proc. of* NTCIR-9 Workshop Meeting, pages 559-578.

Philipp Koehn, Franz J. Och, and Daniel Marcu. 2003. Statistical phrase-based translation. In *Proc. of* HLT/NAACL 2003, pages 127-133.

Philipp Koehn, Hieu Hoang, Alexandra Birch, Chris Callison-Burch, Marcello Federico, Nicola Bertoldi, Brooke Cowan, Wade Shen, Christine Moran, Richard Zens, Chris Dyer, Ondej Bojar, Alexandra Constantin, and Evan Herbst. 2007. Moses: Open Source Toolkit for Statistical Machine Translation. In *Proc. of* ACL 2007, pages 177–180.

Zhifei Li, Chris Callison-Burch, Chris Dyer, Sanjeev Khudanpur, Lane Schwartz, Wren Thornton, Jonathan Weese, and Omar Zaidan. 2009. Joshua: An Open Source Toolkit for Parsing-Based Machine Translation. In *Proc. of* the Workshop on Statistical Machine Translation, pages 135–139.

Yang Liu, Qun Liu and Shouxun Lin. 2006. Tree-to-String Alignment Template for Statistical Machine Translation. In *Proc. of* ACL 2006, pages 609-616.

Haitao Mi, Liang Huang and Qun Liu. 2008. Forest-Based Translation. In *Proc. of* ACL 2008, pages 192-199.

Franz Josef Och. 2003. Minimum error rate training in statistical machine translation. In *Proc. of* ACL 2003, pages 160-167.

Adam Pauls and Dan Klein. 2011. Faster and Smaller N-Gram Language Models. In *Proc. of* ACL 2011, pages 258–267.

David Vilar, Daniel Stein, Matthias Huck and Hermann Ney. 2010. Jane: Open Source Hierarchical Translation, Extended with Reordering and Lexicon Models. In *Proc. of* the Joint 5th Workshop on Statistical Machine Translation and MetricsMATR, pages 262-270.

Dekai Wu. 1996. A polynomial-time algorithm for statistical machine translation. In *Proc. of* ACL1996, pages 152–158.

Deyi Xiong, Qun Liu and Shouxun Lin. 2006. Maximum Entropy Based Phrase Reordering Model for Statistical Machine Translation. In *Proc. of* ACL 2006, pages 521-528.

Andreas Zollmann and Ashish Venugopal. 2006. Syntax Augmented Machine Translation via Chart Parsing. In *Proc. of* HLT/NAACL 2006, pages 138-141.

`langid.py`: An Off-the-shelf Language Identification Tool

Marco Lui and Timothy Baldwin
NICTA VRL
Department of Computing and Information Systems
University of Melbourne, VIC 3010, Australia
mhlui@unimelb.edu.au, tb@ldwin.net

Abstract

We present `langid.py`, an off-the-shelf language identification tool. We discuss the design and implementation of `langid.py`, and provide an empirical comparison on 5 long-document datasets, and 2 datasets from the microblog domain. We find that `langid.py` maintains consistently high accuracy across all domains, making it ideal for end-users that require language identification without wanting to invest in preparation of in-domain training data.

1 Introduction

Language identification (LangID) is the task of determining the natural language that a document is written in. It is a key step in automatic processing of real-world data, where a multitude of languages may be present. Natural language processing techniques typically pre-suppose that all documents being processed are written in a given language (e.g. English), but as focus shifts onto processing documents from internet sources such as microblogging services, this becomes increasingly difficult to guarantee. Language identification is also a key component of many web services. For example, the language that a web page is written in is an important consideration in determining whether it is likely to be of interest to a particular user of a search engine, and automatic identification is an essential step in building language corpora from the web. It has practical implications for social networking and social media, where it may be desirable to organize comments and other user-generated content by language. It also has implications for accessibility, since it enables automatic determination of the target language for automatic machine translation purposes.

Many applications could potentially benefit from automatic language identification, but building a customized solution per-application is prohibitively expensive, especially if human annotation is required to produce a corpus of language-labelled training documents from the application domain. What is required is thus a generic language identification tool that is usable *off-the-shelf*, i.e. with no end-user training and minimal configuration.

In this paper, we present `langid.py`, a LangID tool with the following characteristics: (1) fast, (2) usable off-the-shelf, (3) unaffected by domain-specific features (e.g. HTML, XML, markdown), (4) single file with minimal dependencies, and (5) flexible interface

2 Methodology

`langid.py` is trained over a naive Bayes classifier with a multinomial event model (McCallum and Nigam, 1998), over a mixture of byte n-grams ($1 \leq n \leq 4$). One key difference from conventional text categorization solutions is that `langid.py` was designed to be used *off-the-shelf*. Since `langid.py` implements a supervised classifier, this presents two primary challenges: (1) a pre-trained model must be distributed with the classifier, and (2) the model must generalize to data from different *domains*, meaning that in its default configuration, it must have good accuracy over inputs as diverse as web pages, newspaper articles and microblog messages. (1) is mostly a practical consideration, and so we will address it in Section 3. In order to address (2), we integrate information about the language identification task from a variety of domains by using $\mathcal{LD}$ feature selection (Lui and Baldwin, 2011).

Lui and Baldwin (2011) showed that it is relatively easy to attain high accuracy for language iden-

Proceedings of the 50th Annual Meeting of the Association for Computational Linguistics, pages 25–30,
Jeju, Republic of Korea, 8-14 July 2012.

Dataset	Documents	Langs	Doc Length (bytes)
EuroGOV	1500	10	$1.7\times10^4 \pm3.9\times10^4$
TCL	3174	60	$2.6\times10^3 \pm3.8\times10^3$
Wikipedia	4963	67	$1.5\times10^3 \pm4.1\times10^3$
EMEA	19988	22	$2.9\times10^5 \pm7.9\times10^5$
EuroPARL	20828	22	$1.7\times10^2 \pm1.6\times10^2$
T-BE	9659	6	$1.0\times10^2 \pm3.2\times10^1$
T-SC	5000	5	$8.8\times10^1 \pm3.9\times10^1$

Table 1: Summary of the LangID datasets

tification in a traditional text categorization setting, where we have in-domain training data. The task becomes much harder when trying to perform *domain adaptation*, that is, trying to use model parameters learned in one domain to classify data from a different domain. $\mathcal{LD}$ feature selection addresses this problem by focusing on key features that are relevant to the language identification task. It is based on Information Gain (IG), originally introduced as a splitting criteria for decision trees (Quinlan, 1986), and later shown to be effective for feature selection in text categorization (Yang and Pedersen, 1997; Forman, 2003). $\mathcal{LD}$ represents the difference in IG with respect to language and domain. Features with a high $\mathcal{LD}$ score are informative about language without being informative about domain. For practical reasons, before the IG calculation the candidate feature set is pruned by means of a term-frequency based feature selection.

Lui and Baldwin (2011) presented empirical evidence that $\mathcal{LD}$ feature selection was effective for domain adaptation in language identification. This result is further supported by our evaluation, presented in Section 5.

3 System Architecture

The full `langid.py` package consists of the language identifier `langid.py`, as well as two support modules `LDfeatureselect.py` and `train.py`.

`langid.py` is the single file which packages the language identification tool, and the only file needed to use `langid.py` for off-the-shelf language identification. It comes with an embedded model which covers 97 languages using training data drawn from 5 domains. Tokenization and feature selection are carried out in a single pass over the input document via Aho-Corasick string matching (Aho and Corasick, 1975). The Aho-Corasick string matching algorithm processes an input by means of a deterministic finite automaton (DFA). Some states of the automaton are associated with the completion of one of the n-grams selected through $\mathcal{LD}$ feature selection. Thus, we can obtain our document representation by simply counting the number of times the DFA enters particular states while processing our input. The DFA and the associated mapping from state to n-gram are constructed during the training phase, and embedded as part of the pre-trained model.

The naive Bayes classifier is implemented using `numpy`,[1] the de-facto numerical computation package for Python. `numpy` is free and open source, and available for all major platforms. Using `numpy` introduces a dependency on a library that is not in the Python standard library. This is a reasonable tradeoff, as `numpy` provides us with an optimized implementation of matrix operations, which allows us to implement fast naive Bayes classification while maintaining the single-file concept of `langid.py`.

`langid.py` can be used in the three ways:

Command-line tool: `langid.py` supports an interactive mode with a text prompt and line-by-line classification. This mode is suitable for quick interactive queries, as well as for demonstration purposes. `langid.py` also supports language identification of entire files via redirection. This allows a user to interactively explore data, as well as to integrate language identification into a pipeline of other `unix`-style tools. However, use via redirection is not recommended for large quantities of documents as each invocation requires the trained model to be unpacked into memory. Where large quantities of documents are being processed, use as a library or web service is preferred as the model will only be unpacked once upon initialization.

Python library: `langid.py` can be imported as a Python module, and provides a function that accepts text and returns the identified language of the text. This use of `langid.py` is the fastest in a single-processor setting as it incurs the least overhead.

Web service: `langid.py` can be started as a web service with a command-line switch. This

[1] `http://numpy.scipy.org`

allows language identitication by means of HTTP PUT and HTTP POST requests, which return JSON-encoded responses. This is the preferred method of using `langid.py` from other programming environments, as most languages include libraries for interacting with web services over HTTP. It also allows the language identification service to be run as a network/internet service. Finally, `langid.py` is WSGI-compliant,[2] so it can be deployed in a WSGI-compliant web server. This provides an easy way to achieve parallelism by leveraging existing technologies to manage load balancing and utilize multiple processors in the handling of multiple concurrent requests for a service.

`LDfeatureselect.py` implements the $\mathcal{LD}$ feature selection. The calculation of term frequency is done in constant memory by index inversion through a MapReduce-style sharding approach. The calculation of information gain is also chunked to limit peak memory use, and furthermore it is parallelized to make full use of modern multiprocessor systems. `LDfeatureselect.py` produces a list of byte n-grams ranked by their $\mathcal{LD}$ score.

`train.py` implements estimation of parameters for the multinomial naive Bayes model, as well as the construction of the DFA for the Aho-Corasick string matching algorithm. Its input is a list of byte patterns representing a feature set (such as that selected via `LDfeatureselect.py`), and a corpus of training documents. It produces the final model as a single compressed, encoded string, which can be saved to an external file and used by `langid.py` via a command-line option.

4 Training Data

`langid.py` is distributed with an embedded model trained using the multi-domain language identification corpus of Lui and Baldwin (2011). This corpus contains documents in a total of 97 languages. The data is drawn from 5 different domains: government documents, software documentation, newswire, online encyclopedia and an internet crawl, though no domain covers the full set of languages by itself, and some languages are present only in a single domain. More details about this corpus are given in Lui and Baldwin (2011).

[2] `http://www.wsgi.org`

We do not perform explicit encoding detection, but we do not assume that all the data is in the same encoding. Previous research has shown that explicit encoding detection is not needed for language identification (Baldwin and Lui, 2010). Our training data consists mostly of UTF8-encoded documents, but some of our evaluation datasets contain a mixture of encodings.

5 Evaluation

In order to benchmark `langid.py`, we carried out an empirical evaluation using a number of language-labelled datasets. We compare the empirical results obtained from `langid.py` to those obtained from other language identification toolkits which incorporate a pre-trained model, and are thus usable *off-the-shelf* for language identification. These tools are listed in Table 3.

5.1 Off-the-shelf LangID tools

`TextCat` is an implementation of the method of Cavnar and Trenkle (1994) by Gertjan van Noord. It has traditionally been the de facto LangID tool of choice in research, and is the basis of language identification/filtering in the ClueWeb09 Dataset (Callan and Hoy, 2009) and CorpusBuilder (Ghani et al., 2004). It includes support for training with user-supplied data.

`LangDetect` implements a Naive Bayes classifier, using a character n-gram based representation without feature selection, with a set of normalization heuristics to improve accuracy. It is trained on data from Wikipedia,[3] and can be trained with user-supplied data.

`CLD` is a port of the embedded language identifier in Google's Chromium browser, maintained by Mike McCandless. Not much is known about the internal design of the tool, and there is no support provided for re-training it.

The datasets come from a variety of domains, such as newswire (TCL), biomedical corpora (EMEA), government documents (EUROGOV, EUROPARL) and microblog services (T-BE, T-SC). A number of these datasets have been previously used in language identification research. We provide a

[3] `http://www.wikipedia.org`

Test Dataset	langid.py Accuracy	langid.py docs/s	LangDetect ΔAcc	LangDetect Slowdown	TextCat ΔAcc	TextCat Slowdown	CLD ΔAcc	CLD Slowdown
EUROGOV	0.987	70.5	+0.005	1.1×	−0.046	31.1×	−0.004	0.5×
TCL	0.904	185.4	−0.086	2.1×	−0.299	24.2×	−0.172	0.5×
WIKIPEDIA	0.913	227.6	−0.046	2.5×	−0.207	99.9×	−0.082	0.9×
EMEA	0.934	7.7	−0.820	0.2×	−0.572	6.3×	+0.044	0.3×
EUROPARL	0.992	294.3	+0.001	3.6×	−0.186	115.4×	−0.010	0.2×
T-BE	0.941	367.9	−0.016	4.4×	−0.210	144.1×	−0.081	0.7×
T-SC	0.886	298.2	−0.038	2.9×	−0.235	34.2×	−0.120	0.2×

Table 2: Comparison of standalone classification tools, in terms of accuracy and speed (documents/second), relative to langid.py

Tool	Languages	URL
langid.py	97	http://www.csse.unimelb.edu.au/research/lt/resources/langid/
LangDetect	53	http://code.google.com/p/language-detection/
TextCat	75	http://odur.let.rug.nl/vannoord/TextCat/
CLD	64+	http://code.google.com/p/chromium-compact-language-detector/

Table 3: Summary of the LangID tools compared

brief summary of the characteristics of each dataset in Table 1.

The datasets we use for evaluation are different from and independent of the datasets from which the embedded model of `langid.py` was produced. In Table 2, we report the accuracy of each tool, measured as the proportion of documents from each dataset that are correctly classified. We present the absolute accuracy and performance for `langid.py`, and relative accuracy and slowdown for the other systems. For this experiment, we used a machine with 2 Intel Xeon E5540 processors and 24GB of RAM. We only utilized a single core, as none of the language identification tools tested are inherently multicore.

5.2 Comparison on standard datasets

We compared the four systems on datasets used in previous language identification research (Baldwin and Lui, 2010) (EUROGOV, TCL, WIKIPEDIA), as well as an extract from a biomedical parallel corpus (Tiedemann, 2009) (EMEA) and a corpus of samples from the Europarl Parallel Corpus (Koehn, 2005) (EUROPARL). The sample of EUROPARL we use was originally prepared by Shuyo Nakatani (author of `LangDetect`) as a validation set.

`langid.py` compares very favorably with other language identification tools. It outperforms `TextCat` in terms of speed and accuracy on all of the datasets considered. `langid.py` is generally orders of magnitude faster than `TextCat`, but this advantage is reduced on larger documents. This is primarily due to the design of `TextCat`, which requires that the supplied models be read from file for each document classified.

`langid.py` generally outperforms `LangDetect`, except in datasets derived from government documents (EUROGOV, EUROPARL). However, the difference in accuracy between `langid.py` and `LangDetect` on such datasets is very small, and `langid.py` is generally faster. An abnormal result was obtained when testing `LangDetect` on the EMEA corpus. Here, `LangDetect` is much faster, but has extremely poor accuracy (0.114). Analysis of the results reveals that the majority of documents were classified as Polish. We suspect that this is due to the early termination criteria employed by `LangDetect`, together with specific characteristics of the corpus. `TextCat` also performed very poorly on this corpus (accuracy 0.362). However, it is important to note that `langid.py` and `CLD` both performed very well, providing evidence that it is possible to build a generic language identifier that is insensitive to domain-specific characteristics.

`langid.py` also compares well with `CLD`. It is generally more accurate, although `CLD` does better on the EMEA corpus. This may reveal some insight into the design of `CLD`, which is likely to have been tuned for language identification of web pages. The EMEA corpus is heavy in XML markup, which `CLD` and `langid.py` both successfully ignore. One area where `CLD` outperforms all other systems is in its speed. However, this increase in speed comes at the cost of decreased accuracy in other domains, as we will see in Section 5.3.

5.3 Comparison on microblog messages

The size of the input text is known to play a significant role in the accuracy of automatic language identification, with accuracy decreasing on shorter input documents (Cavnar and Trenkle, 1994; Sibun and Reynar, 1996; Baldwin and Lui, 2010).

Recently, language identification of short strings has generated interest in the research community. Hammarstrom (2007) described a method that augmented a dictionary with an affix table, and tested it over synthetic data derived from a parallel bible corpus. Ceylan and Kim (2009) compared a number of methods for identifying the language of search engine queries of 2 to 3 words. They develop a method which uses a decision tree to integrate outputs from several different language identification approaches. Vatanen et al. (2010) focus on messages of 5–21 characters, using n-gram language models over data drawn from UDHR in a naive Bayes classifier.

A recent application where language identification is an open issue is over the rapidly-increasing volume of data being generated by social media. Microblog services such as Twitter[4] allow users to post short text messages. Twitter has a worldwide user base, evidenced by the large array of languages present on Twitter (Carter et al., to appear). It is estimated that half the messages on Twitter are not in English. [5]

This new domain presents a significant challenge for automatic language identification, due to the much shorter 'documents' to be classified, and is compounded by the lack of language-labelled in-domain data for training and validation. This has led to recent research focused specifically on the task of language identification of Twitter messages. Carter et al. (to appear) improve language identification in Twitter messages by augmenting standard methods with language identification priors based on a user's previous messages and by the content of links embedded in messages. Tromp and Pechenizkiy (2011) present a method for language identification of short text messages by means of a graph structure.

Despite the recently published results on language identification of microblog messages, there is no dedicated off-the-shelf system to perform the task. We thus examine the accuracy and performance of using generic language identification tools to identify the language of microblog messages. It is important to note that none of the systems we test have been specifically tuned for the microblog domain. Furthermore, they do not make use of any non-textual information such as author and link-based priors (Carter et al., to appear).

We make use of two datasets of Twitter messages kindly provided to us by other researchers. The first is T-BE (Tromp and Pechenizkiy, 2011), which contains 9659 messages in 6 European languages. The second is T-SC (Carter et al., to appear), which contains 5000 messages in 5 European languages.

We find that over both datasets, `langid.py` has better accuracy than any of the other systems tested. On T-BE, Tromp and Pechenizkiy (2011) report accuracy between 0.92 and 0.98 depending on the parametrization of their system, which was tuned specifically for classifying short text messages. In its *off-the-shelf* configuration, `langid.py` attains an accuracy of 0.94, making it competitive with the customized solution of Tromp and Pechenizkiy (2011).

On T-SC, Carter et al. (to appear) report overall accuracy of 0.90 for `TextCat` in the off-the-shelf configuration, and up to 0.92 after the inclusion of priors based on (domain-specific) extra-textual information. In our experiments, the accuracy of `TextCat` is much lower (0.654). This is because Carter et al. (to appear) constrained `TextCat` to output only the set of 5 languages they considered. Our results show that it is possible for a generic language identification tool to attain reasonably high accuracy (0.89) without artificially constraining the set of languages to be considered, which corresponds more closely to the demands of automatic language identification to real-world data sources, where there is generally no prior knowledge of the languages present.

[4] `http://www.twitter.com`

[5] `http://semiocast.com/downloads/Semiocast_Half_of_messages_on_Twitter_are_not_in_English_20100224.pdf`

We also observe that while CLD is still the fastest classifier, this has come at the cost of accuracy in an alternative domain such as Twitter messages, where both langid.py and LangDetect attain better accuracy than CLD.

An interesting point of comparison between the Twitter datasets is how the accuracy of all systems is generally higher on T-BE than on T-SC, despite them covering essentially the same languages (T-BE includes Italian, whereas T-SC does not). This is likely to be because the T-BE dataset was produced using a semi-automatic method which involved a language identification step using the method of Cavnar and Trenkle (1994) (E Tromp, personal communication, July 6 2011). This may also explain why TextCat, which is also based on Cavnar and Trenkle's work, has unusually high accuracy on this dataset.

6 Conclusion

In this paper, we presented langid.py, an off-the-shelf language identification solution. We demonstrated the robustness of the tool over a range of test corpora of both long and short documents (including micro-blogs).

Acknowledgments

NICTA is funded by the Australian Government as represented by the Department of Broadband, Communications and the Digital Economy and the Australian Research Council through the ICT Centre of Excellence program.

References

Alfred V. Aho and Margaret J. Corasick. 1975. Efficient string matching: an aid to bibliographic search. *Communications of the ACM*, 18(6):333–340, June.

Timothy Baldwin and Marco Lui. 2010. Language identification: The long and the short of the matter. In *Proceedings of NAACL HLT 2010*, pages 229–237, Los Angeles, USA.

Jamie Callan and Mark Hoy, 2009. *ClueWeb09 Dataset*. Available at http://boston.lti.cs.cmu.edu/Data/clueweb09/.

Simon Carter, Wouter Weerkamp, and Manos Tsagkias. to appear. Microblog language identification: Overcoming the limitations of short, unedited and idiomatic text. *Language Resources and Evaluation Journal*.

William B. Cavnar and John M. Trenkle. 1994. N-gram-based text categorization. In *Proceedings of the Third Symposium on Document Analysis and Information Retrieval*, Las Vegas, USA.

Hakan Ceylan and Yookyung Kim. 2009. Language identification of search engine queries. In *Proceedings of ACL2009*, pages 1066–1074, Singapore.

George Forman. 2003. An Extensive Empirical Study of Feature Selection Metrics for Text Classification. *Journal of Machine Learning Research*, 3(7-8):1289–1305, October.

Rayid Ghani, Rosie Jones, and Dunja Mladenic. 2004. Building Minority Language Corpora by Learning to Generate Web Search Queries. *Knowledge and Information Systems*, 7(1):56–83, February.

Harald Hammarstrom. 2007. A Fine-Grained Model for Language Identication. In *Proceedings of iNEWS07*, pages 14–20.

Philipp Koehn. 2005. Europarl: A parallel corpus for statistical machine translation. *MT summit*, 11.

Marco Lui and Timothy Baldwin. 2011. Cross-domain feature selection for language identification. In *Proceedings of 5th International Joint Conference on Natural Language Processing*, pages 553–561, Chiang Mai, Thailand.

Andrew McCallum and Kamal Nigam. 1998. A comparison of event models for Naive Bayes text classification. In *Proceedings of the AAAI-98 Workshop on Learning for Text Categorization*, Madison, USA.

J.R. Quinlan. 1986. Induction of Decision Trees. *Machine Learning*, 1(1):81–106, October.

Penelope Sibun and Jeffrey C. Reynar. 1996. Language determination: Examining the issues. In *Proceedings of the 5th Annual Symposium on Document Analysis and Information Retrieval*, pages 125–135, Las Vegas, USA.

Jörg Tiedemann. 2009. News from OPUS - A Collection of Multilingual Parallel Corpora with Tools and Interfaces. *Recent Advances in Natural Language Processing*, V:237–248.

Erik Tromp and Mykola Pechenizkiy. 2011. Graph-Based N-gram Language Identification on Short Texts. In *Proceedings of Benelearn 2011*, pages 27–35, The Hague, Netherlands.

Tommi Vatanen, Jaakko J. Vayrynen, and Sami Virpioja. 2010. Language identification of short text segments with n-gram models. In *Proceedings of LREC 2010*, pages 3423–3430.

Yiming Yang and Jan O. Pedersen. 1997. A comparative study on feature selection in text categorization. In *Proceedings of ICML 97*.

Personalized Normalization for a Multilingual Chat System

Ai Ti Aw and Lian Hau Lee
Human Language Technology
Institute for Infocomm Research
1 Fusionopolis Way, #21-01 Connexis, Singapore 138632
aaiti@i2r.a-star.edu.sg

Abstract

This paper describes the personalized normalization of a multilingual chat system that supports chatting in user defined short-forms or abbreviations. One of the major challenges for multilingual chat realized through machine translation technology is the normalization of non-standard, self-created short-forms in the chat message to standard words before translation. Due to the lack of training data and the variations of short-forms used among different social communities, it is hard to normalize and translate chat messages if user uses vocabularies outside the training data and create short-forms freely. We develop a personalized chat normalizer for English and integrate it with a multilingual chat system, allowing user to create and use personalized short-forms in multilingual chat.

1 Introduction

Processing user-generated textual content on social media and networking usually encounters challenges due to the language used by the online community. Though some jargons of the online language has made their way into the standard dictionary, a large portion of the abbreviations, slang and context specific terms are still uncommon and only understood within the user community. Consequently, content analysis or translation techniques developed for a more formal genre like news or even conversations cannot apply directly and effectively to the social media content. In recent years, there are many works (Aw et al., 2006; Cook et al., 2009; Han et al., 2011) on text normalization to preprocess user generated content such as tweets and short messages before further processing. The approaches include supervised or unsupervised methods based on morphological and phonetic variations. However, most of the multilingual chat systems on the Internet have not yet integrated this feature into their systems but requesting users to type in proper language so as to have good translation. This is because the current techniques are not robust enough to model the different characteristics featured in the social media content. Most of the techniques are developed based on observations and assumptions made on certain datasets. It is also difficult to unify the language uniqueness among different users into a single model.

We propose a practical and effective method, exploiting a personalized dictionary for each user, to support the use of user-defined short-forms in a multilingual chat system - *AsiaSpik*. The use of this personalized dictionary reduces the reliance on the availability and dependency of training data and empowers the users with the flexibility and interactivity to include and manage their own vocabularies during chat.

2 ASIASPIK System Overview

AsiaSpik is a web-based multilingual instant messaging system that enables online chats written in one language to be readable in other languages by other users. Figure 1 describes the system process. It describes the process flow between *Chat Client*, *Chat Server*, *Translation Bot* and *Normalization Bot* whenever *Chat Client* starts chat module.

When *Chat Client* starts chat module, the *Chat Client* checks if the normalization option for that language used by the user is active and activated. If

Proceedings of the 50th Annual Meeting of the Association for Computational Linguistics, pages 31–36,
Jeju, Republic of Korea, 8-14 July 2012.

so, any message sent by the user will be routed to the *Normalization Bot* for normalization before reaching the *Chat Server*. The *Chat Server* then directs the message to the designated recipients. *Chat Client* at each recipient invokes a translation request to the *Translation Bot* to translate the message to the language set by the recipient. This allows the same source message to be received by different recipients in different target languages.

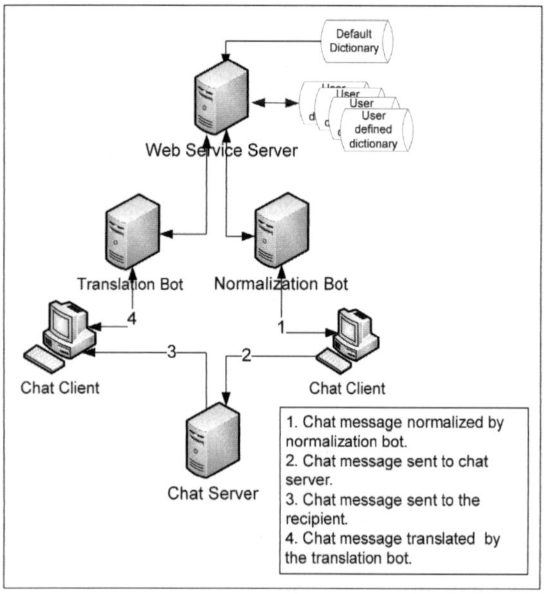

Figure 1. AsiaSpik Chat Process Flow

In this system, we use *Openfire Chat Server* by *Ignite Realtime* as our *Chat Server*. We custom build a web-based *Chat Client* to communicate with the *Chat Server* based on Jabber/XMPP to receive presence and messaging information. We also develop a user management plug-in to synchronize and authenticate user login. The translation and normalization function used by the *Translation Bot* and *Normalization Bot* are provided through *Web Services*.

The *Translation Web Service* uses in-house translation engines and supports the translation from Chinese, Malay and Indonesian to English and vice versa. Multilingual chat among these languages is achieved through pivot translation using English as the pivot language. The *Normalization Web Service* supports only English normalization. Both web services are running on *Apache Tomcat* web server with *Apache Axis2*.

3 Personalized Normalization

Personalized Normalization is the main distinction of *AsiaSpik* among other multilingual chat system. It gives the flexibility for user to personalize his/her short-forms for messages in English.

3.1 Related Work

The traditional text normalization strategy follows the noisy channel model (Shannon, 1948). Suppose the chat message is C and its corresponding standard form is S, the approach aims to find $\arg\max P(S \mid C)$ by computing $\arg\max P(C \mid S)$ in which $P(S)$ is usually a language model and $P(C \mid S)$ is an error model. The objective of using model in the chat message normalization context is to develop an appropriate error model for converting the non-standard and unconventional words found in chat messages into standard words.

$$\hat{S} = \arg\max_{S} P(S \mid C) = \arg\max_{S} P(C \mid S) P(S)$$

Recently, Aw et al. (2006) model text message normalization as translation from the texting language into the standard language. Choudhury et al. (2007) model the word-level text generation process for SMS messages, by considering graphemic/phonetic abbreviations and unintentional typos as hidden Markov model (HMM) state transitions and emissions, respectively. Cook and Stevenson (2009) expand the error model by introducing inference from different erroneous formation processes, according to the sample error distribution. Han and Baldwin (2011) use a classifier to detect ill-formed words, and generate correction candidates based on morphophonemic similarity. These models are effective on their experiments conducted, however, much works remain to be done to handle the diversity and dynamic of content and fast evolution of words used in social media and networking.

As we notice that unlike spelling errors which are made mostly unintentionally by the writers, abbreviations or slangs found in chat messages are introduced intentionally by the senders most of the time. This leads us to suggest that if facilities are given to users to define their abbreviations, the dynamic of the social content and the fast evolution of words could be well captured and managed by the user. In this way, the normalization model could be evolved together with the social media language and chat message could also be personalized for each user dynamically and interactively.

3.2 Personalized Normalization Model

We employ a simple but effective approach for chat normalization. We express normalization using a probabilistic model as below

$$s_{best} = \arg\max_{s} P(s \mid c)$$

and define the probability using a linear combination of features

$$P(s \mid c) \propto \exp \sum_{k=1}^{m} \lambda_k h_k(s,c)$$

where $h_k(s,c)$ are two feature functions namely the log probability $P(s_{i,j} \mid c_i)$ of a short-form, c_i, being normalized to a standard form, $s_{i,j}$; and the language model log probability. λ_k are weights of the feature functions.

We define $P(s_{i,j} \mid c_i)$ as a uniform distribution computed through a set of dictionary collected from corpus, SMS messages and Internet sources. A total of 11,119 entries are collected and each entry is assigned with an initial probability, $P_s(s_{i,j} \mid c_i) = \frac{1}{|c_i|}$, where $|c_i|$ is the number of c_i entries defined in the dictionary. We adjust the probability manually for some entries that are very common and occur more than a certain threshold, t, in the NUS SMS corpus (How and Kan, 2005) with a higher weight-age, w. This model, together with the language model, forms our baseline system for chat normalization.

$$P_s(s_{i,j} \mid c_i) = \begin{cases} \frac{1}{|c_i|} + w & \text{if } |(s_{i,j}, c_i)| \geq t \\ \frac{1}{|c_i|} - \frac{w \times \|(s_{i,j}, c_i)| \geq t|}{\|(s_{i,j}, c_i)| < t|} & \text{if } |(s_{i,j}, c_i)| < t \end{cases}$$

To enable personalized real-time management of user-defined abbreviations and short-forms, we define a personalized model $P_{user\_i}(s_{i,j} \mid c_i)$ for each user based on his/her dictionary profile. Each personalized model is loaded into the memory once the user activates the normalization option. Whenever there is a change in the entry, the entry's probability will be re-distributed and updated based on the following model. This characterizes the *AsiaSpik* system which supports personalized and dynamic chat normalization.

$$P_{user\_i}(s_{i,j} \mid c_i) = \begin{cases} P_s(s_{i,j} \mid c_i) \times \frac{N}{N+M} & \text{if } c_i, s_{i,j} \in SD \\ \frac{1}{N+M} & \text{if } c_i \in \text{SD}, s_{i,j} \notin \text{SD} \\ \frac{1}{\text{M}} & \text{if } c_i \notin \text{SD} \end{cases}$$

where

SD denotes default dictionary;

N denotes the number of c_i entries in SD

M denotes the number of c_i entries in user dictionary.

The feature weights in the normalization model are optimized by minimum error rate training (Och, 2003), which searches for weights maximizing the normalization accuracy using a small development set. We use standard state-of-the-art open source tools, Moses (Koehn, 2007), to develop the system and the SRI language modeling toolkit (Stolcke,2003) to train a trigram language model on the English portion of the Europarl Corpus (Koehn, 2005).

3.3 Experiments

We conducted a small experiment using 134 chat messages sent by high school students. Out of these messages, 73 short-forms are uncommon and not found in our default dictionary. Most of these short-forms are very irregular and hard to predict their standard forms using morphological and phonetic similarity. It is also hard to train a statistical model if training data is not available. We asked the students to define their personal abbreviations in the system and run through the system with and without the user dictionary. We asked them to give a score of *1* if the output is acceptable to them as proper English, otherwise a *0* will be given. We compared the results using both the baseline model and the model implemented using the same training data as in Aw et al. (2006).

Table 1 shows the number of accepted output between the two models. Both models show improvement with the use of user dictionary. It also shows that it is very critical to have similar training data for the targeted domain to have good normalization performance. A simple model helps if such training data is unavailable. Nevertheless, the use of a dictionary driven by the user is an alternative to improve the overall performance. One reason for the inability of both models to capture the variations fully is because many messages require some degree of rephrasing in addition to insertion and deletion to make it readable and acceptable. For example, the ideal output for "*haiz, I wanna pontang school*" is "*Sigh, I do not feel like going to school*", which may not be just a normalization problem.

Baseline Model	Baseline + User Dictionary	Aw et al. (2006)	Aw et al. (2006) + user Dictionary
40	72	17	42

Table 1. Number of Correct Normalization Output

In the examples showed in Table 2, '*din*' and '*dnr*' are normalized to '*didn't*' and '*do not reply*' based on the entries captured in the default dictionary. With the extension of normalization hypotheses in the user dictionary, the system produces the correct expansion to 'dinner'.

Chat Message	**Chat Message normalized using the Default dictionary**	**Chat Message normalized with the supplement of user dictionary**
buy *din* 4 urself.	Buy *didn't* for yourself.	Buy *dinner* for yourself.
dun cook *dnr* 4 me 2nite	Don't cook *do not reply* for me tonight	Don't cook *dinner* for me tonight
gtg *bb* ttyl ttfn	Got to go *bb ttyl ttfn*	Got to go *bye talk to you later bye bye*
I dun feel lyk riting	I don't feel *lyk riting*	I don't feel *like writing*
im gng hme 2 mug	I'm going *hme two mug*	I'm going *home to study*
msg me *wh u rch*	Message me *wh you rch*	Message me *when you reach*
so sian I dun wanna do hw now	So *sian* I don't want to do *how* now	So *bored* I don't want to do *homework* now

Table 2. Normalized chat messages

AsiaSpik Multilingual Chat

Figure 2 and Figure 3 show the personal lingo defined by two users. Note that expansions for "gtg" and "tgt" are defined differently and expanded differently for the two users. 'Me' in the message box indicates the message typed by the user while 'Expansion' is the message expanded by the system.

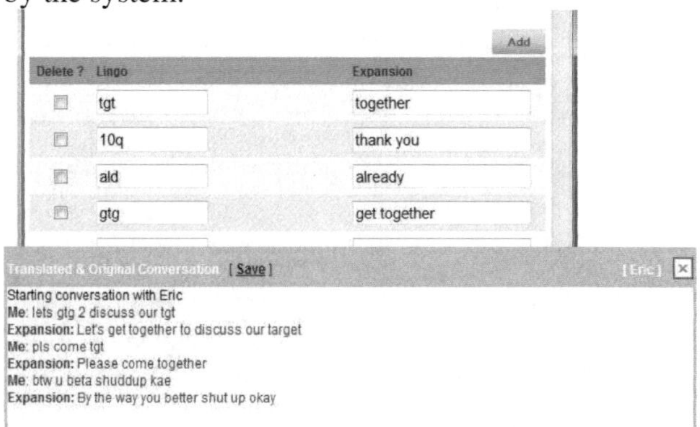

Figure 2. Short-forms defined and messages expanded for user 1

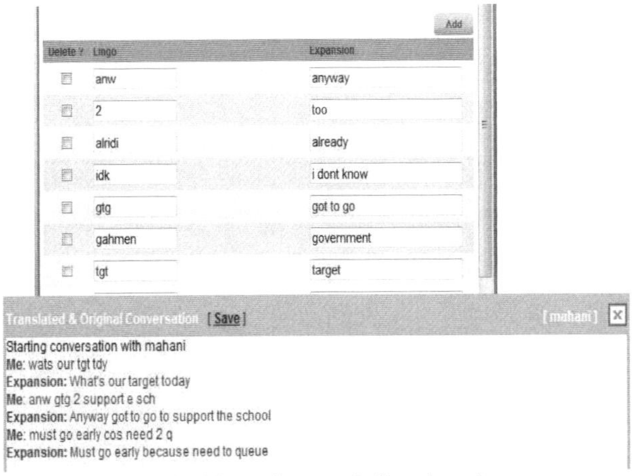

Figure 3. Short-forms defined and messages expanded for user 2

Figure 4 shows the multilingual chat exchange between a Malay language user (Mahani) and an English user (Keith). The figure shows the messages are first expanded to the correct forms before translated to the recipient language.

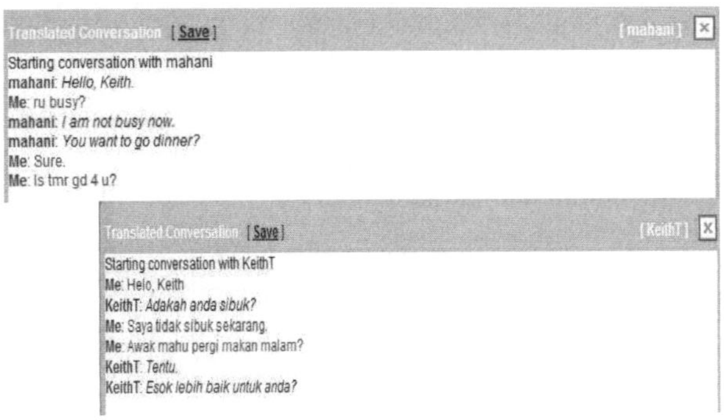

Figure 4. Conversion between a Malay user & an English user

4 Conclusions

AsiaSpik system provides an architecture for performing chat normalization for each user such that user can chat as usual and does not need to pay special attention to type in proper language when involving translation for multilingual chat. The system aims to overcome the limitations of normalizing social media content universally through a personalized normalization model. The proposed strategy makes user the active contributor in defining the chat language and enables the system to model the user chat language dynamically.

The normalization approach is a simple probabilistic model making use of the normalization probability defined for each short-form and the language model probability. The model can be further improved by fine-tuning the normalization probability and incorporate other feature functions. The baseline model can also be further improved with more sophisticated method without changing the architecture of the full system.

AsiaSpik is a demonstration system. We would like to expand the normalization model to include more features and support other languages such as Malay and Chinese. We would also like to further enhance the system to convert the translated English chat messages back to the social media language as defined by the user.

References

AiTi Aw, Min Zhang, Juan Xiao, and Jian Su. 2006. A Phrase-based statistical model for SMS text normalization. *In Proc. Of the COLING/ACL 2006 Main Conference Poster Sessions*, pages 33-40. Sydney.

Monojit Choudhury, Rahul Saraf, Vijit Jain, Animesh Mukherjee, Sudeshna Sarkar, and Anupam Basu. 2007. Investigation and modeling of the structure of texting language. *International Journal on Document Analysis and Recognition*, 10:157–174.

Paul Cook and Suzanne Stevenson. 2009. An unsupervised model for text message normalization. In *CALC '09: Proceedings of the Workshop on Computational Approaches to Linguistic Creativity*, pages 71–78, Boulder, USA.

Bo Han and Timothy Baldwin. 2011. Leixcal Normalisation of Short Text Messages: Makn Sens a #twitter. *In Proc. Of the 49th Annual Meeting of the Association for Computational Linguistics*, pages 368-378, Portland, Oregon, USA.

Yijue How and Min-Yen Kan. 2005. Optimizing predictive text entry for short message service on mobile phones. *In Proceedings of HCII.*

Philipp Koehn &al. Moses: Open Source Toolkit for Statistical Machine Translation, *ACL 2007*, demonstration session.

Koehn, P. (2005). Europarl: A Parallel Corpus for Statistical Machine Translation. In *Machine Translation Summit X* (pp. 79{86). Phuket, Thailand.

Franz Josef Och. 2003. Minimum error rate training for statistical machine translation. *In Proceedings of the*

41th Annual Meeting of the Association for Computational Linguistics, Sapporo, July.

C. Shannon. 1948. *A mathematical theory of communication*. Bell System Technical Journal 27(3): 379-423

A. Stolcke. 2003 SRILM – an Extensible Language Modeling Toolkit. *In International Conference on Spoken Language Processing*, Denver, USA.

IRIS: a Chat-oriented Dialogue System based on the Vector Space Model

Rafael E. Banchs
Human Language Technology
Institute for Infocomm Research
Singapore 138632
rembanchs@i2r.a-star.edu.sg

Haizhou Li
Human Language Technology
Institute for Infocomm Research
Singapore 138632
hli@i2r.a-star.edu.sg

Abstract

This system demonstration paper presents IRIS (Informal Response Interactive System), a chat-oriented dialogue system based on the vector space model framework. The system belongs to the class of example-based dialogue systems and builds its chat capabilities on a dual search strategy over a large collection of dialogue samples. Additional strategies allowing for system adaptation and learning implemented over the same vector model space framework are also described and discussed.

1 Introduction

Dialogue systems have been gaining popularity recently as the demand for such kind of applications have increased in many different areas. Additionally, recent advances in other related language technologies such as speech recognition, discourse analysis and natural language understanding have made possible for dialogue systems to find practical applications that are commercially exploitable (Pieraccini *et al.*, 2009; Griol *et al.*, 2010).

From the application point of view, dialogue systems can be categorized into two major classes: task-oriented and chat-oriented. In the case of task-oriented dialogue systems, the main objective of such a system is to help the user to complete a task, which typically includes booking transportation or accommodation services, requesting specific information from a service facility, etc. (Busemann *et al.*, 1997; Seneff and Polifroni, 2000; Stallard, 2000). On the other hand, chat-oriented systems are not intended to help the user completing any specific task, but to provide a means for participating in a game, or just for chitchat or entertainment. Typical examples of chat-oriented dialogue systems are the so called chat bots (Weizenbaum, 1966; Ogura *et al.*, 2003, Wallis, 2010).

In this paper, we introduce IRIS (Informal Response Interactive System), a chat-oriented dialogue system that is based on the vector space model framework (Salton *et al.*, 1975; van Rijsbergen, 2005). From the operational point of view, IRIS belongs to the category of example-based dialogue systems (Murao *et al.*, 2003). Its dialogue strategy is supported by a large database of dialogues that is used to provide candidate responses to a given user input. The search for candidate responses is performed by computing the cosine similarity metric into the vector space model representation, in which each utterance in the dialogue database is represented by a vector.

Different from example-based question answering systems (Vicedo, 2002; Xue *et al.*, 2008), IRIS uses a dual search strategy. In addition to the current user input, which is compared with all existent utterances in the database, a vector representation of the current dialogue history is also compared with vector representations of full dialogues in the database. Such a dual search strategy allows for incorporating information about the dialogue context into the response selection process.

The rest of the paper is structured as follows. Section 2 presents the architecture of IRIS as well as provides a general description of the dataset that has been used for its implementation. Section 3 presents some illustrative examples of dialogues generated by IRIS, and Section 4 presents the main conclusions of this work.

Proceedings of the 50th Annual Meeting of the Association for Computational Linguistics, pages 37–42,
Jeju, Republic of Korea, 8-14 July 2012. ©2012 Association for Computational Linguistics

2 The IRIS Implementation

In this section we first provide a detailed description of the IRIS architecture along with the most relevant issues behind its implementation. Then, we describe the specific dialogue dataset that supports the IRIS implementation.

2.1 Architecture

As already mentioned, IRIS architecture is heavily based on a vector space model framework, which includes a standard similarity search module from vector-based information retrieval systems (Salton and McGill, 1983). However, it also implements some additional modules that provide the system with capabilities for automatic chatting.

Figure 1 depicts a block diagram that illustrates the main modules in the IRIS architecture. As seen from the picture, the whole system comprises seven processing modules and three repositories.

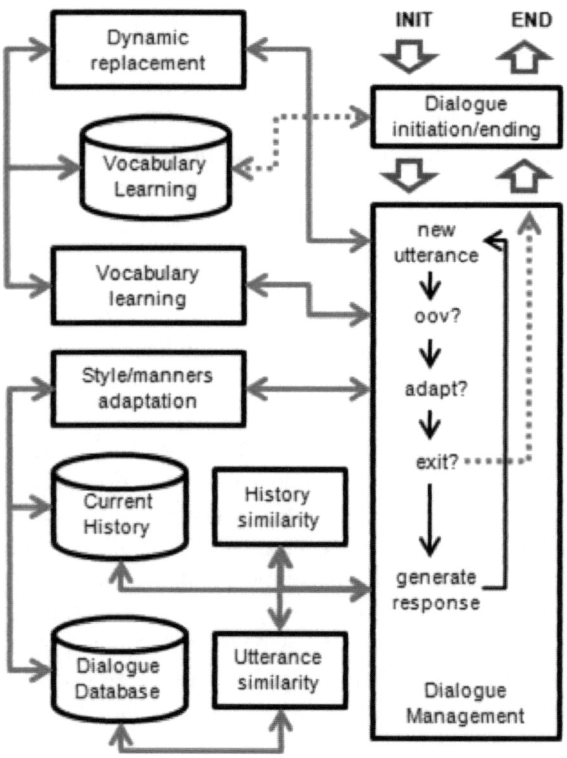

Figure 1: General block diagram for IRIS

The main operation of IRIS can be described as follows. When a new dialogue starts, the control of the dialogue is passed from the dialogue management module to the initiation/ending module. This module implements a two-state dialogue strategy which main objectives are: first, to greet the user and self-introduce IRIS and, second, to collect the name of the user. This module uses a basic parsing algorithm that is responsible for extracting the user's name from the provided input. The name is the first vocabulary term learned by IRIS, which is stored in the vocabulary learning repository.

Once the dialogue initiation has been concluded the dialogue management system gains back the control of the dialogue and initializes the current history vector. Two types of vector initializations are possible here. If the user is already know by IRIS, it will load the last stored dialogue history for that user; otherwise, IRIS will randomly select one dialogue history vector from the dialogue database. After this initialization, IRIS prompts the user for what he desires to do. From this moment, the example-based chat strategy starts.

For each new input from the user, the dialogue management module makes a series of actions that, after a decision process, can lead to different types of responses. In the first action, the dynamic replacement module searches for possible matches between the terms within the vocabulary learning repository and the input string. In a new dialogue, the only two terms know by IRIS are its own name and the user name. If any of this two terms are identified, they are automatically replaced by the placeholders <*self-name*> and <*other-name*>, respectively.

In the case of a mature dialogue, when there are more terms into the vocabulary learning repository, every term matched in the input is replaced by its corresponding definition stored in the vocabulary learning database.

Just after the dynamic replacement is conducted, tokenization and vectorization of the user input is carried out. During tokenization, an additional checking is conducted by the dialogue manager. It looks for any adaptation command that could be possibly inserted at the beginning of the user input. More details on adaptation commands will be given when describing the style/manner adaptation module. Immediately after tokenization, unknown vocabulary terms (OOVs) are identified. IRIS will consider as OOV any term that is not contained in either the dialogue or vocabulary learning databases. In case an OOV is identified, a set of heuristics (aiming at avoiding confusing misspellings with OOVs) are applied to decide whether IRIS should ask the user for the meaning of such a term.

If IRIS decides to ask for the meaning of the term, the control of the dialogue is passed to the vocabulary learning module which is responsible for collecting the meaning of the given term from the user or, alternatively, from an external source of information. Once the definition is collected and validated, it is stored along with the OOV term into the vocabulary learning repository. After completing a learning cycle, IRIS acknowledges the user about having "understood" the meaning of the term and control is passed back to the dialogue management module, which waits for a new user input.

If IRIS decides not to ask for the meaning of the OOV term, or if no OOV term has been identified, vectorization of the user input is completed by the vector similarity modules and similarity scores are computed for retrieving best matches from the dialogue database. Two different similarity scores are actually used by IRIS. The first score is applied at the utterance level. It computes the cosine similarities between the current user input vector and all single utterances stored in the database. This score is used for retrieving a large amount of candidate utterances from the dialogue database, generally between 50 and 100, depending on the absolute value of the associated scores.

The second score is computed over history vectors. The current dialogue history, which is available from the current history repository, includes all utterances interchanged by the current user and IRIS. In other to facilitate possible topic changes along the dialogue evolution, a damping or "forgetting" factor is used for giving more importance to the most recent utterances in the dialogue history. A single vector representation is then computed for the currently updated dialogue history after applying the damping factor. The cosine similarity between this vector and the vector representations for each full dialogue stored in the dialogue database are computed and used along with the utterance-level score for generating a final rank of candidate utterances. A log-linear combination scheme is used for combining the two scores. The dialogue management module randomly selects one of the top ranked utterances and prompts back to the user the corresponding reply (from the dialogue database) to the wining utterance.

Just immediately before prompting back the response to the user, the dynamic replacement module performs an inverse operation for replacing the two placeholders *<self-name>* and *<other-name>*, in case they occur in the response, by their actual values.

The final action taken by IRIS is related to the style/manner adaptation module. For this action to take place the user has to include one of three possible adaptations commands at the beginning of her/his new turn. The three adaptation commands recognized by IRIS are: ban (*), reinforce (+), and discourage (–). By using any of these three characters as the first character in the new turn, the user is requesting IRIS to modify the vector space representation of the previous selected response as follows:

- Ban (*): IRIS will mark its last response as a prohibited response and will not show such response ever again.
- Reinforce (+): IRIS will pull the vector space representation of its last selected utterance towards the vector space representation of the previous user turn, so that the probability of generating the same response given a similar user input will be increased.
- Discourage (–): IRIS will push the vector space representation of its last selected utterance apart from the vector space representation of the previous user turn, so that the probability of generating the same response given a similar user input will be decreased.

2.2 Dialogue Data Collection

For the current implementation of IRIS, a subset of the Movie-DiC dialogue data collection has been used (Banchs, 2012). Movie-DiC is a dialogue corpus that has been extracted from movie scripts which are freely available at The Internet Movie Script Data Collection (http://www.imsdb.com/). In this subsection, we present a brief description on the specific data subset used for the implementation of IRIS, as well as we briefly review the process followed for collecting the data and extracting the dialogues.

First of all, dialogues have to be identified and parsed from the collected html files. Three basic elements are extracted from the scripts: speakers, utterances and context. The speaker and utterance elements contain information about the characters who speak and what they said at each dialogue turn. On the other hand, context elements contain all the additional information (explanations and descriptions) appearing in the scripts.

The extracted dialogues are stored into a data structure such that the information about turn sequences within the dialogues and dialogue sequences within the scripts are preserved.

Some post-processing is also necessary to filter out and/or repair the most common parsing errors occurring during the dialogue extraction phase. Some of these errors include: bad script formatting, same-speaker turn continuations, explanatory notes inserted within the turns, misspelling of names in the speaker headers, changes in the encoding format, etc.

The final dialogue collection used in the IRIS implementation consists of dialogues from 153 movie scripts, mainly belonging to the comedy, action and family genres. Table 1 summarizes the main statistics of the resulting dataset.

Total number of movie scripts	153
Total number of dialogues	24,265
Total number of speaker turns	159,182
Average amount of dialogues per movie	158.59
Average amount of turns per dialogue	6.56
Total number of running words	1,670,879
Overall vocabulary size	34,903

Table 2: Main statistics of the movie dialogue dataset used in the IRIS implementation

For each turn in the dialogue collection, a vector space model representation was constructed. For this, the standard bag-of-words weighting scheme known as TF-IDF was used (Spark, 1972; Salton and Buckley, 1988).

Before performing the vectorization, word tokenization was conducted. In this step, all punctuation marks were removed, with the exception of the question "?" and exclamation "!" marks. Similarly, all other non-alphanumeric characters occurring in the utterances were removed as well. Also during the tokenization phase, all self-references to current speaker names in the utterances were replaced by the *<self-name>* placeholder, as well as all references to the names of other speakers participating in the same dialogue were replaced by the *<other-name>* place-holder.

Finally, a vector space model representation was also computed for each full dialogue in the collection. For this bag-of-words model at the dialogue level, both utterance and context information were taken into account. Again, the TF-IDF weighting scheme was used.

3 Some Dialogue Examples

In this section we show some real examples of interactions between IRIS and human users. First, we present some interesting examples of good performance, as well as illustrate some of the learning capabilities of IRIS. Then, we present some of the common failures which identify specific points of attention for further improvements.

3.1 Good Performance Examples

Our first example illustrates the beginning of a typical chat session between IRIS and a new user. This example is depicted in Table 2.

#	Spkr.	Turn
1	IRIS	Hi, I'm IRIS… What's your name?
2	USER	Hi Iris, I am Peter
3	IRIS	Nice name Peter... What do you want to talk about?
4	USER	Sports?
5	IRIS	How come in all that time I was trying to get you a date, you never asked me out?
6	USER	ok, do you want to go for dinner tonight?
7	IRIS	Yes.
8	USER	What kind of food do you like?
9	IRIS	Anything but guts and mushrooms.
10	USER	Ok pick you up at seven!
11	IRIS	Ok. Pick me up at seven.

Table 2: Beginning of a chat session between IRIS and a new user

For the dialogue depicted in Table 2, turn numbers 1, 2 and 3 are processed by the dialogue intiation/ending module. The example-based dialogue management strategy starts from turn 4 onwards. Notice that as far as this is a new user, not previous dialogue history exists, so in this case a random history vector has been selected and instead of focusing in the *sports* topic suggested by the user, IRIS "takes the initiative" of asking for a date.

In our second example, which is presented in Table 3, we illustrate the beginning of a typical chat session between IRIS and a returning user. For this particular user, her last interaction with IRIS was about sports.

Similar to the previous example, turn 1 is processed by the dialogue intiation/ending module and the example-based dialogue management strategy starts from turn 2 onwards. In this particular case, IRIS is much more centered on the *sports* topic as this context information has been already provided by the stored dialogue history of the previous chat session with this particular user.

#	Spkr.	Turn
1	IRIS	Hey, Helen... welcome back! How are you doing?
2	USER	fine and you?
3	IRIS	Is there more?
4	USER	Yes, I finally went to that tennis match I told you the last time.
5	IRIS	The match!
6	USER	Yes, have you seen some sports recently?
7	IRIS	I hate sports.

Table 3: Beginning of a chat session between IRIS and a returning user

In our third example, which is presented in Table 4, we illustrate the learning of a new vocabulary word by IRIS. In this example, when the unknown term *paella* is detected, the control of the dialogue is passed to the vocabulary learning module, which takes care of turns 7, 8, 9 and 10.

#	Spkr.	Turn
1	USER	do you cook anything Iris?
2	IRIS	Eggs.
3	USER	ha ha ha!
4	IRIS	Ha-ha-ha! Ha-ha-ha!
5	USER	Can you cook anything else?
6	IRIS	Do you cook?
7	USER	Paella
8	IRIS	What the hell is that????
9	USER	It is a Spanish food. Yellow rice with some seafood on it.
10	IRIS	Ok, I see... thanks!
11	USER	So, do you want some paella today?
12	IRIS	Well, it beats working in a seafood restaurant...

Table 4: Chat segment in which IRIS learns the new vocabulary term *paella*

Notice that when the user asks IRIS about having some *paella* today, IRIS is already able to associate it with *seafood* as it was stated in the user's provided definition. The process actually occurs as follows: after tokenization, but before vectorization of the user input in turn 11, the dynamic replacement module substitutes the term *paella* by its definition, which has been previously stored in the vocabulary learning repository when turn 9 was processed. The actual user input that is finally vectorized in turn 11 is the following one: *so do you want some it is a spanish food yellow rice with some seafood on it today ?*, which is the utterance used by IRIS to retrieve and select the response it provides in turn 12.

3.2 Common Failure Examples

In this subsection we focus our attention in the most common failures exhibited by IRIS. Some of these failures put in evidence specific points of attention that should be taken into account for further improvements of the system.

Our first example illustrates the problem of IRIS lack of consistency in issues for which consistent answers are required. Two specific chat segments in which IRIS provides inconsistent responses are presented in Table 5.

#	Spkr.	Turn
1	USER	how old are you Iris?
2	IRIS	I'm thirteen, how old are you?
3	USER	I am 40
4	IRIS	Only I did better... 40 crates a day.
5	USER	how old are you Iris?
6	IRIS	Ten.
#	**Spkr.**	**Turn**
1	USER	Yes, have you seen some sports recently?
2	IRIS	I hate sports.
3	USER	Really, what about soccer?
4	IRIS	I'd sooner watch soccer.
5	USER	what do you prefer soccer or football?
6	IRIS	Football is my life.

Table 5: IRIS incapability to being consistent

The first example presented in Table 5 constitutes a serious consistency problem. In this case IRIS has reported two different ages in the same chat session. The second case, although not so serious as the previous one, also constitutes a consistency failure. In this case IRIS states *Football is my life* just two turns after saying *I hate sports*.

Our second example, which is presented in Table 6, illustrates a problem derived from the noise that is still present in the dataset.

#	Spkr.	Turn
1	IRIS	You watching the ballgame?
2	USER	No
3	IRIS	Bianca stares at him for a moment.

Table 6: Example of noise in the dialogue dataset

In the particular example illustrated in Table 6, as seen from turn 3, a context element has been mistakenly stored in the data collection as an utterance during the dataset preparation phase. Several problems similar to this one, which are related to noise in the database, have been detected already. To tackle this problem we need to refine the parsing and post-processing algorithms used during the dialogue dataset construction phase.

4 Conclusions and Future Work

In this paper, we have presented IRIS (Informal Response Interactive System), a chat-oriented dialogue system that is based on the vector space model framework. The system belongs to the class of example-based dialogue systems and builds its chat capabilities on a dual search strategy over a large collection of movie dialogues.

Additional strategies allowing for system adaptation and learning have been also implemented over the same vector space model framework. More specifically, IRIS is capable of learning new vocabulary terms and semantically relating them to previous knowledge, as well as adapting its dialogue decisions to some stated user preferences.

We have also described the main characteristics of the architecture of IRIS and the most important functions performed by each of its constituent modules. Finally, we have provided some examples of good chat performance and some examples of the common failures exhibited by IRIS.

As future work, we intend to improve IRIS performance by addressing some of the already identified common failures. Similarly, we intend to augment IRIS chatting capabilities by extending the size of the current dialogue database and integrating a strategy for group chatting.

Acknowledgments

The authors would like to thank the Institute for Infocomm Research for its support and permission to publish this work.

References

Banchs R E (2012) Movie-DiC: a movie dialogue corpus for research and development. In Proc. of the 50th Annual Meeting of the ACL.

Busemann S, Declerck T, Diagne A, Dini L, Klein J, Schmeier S (1997) Natural language dialogue service for appointment scheduling agents. In Proc. of the 5th Conference on Applied NLP, pp 25-32.

Griol D, Callejas Z, Lopez-Cozar R (2010) Statistical dialog management methodologies for real applications. In Proc. of SIGDIAL'10, pp 269-272.

Murao H, Kawaguchi N, Matsubara S, Yamaguchi Y, Inagaki Y (2003) Example-based spoken dialogue system using WOZ system log. In Proc. of the 4th SIGDIAL, pp 140-148.

Ogura K, Masuda T, Ishizaki M (2003) Building a new Internet chat system for sharing timing information. In Proc. of the 4th SIGDIAL, pp 97-104.

Pieraccini R, Suendermann D, Dayanidhi K, Liscombe J (2009) Are we there yet? Research in commercial spoken dialog systems. In Proc. of TSD'09, pp 3-13.

Salton G, Wong A, Yang C (1975) A vector space model for automatic indexing. Communications of the ACM 18(11):613-620.

Salton G, McGill M (1983) Introduction to modern information retrieval. McGraw-Hill.

Salton G, Buckley C (1988) Term-weighting approaches in automatic text retrieval. Information Processing & Management 24(5):513-523

Seneff S, Polifroni J (2000) Dialogue management in the Mercury flight reservation system. In Proc. of the ANLP-NAACL 2000 Workshop on Conversational Systems, pp 11-16.

Spark K (1972) A statistical interpretation of term specificity and its application in retrieval. Journal of Documentation 28(1):11-21

Stallard D (2000) Talk'n'travel: a conversational system for air travel planning. In Proc. of the 6th Conference on Applied NLP, pp 68-75.

van Rijsbergen C (2005) A probabilistic logic for information retrieval. In Advances in Information Retrieval, Lecture Notes in Computer Science 3408:1-6.

Vicedo J (2002) SEMQA: A semantic model applied to question answering systems. PhD Thesis, University of Alicante.

Wallis P (2010) A robot in the kitchen. In Proceedings of the ACL 2010 Workshop on Companionable Dialogue Systems, pp 25-30.

Weizenbaum J (1966) ELIZA – A computer program for the study of natural language communication between man and machine. Communications of the ACM 9(1):36-45.

Xue X, Jeon J, Croft W (2008) Retrieval models for question and answer archives. In Proc. of the 31st Annual International ACM SIGIR Conference on R&D in Information Retrieval, pp 475-482.

LetsMT!: A Cloud-Based Platform for Do-It-Yourself Machine Translation

Andrejs Vasiļjevs
TILDE
Vienbas gatve 75a, Riga
LV-1004, LATVIA
andrejs@tilde.com

Raivis Skadiņš
TILDE
Vienbas gatve 75a, Riga
LV-1004, LATVIA
raivis.skadins@tilde.lv

Jörg Tiedemann
Uppsala University
Box 635, Uppsala
SE-75126, SWEDEN
jorg.tiedemann@lingfil.uu.se

Abstract

To facilitate the creation and usage of custom SMT systems we have created a cloud-based platform for do-it-yourself MT. The platform is developed in the EU collaboration project LetsMT!. This system demonstration paper presents the motivation in developing the LetsMT! platform, its main features, architecture, and an evaluation in a practical use case.

1 Introduction

Current mass-market and online MT systems are of a general nature and perform poorly for smaller languages and domain specific texts. The European Union ICT-PSP Programme project LetsMT! develops a user-driven MT "factory in the cloud" enabling web users to get customised MT that better fits their needs. Harnessing the huge potential of the web together with open statistical machine translation (SMT) technologies, LetsMT! has created an online collaborative platform for data sharing and MT building.

The goal of the LetsMT! project is to facilitate the use of open source SMT tools and to involve users in the collection of training data. The LetsMT! project extends the use of existing state-of-the-art SMT methods by providing them as cloud-based services. An easy-to-use web interface empowers users to participate in data collection and MT customisation to increase the quality, domain coverage, and usage of MT.

The LetsMT! project partners are companies TILDE (coordinator), Moravia, and SemLab, and the Universities of Edinburgh, Zagreb, Copenhagen, and Uppsala.

2 LetsMT! Key Features

The LetsMT! platform[1] (Vasiļjevs et al., 2011) gathers public and user-provided MT training data and enables generation of multiple MT systems by combining and prioritising this data. Users can upload their parallel corpora to an online repository and generate user-tailored SMT systems based on data selected by the user.

Authenticated users with appropriate permissions can also store private corpora that can be seen and used only by this user (or a designated user group). All data uploaded into the LetsMT! repository is kept in internal format, and only its metadata is provided to the user. Data cannot be downloaded or accessed for reading by any means. The uploaded data can only be used for SMT training. In such a way, we encourage institutions and individuals to contribute their data to be publicly used for SMT training, even if they are not willing to share the content of the data.

A user creates SMT system definition by specifying a few basic parameters like system name, source/target languages, domain, and choosing corpora (parallel for translation models or monolingual for language models) to use for the particular system. Tuning and evaluation data can be automatically extracted from the training corpora or specified by the user. The access level of the system can also be specified - whether it will be public or accessible only to the particular user or user group.

[1] http://letsmt.com

Proceedings of the 50th Annual Meeting of the Association for Computational Linguistics, pages 43–48,
Jeju, Republic of Korea, 8-14 July 2012. ©2012 Association for Computational Linguistics

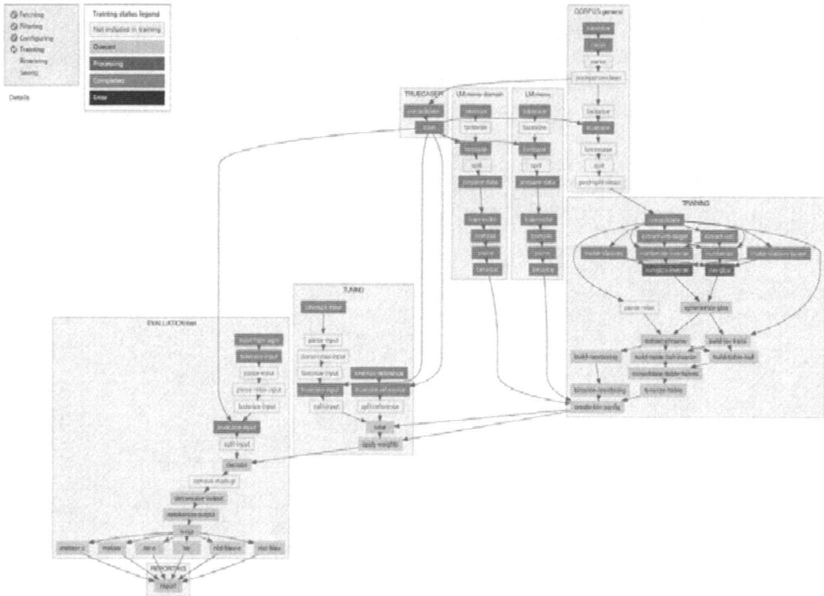

Figure 1. Training chart providing dynamic representation of training steps.

When the system is specified, the user can begin training it. Progress of the training can be monitored on the dynamic training chart (Figure 1). It provides a detailed visualisation of the training process showing (i) steps queued for execution of a particular training task, (ii) current execution status of active training steps, and (iii) steps where any errors have occurred. The training chart remains available after the training to facilitate analysis of the performed trainings. The last step of the training task is automatic evaluation using BLEU, NIST, TER, and METEOR scores.

A successfully trained SMT system can be started and used for translation in several ways:

- on the translation webpage of LetsMT! for testing and short translations;
- using LetsMT! plug-ins in computer-assisted translation (CAT) tools for professional translation;
- integrating the LetsMT! widget for web-site translation;
- using LetsMT! plug-ins for IE and FireFox to integrate translation into the browsers;
- using LetsMT! API for MT integration into different applications.

LetsMT! allows for several system instances to run simultaneously to speed up translation and balance the workload from numerous translation requests.

LetsMT! user authentication and authorisation mechanisms control access rights to private training data, trained models and SMT systems, permissions to initiate and manage training tasks, run trained systems, and access LetsMT! services through external APIs.

The LetsMT! platform is populated with initial SMT training data collected and prepared by the project partners. It currently contains more than 730 million parallel sentences in almost 50 languages. In the first 4 months since launching the invitation only beta version of the platform, 82 SMT systems have been successfully trained.

3 SMT Training and Decoding Facilities

The SMT training and decoding facilities of LetsMT! are based on the open source toolkit Moses. One of the important achievements of the project is the adaptation of the Moses toolkit to fit into the rapid training, updating, and interactive access environment of the LetsMT! platform.

The Moses SMT toolkit (Koehn et al., 2007) provides a complete statistical translation system distributed under the LGPL license. Moses includes all of the components needed to pre-process data and to train language and translation models. Moses is widely used in the research community and has also reached the commercial sector. While the use of the software is not closely monitored, Moses is known to be in commercial use by companies such as Systran (Dugast et al., 2009), Asia Online, Autodesk (Plitt and Masselot, 2010), Matrixware[2], Adobe, Pangeanic, Logrus[3], and Applied Language Solutions (Way et al., 2011).

The SMT training pipeline implemented in Moses involves a number of steps that each require a separate program to run. In the framework of

[2] Machine Translation at Matrixware: http://ir-facility.net/downloads/mxw_factsheet_smt_200910.pdf

[3] TDA Members doing business with Moses: http://www.tausdata.org/blog/2010/10/doing-business-with-moses-open-source-translation/

LetsMT!, this process is streamlined and made automatically configurable given a set of user-specified variables (training corpora, language model data, tuning sets). SMT training is automated using the Moses experiment management system (Koehn, 2010). Other improvements of Moses, implemented by the University of Edinburgh as part of LetsMT! project, are:

- the incremental training of SMT models (Levenberg et al., 2010);
- randomised language models (Levenberg et al., 2009);
- a server mode version of the Moses decoder and multithreaded decoding;
- multiple translation models;
- distributed language models (Brants et al., 2007).

Many improvements in the Moses experiment management system were implemented to speed up SMT system training and to use the full potential of the HPC cluster. We revised and improved Moses training routines (i) by finding tasks that are executed sequentially but can be executed in parallel and (ii) by splitting big training tasks into smaller ones and executing them in parallel.

4 Multitier Architecture

The LetsMT! system has a multitier architecture (Figure 2). It has (i) an interface layer implementing the user interface and APIs with external systems, (ii) an application logic layer for the system logic, (iii) a data storage layer consisting of file and database storage, and (iv) a high performance computing (HPC) cluster. The LetsMT! system performs various time and resource consuming tasks; these tasks are defined by the application logic and data storage and are sent to the HPC cluster for execution.

The Interface layer provides interfaces between the LetsMT! system and external users. The system has both human and machine users. Human users can access the system through web browsers by using the LetsMT! web page interface. External systems such as Computer Aided Translation (CAT) tools and web browser plug-ins can access the LetsMT! system through a public API. The public API is available through both REST/JSON and SOAP protocol web services. An HTTPS protocol is used to ensure secure user authentication and secure data transfer.

The application logic layer contains a set of modules responsible for the main functionality and logic of the system. It receives queries and commands from the interface layer and prepares answers or performs tasks using data storage and the HPC cluster. This layer contains several modules such as the Resource Repository Adapter, the User Manager, the SMT Training Manager, etc. The interface layer accesses the application logic layer through the REST/JSON and SOAP protocol web services. The same protocols are used for communication between modules in the application logic layer.

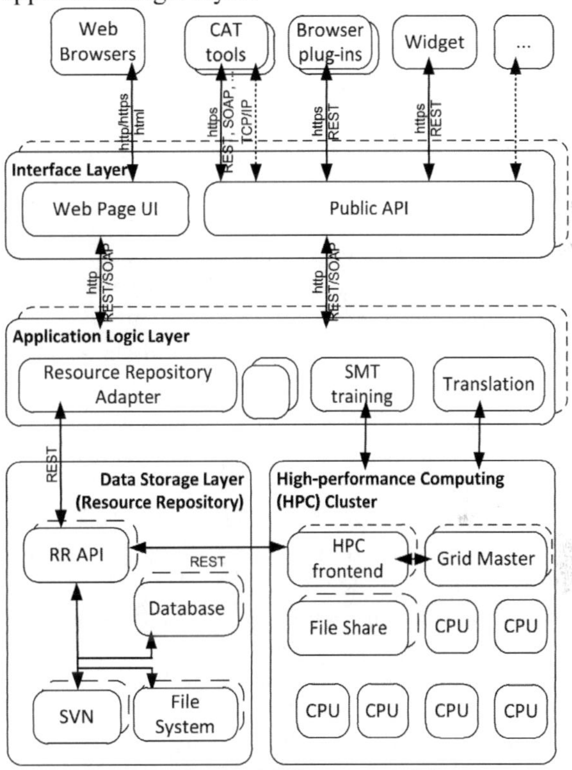

Figure 2. The LetsMT! system architecture

The data is stored in one central Resource Repository (RR). As training data may change (for example, grow), the RR is based on a version-controlled file system (currently we use SVN as the backend system). A key-value store is used to keep metadata and statistics about training data and trained SMT systems. Modules from the application logic layer and HPC cluster access RR through a REST-based web service interface.

A High Performance Computing Cluster is used to execute many different computationally heavy data processing tasks – SMT training and running, corpora processing and converting, etc. Modules from the application logic and data storage layers create jobs and send them to the HPC cluster for execution. The HPC cluster is responsible for accepting, scheduling, dispatching, and managing remote and distributed execution of large numbers of standalone, parallel, or interactive jobs. It also manages and schedules the allocation of distributed resources such as processors, memory, and disk space. The LetsMT! HPC cluster is based on the Oracle Grid Engine (SGE).

The hardware infrastructure of the LetsMT! platform is heterogeneous. The majority of services run on Linux platforms (Moses, RR, data processing tools, etc.). The Web server and application logic services run on a Microsoft Windows platform.

The system hardware architecture is designed to be highly scalable. The LetsMT! platform contains several machines with both continuous and on-demand availability:

- Continuous availability machines are used to run the core frontend and backend services and the HPC grid master to guarantee stable system functioning;
- On-demand availability machines are used (i) to scale up the system by adding more computing power to training, translation, and data import services (HPC cluster nodes) and (ii) to increase performance of frontend and backend server instances.

To ensure scalability of the system, the whole LetsMT! system including the HPC cluster is hosted by Amazon Web Services infrastructure, which provides easy access to on-demand computing and storage resources.

5 Data Storage and Processing Facilities

As a data sharing and MT platform, the LetsMT! system has to store and process large amounts of SMT training data (parallel and monolingual corpora) as well as trained models of SMT systems. The Resource Repository (RR) software is fully integrated into the LetsMT! Platform and provides the following major components:

- Scalable data storage based on version-controlled file systems;
- A flexible key-value store for metadata;
- Access-control mechanisms defining three levels of permission (private data, public data, shared data);
- Data import modules that include tools for data validation, conversion and automatic sentence alignment for a variety of popular document formats.

The general architecture of the Resource Repository is illustrated in Figure 3. It is implemented in terms of a modular package that can easily be installed in a distributed environment. RR services are provided via Web API's and secure HTTP requests. Data storage can be distributed over several servers as is illustrated in Figure 3. Storage servers communicate with the central database server that manages all metadata records attached to resources in the RR. Data resources are organised in slots that correspond to file systems with user-specific branches. Currently, the RR package implements two storage backends: a plain file system and a version-controlled file system based on subversion (SVN). The latter is the default mode, which has several advantages over non-revisioned data storage. Revision control systems are designed to handle dynamically growing collections of mainly textual data in a multi-user environment. Furthermore, they keep track of modifications and file histories to make it possible to backtrack to prior revisions. This can be a strong advantage, especially in cases of shared data access. Another interesting feature is the possibility to create cheap copies of entire branches that can be used to enable data modifications by other users without compromising data integrity for others. Finally, SVN also naturally stores data in a compressed format, which is useful for large-scale document collections. In general, the RR implementation is modular, other storage backends may be added later, and each individual slot can use its own backend type.

Another important feature of the RR is the support of a flexible database for metadata. We decided to integrate a modern key-value store into the platform in order to allow a maximum of flexibility. In contrast to traditional relational databases, key-value stores allow the storage of arbitrary data sets based on pairs of keys and values without being restricted to a pre-defined schema or a fixed data model. Our implementation relies on TokyoCabinet[4], a modern implementation of schema-less databases that supports all of our

[4] https://fallabs/tokyocabinet

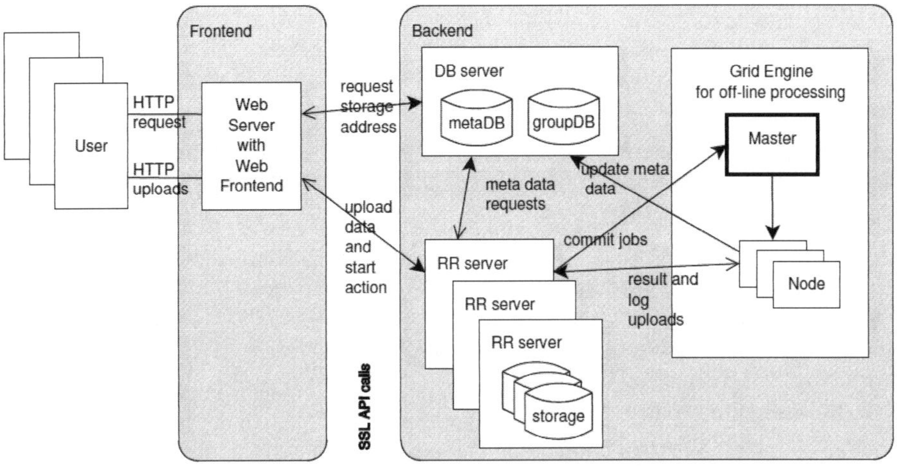

Figure 3. Resource repository overview

requirements in terms of flexibility and efficiency. In particular, we use the table mode of TokyoCabinet that supports storage of arbitrary data records connected to a single key in the database. We use resource URL's in our repository to define unique keys in the database, and data records attached to these keys may include any number of key-value pairs. In this way, we can add any kind of information to each addressable resource in the RR. The software also supports keys with unordered lists of values, which is useful for metadata such as languages (in a data collection) and for many other purposes. Moreover, TokyoCabinet provides powerful query language and software bindings for the most common programming languages. It can be run in client-server mode, which ensures robustness in a multi-user environment and natively supports data replication. Using TokyoCabinet as our backend, we implemented a key-value store for metadata in the RR that can easily be extended and queried from the frontend of the LetsMT! Platform via dedicated web-service calls.

Yet another important feature of the RR is the collection of import modules that take care of validation and conversion of user-provided SMT training material. Our main goal was to make the creation of appropriate data resources as painless as possible. Therefore, we included support for the most common data formats to be imported into LetsMT!. Pre-aligned parallel data can be uploaded in TMX, XLIFF, and Moses formats. Monolingual data can be provided in plain text, PDF, and MS Word formats. We also support the upload of compressed archives in zip and tar format. In the future, other formats can easily be integrated in our modular implementation.

Validation of such a variety of formats is important. Therefore among others, we included XML/DTD validation, text encoding detection software, and language identification tools with pre-trained models for over 60 languages.

Furthermore, our system also includes tools for automatic sentence alignment. Import processes automatically align translated documents with each other using standard length-based sentence alignment methods (Gale and Church, 1993; Varga et al., 2005).

Finally, we also integrated a general batch-queuing system (SGE) to run off-line processes such as import jobs. In this way, we further increase the scalability of the system by taking the load off repository servers. Data uploads automatically trigger appropriate import jobs that will be queued on the grid engine using a dedicated job web-service API.

6 Evaluation for Usage in Localisation

One of the usage scenarios particularly targeted by the project is application in the localisation and translation industry. Localisation companies usually have collected significant amounts of parallel data in the form of translation memories. They are interested in using this data to create customised MT engines that can increase productivity of translators. Productivity is usually measured as an average number of words translated per hour. For this use case, LetsMT! has developed plug-ins for integration into CAT tools. In addition to translation candidates from translation memories, translators receive translation suggestions provided by the selected MT engine running on LetsMT!.

As part of the system evaluation, project partner Moravia used the LetsMT! platform to train and evaluate SMT systems for Polish and Czech. An English-Czech engine was trained on 0.9M parallel sentences coming from Moravia translation memories in the IT and tech domain part of the Czech National Corpus. The resulting system increased translator productivity by 25.1%. An English-Polish system was trained on 1.5M parallel sentences from Moravia production data in the IT domain. Using this system, translator productivity increased by 28.5%.

For evaluation of English-Latvian translation, TILDE created a MT system using a significantly larger corpus of 5.37M parallel sentence pairs, including 1.29M pairs in the IT domain. Additional tweaking was made by manually adding a factored model over disambiguated morphological tags. The resulting system increased translator productivity by 32.9% (Skadiņš et al., 2011).

7 Conclusions

The results described in this paper show that the LetsMT! project is on track to fulfill its goal to democratise the creation and usage of custom SMT systems. LetsMT! demonstrates that the open source SMT toolkit Moses is reaching maturity to serve as a base for large scale and heavy use production purposes. The architecture of the platform and Resource Repository enables scalability of the system and very large amounts of data to be handled in a variety of formats. Evaluation shows a strong increase in translation productivity by using LetsMT! systems in IT localisation.

Acknowledgments

The research within the LetsMT! project has received funding from the ICT Policy Support Programme (ICT PSP), Theme 5 – Multilingual web, grant agreement 250456.

References

L. Dugast, J. Senellart, P. Koehn. 2009. Selective addition of corpus-extracted phrasal lexical rules to a rule-based machine translation system. Proceedings of MT Summit XII.

T. Brants, A.C. Popat, P. Xu, F.J Och, J. Dean. 2007. Large Language Models in Machine Translation. Proceedings of the 2007 Joint Conference on Empirical Methods in Natural Language Processing and Computational Natural Language Learning (EMNLP-CoNLL), 858-867. Prague, Czech Republic

W. A. Gale, K. W. Church. 1993. A Program for Aligning Sentences in Bilingual Corpora. Computational Linguistics 19 (1): 75–102

P. Koehn, M. Federico, B. Cowan, R. Zens, C. Duer, O. Bojar, A. Constantin, E. Herbst. 2007. Moses: Open Source Toolkit for Statistical Machine Translation. Proceedings of the ACL 2007 Demo and Poster Sessions, 177-180. Prague.

P. Koehn. 2010. An experimental management system. The Prague Bulletin of Mathematical Linguistics, 94.

A. Levenberg, M. Osborne. 2009. Stream-based Randomised Language Models for SMT. Proceedings of the 2009 Conference on Empirical Methods in Natural Language Processing.

A. Levenberg, C. Callison-Burch, M. Osborne. 2010. Stream-based Translation Models for Statistical Machine Translation. Human Language Technologies: The 2010 Annual Conference of the North American Chapter of the Association for Computational Linguistics (HLT '10)

M. Plitt, F. Masselot. 2010. A Productivity Test of Statistical Machine Translation Post-Editing in a Typical Localisation Context. The Prague Bulletin of Mathematical Linguistics, 93(January 2010): –16

R. Skadiņš, M. Puriņš, I. Skadiņa, A. Vasiļjevs. 2011. Evaluation of SMT in localization to under-resourced inflected language. Proceedings of the 15th International Conference of the European Association for Machine Translation EAMT 2011, 35-40. Leuven, Belgium

A. Vasiļjevs, R. Skadiņš, I. Skadiņa. 2011. Towards Application of User-Tailored Machine Translation in Localization. Proceedings of the Third Joint EM+/CNGL Workshop "Bringing MT to the User: Research Meets Translators" JEC 2011, 23-31. Luxembourg

D. Varga, L. Németh, P. Halácsy, A. Kornai, V. Trón, V. Nagy. 2005. Parallel corpora for medium density languages. Recent Advances in Natural Language Processing IV Selected papers from RANLP05, 590-596

A. Way, K. Holden, L. Ball, G. Wheeldon. 2011. SmartMATE: online self-serve access to state-of-the-art SMT. Proceedings of the Third Joint EM+/CNGL Workshop "Bringing MT to the User: Research Meets Translators" (JEC '11), 43-52. Luxembourg

A Web-based Evaluation Framework for Spatial Instruction-Giving Systems

Srinivasan Janarthanam, Oliver Lemon, and Xingkun Liu
Interaction Lab
School of Mathematical and Computer Sciences
Heriot Watt University, Edinburgh
sc445,o.lemon,x.liu@hw.ac.uk

Abstract

We demonstrate a web-based environment for development and testing of different pedestrian route instruction-giving systems. The environment contains a City Model, a TTS interface, a game-world, and a user GUI including a simulated street-view. We describe the environment and components, the metrics that can be used for the evaluation of pedestrian route instruction-giving systems, and the shared challenge which is being organised using this environment.

1 Introduction

Generating navigation instructions in the real world for pedestrians is an interesting research problem for researchers in both computational linguistics and geo-informatics (Dale et al., 2003; Richter and Duckham, 2008). These systems generate verbal route directions for users to go from A to B, and techniques range from giving 'a priori' route directions (i.e. all route information in a single turn) and incremental 'in-situ' instructions, to full interactive dialogue systems (see section 4). One of the major problems in developing such systems is in evaluating them with real users in the real world. Such evaluations are expensive, time consuming and painstaking to organise, and are carried out not just at the end of the project but also during the development cycle. Consequently, there is a need for a common platform to effectively compare the performances of verbal navigation systems developed by different teams using a variety of techniques (e.g. a priori vs. in-situ or rule-based vs. machine learning).

This demonstration system brings together existing online data resources and software toolkits to create a low-cost framework for evaluation of pedestrian route instruction systems. We have built a web-based environment containing a *simulated real world* in which users can simulate walking on the streets of real cities whilst interacting with different navigation systems. This evaluation framework will be used in the near future to evaluate a series of instruction-giving dialogue systems.

2 Related work

The GIVE challenge developed a 3D virtual indoor environment for development and evaluation of indoor pedestrian navigation instruction systems (Koller et al., 2007; Byron et al., 2007). In this framework, users can walk through a building with rooms and corridors, similar to a first-person shooter game. The user is instructed by a navigation system that generates route instructions. The basic idea was to have several such navigation systems hosted on the GIVE server and evaluate them in the same game worlds, with a number of users over the internet. Conceptually our work is very similar to the GIVE framework, but its objective is to evaluate systems that instruct pedestrian users in the real world. The GIVE framework has been successfully used for comparative evaluation of several systems generating instructions in virtual indoor environments.

Another system, "Virtual Navigator", is a simulated 3D environment that simulates the real world for training blind and visually impaired people to learn often-used routes and develop basic navigation skills (McGookin et al., 2010). The framework

Proceedings of the 50th Annual Meeting of the Association for Computational Linguistics, pages 49–54,
Jeju, Republic of Korea, 8-14 July 2012. ©2012 Association for Computational Linguistics

uses haptic force-feedback and spatialised auditory feedback to simulate the interaction between users and the environment they are in. The users simulate walking by using arrow keys on a keyboard and by using a device that works as a 3D mouse to simulate a virtual white cane. Auditory clues are provided to the cane user to indicate for example the difference between rush hour and a quiet evening in the environment. While this simulated environment focusses on the providing the right kind of tactile and auditory feedback to its users, we focus on providing a simulated environment where people can look at landmarks and navigate based on spatial and visual instructions provided to them.

User simulation modules are usually developed to train and test reinforcement learning based interactive spoken dialogue systems (Janarthanam and Lemon, 2009; Georgila et al., 2006; Schatzmann et al., 2006). These agents replace real users in interaction with dialogue systems. However, these models simulate the users' behaviours in addition to the environment in which they operate. Users' dialogue and physical behaviour are dependent on a number of factors such as a user's preferences, goals, knowledge of the environment, environmental constraints, etc. Simulating a user's behaviour realistically based on many such features requires large amounts of data. In contrast to this approach, we propose a system where only the spatial and visual environment is simulated.

See section 4 for a discussion of different pedestrian navigation systems.

3 Architecture

The evaluation framework architecture is shown in figure 1. The server side consists of a broker module, navigation system, gameworld server, TTS engine, and a city model. On the user's side is a web-based client that consists of the simulated real-world and the interaction panel.

3.1 Game-world module

Walking aimlessly in the simulated real world can be a boring task. Therefore, instead of giving web users navigation tasks from A to B, we embed navigation tasks in a game-world overlaid on top of the simulated real world. We developed a "treasure hunting" game which consists of users solving several pieces of a puzzle to discover the location of the treasure chest. In order to solve the puzzle, they interact with game characters (e.g. a pirate) to obtain clues as to where the next clue is. This sets the user a number of navigation tasks to acquire the next clues until they find the treasure. In order to keep the game interesting, the user's energy depletes as time goes on and they therefore have limited time to find the treasure. Finally, the user's performance is scored to encourage users to return. The game characters and entities like keys, chests, etc. are laid out on real streets making it easy to develop a game without developing a game-world. New game-worlds can be easily scripted using Javascript, where the location (latitude and longitude) and behaviour of the game characters are defined. The game-world module serves game-world specifications to the web-based client.

3.2 Broker

The broker module is a web server that connects the web clients to their corresponding different navigation systems. This module ensures that the framework works for multiple users. Navigation systems are instantiated and assigned to new users when they first connect to the broker. Subsequent messages from the users will be routed to the assigned navigation system. The broker communicates with the navigation systems via a communication platform thereby ensuring that different navigation systems developed using different languages (such as C++, Java, Python, etc) are supported.

3.3 Navigation system

The navigation system is the central component of this architecture, which provides the user instructions to reach their destinations. Each navigation system is run as a server remotely. When a user's client connects to the server, it instantiates a navigation system object and assigns it to the user exclusively. Every user is identified using a unique id (UUID), which is used to map the user to his/her respective navigation system. The navigation system is introduced in the game scenario as a buddy system that will help the user in his objective: find the treasure. The web client sends the user's location to the system periodically (every few seconds).

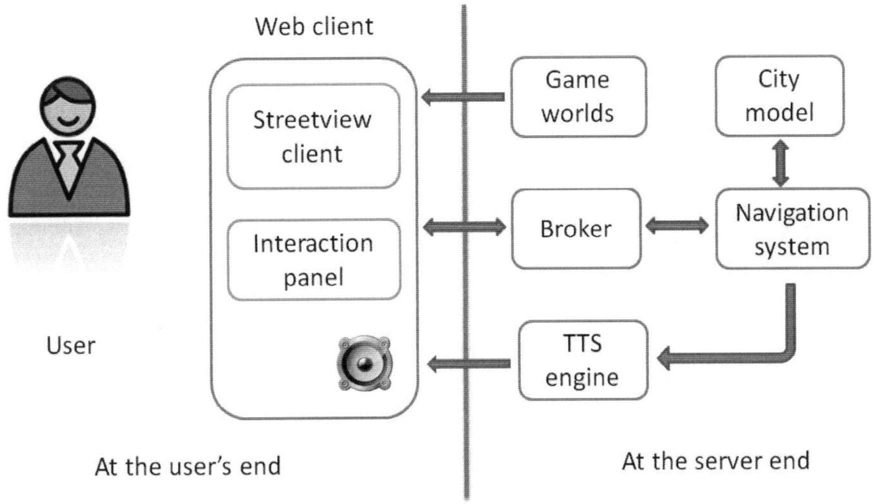

Figure 1: Evaluation framework architecture

3.4 TTS engine

Alongside the navigation system we use the Cereproc text-to-speech engine that converts the utterances of the system into speech. The URL of the audio file is then sent to the client's browser which then uses the audio plugin to play the synthesized speech to the user. The TTS engine need not be used if the output modality of the system is just text.

3.5 City Model

The navigation system is supported by a database called the City Model. The City Model is a GIS database containing a variety of data required to support navigation tasks. It has been derived from an open-source data source called OpenStreetMaps[1]. It consists of the following:

- Street network data: the street network data consists of nodes and ways representing junctions and streets.
- Amenities: such as ATMs, public toilets, etc.
- Landmarks: other structures that can serve as landmarks. E.g. churches, restaurants, etc.

The amenities and landmarks are represented as nodes (with latitude and longitude information). The City Model interface API consists of a number of subroutines to access the required information such as the nearest amenity, distance or route from A to B, etc. These subroutines provide the interface between the navigation systems and the database.

[1] www.openstreetmaps.org

3.6 Web-based client

The web-based client is a JavaScript/HTML program running on the user's web browser software (e.g. Google Chrome). A snapshot of the webclient is shown in figure 2. It has two parts: the streetview panel and the interaction panel.

Streetview panel: the streetview panel presents a simulated real world visually to the user. When the page loads, a Google Streetview client (Google Maps API) is created with an initial user coordinate. Google Streetview is a web service that renders a panoramic view of real streets in major cities around the world. This client allows the web user to get a panoramic view of the streets around the user's virtual location. A gameworld received from the server is overlaid on the simulated real world. The user can walk around and interact with game characters using the arrow keys on his keyboard or the mouse. As the user walks around, his location (stored in the form of latitude and longitude coordinates) gets updated locally. Streetview also returns the user's point of view (0-360 degrees), which is also stored locally.

Interaction panel: the web-client also includes an

interaction panel that lets the user interact with his buddy navigation system. In addition to user location information, users can also interact with the navigation system using textual utterances or their equivalents. We provide users with two types of interaction panel: a GUI panel and a text panel. In the GUI panel, there are GUI objects such as buttons, drop-down lists, etc. which can be used to construct requests and responses to the system. By clicking the buttons, users can send abstract semantic representations (dialogue actions) that are equivalent to their textual utterances. For example, the user can request a route to a destination by selecting the street name from a drop down list and click on the Send button. Similarly, users can click on 'Yes', 'No', 'OK', etc. buttons to respond to the system's questions and instructions. In the text panel, on the other hand, users are free to type any request or response they want. Of course, both types of inputs are parsed by the navigation system. We also plan to add an additional input channel that can stream user speech to the navigation system in the future.

4 Candidate Navigation Systems

This framework can be used to evaluate a variety of navigation systems. Route navigation has been an interesting research topic for researchers in both geoinformatics and computational linguistics alike. Several navigation prototype systems have been developed over the years. Although there are several systems that do not use language as a means of communication for navigation tasks (instead using geotagged photographs (Beeharee and Steed, 2006; Hiley et al., 2008), haptics (Bosman et al., 2003), music (Holland et al., 2002; Jones et al., 2008), etc), we focus on systems that generate instructions in natural language. Therefore, our framework does not include systems that generate routes on 2D/3D maps as navigation aids.

Systems that generate text/speech can be further classified as follows:

- 'A priori' systems: these systems generate route instructions prior to the users touring the route. These systems describe the entire route before the user starts navigating. Several web services exist that generate such lists of step-by-step instructions (e.g. Google/Bing directions).
- 'In-situ' or incremental route instruction systems: these systems generate route instructions incrementally along the route. e.g. CORAL (Dale et al., 2003). They keep track of the user's location and issue the next instruction when the user reaches the next node on the planned route. The next instruction tells the user how to reach the new next node. Some systems do not keep track of the user, but require the user to request the next instruction when they reach the next node.
- Interactive navigation systems: these systems are both incremental and interactive. e.g. DeepMap (Malaka and Zipf, 2000). These systems keep track of the user's location and proactively generate instructions based on user proximity to the next node. In addition, they can interact with users by asking them questions about entities in their viewshed. For example "Can you see a tower at about 100 feet away?". Questions like these will let the system assess the user's location and thereby adapt its instruction to the situated context.

5 Evaluation metrics

Navigation systems can be evaluated using two kinds of metrics using this framework. Objective metrics such as *time taken* by the user to finish each navigation task and the game, *distance travelled*, number of *wrong turns*, etc. can be directly measured from the environment. Subjective metrics based on each user's ratings of different features of the system can be obtained through user satisfaction questionnaires. In our framework, users are requested to fill in a questionnaire at the end of the game. The questionnaire consists of questions about the game, the buddy, and the user himself, for example:

- Was the game engaging?
- Would you play it again (i.e. another similar gameworld)?
- Did your buddy help you enough?

Figure 2: Snapshot of the web client

- Were the buddy instructions easy to understand?
- Were the buddy instructions ever wrong or mis-placed?
- If you had the chance, will you choose the same buddy in the next game?
- How well did you know the neighbourhood of the gameworld before the game?

6 Evaluation scenarios

We aim to evaluate navigation systems under a variety of scenarios.

- Uncertain GPS: GPS positioning available in smartphones is erroneous (Zandbergen and Barbeau, 2011). Therefore, one scenario for evaluation would be to test how robustly navigation systems handle erroneous GPS signals from the user's end.
- Output modalities: the output of navigation systems can be presented in two modalities: text and speech. While speech may enable a hands-free eyes-free navigation, text displayed on navigation aids like smartphones may increase cognitive load. We therefore believe it will be interesting to evaluate the systems in both conditions and compare the results.
- Noise in user speech: for systems that take as input user speech, it is important to handle noise in such a channel. Noise due to wind and traffic is most common in pedestrian scenarios. Scenarios with different levels of noise settings can be evaluated.
- Adaptation to users: returning users may have learned the layout of the game world. An interesting scenario is to examine how navigation systems adapt to user's increasing spatial and visual knowledge.

Errors in GPS positioning of the user and noise in user speech can be simulated at the server end, thereby creating a range of challenging scenarios to evaluate the robustness of the systems.

7 The Shared Challenge

We plan to organise a shared challenge for outdoor pedestrian route instruction generation, in which a variety of systems can be evaluated. Participating research teams will be able to use our interfaces and modules to develop navigation systems. Each team will be provided with a development toolkit and documentation to setup the framework in their local premises for development purposes. Developed systems will be hosted on our challenge server and a web based evaluation will be organised in consultation with the research community (Janarthanam and Lemon, 2011).

8 Demonstration system

At the demonstration, we will present the evaluation framework along with a demo navigation dialogue system. The web-based client will run on a laptop using a high-speed broadband connection. The navigation system and other server modules will run on a remote server.

Acknowledgments

The research has received funding from the European Community's Seventh Framework Programme (FP7/2007-2013) under grant agreement no. 216594 (SPACEBOOK project www.spacebookproject.org).

References

Ashweeni K. Beeharee and Anthony Steed. 2006. A natural wayfinding exploiting photos in pedestrian navigation systems. In *Proceedings of the 8th conference on Human-computer interaction with mobile devices and services (2006)*.

S. Bosman, B. Groenendaal, J. W. Findlater, T. Visser, M. de Graaf, and Panos Markopoulos. 2003. GentleGuide: An Exploration of Haptic Output for Indoors Pedestrian Guidance. In *Proceedings of 5th International Symposium, Mobile HCI 2003, Udine, Italy*.

D. Byron, A. Koller, J. Oberlander, L. Stoia, and K. Striegnitz. 2007. Generating Instructions in Virtual Environments (GIVE): A challenge and evaluation testbed for NLG. In *Proceedings of the Workshop on Shared Tasks and Comparative Evaluation in Natural Language Generation*.

Robert Dale, Sabine Geldof, and Jean-Philippe Prost. 2003. CORAL : Using Natural Language Generation for Navigational Assistance. In *Proceedings of the Twenty-Sixth Australasian Computer Science Conference (ACSC2003), 4th7th February, Adelaide, South Australia*.

Kallirroi Georgila, James Henderson, and Oliver Lemon. 2006. User simulation for spoken dialogue systems: Learning and evaluation. In *Proceedings of Interspeech/ICSLP*, pages 1065–1068.

Harlan Hiley, Ramakrishna Vedantham, Gregory Cuellar, Alan Liuy, Natasha Gelfand, Radek Grzeszczuk, and Gaetano Borriello. 2008. Landmark-based pedestrian navigation from collections of geotagged photos. In *Proceedings of the 7th International Conference on Mobile and Ubiquitous Multimedia (MUM) 2008*.

S. Holland, D. Morse, and H. Gedenryd. 2002. Audiogps: Spatial audio navigation with a minimal attention interface. *Personal and Ubiquitous Computing*, 6(4):253–259.

Srini Janarthanam and Oliver Lemon. 2009. A User Simulation Model for learning Lexical Alignment Policies in Spoken Dialogue Systems. In *European Workshop on Natural Language Generation*.

Srini Janarthanam and Oliver Lemon. 2011. The GRUVE Challenge: Generating Routes under Uncertainty in Virtual Environments. In *Proceedings of ENLG / Generation Challenges*.

M. Jones, S. Jones, G. Bradley, N. Warren, D. Bainbridge, and G. Holmes. 2008. Ontrack: Dynamically adapting music playback to support navigation. *Personal and Ubiquitous Computing*, 12(7):513–525.

A. Koller, J. Moore, B. Eugenio, J. Lester, L. Stoia, D. Byron, J. Oberlander, and K. Striegnitz. 2007. Shared Task Proposal: Instruction Giving in Virtual Worlds. In *Workshop on Shared Tasks and Comparative Evaluation in Natural Language Generation*.

Rainer Malaka and Er Zipf. 2000. Deep Map - challenging IT research in the framework of a tourist information system. In *Information and Communication Technologies in Tourism 2000*, pages 15–27. Springer.

D. McGookin, R. Cole, and S. Brewster. 2010. Virtual navigator: Developing a simulator for independent route learning. In *Proceedings of Workshop on Haptic Audio Interaction Design 2010, Denmark*.

Kai-Florian Richter and Matt Duckham. 2008. Simplest instructions: Finding easy-to-describe routes for navigation. In *Proceedings of the 5th international conference on Geographic Information Science*.

Jost Schatzmann, Karl Weilhammer, Matt Stuttle, and Steve Young. 2006. A survey of statistical user simulation techniques for reinforcement-learning of dialogue management strategies. *The Knowledge Engineering Review*, 21:97–126.

P. A. Zandbergen and S. J. Barbeau. 2011. Positional accuracy of assisted gps data from high-sensitivity gps-enabled mobile phones. *Journal of Navigation*, 64(3):381–399.

DOMCAT: A Bilingual Concordancer for Domain-Specific Computer Assisted Translation

Ming-Hong Bai[1,2] **Yu-Ming Hsieh**[1,2] **Keh-Jiann Chen**[1] **Jason S. Chang**[2]
1 Institute of Information Science, Academia Sinica, Taiwan
2 Department of Computer Science, National Tsing-Hua University, Taiwan
mhbai@sinica.edu.tw, morris@iis.sinica.edu.tw,
kchen@iis.sinica.edu.tw, jason.jschang@gmail.com

Abstract

In this paper, we propose a web-based bilingual concordancer, DOMCAT [1], for domain-specific computer assisted translation. Given a multi-word expression as a query, the system involves retrieving sentence pairs from a bilingual corpus, identifying translation equivalents of the query in the sentence pairs (translation spotting) and ranking the retrieved sentence pairs according to the relevance between the query and the translation equivalents. To provide high-precision translation spotting for domain-specific translation tasks, we exploited a normalized correlation method to spot the translation equivalents. To ranking the retrieved sentence pairs, we propose a correlation function modified from the Dice coefficient for assessing the correlation between the query and the translation equivalents. The performances of the translation spotting module and the ranking module are evaluated in terms of precision-recall measures and coverage rate respectively.

1 Introduction

A bilingual concordancer is a tool that can retrieve aligned sentence pairs in a parallel corpus whose source sentences contain the query and the translation equivalents of the query are identified in the target sentences. It helps not only on finding translation equivalents of the query but also presenting various contexts of occurrence. As a result, it is extremely useful for bilingual lexicographers, human translators and second language learners (Bowker and Barlow 2004; Bourdaillet et al., 2010; Gao 2011).

Identifying the translation equivalents, *translation spotting*, is the most challenging part of a bilingual concordancer. Recently, most of the existing bilingual concordancers spot translation equivalents in terms of word alignment-based method. (Jian et al., 2004; Callison-Burch et al., 2005; Bourdaillet et al., 2010). However, word alignment-based translation spotting has some drawbacks. First, aligning a rare (low frequency) term may encounter the *garbage collection effect* (Moore, 2004; Liang et al., 2006) that cause the term to align to many unrelated words. Second, the statistical word alignment model is not good at many-to-many alignment due to the fact that translation equivalents are not always correlated in lexical level. Unfortunately, the above effects will be intensified in a domain-specific concordancer because the queries are usually domain-specific terms, which are mostly multi-word low-frequency terms and semantically non-compositional terms.

Wu et al. (2003) employed a statistical association criterion to spot translation equivalents in their bilingual concordancer. The association-based criterion can avoid the above mentioned effects. However, it has other drawbacks in translation spotting task. First, it will encounter the *contextual effect* that causes the system incorrectly spot the translations of the strongly collocated context. Second, the association-based translation spotting tends to spot the *common subsequence* of a set of similar translations instead of the full translations. Figure 1 illustrates an example of *contextual effect*, in which 'Fan K'uan' is incorrectly spotted as part of the translation of the query term '谿山行旅圖' (Travelers Among Mountains and Streams), which is the name of the

[1] http://ckip.iis.sinica.edu.tw/DOMCAT/

Proceedings of the 50th Annual Meeting of the Association for Computational Linguistics, pages 55–60, Jeju, Republic of Korea, 8-14 July 2012. ©2012 Association for Computational Linguistics

painting painted by 'Fan K'uan/范寬' since the painter's name is strongly collocated with the name of the painting.

Sung , Travelers Among Mountains and Streams , Fan K'uan 宋谿山行旅圖范寬

Figure 1. 'Fan K'uan' may be incorrectly spotted as part of the translation of '谿山行旅圖', if pure association method is applied.

Figure 2 illustrates an example of *common subsequence effect*, in which '清明上河圖' (the River During the Qingming Festival/ Up the River During Qingming) has two similar translations as quoted, but the Dice coefficient tends to spot the *common subsequences* of the translations. (Function words are ignored in our translation spotting.)

Expo 2010 Shanghai-Treasures of Chinese Art Along the River During the Qingming Festival 2010 上海世博會華夏百寶篇清院本清明上河圖 Oversized Hanging Scrolls and Handscrolls Up the River During Qingming 巨幅名畫清沈源清明上河圖

Figure 2. The Dice coefficient tends to spot the common subsequences 'River During Qingming'.

Bai et al. (2009) proposed a *normalized frequency* criterion to extract translation equivalents form sentence aligned parallel corpus. This criterion takes lexical-level contexture effect into account, so it can effectively resolve the above mentioned effect. But the goal of their method is to find most common translations instead of spotting translations, so the normalized frequency criterion tends to ignore rare translations.

In this paper, we propose a bilingual concordancer, DOMCAT, for computer assisted domain-specific term translation. To remedy the above mentioned effects, we extended the *normalized frequency* of Bai et al. (2009) to a *normalized correlation* criterion to spot translation equivalents. The *normalized correlation* inherits the characteristics of normalized frequency and is adjusted for spotting rare translations. These characteristics are especially important for a domain-specific bilingual concordancer to spot translation pairs of low-frequency and semantically non-compositional terms.

The remainder of this paper is organized as follows. Section 2 describes the DOMCAT system. In Section 3, we describe the evaluation of the DOMCAT system. Section 4 contains some concluding remarks.

2 The DOMCAT System

Given a query, the DOMCAT bilingual concordancer retrieves sentence pairs and spots translation equivalents by the following steps:

1. Retrieve the sentence pairs whose source sentences contain the query term.
2. Extract translation candidate words from the retrieved sentence pairs by the normalized correlation criterion.
3. Spot the candidate words for each target sentence and rank the sentences by normalized the Dice coefficient criterion.

In step 1, the query term can be a single word, a phrase, a gapped sequence and even a regular expression. The parallel corpus is indexed by the suffix array to efficiently retrieve the sentences.

The step 2 and step 3 are more complicated and will be described from Section 2.1 to Section 2.3.

2.1 Extract Translation Candidate Words

After the queried sentence pairs retrieved from the parallel corpus, we can extract translation candidate words from the sentence pairs. We compute the *local normalized correlation* with respect to the query term for each word *e* in each target sentence. The *local normalized correlation* is defined as follows:

$$lnc(e;\mathbf{q},\mathbf{e},\mathbf{f}) = \frac{\sum_{\forall f_i \in \mathbf{q}} p(e \mid f_i) + \Delta \mid \mathbf{q} \mid}{\sum_{\forall f_j \in \mathbf{f}} p(e \mid f_j) + \Delta \mid \mathbf{f} \mid} \quad (1)$$

where **q** denotes the query term, **f** denotes the source sentence and **e** denotes the target sentence, Δ is a small smoothing factor. The probability $p(e|f)$ is the word translation probability derived from the entire parallel corpus by IBM Model 1 (Brown et al., 1993). The sense of *local normalized correlation* of *e* can be interpreted as the probability of word *e* being part of translation of the query term **q** under the condition of sentence pair (**e, f**).

Once the local normalized correlation is computed for each word in retrieved sentences, we compute the normalized correlation on the retrieved sentences. The normalized correlation is the average of all *lnc* values and defined as follows:

$$nc(e;\mathbf{q}) = \frac{1}{n}\sum_{i=1}^{n} lnc(e;\mathbf{q},\mathbf{e}^{(i)},\mathbf{f}^{(i)}) \qquad (2)$$

where n is the number of retrieved sentence pairs.

After the *nc* values for the words of the retrieved target sentences are computed, we can obtain a translation candidate list by filtering out the words with lower *nc* values.

To compare with the association-based method, we also sorted the word list by the Dice coefficient defined as follows:

$$dice(e,\mathbf{q}) = \frac{2freq(e,\mathbf{q})}{freq(e)+freq(\mathbf{q})} \qquad (3)$$

where *freq* is frequency function which computes frequencies from the parallel corpus.

Candidate words	NC
mountain	0.676
stream	0.442
traveler	0.374
among	0.363
sung	0.095
k'uan	0.090

Figure 3(a). Candidate words sorted by *nc* values.

Candidate words	Dice
traveler	0.385
reduced	0.176
stream	0.128
k'uan	0.121
fan	0.082
among	0.049
mountain	0.035

Figure 3(b). Candidate words sorted by Dice coefficient values.

Figure 3(a) and (b) illustrate examples of translation candidate words of the query term '谿山行旅圖' (Travelers Among Mountains and Streams) sorted by the *nc* values, *NC*, and the Dice coefficients respectively. The result shows that the normalized correlation separated the related words from unrelated words much better than the Dice coefficient.

The rationale behind the normalized correlation is that the *nc* value is the strength of word *e* generated by the query compared to that of generated by the whole sentence. As a result, the normalized correlation can easily separate the words generated by the query term from the words generated by the context. On the contrary, the Dice coefficient counts the frequency of a co-occurred word without considering the fact that it could be generated by the strongly collocated context.

2.2 Translation Spotting

Once we have a translation candidate list and respective *nc* values, we can spot the translation equivalents by the following spotting algorithm. For each target sentence, first, spot the word with highest *nc* value. Then extend the spotted sequence to the neighbors of the word by checking their *nc* values of neighbor words but skipping function words. If the *nc* value is greater than a threshold θ, add the word into spotted sequence. Repeat the extending process until no word can be added to the spotted sequence.

The following is the pseudo-code for the algorithm:

```
S is the target sentence
H is the spotted word sequence
θ is the threshold of translation candidate words

Initialize:
    H←∅
    e_max←S[0]
Foreach e_i in S:
    If nc(e_i) > nc(e_max):
        e_max ← e_i
If nc(e_max )> θ :
    add e_max to H
Repeat until no word add to H
    e_j←left neighbor of H
    If nc(e_j )> θ :
        add e_j to H
    e_k←right neighbor of H
    If nc( e_k ) > θ :
        add e_k to H
```

Figure 4: Pseudo-code of translation spotting process.

2.3 Ranking

The ranking mechanism of a bilingual concordancer is used to provide the most related translation of the query on the top of the outputs for the user. So, an association metric is needed to evaluate the relations between the query and the spotted translations. The Dice coefficient is a widely used measure for assessing the association strength between a multi-word expression and its translation candidates. (Kupiec, 1993; Smadja et al., 1996; Kitamura and Matsumoto, 1996; Yamamoto and Matsumoto, 2000; Melamed, 2001) The following is the definition of the Dice coefficient:

$$dice(\mathbf{t},\mathbf{q}) = \frac{2freq(\mathbf{t},\mathbf{q})}{freq(\mathbf{t}) + freq(\mathbf{q})} \quad (4)$$

where **q** denotes a multi-word expression to be translated, **t** denotes a translation candidate of **q**. However, the Dice coefficient has the *common subsequence effect* (as mentioned in Section 1) due to the fact that the co-occurrence frequency of the common subsequence is usually larger than that of the full translation; hence, the Dice coefficient tends to choose the common subsequence.

To remedy the common subsequence effect, we introduce a *normalized frequency* for a spotted sequence defined as follows:

$$nf(\mathbf{t},\mathbf{q}) = \sum_{i=1}^{n} lnf(\mathbf{t};\mathbf{q},\mathbf{e}^{(i)},\mathbf{f}^{(i)}) \quad (5)$$

where *lnf* is a function which compute normalized frequency locally in each sentence. The following is the definition of *lnf*:

$$lnf(\mathbf{t};\mathbf{q},\mathbf{e},\mathbf{f}) = \prod_{\forall e \in \mathbf{H}-\mathbf{t}} (1 - lnc(e;\mathbf{q},\mathbf{e},\mathbf{f})) \quad (6)$$

where ***H*** is the spotted sequence of the sentence pair (**e**,**f**), ***H*-*t*** are the words in **H** but not in **t**. The rationale behind *lnf* function is that: when counting the local frequency of **t** in a sentence pair, if **t** is a subsequence of **H**, then the count of **t** should be reasonably reduced by considering the strength of the correlation between the words in **H**-**t** and the query.

Then, we modify the Dice coefficient by replacing the co-occurrence frequency with normalized frequency as follows:

$$nf\_dice(\mathbf{t},\mathbf{q}) = \frac{2nf(\mathbf{t},\mathbf{q})}{freq(\mathbf{t}) + freq(\mathbf{q})} \quad (7)$$

The new scoring function, *nf_dice*(**t**,**q**), is exploited as our criterion for assessing the association strength between the query and the spotted sequences.

3 Experimental Results

3.1 Experimental Setting

We use the Chinese/English web pages of the National Palace Museum [2] as our underlying parallel corpus. It contains about 30,000 sentences in each language. We exploited the Champollion Toolkit (Ma et al., 2006) to align the sentence pairs. The English sentences are tokenized and lemmatized by using the NLTK (Bird and Loper, 2004) and the Chinese sentences are segmented by the CKIP Chinese segmenter (Ma and Chen, 2003).

To evaluate the performance of the translation spotting, we selected 12 domain-specific terms to query the concordancer. Then, the returned spotted translation equivalents are evaluated against a manually annotated gold standard in terms of recall and precision metrics. We also build two different translation spotting modules by using the GIZA++ toolkit (Och and Ney, 2000) with the intersection/union of the bidirectional word alignment as baseline systems.

To evaluate the performance of the ranking criterion, we compiled a reference translation set for each query by collecting the manually annotated translation spotting set and selecting 1 to 3 frequently used translations. Then, the outputs of each query are ranked by the *nf_dice* function and evaluated against the reference translation set. We also compared the ranking performance with the Dice coefficient.

3.2 Evaluation of Translation Spotting

We evaluate the translation spotting in terms of the Recall and Precision metrics defined as follows:

[2] http://www.npm.gov.tw

$$Recall = \frac{\sum_{i=1}^{n} | H_g^{(i)} \cap H^{(i)} |}{\sum_{i=1}^{n} | H_g^{(i)} |} \quad (8)$$

$$Precision = \frac{\sum_{i=1}^{n} | H_g^{(i)} \cap H^{(i)} |}{\sum_{i=1}^{n} | H^{(i)} |} \quad (9)$$

where i denotes the index of the retrieved sentence, $H^{(i)}$ is the spotted sequences of the ith sentence returned by the concordancer, and $H_g^{(i)}$ is the gold standard spotted sequences of the ith sentence. Table 1 shows the evaluation of translation spotting for normalized correlation, *NC*, compared with the intersection and union of GIZA++ word alignment. The F-score of the normalized correlation is much higher than that of the word alignment methods. It is noteworthy that the normalized correlation increased the recall rate without losing the precision rate. This may indicate that the normalized correlation can effectively conquer the drawbacks of the word alignment-based translation spotting and the association-based translation spotting mentioned in Section 1.

	Recall	Precision	F-score
Intersection	0.4026	0.9498	0.5656
Union	0.7061	0.9217	0.7996
NC	0.8579	0.9318	0.8933

Table 1. Evaluation of the translation spotting queried by 12 domain-specific terms.

We also evaluate the queried results of each term individually (as shown in Table 2). As it shows, the normalized correlation is quite stable for translation spotting.

Query terms	GIZA Intersection			GIZA Union			NC		
	R	P	F	R	P	F	R	P	F
毛公鼎 (Maogong cauldron)	0.27	0.86	0.41	0.87	0.74	0.80	0.92	0.97	**0.94**
翠玉白菜(Jadeite cabbage)	0.48	1.00	0.65	1.00	0.88	0.94	0.98	0.98	**0.98**
谿山行旅圖(Travelers Among Mountains and Streams)	0.28	0.75	0.41	1.00	0.68	0.81	0.94	0.91	**0.92**
清明上河圖(Up the River During Qingming)	0.22	0.93	0.35	0.97	0.83	0.89	0.99	0.91	**0.95**
景德鎮(Ching-te-chen)	0.50	0.87	0.63	0.73	0.31	0.44	1.00	0.69	**0.82**
瓷器(porcelain)	0.53	0.99	0.69	0.93	0.64	0.76	0.78	0.96	**0.86**
霽青(cobalt blue glaze)	0.12	1.00	0.21	0.85	0.58	0.69	0.94	0.86	**0.90**
銘文(inscription)	0.20	0.89	0.32	0.71	0.34	0.46	0.88	0.95	**0.91**
三友百禽(Three Friends and a Hundred Birds)	0.58	0.99	0.73	1.00	0.97	**0.99**	1.00	0.72	0.84
狂草(wild cursive script)	0.42	1.00	0.59	0.63	0.80	0.71	0.84	1.00	**0.91**
蘭亭序(Preface to the Orchid Pavilion Gathering)	0.33	0.75	0.46	0.56	0.50	0.53	0.78	1.00	**0.88**
後赤壁賦(Latter Odes to the Red Cliff)	0.19	0.50	0.27	0.75	0.46	0.57	0.94	0.88	**0.91**

Table 2. Evaluation of the translation spotting for each term

3.3 Evaluation of Ranking

To evaluate the performance of a ranking function, we ranked the retrieved sentences of the queries by the function. Then, the top-n sentences of the output are evaluated in terms of the coverage rate defined as follows:

$$\text{coverage} = \frac{\#\text{ of queries can find a translation in top-n}}{\#\text{ of queries}} \quad (10)$$

The meaning of the coverage rate can be interpreted as: how many percent of the query can find an acceptable translation in the top-n results. We use the reference translations, as described in Section 3.1, as acceptable translation set for each query of our experiment. Table 3 shows the coverage rate of the *nf_dice* function compared with the Dice coefficient. As it shows, in the outputs ranked by the Dice coefficient, uses usually have to look up more than 3 sentences to find an acceptable translation; while in the outputs ranked by the *nf_dice* function, users can find an acceptable translation in top-2 sentences.

	dice	nf_dice
top-1	0.42	0.92
top-2	0.75	1.00
top-3	0.92	1.00

Table 3. Evaluation of the ranking criteria.

4 Conclusion and Future Works

In this paper, we proposed a bilingual concordancer, DOMCAT, designed as a domain-specific computer assisted translation tool. We exploited a normalized correlation which incorporate lexical level information into association-based method that effectively avoid the drawbacks of the word alignment-based translation spotting as well as the association-based translation spotting.

In the future, it would be interesting to extend the parallel corpus to the internet to retrieve more rich data for the computer assisted translation.

References

Bai, Ming-Hong, Jia-Ming You, Keh-Jiann Chen, Jason S. Chang. 2009. Acquiring Translation Equivalences of Multiword Expressions by Normalized Correlation Frequencies. In *Proceedings of EMNLP*, pages 478-486.

Bird, Steven and Edward Loper. 2004. NLTK: The Natural Language Toolkit. In *Proceedings of ACL*, pages 214-217.

Bourdaillet, Julien, Stéphane Huet, Philippe Langlais and Guy Lapalme. 2010. TRANSSEARCH: from a bilingual concordancer to a translation finder. *Machine Translation*, 24(3-4): 241–271.

Bowker, Lynne, Michael Barlow. 2004. Bilingual concordancers and translation memories: A comparative evaluation. In *Proceedings of the Second International Workshop on Language Resources for Translation Work, Research and Training* , pages. 52-61.

Brown, Peter F., Stephen A. Della Pietra, Vincent J. Della Pietra, Robert L. Mercer. 1993. The Mathematics of Statistical Machine Translation: Parameter Estimation. *Computational Linguistics*, 19(2):263-311.

Callison-Burch, Chris, Colin Bannard and Josh Schroeder. 2005. A Compact Data Structure for Searchable Translation Memories. In *Proceedings of EAMT*.

Gao, Zhao-Ming. 2011. Exploring the effects and use of a Chinese–English parallel concordancer. *Computer-Assisted Language Learning* 24.3 (July 2011): 255-275.

Jian, Jia-Yan, Yu-Chia Chang and Jason S. Chang. 2004. TANGO: Bilingual Collocational Concordancer. In *Proceedings of ACL*, pages 166-169.

Kitamura, Mihoko and Yuji Matsumoto. 1996. Automatic Extraction of Word Sequence Correspondences in Parallel Corpora. In *Proceedings of WVLC-4* pages 79-87.

Kupiec, Julian. 1993. An Algorithm for Finding Noun Phrase Correspondences in Bilingual Corpora. In *Proceedings of ACL*, pages 17-22.

Liang, Percy, Ben Taskar, Dan Klein. 2006. Alignment by Agreement. In *Proceedings of HLT-NAACL 2006*, pages 104-111, New York, USA.

Ma, Wei-Yun and Keh-Jiann Chen. 2003. Introduction to CKIP Chinese word segmentation system for the first international Chinese word segmentation bakeoff. In *Proceedings of the second SIGHAN workshop on Chinese language processing*, pages 168-171.

Ma, Xiaoyi. 2006. Champollion: A Robust Parallel Text Sentence Aligner. In *Proceedings of the Fifth International Conference on Language Resources and Evaluation.*

Melamed, Ilya Dan. 2001. Empirical Methods for Exploiting parallel Texts. *MIT press*.

Moore, Robert C. 2004. Improving IBM Word-Alignment Model 1. In *Proceedings of ACL*, pages 519-526, Barcelona, Spain.

Och, Franz J., Hermann Ney., 2000, Improved Statistical Alignment Models, In *Proceedings of ACL*, pages 440-447. Hong Kong.

Smadja, Frank, Kathleen R. McKeown, and Vasileios Hatzivassiloglou. 1996. Translating Collocations for Bilingual Lexicons: A Statistical Approach. *Computational Linguistics*, 22(1):1-38.

Wu, Jian-Cheng, Kevin C. Yeh, Thomas C. Chuang, Wen-Chi Shei, Jason S. Chang. 2003. TotalRecall: A Bilingual Concordance for Computer Assisted Translation and Language Learning. In *Proceedings of ACL*, pages 201-204.

Yamamoto, Kaoru, Yuji Matsumoto. 2000. Acquisition of Phrase-level Bilingual Correspondence using Dependency Structure. In *Proceedings of COLING*, pages 933-939.

The OpenGrm open-source finite-state grammar software libraries

Brian Roark[†] **Richard Sproat**[†○] **Cyril Allauzen**[○] **Michael Riley**[○] **Jeffrey Sorensen**[○] **& Terry Tai**[○]
[†]Oregon Health & Science University, Portland, Oregon [○]Google, Inc., New York

Abstract

In this paper, we present a new collection of open-source software libraries that provides command line binary utilities and library classes and functions for compiling regular expression and context-sensitive rewrite rules into finite-state transducers, and for n-gram language modeling. The OpenGrm libraries use the OpenFst library to provide an efficient encoding of grammars and general algorithms for building, modifying and applying models.

1 Introduction

The OpenGrm libraries[1] are a (growing) collection of open-source software libraries for building and applying various kinds of formal grammars. The C++ libraries use the OpenFst library[2] for the underlying finite-state representation, which allows for easy inspection of the resulting grammars and models, as well as straightforward combination with other finite-state transducers. Like OpenFst, there are easy-to-use command line binaries for frequently used operations, as well as a C++ library interface, allowing library users to create their own algorithms from the basic classes and functions provided.

The libraries can be used for a range of common string processing tasks, such as text normalization, as well as for building and using large statistical models for applications like speech recognition. In the rest of the paper, we will present each of the two libraries, starting with the Thrax grammar compiler and then the NGram library. First, though, we will briefly present some preliminary (informal) background on weighted finite-state transducers (WFST), just as needed for this paper.

[1]`http://www.opengrm.org/`
[2]`http://www.openfst.org/`

2 Informal WFST preliminaries

A weighted finite-state transducer consists of a set of states and transitions between states. There is an initial state and a subset of states are final. Each transition is labeled with an input symbol from an input alphabet; an output symbol from an output alphabet; an origin state; a destination state; and a weight. Each final state has an associated final weight. A path in the WFST is a sequence of transitions where each transition's destination state is the next transition's origin state. A valid path through the WFST is a path where the origin state of the first transition is an initial state, and the the last transition is to a final state. Weights combine along the path according to the semiring of the WFST.

If every transition in the transducer has the same input and output symbol, then the WFST represents a weighted finite-state automaton. In the OpenFst library, there are a small number of special symbols that can be used. The ϵ symbol represents the empty string, which allows the transition to be traversed without consuming any symbol. The ϕ (or failure) symbol on a transition also allows it to be traversed without consuming any symbol, but it differs from ϵ in only allowing traversal if the symbol being matched does not label any other transition leaving the same state, i.e., it encodes the semantics of *otherwise*, which is useful for language models. For a more detailed presentation of WFSTs, see Allauzen et al. (2007).

3 The Thrax Grammar Compiler

The Thrax grammar compiler[3] compiles grammars that consist of regular expressions, and context-dependent rewrite rules, into FST archives (fars) of weighted finite state transducers. Grammars may

[3]The compiler is named after Dionysius Thrax (170–90BCE), the reputed first Greek grammarian.

Proceedings of the 50th Annual Meeting of the Association for Computational Linguistics, pages 61–66,
Jeju, Republic of Korea, 8-14 July 2012.

be split over multiple files and *imported* into other grammars. Strings in the rules may be parsed in one of three different ways: as a sequence of bytes (the default), as utf8 encodings, or according to a user-provided symbol table. With the `--save_symbols` flag, the transducers can be saved out into fars with appropriate symbol tables.

The Thrax libraries provide full support for different weight (semiring) classes. The command-line flag `--semiring` allows one to set the semiring, currently to one of: tropical (default), log or log64 semirings.

3.1 General Description

Thrax revolves around rules which, typically, construct an FST based on a given input. In the simplest case, we can just provide a string that represents a (trivial) transducer and name it using the assignment operator:

```
pear = "pear";
```

In this example, we have an FST consisting of the characters "p", "e", "a", and "r" in a chain, assigned to the identifier `pear`:

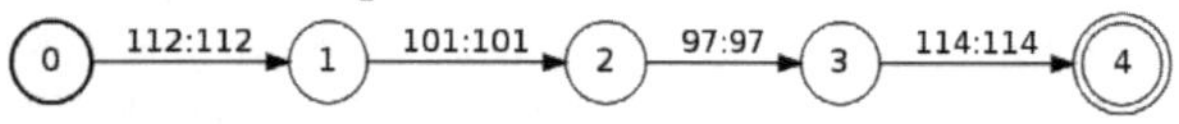

This identifier can be used later in order to build further FSTs, using built-in operators or using custom functions:

```
kiwi = "kiwi";
fruits = pear | kiwi; # union
```

In Thrax, string FSTs are enclosed by double-quotes (") whereas simple strings (often used as pathnames for functions) are enclosed in single-quotes (').

Thrax provides a set of built-in functions that aid in the construction of more complex expressions. We have already seen the disjunction "|" in the previous example. Other standard regular operations are *expr**, *expr+*, *expr?* and *expr{m,n}*, the latter repeating *expr* between *m* and *n* times, inclusive. Composition is notated with "@" so that *expr1 @ expr2* denotes the composition of *expr1* and *expr2*. Rewriting is denoted with ":" where *expr1 : expr2* rewrites strings that match *expr1* into *expr2*. Weights can be added to expressions using the notation "<>": thus, *expr<2.4>* adds weight *2.4* to *expr*. Various operations on FSTs are also provided by built-in functions, including `Determinize`, `Minimize`, `Optimize` and `Invert`, among many others.

3.2 Detailed Description

A Thrax grammar consists of a set of one or more source files, each of which must have the extension `.grm`. The compiler compiles each source file to a single *FST archive* with the extension `.far`. Each grammar file has sections: Imports and Body, each of which is optional. The body section can include statements interleaved with functions, as specified below. Comments begin with a single pound sign (#) and last until the next newline.

3.2.1 Imports

The Thrax compiler compiles source files (with the extension `.grm`) into *FST archive* files (with the extension `.far`). FST archives are an OpenFst storage format for a series of one or more FSTs. The FST archive and the original source file then form a pair which can be imported into other source files, allowing a Python-esque include system that is hopefully familiar to many. Instead of working with a monolithic file, Thrax allows for a modular construction of the final rule set as well as sharing of common elements across projects.

3.2.2 Functions

Thrax has extensive support for functions that can greatly augment the capabilities of the language. Functions in Thrax can be specified in two ways. The first is inline via the *func* keyword within `grm` files. These functions can take any number of input arguments and must return a single result (usually an FST) to the caller via the *return* keyword:

```
func DumbPluralize[fst] {
  # Concatenate with "s"...
  result = fst "s";
  # ...and then return to caller.
  return result;
}
```

Alternatively, functions can be written C++ and added to the language. Regardless of the function implementation method (inline in Thrax or subclassed in C++), functions are integrated into the Thrax environment and can be called directly by using the function name and providing the necessary arguments. Thus, assuming someone has written a function called `NetworkPluralize` that retrieves the plural of a word from some website, one could write a grammar fragment as follows:

```
apple = "apple";
plural_apple = DumbPluralize[apple];

plural_tomato = NetworkPluralize[
    "tomato",
    'http://server:port/...'];
```

3.2.3 Statements

Functions can be interleaved with grammar statements that generate the FSTs that are exported to the FST archive as output. Each statement consists of an assignment terminating with a semicolon:

```
foo = "abc";
export bar = foo | "xyz";
```

Statements preceded with the *export* keyword will be written to the final output archive. Statements lacking this keyword define temporaries that be used later, but are themselves not output.

The basic elements of any grammar are string FSTs, which, as mentioned earlier, are defined by text enclosed by double quotes ("), in contrast to raw strings, which are enclosed by single quotes ('). String FSTs can be parsed in one of three ways, which are denoted using a dot (.) followed by either *byte*, *utf8*, or an identifier holding a symbol table. Note that within strings, the backslash character (\) is used to escape the next character. Of particular note, '\n' translates into a newline, '\r' into a line feed, and '\t' into the tab character. Literal left and right square brackets also need escaping, as they are used to generate symbols (see below). All other characters following the backslash are uninterpreted, so that we can use \" and \' to insert an actual quote (double) quote symbol instead of terminating the string.

Strings, by default, are interpreted as sequences of bytes, each transition of the resulting FST corresponding to a single 1-byte character of the input. This can be specified either by leaving off the parse mode ("abc") or by explicitly using the byte mode ("abc".byte). The second way is to use UTF8 parsing by using the special keyword, e.g.:

```
kimchi = "김치".utf8;
```

Finally, we can load a symbol table and split the string using the fst_field_separator flag (found in fst/src/lib/symbol-table.cc) and then perform symbol table lookups. Symbol tables can be loaded using the SymbolTable built-in function:

```
arctic_symbol_table =
  SymbolTable['/path/to/bears.symtab'];
pb = "polar bear".arctic_symbol_table;
```

One can also create temporary symbols on the fly by enclosing a symbol name inside brackets within an FST string. All of the text inside the brackets will be taken to be part of the symbol name, and future encounters of the same symbol name will map to the same label. By default, labels use "Private Use Area B" of the unicode table (0x100000 - 0x10FFFD), except that the last two code points 0x10FFFC and 0x10FFFD are reserved for the "[BOS]" and "[EOS]" tags discussed below.

```
cross_pos = "cross" ("" : "_[s_noun]");
pluralize_nouns = "_[s_noun]" : "es";
```

3.3 Standard Library Functions and Operations

Built-in functions are provided that operate on FSTs and perform most of the operations that are available in the OpenFst library. These include: closure, concatenation, difference, composition and union. In most cases the notation of these functions follows standard conventions. Thus, for example, for closure, the following syntax applies: fst* (accepts fst 0 or more times); fst+ (accepts fst 1 or more times); fst? (accepts fst 0 or 1 times) fst{x,y} (accepts fst at least x but no more than y times).

The operator "@" is used for composition: `a @ b` denotes `a` composed with `b`. A ":" is used to denote *rewrite*, where `a : b` denotes a transducer that deletes `a` and inserts `b`. Most functions can also be expressed using functional notation:

```
b = Rewrite["abc", "def"];
```

The delimiters < and > add a weight to an expression in the chosen semiring: `a<3>` adds the weight 3 (in the tropical semiring by default) to `a`.

Functions lacking operators (hence only called by function name) include: `ArcSort`, `Connect`, `Determinize`, `RmEpsilon`, `Minimize`, `Optimize`, `Invert`, `Project` and `Reverse`. Most of these call the obvious underlying OpenFst function.

One function in particular, `CDRewrite` is worth further discussion. This function takes a transducer and two context acceptors (and the alphabet machine), and generates a new FST that performs a context dependent rewrite everywhere in the provided contexts. The context-dependent rewrite algorithm used is that of Mohri and Sproat (1996), and see also Kaplan and Kay (1994). The fourth argument (`sigma_star`) needs to be a minimized machine. The fifth argument selects the direction of rewrite; we can either rewrite left-to-right or right-to-left or simultaneously. The sixth argument selects whether the rewrite is optional.

```
CDRewrite[tau, lambda, rho,
          sigma_star,
          'ltr'|'rtl'|'sim',
          'obl'|'opt']
```

For context-dependent rewrite rules, two built-in symbols "[BOS]" and "[EOS]" have a special meaning in the context specifications: they refer to the beginning and end of string, respectively.

There are also built-in functions that perform other tasks. In the interest of space we concentrate here on the `StringFile` function, which loads a file consisting of a list of strings, or tab-separated *pairs* of strings, and compiles them to an acceptor that represents the union of the strings.

```
StringFile['strings_file']
```

While it is equivalent to the union of the individual string (pairs), `StringFile` uses an efficient algorithm for constructing a prefix tree (trie) from the list and can be *significantly* more efficient than computing a union for large lists. If a line consists of a tab-separated pair of strings *a*, *b*, a transducer equivalent to `Rewrite[a, b]` is compiled.

The optional keywords `byte` (default), `utf8` or the name of a symbol table can be used to specify the parsing mode for the strings. Thus

```
StringFile['strings_file', utf8, my_symtab]
```

would parse a sequence of tab-separated pairs, using utf8 parsing for the left-hand string, and the symbol table `my_symtab` for the right-hand string.

4 NGram Library

The OpenGrm NGram library contains tools for building, manipulating and using n-gram language models represented as weighted finite-state transducers. The same finite-state topology is used to encode raw counts as well as smoothed models. Here we briefly present this structure, followed by details on the operations manipulating it.

An n-gram is a sequence of n symbols: $w_1 \dots w_n$. Each state in the model represents a prefix *history* of the n-gram ($w_1 \dots w_{n-1}$), and transitions in the model represent either n-grams or backoff transitions following that history. Figure 1 lists conventions for states and transitions used to encode the n-grams as a WFST.

This representation is similar to that used in other WFST-based n-gram software libraries, such as the AT&T GRM library (Allauzen et al., 2005). One key difference is the implicit representation of <s> and </s>, as opposed to encoding them as symbols in the grammar. This has the benefit of including all start and stop symbol functionality while avoiding common pitfalls that arise with explicit symbols.

Another difference from the GRM library representation is explicit inclusion of failure links from states to their backoff states even in the raw count files. The OpenGrm n-gram FST format is consistent through all stages of building the models, meaning that model manipulation (e.g., merging of two

Figure 1: List of state and transition conventions used to encode collection of n-grams in WFST.

An n-gram is a sequence of n symbols: $w_1 \dots w_n$. Its proper prefixes include all sequences $w_1 \dots w_k$ for $k < n$.

- There is a *unigram* state in every model, representing the empty string.
- Every proper prefix of every n-gram in the model has an associated state in the model.
- The state associated with an n-gram $w_1 ... w_n$ has a backoff transition (labeled with ϵ) to the state associated with its suffix $w_2 ... w_n$.
- An n-gram $w_1 ... w_n$ is represented as a transition, labeled with w_n, from the state associated with its prefix $w_1 ... w_{n-1}$ to a destination state defined as follows:
  - If $w_1 ... w_n$ is a proper prefix of an n-gram in the model, then the destination of the transition is the state associated with $w_1 ... w_n$
  - Otherwise, the destination of the transition is the state associated with the suffix $w_2 ... w_n$.
- Start and end of the sequence are not represented via transitions in the automaton or symbols in the symbol table. Rather
  - The start state of the automaton encodes the "start of sequence" n-gram prefix (commonly denoted <s>).
  - The end of the sequence (often denoted </s>) is included in the model through state final weights, i.e., for a state associated with an n-gram prefix $w_1 ... w_n$, the final weight of that state represents the weight of the n-gram $w_1 ... w_n$</s>.

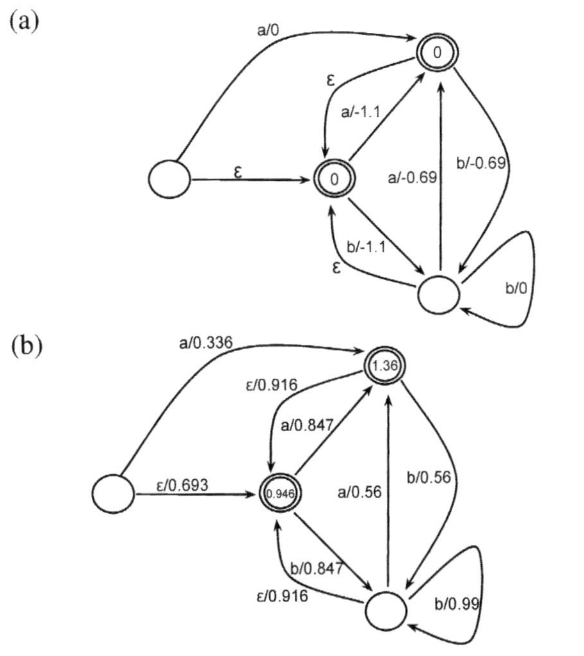

Figure 2: FST representations of (a) bigram and unigram counts; and (b) smoothed bigram model, when trained on the single string "a b a b b a"

models or count files, or pruning them) can be processed by the same operations. By convention, all counts and probabilities are stored as negative logs, and the FSTs are in the Tropical semiring. The symbol table provided during counting is kept with the model FSTs.

4.1 N-gram Counting

The command line binary `ngramcount` takes as input an FST archive (far) consisting of a collection of acyclic WFSTs and outputs an n-gram WFST of the specified order. The acyclic WFSTs can be linear automata representing strings from a corpus – easily compiled using the `farcompilestrings` command of OpenFst – or weighted word lattices output from, say, a speech recognition or machine translation system. In such a way, expected frequencies of n-grams can be counted. To count all trigrams, bigrams and unigrams in the compiled (far) corpus:

```
ngramcount -order=3 in.far >3g.cnt.fst
```

For example, counting with the `-order=2` flag (bigrams) from a corpus consisting of a single string "a b a b b a" yields the FST in Figure 2(a). Each state represents a prefix history: the leftmost state is the initial state, representing the <s> history; the central state is the *unigram* state, representing the ϵ history; the topmost state represents the history 'a'; and the bottom state represents the history 'b'. Since this is a bigram model, histories consist of at most one prior symbol from the vocabulary. Double circles represent final states, which come with a final weight encoding the negative log count of ending the string at that state. Only the 'a' history state and the unigram state are final states, since our example string ends with the symbol 'a'. (The unigram state is always final.) The ϵ transitions are backoff transitions, and the weights on each n-gram transition are negative log counts of that symbol occurring following the history that the state represents. Hence the bigram "b b" occurs once, yielding a negative log of zero for the transition labeled with 'b' leaving the state representing the history 'b'.

4.2 N-gram Model Parameter Estimation

Given counts, one can build a smoothed n-gram model by normalizing and smoothing, which is accomplished with the `ngrammake` command line binary. The library has several available smoothing methods, including Katz (1987), absolute discounting (Ney et al., 1994), Kneser-Ney (1995) and (the default) Witten-Bell (1991). See Chen and Goodman (1998) for a detailed presentation of these smoothing methods. Each of these smoothing methods is implemented as a relatively simple derived subclass, thus allowing for straightforward extension to new and different smoothing methods. To make a smoothed n-gram model from counts:

```
ngrammake 3g.cnt.fst >3g.mod.fst
```

Figure 2(b) shows the model built using the default Witten-Bell smoothing from the count FST in 2(a). The topology remains identical, but now the n-gram transition weights and final weights are negative log probabilities. The backoff transitions (labeled with ϵ) have the negative log backoff weights, which ensure that the model is correctly normalized.

Models, by default, are smoothed by interpolating higher- and lower-order probabilities. This is even true for methods more typically associated with backoff (rather than mixture) smoothing styles, such as Katz. While the smoothing values are estimated using interpolation, the model is encoded as a backoff model by pre-summing the interpolated probabilities, so that the backoff transitions are to be traversed only for symbols without transitions out of the current state. While these backoff transitions are labeled with ϵ, see Section 4.4 for discussion of applying them as failure transitions.

4.3 N-gram Model Merging and Pruning

Two n-gram count FSTs or two model FSTs can be merged into a single FST using `ngrammerge`, with command line flags to allow for scaling of each of the two, and to indicate whether to carry out full normalization. This approach allows for various sorts of MAP adaptation approaches for the n-gram models (Bacchiani et al., 2006). To merge two input FST models with no scaling:

```
ngrammerge in.mod1 in.mod2 >mrg.mod
```

N-gram model pruning is provided with three different methods: count pruning based on a threshold; the method from Seymore and Rosenfeld (1996); and relative entropy pruning of Stolcke (1998). Like smoothing, each of these pruning methods is implemented as a relatively simple derived subclass, thus allowing for straightforward extension to new and different pruning methods. To prune a smoothed n-gram model:

```
ngramshrink -theta=4 in.mod >prn.mod
```

4.4 N-gram Utilities

In addition to the above detailed core operations on language models, the OpenGrm NGram library has a number of utilities that make building and using the models very easy. There are utilities related to input and output, including `ngramsymbols`, which produces a symbol table from a corpus; `ngramread`, which reads in textual count files and models in ARPA format and encodes them as an FST; `ngramprint` which prints n-gram counts or ARPA format text files; and `ngraminfo` which displays information about the model, such as number of n-grams of various orders. There are also utilities related to the use of the models, including `ngramapply`, which applies the model to an input FST archive (far); `ngramrandgen` which randomly generates strings from the model; and `ngramperplexity` which calculates the perplexity of a corpus given the model. Note that `ngramapply` includes options for interpreting the backoff transitions as failure transitions.

Acknowledgments

This work was supported in part by a Google Faculty Research Award, NSF grant #IIS-0811745 and DARPA #HR0011-09-1-0041. Any opinions, findings, conclusions or recommendations expressed in this publication are those of the authors and do not necessarily reflect the views of the NSF or DARPA.

References

Cyril Allauzen, Mehryar Mohri, and Brian Roark. 2005. The design principles and algorithms of a weighted grammar library. *International Journal of Foundations of Computer Science*, 16(3):403–421.

Cyril Allauzen, Michael Riley, Johan Schalkwyk, Wojciech Skut, and Mehryar Mohri. 2007. OpenFst: A general and efficient weighted finite-state transducer library. In *Proceedings of the Twelfth International Conference on Implementation and Application of Automata (CIAA 2007), Lecture Notes in Computer Science*, volume 4793, pages 11–23.

Michiel Bacchiani, Michael Riley, Brian Roark, and Richard Sproat. 2006. MAP adaptation of stochastic grammars. *Computer Speech and Language*, 20(1):41–68.

Stanley Chen and Joshua Goodman. 1998. An empirical study of smoothing techniques for language modeling. Technical report, TR-10-98, Harvard University.

Ronald M. Kaplan and Martin Kay. 1994. Regular models of phonological rule systems. *Computational Linguistics*, 20:331–378.

Slava M. Katz. 1987. Estimation of probabilities from sparse data for the language model component of a speech recogniser. *IEEE Transactions on Acoustics, Speech, and Signal Processing*, 35(3):400–401.

Reinhard Kneser and Hermann Ney. 1995. Improved backing-off for m-gram language modeling. In *Proceedings of the IEEE International Conference on Acoustics, Speech, and Signal Processing (ICASSP)*, pages 181–184.

Mehryar Mohri and Richard Sproat. 1996. An efficient compiler for weighted rewrite rules. In *Proceedings of the 34th Annual Meeting of the Association for Computational Linguistics*, pages 231–238.

Hermann Ney, Ute Essen, and Reinhard Kneser. 1994. On structuring probabilistic dependences in stochastic language modeling. *Computer Speech and Language*, 8:1–38.

Kristie Seymore and Ronald Rosenfeld. 1996. Scalable backoff language models. In *Proceedings of the International Conference on Spoken Language Processing (ICSLP)*.

Andreas Stolcke. 1998. Entropy-based pruning of backoff language models. In *Proc. DARPA Broadcast News Transcription and Understanding Workshop*, pages 270–274.

Ian H. Witten and Timothy C. Bell. 1991. The zero-frequency problem: Estimating the probabilities of novel events in adaptive text compression. *IEEE Transactions on Information Theory*, 37(4):1085–1094.

Multilingual WSD with Just a Few Lines of Code: the BabelNet API

Roberto Navigli and **Simone Paolo Ponzetto**
Dipartimento di Informatica
Sapienza Università di Roma
{navigli,ponzetto}@di.uniroma1.it

Abstract

In this paper we present an API for programmatic access to BabelNet – a wide-coverage multilingual lexical knowledge base – and multilingual knowledge-rich Word Sense Disambiguation (WSD). Our aim is to provide the research community with easy-to-use tools to perform multilingual lexical semantic analysis and foster further research in this direction.

1 Introduction

In recent years research in Natural Language Processing (NLP) has been steadily moving towards multilingual processing: the availability of ever growing amounts of text in different languages, in fact, has been a major driving force behind research on multilingual approaches, from morpho-syntactic (Das and Petrov, 2011) and syntactico-semantic (Peirsman and Padó, 2010) phenomena to high-end tasks like textual entailment (Mehdad et al., 2011) and sentiment analysis (Lu et al., 2011).

These research trends would seem to indicate the time is ripe for developing methods capable of performing semantic analysis of texts written in any language: however, this objective is still far from being attained, as is demonstrated by research in a core language understanding task such as Word Sense Disambiguation (Navigli, 2009, WSD) continuing to be focused primarily on English. While the lack of resources has hampered the development of effective multilingual approaches to WSD, recently this idea has been revamped with the organization of SemEval tasks on cross-lingual WSD (Lefever and Hoste, 2010) and cross-lingual lexical substitution (Mihalcea et al., 2010). In addition, new research on the topic has explored the translation of sentences into many languages (Navigli and Ponzetto, 2010; Lefever et al., 2011; Banea and Mihalcea, 2011), as well as the projection of monolingual knowledge onto another language (Khapra et al., 2011).

In our research we focus on knowledge-based methods and tools for multilingual WSD, since knowledge-rich WSD has been shown to achieve high performance across domains (Agirre et al., 2009; Navigli et al., 2011) and to compete with supervised methods on a variety of lexical disambiguation tasks (Ponzetto and Navigli, 2010). Our vision of knowledge-rich multilingual WSD requires two fundamental components: first, a wide-coverage multilingual lexical knowledge base; second, tools to effectively query, retrieve and exploit its information for disambiguation. Nevertheless, to date, no integrated resources and tools exist that are freely available to the research community on a multilingual scale. Previous endeavors are either not freely available (EuroWordNet (Vossen, 1998)), or are only accessible via a Web interface (cf. the Multilingual Research Repository (Atserias et al., 2004) and MENTA (de Melo and Weikum, 2010)), thus providing no programmatic access. And this is despite the fact that the availability of easy-to-use libraries for efficient information access is known to foster top-level research – cf. the widespread use of semantic similarity measures in NLP, thanks to the availability of `WordNet::Similarity` (Pedersen et al., 2004).

With the present contribution we aim to fill this gap in multilingual tools, providing a multi-tiered contribution consisting of (a) an Application Programming Interface (API) for efficiently accessing the information available in BabelNet (Navigli and

Proceedings of the 50th Annual Meeting of the Association for Computational Linguistics, pages 67–72,
Jeju, Republic of Korea, 8-14 July 2012.

```
bn:00008364n WIKIWN 08420278n 85 WN:EN:bank WIKI:EN:Bank WIKI:DE:Bank WIKI:IT:Banca
                                 WIKIRED:DE:Finanzinstitut WN:EN:banking_company
                                 WNTR:ES:banco WNTR:FR:société_bancaire WIKI:FR:Banque ...
                              35 1_7 2_3,4,9 6_8 ...
                             228 r bn:02945246n r bn:02854884n|FROM_IT @ bn:00034537n ...
```

Figure 1: The Babel synset for bank_n^2, i.e. its 'financial' sense (excerpt, formatted for ease of readability).

Ponzetto, 2010), a very large knowledge repository with concept lexicalizations in 6 languages (Catalan, English, French, German, Italian and Spanish), at the lexicographic (i.e., word senses), encyclopedic (i.e., named entities) and conceptual (i.e., concepts and semantic relations) levels; (b) an API to perform graph-based WSD with BabelNet, thus providing, for the first time, a freely-available toolkit for performing knowledge-based WSD in a multilingual and cross-lingual setting.

2 BabelNet

BabelNet follows the structure of a traditional lexical knowledge base and accordingly consists of a labeled directed graph where nodes represent concepts and named entities and edges express semantic relations between them. Concepts and relations are harvested from the largest available semantic lexicon of English, i.e., WordNet (Fellbaum, 1998), and a wide-coverage collaboratively-edited encyclopedia, i.e., Wikipedia[1], thus making BabelNet a multilingual 'encyclopedic dictionary' which automatically integrates fine-grained lexicographic information with large amounts of encyclopedic knowledge by means of a high-performing mapping algorithm (Navigli and Ponzetto, 2010). In addition to this conceptual backbone, BabelNet provides a multilingual lexical dimension. Each of its nodes, called *Babel synsets*, contains a set of lexicalizations of the concept for different languages, e.g., $\{$ bank_{EN}, Bank_{DE}, banca_{IT}, $\ldots$, banco_{ES} $\}$.

Similar in spirit to WordNet, BabelNet consists, at its lowest level, of a plain text file. An excerpt of the entry for the Babel synset containing bank_n^2 is shown in Figure 1[2]. The record contains (a) the synset's `id`; (b) the `region` of BabelNet where it lies (e.g., `WIKIWN` means at the intersection of WordNet and Wikipedia); (c) the corresponding (possibly empty) WordNet 3.0 synset `offset`; (d) the number of `senses` in all languages and their full listing; (e) the number of translation relations and their full listing; (f) the number of semantic `pointers` (i.e., relations) to other Babel synsets and their full listing. Senses encode information about their source – i.e., whether they come from WordNet (`WN`), Wikipedia pages (`WIKI`) or their redirections (`WIKIRED`), or are automatic translations (`WNTR / WIKITR`) – and about their language and lemma. In addition, translation relations among lexical items are represented as a mapping from source to target senses – e.g., `2_3,4,9` means that the second element in the list of senses (the English word bank) translates into items #3 (German Bank), #4 (Italian banca), and #9 (French banque). Finally, semantic relations are encoded using WordNet's pointers and an additional symbol for Wikipedia relations (`r`), which can also specify the source of the relation (e.g., `FROM_IT` means that the relation was harvested from the Italian Wikipedia). In Figure 1, the Babel synset inherits the WordNet hypernym (`@`) relation to $\text{financial institution}_n^1$ (offset `bn:00034537n`), as well as Wikipedia relations to the synsets of FINANCIAL INSTRUMENT (`bn:02945246n`) and ETHICAL BANKING (`bn:02854884n`, from Italian).

3 An API for multilingual WSD

BabelNet API. BabelNet can be effectively accessed and automatically embedded within applications by means of a programmatic access. In order to achieve this, we developed a Java API, based on Apache Lucene[3], which indexes the BabelNet textual dump and includes a variety of methods to access the four main levels of information encoded in BabelNet, namely: (a) lexicographic (information about word senses), (b) encyclopedic (i.e. named en-

[1] `http://www.wikipedia.org`

[2] We denote with w_p^i the i-th WordNet sense of a word w with part of speech p.

[3] `http://lucene.apache.org`

```
1  BabelNet bn = BabelNet.getInstance();
2  System.out.println("SYNSETS WITH English word: \"bank\"");
3  List<BabelSynset> synsets = bn.getSynsets(Language.EN, "bank");
4  for (BabelSynset synset : synsets) {
5    System.out.print("  =>(" + synset.getId() + ") SOURCE: " + synset.getSource() +
6                     "; WN SYNSET: " + synset.getWordNetOffsets() + ";\n" +
7                     "  MAIN LEMMA: " + synset.getMainLemma() + ";\n  SENSES (IT): { ");
8    for (BabelSense sense : synset.getSenses(Language.IT))
9      System.out.print(sense.toString()+" ");
10   System.out.println("}\n  -----");
11   Map<IPointer, List<BabelSynset>> relatedSynsets = synset.getRelatedMap();
12   for (IPointer relationType : relatedSynsets.keySet()) {
13     List<BabelSynset> relationSynsets = relatedSynsets.get(relationType);
14     for (BabelSynset relationSynset : relationSynsets) {
15       System.out.println("    EDGE " + relationType.getSymbol() +
16                          " " + relationSynset.getId() +
17                          " " + relationSynset.toString(Language.EN));
18     }
19   }
20   System.out.println("  -----");
21 }
```

Figure 2: Sample BabelNet API usage.

tities), (c) conceptual (the semantic network made up of its concepts), (d) and multilingual level (information about word translations). Figure 2 shows a usage example of the BabelNet API. In the code snippet we start by querying the Babel synsets for the English word bank (line 3). Next, we access different kinds of information for each synset: first, we print their id, source (WordNet, Wikipedia, or both), the corresponding, possibly empty, WordNet offsets, and 'main lemma' – namely, a compact string representation of the Babel synset consisting of its corresponding WordNet synset in stringified form, or the first non-redirection Wikipedia page found in it (lines 5–7). Then, we access and print the Italian word senses they contain (lines 8–10), and finally the synsets they are related to (lines 11–19). Thanks to carefully designed Java classes, we are able to accomplish all of this in about 20 lines of code.

Multilingual WSD API. We use the BabelNet API as a framework to build a toolkit that allows the user to perform multilingual graph-based lexical disambiguation – namely, to identify the most suitable meanings of the input words on the basis of the semantic connections found in the lexical knowledge base, along the lines of Navigli and Lapata (2010). At its core, the API leverages an in-house Java library to query paths and create semantic graphs with BabelNet. The latter works by pre-computing off-line paths connecting any pair of Babel synsets, which are collected by iterating through each synset in turn, and performing a depth-first search up to a maximum depth – which we set to 3, on the basis of experimental evidence from a variety of knowledge base linking and lexical disambiguation tasks (Navigli and Lapata, 2010; Ponzetto and Navigli, 2010). Next, these paths are stored within a Lucene index, which ensures efficient lookups for querying those paths starting and ending in a specific synset. Given a set of words as input, a semantic graph factory class searches for their meanings within BabelNet, looks for their connecting paths, and merges such paths within a single graph. Optionally, the paths making up the graph can be filtered – e.g., it is possible to remove loops, weighted edges below a certain threshold, etc. – and the graph nodes can be scored using a variety of methods – such as, for instance, their outdegree or PageRank value in the context of the semantic graph. These graph connectivity measures can be used to rank senses of the input words, thus performing graph-based WSD on the basis of the structure of the underlying knowledge base.

We show in Figure 3 a usage example of our disambiguation API. The method which performs WSD (`disambiguate`) takes as input a collection of words (i.e., typically a sentence), a `KnowledgeBase` with which to perform dis-

```
1  public static void disambiguate(Collection<Word> words,
2                                  KnowledgeBase kb, KnowledgeGraphScorer scorer) {
3    KnowledgeGraphFactory factory = KnowledgeGraphFactory.getInstance(kb);
4    KnowledgeGraph kGraph = factory.getKnowledgeGraph(words);
5    Map<String, Double> scores = scorer.score(kGraph);
6    for (String concept : scores.keySet()) {
7      double score = scores.get(concept);
8      for (Word word : kGraph.wordsForConcept(concept))
9        word.addLabel(concept, score);
10   }
11   for (Word word : words) {
12     System.out.println("\n\t" + word.getWord() + " -- ID " + word.getId() +
13                        " => SENSE DISTRIBUTION: ");
14     for (ScoredItem<String> label : word.getLabels()) {
15       System.out.println("\t   [" + label.getItem() + "]:" +
16                          Strings.format(label.getScore()));
17     }
18   }
19 }
20
21 public static void main(String[] args) {
22   List<Word> sentence = Arrays.asList(
23     new Word[]{new Word("bank", 'n', Language.EN), new Word("bonus", 'n', Language.EN),
24                new Word("pay", 'v', Language.EN), new Word("stock", 'n', Language.EN)});
25   disambiguate(sentence, KnowledgeBase.BABELNET, KnowledgeGraphScorer.DEGREE);
26 }
```

Figure 3: Sample Word Sense Disambiguation API usage.

ambiguation, and a `KnowledgeGraphScorer`, namely a value from an enumeration of different graph connectivity measures (e.g., node outdegree), which are responsible for scoring nodes (i.e., concepts) in the graph. `KnowledgeBase` is an enumeration of supported knowledge bases: currently, it includes BabelNet, as well as WordNet++ (namely, an English WordNet-based subset of it (Ponzetto and Navigli, 2010)) and WordNet. Note that, while BabelNet is presently the only lexical knowledge base which allows for multilingual processing, our framework can easily be extended to work with other existing lexical knowledge resources, provided they can be wrapped around Java classes and implement interface methods for querying senses, concepts, and their semantic relations. In the snippet we start in line 3 by obtaining an instance of the factory class which creates the semantic graphs for a given knowledge base. Next, we use this factory to create the graph for the input words (line 4). We then score the senses of the input words occurring within this graph (line 5–10). Finally, we output the sense distributions of each word in lines 11–18. The disambiguation method, in turn, can be called by any other Java program in a way similar to the one highlighted by the `main` method of lines 21–26, where we disambiguate the sample sentence '*bank bonuses are paid in stocks*' (note that each input word can be written in any of the 6 languages, i.e. we could mix languages).

4 Experiments

We benchmark our API by performing knowledge-based WSD with BabelNet on standard SemEval datasets, namely the SemEval-2007 coarse-grained all-words (Navigli et al., 2007, Coarse-WSD, henceforth) and the SemEval-2010 cross-lingual (Lefever and Hoste, 2010, CL-WSD) WSD tasks. For both experimental settings we use a standard graph-based algorithm, Degree (Navigli and Lapata, 2010), which has been previously shown to yield a highly competitive performance on different lexical disambiguation tasks (Ponzetto and Navigli, 2010). Given a semantic graph for the input context, Degree selects the sense of the target word with the highest vertex degree. In addition, in the CL-WSD setting we need to output appropriate lexicalization(s) in different languages. Since the selected Babel synset can contain multiple translations in a target language for the given English word, we use for this task an

Algorithm	Nouns only	All words
NUS-PT	82.3	82.5
SUSSX-FR	81.1	77.0
Degree	84.7	82.3
MFS BL	77.4	78.9
Random BL	63.5	62.7

Table 1: Performance on SemEval-2007 coarse-grained all-words WSD (Navigli et al., 2007).

	Degree	T3-Coleur	UvT-v
Dutch	15.52	10.56	17.70
French	22.94	21.75	–
German	17.15	13.05	–
Italian	18.03	14.67	–
Spanish	22.48	19.64	23.39

Table 2: Performance on SemEval-2010 cross-lingual WSD (Lefever and Hoste, 2010).

unsupervised approach where we return for each test instance only the most frequent translation found in the synset, as given by its frequency of alignment obtained from the Europarl corpus (Koehn, 2005).

Tables 1 and 2 summarize our results in terms of recall (the primary metric for WSD tasks): for each SemEval task, we benchmark our disambiguation API against the best unsupervised and supervised systems, namely SUSSX-FR (Koeling and McCarthy, 2007) and NUS-PT (Chan et al., 2007) for Coarse-WSD, and T3-COLEUR (Guo and Diab, 2010) and UvT-v (van Gompel, 2010) for CL-WSD. In the Coarse-WSD task our API achieves the best overall performance on the nouns-only subset of the data, thus supporting previous findings indicating the benefits of using rich knowledge bases like BabelNet. In the CL-WSD evaluation, instead, using BabelNet allows us to surpass the best unsupervised system by a substantial margin, thus indicating the viability of high-performing WSD with a multilingual lexical knowledge base. While our performance still lags behind the application of supervised techniques to this task (cf. also results from Lefever and Hoste (2010)), we argue that further improvements can still be obtained by exploiting more complex disambiguation strategies. In general, using our toolkit we are able to achieve a performance which is competitive with the state of the art for these tasks, thus supporting previous findings on knowledge-rich WSD, and confirming the robustness of our toolkit.

5 Related Work

Our work complements recent efforts focused on visual browsing of wide-coverage knowledge bases (Tylenda et al., 2011; Navigli and Ponzetto, 2012) by means of an API which allows the user to programmatically query and search BabelNet. This knowledge resource, in turn, can be used for easily performing multilingual and cross-lingual WSD out-of-the-box. In comparison with other contributions, our toolkit for multilingual WSD takes previous work from Navigli (2006), in which an online interface for graph-based monolingual WSD is presented, one step further by adding a multilingual dimension as well as a full-fledged API. Our work also complements previous attempts by NLP researchers to provide the community with freely available tools to perform state-of-the-art WSD using WordNet-based measures of semantic relatedness (Patwardhan et al., 2005), as well as supervised WSD techniques (Zhong and Ng, 2010). We achieve this by building upon BabelNet, a multilingual 'encyclopedic dictionary' bringing together the lexicographic and encyclopedic knowledge from WordNet and Wikipedia. Other recent projects on creating multilingual knowledge bases from Wikipedia include WikiNet (Nastase et al., 2010) and MENTA (de Melo and Weikum, 2010): both these resources offer structured information complementary to BabelNet – i.e., large amounts of facts about entities (MENTA), and explicit semantic relations harvested from Wikipedia categories (WikiNet).

Acknowledgments

The authors gratefully acknowledge the support of the ERC Starting Grant MultiJEDI No. 259234.

BabelNet and its API are available for download at `http://lcl.uniroma1.it/babelnet`.

References

Eneko Agirre, Oier Lopez de Lacalle, and Aitor Soroa. 2009. Knowledge-based WSD on specific domains: performing better than generic supervised WSD. In *Proc. of IJCAI-09*, pages 1501–1506.

Jordi Atserias, Luis Villarejo, German Rigau, Eneko Agirre, John Carroll, Bernardo Magnini, and Piek Vossen. 2004. The MEANING multilingual central repository. In *Proc. of GWC-04*, pages 22–31.

Carmen Banea and Rada Mihalcea. 2011. Word Sense Disambiguation with multilingual features. In *Proc. of IWCS-11*, pages 25–34.

Yee Seng Chan, Hwee Tou Ng, and Zhi Zhong. 2007. NUS-ML: Exploiting parallel texts for Word Sense Disambiguation in the English all-words tasks. In *Proc. of SemEval-2007*, pages 253–256.

Dipanjan Das and Slav Petrov. 2011. Unsupervised part-of-speech tagging with bilingual graph-based projections. In *Proc. of ACL-11*, pages 600–609.

Gerard de Melo and Gerhard Weikum. 2010. MENTA: inducing multilingual taxonomies from Wikipedia. In *Proc. of CIKM-10*, pages 1099–1108.

Christiane Fellbaum, editor. 1998. *WordNet: An Electronic Lexical Database*. MIT Press, Cambridge, MA.

Weiwei Guo and Mona Diab. 2010. COLEPL and COLSLM: An unsupervised WSD approach to multilingual lexical substitution, tasks 2 and 3 SemEval 2010. In *Proc. of SemEval-2010*, pages 129–133.

Mitesh M. Khapra, Salil Joshi, Arindam Chatterjee, and Pushpak Bhattacharyya. 2011. Together we can: Bilingual bootstrapping for WSD. In *Proc. of ACL-11*, pages 561–569.

Philipp Koehn. 2005. Europarl: A parallel corpus for statistical machine translation. In *Proceedings of Machine Translation Summit X*.

Rob Koeling and Diana McCarthy. 2007. Sussx: WSD using automatically acquired predominant senses. In *Proc. of SemEval-2007*, pages 314–317.

Els Lefever and Veronique Hoste. 2010. SemEval-2010 Task 3: Cross-lingual Word Sense Disambiguation. In *Proc. of SemEval-2010*, pages 15–20.

Els Lefever, Véronique Hoste, and Martine De Cock. 2011. Parasense or how to use parallel corpora for Word Sense Disambiguation. In *Proc. of ACL-11*, pages 317–322.

Bin Lu, Chenhao Tan, Claire Cardie, and Benjamin K. Tsou. 2011. Joint bilingual sentiment classification with unlabeled parallel corpora. In *Proc. of ACL-11*, pages 320–330.

Yashar Mehdad, Matteo Negri, and Marcello Federico. 2011. Using bilingual parallel corpora for cross-lingual textual entailment. In *Proc. of ACL-11*, pages 1336–1345.

Rada Mihalcea, Ravi Sinha, and Diana McCarthy. 2010. SemEval-2010 Task 2: Cross-lingual lexical substitution. In *Proc. of SemEval-2010*, pages 9–14.

Vivi Nastase, Michael Strube, Benjamin Börschinger, Caecilia Zirn, and Anas Elghafari. 2010. WikiNet: A very large scale multi-lingual concept network. In *Proc. of LREC '10*.

Roberto Navigli and Mirella Lapata. 2010. An experimental study on graph connectivity for unsupervised Word Sense Disambiguation. *IEEE Transactions on Pattern Analysis and Machine Intelligence*, 32(4):678–692.

Roberto Navigli and Simone Paolo Ponzetto. 2010. BabelNet: Building a very large multilingual semantic network. In *Proc. of ACL-10*, pages 216–225.

Roberto Navigli and Simone Paolo Ponzetto. 2012. BabelNetXplorer: a platform for multilingual lexical knowledge base access and exploration. In *Comp. Vol. to Proc. of WWW-12*, pages 393–396.

Roberto Navigli, Kenneth C. Litkowski, and Orin Hargraves. 2007. Semeval-2007 task 07: Coarse-grained English all-words task. In *Proc. of SemEval-2007*, pages 30–35.

Roberto Navigli, Stefano Faralli, Aitor Soroa, Oier Lopez de Lacalle, and Eneko Agirre. 2011. Two birds with one stone: learning semantic models for Text Categorization and Word Sense Disambiguation. In *Proc. of CIKM-11*, pages 2317–2320.

Roberto Navigli. 2006. Online word sense disambiguation with structural semantic interconnections. In *Proc. of EACL-06*, pages 107–110.

Roberto Navigli. 2009. Word Sense Disambiguation: A survey. *ACM Computing Surveys*, 41(2):1–69.

Siddharth Patwardhan, Satanjeev Banerjee, and Ted Pedersen. 2005. SenseRelate::TargetWord – a generalized framework for Word Sense Disambiguation. In *Comp. Vol. to Proc. of ACL-05*, pages 73–76.

Ted Pedersen, Siddharth Patwardhan, and Jason Michelizzi. 2004. WordNet::Similarity – Measuring the relatedness of concepts. In *Comp. Vol. to Proc. of HLT-NAACL-04*, pages 267–270.

Yves Peirsman and Sebastian Padó. 2010. Cross-lingual induction of selectional preferences with bilingual vector spaces. In *Proc. of NAACL-HLT-10*, pages 921–929.

Simone Paolo Ponzetto and Roberto Navigli. 2010. Knowledge-rich Word Sense Disambiguation rivaling supervised system. In *Proc. of ACL-10*, pages 1522–1531.

Tomasz Tylenda, Mauro Sozio, and Gerhard Weikum. 2011. Einstein: physicist or vegetarian? Summarizing semantic type graphs for knowledge discovery. In *Proc. of WWW-11*, pages 273–276.

Maarten van Gompel. 2010. UvT-WSD1: A cross-lingual word sense disambiguation system. In *Proc. of SemEval-2010*, pages 238–241.

Piek Vossen, editor. 1998. *EuroWordNet: A Multilingual Database with Lexical Semantic Networks*. Kluwer, Dordrecht, The Netherlands.

Zhi Zhong and Hwee Tou Ng. 2010. It Makes Sense: A wide-coverage Word Sense Disambiguation system for free text. In *Proc. of ACL-10 System Demonstrations*, pages 78–83.

BIUTEE: A Modular Open-Source System for Recognizing Textual Entailment

Asher Stern
Computer Science Department
Bar-Ilan University
Ramat-Gan 52900, Israel
astern7@gmail.com

Ido Dagan
Computer Science Department
Bar-Ilan University
Ramat-Gan 52900, Israel
dagan@cs.biu.ac.il

Abstract

This paper introduces BIUTEE[1], an open-source system for recognizing textual entailment. Its main advantages are its ability to utilize various types of knowledge resources, and its extensibility by which new knowledge resources and inference components can be easily integrated. These abilities make BIUTEE an appealing RTE system for two research communities: (1) researchers of end applications, that can benefit from generic textual inference, and (2) RTE researchers, who can integrate their novel algorithms and knowledge resources into our system, saving the time and effort of developing a complete RTE system from scratch. Notable assistance for these researchers is provided by a visual tracing tool, by which researchers can refine and "debug" their knowledge resources and inference components.

1 Introduction

Recognizing Textual Entailment (RTE) is the task of identifying, given two text fragments, whether one of them can be inferred from the other (Dagan et al., 2006). This task generalizes a common problem that arises in many tasks at the semantic level of NLP. For example, in *Information Extraction (IE)*, a system may be given a template with variables (e.g., "X is employed by Y") and has to find text fragments from which this template, with variables replaced by proper entities, can be inferred. In *Summarization*, a good summary should be inferred from the given text, and, in addition, should not contain duplicated information, i.e., sentences which can be inferred from other sentences in the summary. Detecting these inferences can be performed by an RTE system.

Since first introduced, several approaches have been proposed for this task, ranging from shallow lexical similarity methods (e.g., (Clark and Harrison, 2010; MacKinlay and Baldwin, 2009)), to complex linguistically-motivated methods, which incorporate extensive linguistic analysis (syntactic parsing, coreference resolution, semantic role labelling, etc.) and a rich inventory of linguistic and world-knowledge resources (e.g., (Iftene, 2008; de Salvo Braz et al., 2005; Bar-Haim et al., 2007)). Building such complex systems requires substantial development efforts, which might become a barrier for new-comers to RTE research. Thus, flexible and extensible publicly available RTE systems are expected to significantly facilitate research in this field. More concretely, two major research communities would benefit from a publicly available RTE system:

1. Higher-level application developers, who would use an RTE system to solve inference tasks in their application. RTE systems for this type of researchers should be adaptable for the application specific data: they should be configurable, trainable, and extensible with inference knowledge that captures application-specific phenomena.

2. Researchers in the RTE community, that would not need to build a complete RTE system for their research. Rather, they may integrate

[1] www.cs.biu.ac.il/~nlp/downloads/biutee

Proceedings of the 50th Annual Meeting of the Association for Computational Linguistics, pages 73–78,
Jeju, Republic of Korea, 8-14 July 2012. ©2012 Association for Computational Linguistics

their novel research components into an existing open-source system. Such research efforts might include developing knowledge resources, developing inference components for specific phenomena such as temporal inference, or extending RTE to different languages. A flexible and extensible RTE system is expected to encourage researchers to create and share their textual-inference components. A good example from another research area is the *Moses* system for *Statistical Machine Translation (SMT)* (Koehn et al., 2007), which provides the core SMT components while being extended with new research components by a large scientific community.

Yet, until now rather few and quite limited RTE systems were made publicly available. Moreover, these systems are restricted in the types of knowledge resources which they can utilize, and in the scope of their inference algorithms. For example, *EDITS*[2] (Kouylekov and Negri, 2010) is a distance-based RTE system, which can exploit only lexical knowledge resources. *NutCracker*[3] (Bos and Markert, 2005) is a system based on logical representation and automatic theorem proving, but utilizes only WordNet (Fellbaum, 1998) as a lexical knowledge resource.

Therefore, we provide our open-source textual-entailment system, BIUTEE. Our system provides state-of-the-art linguistic analysis tools and exploits various types of manually built and automatically acquired knowledge resources, including lexical, lexical-syntactic and syntactic rewrite rules. Furthermore, the system components, including pre-processing utilities, knowledge resources, and even the steps of the inference algorithm, are modular, and can be replaced or extended easily with new components. Extensibility and flexibility are also supported by a *plug-in mechanism*, by which new inference components can be integrated without changing existing code.

Notable support for researchers is provided by *a visual tracing tool, Tracer*, which visualizes every step of the inference process as shown in Figures 2 and 3. We will use this tool to illustrate various inference components in the demonstration session.

[2]`http://edits.fbk.eu/`

[3]`http://svn.ask.it.usyd.edu.au/trac/candc/wiki/nutcracker`

2 System Description

2.1 Inference algorithm

In this section we provide a high level description of the inference components. Further details of the algorithmic components appear in references provided throughout this section.

BIUTEE follows the transformation based paradigm, which recognizes textual entailment by converting the text into the hypothesis via a sequence of transformations. Such a sequence is often referred to as a *proof*, and is performed, in our system, over the syntactic representation of the text - the text's parse tree(s). A transformation modifies a given parse tree, resulting in a generation of a new parse tree, which can be further modified by subsequent transformations.

Consider, for example, the following text-hypothesis pair:

Text: ... Obasanjo invited him to step down as president ... and accept political asylum in Nigeria.

Hypothesis: Charles G. Taylor was offered asylum in Nigeria.

This text-hypothesis pair requires two major transformations: (1) substituting "him" by "Charles G. Taylor" via a coreference substitution to an earlier mention in the text, and (2) inferring that if "X accept Y" then "X was offered Y".

BIUTEE allows many types of transformations, by which any hypothesis can be proven from any text. Given a T-H pair, the system finds a proof which generates H from T, and estimates the proof validity. The system returns a score which indicates how likely it is that the obtained proof is valid, i.e., the transformations along the proof preserve entailment from the meaning of T.

The main type of transformations is application of *entailment-rules* (Bar-Haim et al., 2007). An entailment rule is composed of two sub-trees, termed *left-hand-side* and *right-hand-side*, and is *applied* on a parse-tree fragment that matches its left-hand-side, by substituting the left-hand-side with the right-hand-side. This formalism is simple yet powerful, and captures many types of knowledge. The simplest type of rules is *lexical rules*, like `car` $\rightarrow$

`vehicle`. More complicated rules capture the entailment relation between predicate-argument structures, like `X accept Y` $\rightarrow$ `X was offered Y`. Entailment rules can also encode syntactic phenomena like the semantic equivalence of active and passive structures (`X Verb[active] Y` $\rightarrow$ `Y is Verb[passive] by X`). Various knowledge resources, represented as entailment rules, are freely available in BIUTEE's web-site. The complete formalism of entailment rules, adopted by our system, is described in (Bar-Haim et al., 2007).

Coreference relations are utilized via coreference-substitution transformations: one mention of an entity is replaced by another mention of the same entity, based on coreference relations. In the above example the system could apply such a transformation to substitute "him" with "Charles G. Taylor".

Since applications of entailment rules and coreference substitutions are yet, in most cases, insufficient in transforming T into H, our system allows *on-the-fly* transformations. These transformations include insertions of missing nodes, flipping parts-of-speech, moving sub-trees, etc. (see (Stern and Dagan, 2011) for a complete list of these transformations). Since these transformations are not justified by given knowledge resources, we use linguistically-motivated features to estimate their validity. For example, for on-the-fly lexical insertions we consider as features the named-entity annotation of the inserted word, and its probability estimation according to a unigram language model, which yields lower costs for more frequent words.

Given a (T,H) pair, the system applies a search algorithm (Stern et al., 2012) to find a proof $O = (o_1, o_2, \ldots o_n)$ that transforms T into H. For each proof step o_i the system calculates a *cost* $c(o_i)$. This cost is defined as follows: the system uses a weight-vector w, which is learned in the training phase. In addition, each transformation o_i is represented by a *feature vector* $f(o_i)$ which characterizes the transformation. The cost $c(o_i)$ is defined as $w \cdot f(o_i)$. The *proof cost* is defined as the sum of the costs of the transformations from which it is composed, i.e.:

$$c(O) \triangleq \sum_{i=1}^{n} c(o_i) = \sum_{i=1}^{n} w \cdot f(o_i) = w \cdot \sum_{i=1}^{n} f(o_i) \quad (1)$$

If the proof cost is below a threshold b, then the system concludes that T entails H. The complete description of the cost model, as well as the method for learning the parameters w and b is described in (Stern and Dagan, 2011).

2.2 System flow

The BIUTEE system flow (Figure 1) starts with pre-processing of the text and the hypothesis. BIUTEE provides state-of-the-art pre-processing utilities: *Easy-First parser* (Goldberg and Elhadad, 2010), *Stanford named-entity-recognizer* (Finkel et al., 2005) and *ArkRef coreference resolver* (Haghighi and Klein, 2009), as well as utilities for sentence-splitting and numerical-normalizations. In addition, BIUTEE supports integration of users' own utilities by simply implementing the appropriate interfaces. Entailment recognition begins with a *global processing phase* in which inference related computations that are not part of the proof are performed. Annotating the negation indicators and their scope in the text and hypothesis is an example of such calculation. Next, the system constructs a proof which is a sequence of transformations that transform the text into the hypothesis. Finding such a proof is a sequential process, conducted by the search algorithm. In each step of the proof construction the system examines all possible transformations that can be applied, generates new trees by applying selected transformations, and calculates their costs by constructing appropriate feature-vectors for them.

New types of transformations can be added to BIUTEE by a *plug-in* mechanism, without the need to change the code. For example, imagine that a researcher applies BIUTEE on the medical domain. There might be some well-known domain knowledge and rules that every medical person knows. Integrating them is directly supported by the plug-in mechanism. A plug-in is a piece of code which implements a few interfaces that detect which transformations can be applied, apply them, and construct appropriate feature-vectors for each applied transformation. In addition, a plug-in can perform computations for the global processing phase.

Eventually, the search algorithm finds a (approximately) lowest cost proof. This cost is normalized as a score between 0 and 1, and returned as output.

Training the cost model parameters w and b (see subsection 2.1) is performed by a linear learn-

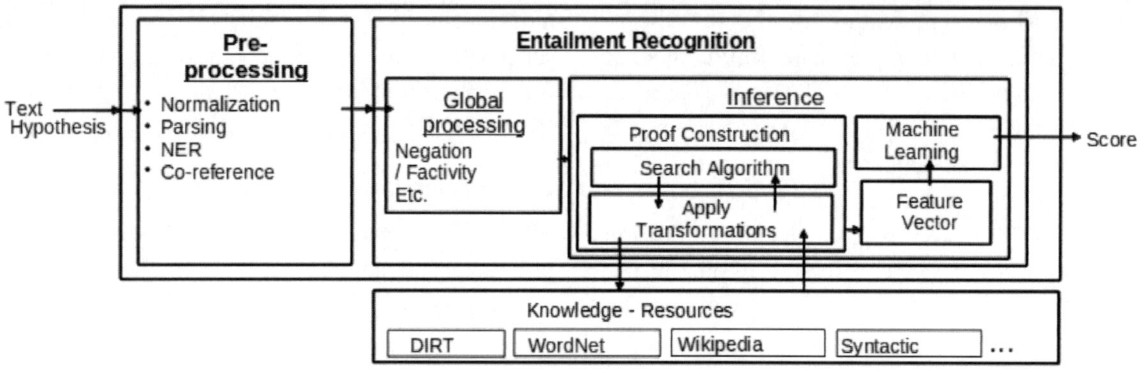

Figure 1: System architecture

RTE challenge	Median	Best	BIUTEE
RTE-6	33.72	48.01	49.09
RTE-7	39.89	48.00	42.93

Table 1: Performance (F1) of BIUTEE on RTE challenges, compared to other systems participated in these challenges. *Median* and *Best* indicate the median score and the highest score of all submissions, respectively.

ing algorithm, as described in (Stern and Dagan, 2011). We use a *Logistic-Regression* learning algorithm, but, similar to other components, alternative learning-algorithms can be integrated easily by implementing an appropriate interface.

2.3 Experimental results

BIUTEE's performance on the last two RTE challenges (Bentivogli et al., 2011; Bentivogli et al., 2010) is presented in Table 1: BIUTEE is better than the median of all submitted results, and in RTE-6 it outperforms all other systems.

3 Visual Tracing Tool

As a complex system, the final score provided as output, as well as the system's detailed logging information, do not expose all the decisions and calculations performed by the system. In particular, they do not show all the potential transformations that could have been applied, but were rejected by the search algorithm. However, such information is crucial for researchers, who need to observe the usage and the potential impact of each component of the system.

We address this need by providing an interactive *visual tracing tool*, *Tracer*, which presents detailed information on each proof step, including potential steps that were not included in the final proof. In the demo session, we will use the visual tracing tool to illustrate all of BIUTEE's components[4].

3.1 Modes

Tracer provides two modes for tracing proof construction: *automatic mode* and *manual mode*. In automatic mode, shown in Figure 2, the tool presents the complete process of inference, as conducted by the system's search: the parse trees, the proof steps, the cost of each step and the final score. For each transformation the tool presents the parse tree before and after applying the transformation, highlighting the impact of this transformation. In manual mode, the user can invoke specific transformations proactively, including transformations rejected by the search algorithm for the eventual proof. As shown in Figure 3, the tool provides a list of transformations that match the given parse-tree, from which the user chooses and applies a single transformation at each step. Similar to automatic mode, their impact on the parse tree is shown visually.

3.2 Use cases

Developers of knowledge resources, as well as other types of transformations, can be aided by *Tracer* as follows. Applying an entailment rule is a process of first *matching* the rule's left-hand-side to the text parse-tree (or to any tree along the proof), and then substituting it by the rule's right-hand-side. To test a

[4]Our demonstration requirements are a large screen and Internet connection.

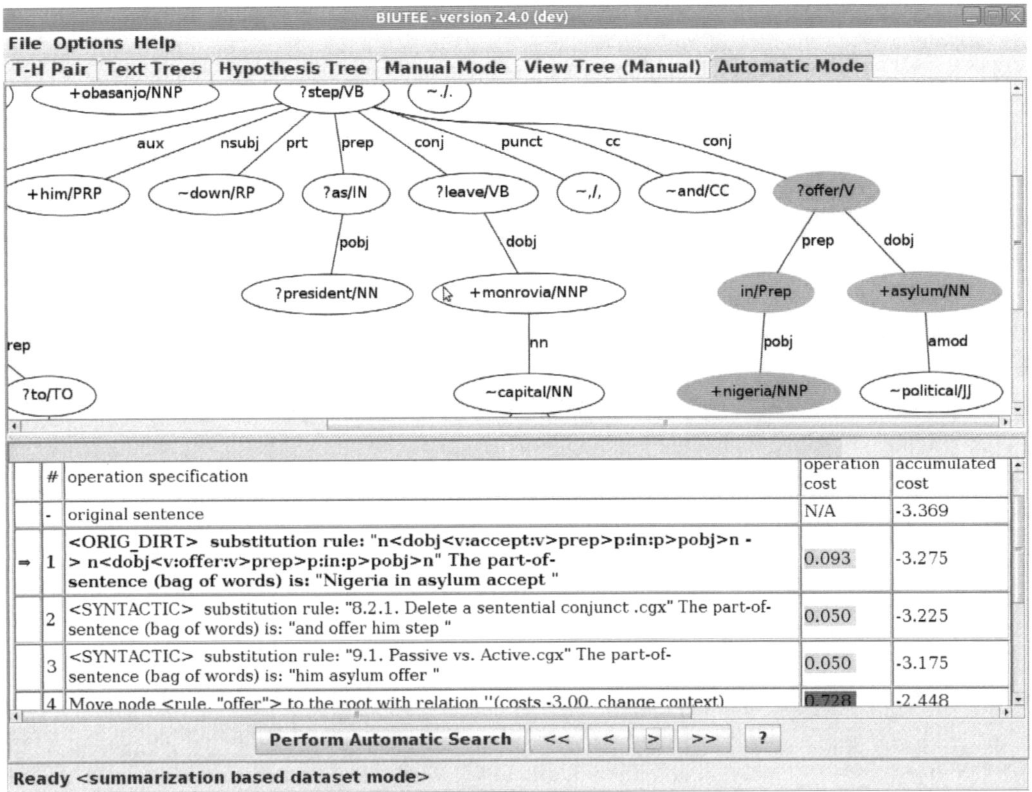

Figure 2: Entailment Rule application visualized in tracing tool. The upper pane displays the parse-tree generated by applying the rule. The rule description is the first transformation (printed in **bold**) of the proof, shown in the lower pane. It is followed by transformations 2 and 3, which are syntactic rewrite rules.

rule, the user can provide a text for which it is supposed to match, examine the list of potential transformations that can be performed on the text's parse tree, as in Figure 3, and verify that the examined rule has been matched as expected. Next, the user can apply the rule, visually examine its impact on the parse-tree, as in Figure 2, and validate that it operates as intended with no side-effects.

The complete inference process depends on the parameters learned in the training phase, as well as on the search algorithm which looks for lowest-cost proof from T to H. Researchers investigating these algorithmic components can be assisted by the tracing tool as well. For a given (T,H) pair, the automatic mode provides the complete proof found by the system. Then, in the manual mode the researcher can try to construct alternative proofs. If a proof with lower cost can be constructed manually it implies a limitation of the search algorithm. On the other hand, if the user can manually construct a better linguistically motivated proof, but it turns out that this proof has higher cost than the one found by the system, it implies a limitation of the learning phase which may be caused either by a limitation of the learning method, or due to insufficient training data.

4 Conclusions

In this paper we described BIUTEE, an open-source textual-inference system, and suggested it as a research platform in this field. We highlighted key advantages of BIUTEE, which directly support researchers' work: (a) modularity and extensibility, (b) a plug-in mechanism, (c) utilization of entailment rules, which can capture diverse types of knowledge, and (d) a visual tracing tool, which visualizes all the details of the inference process.

Acknowledgments

This work was partially supported by the Israel Science Foundation grant 1112/08, the PASCAL-

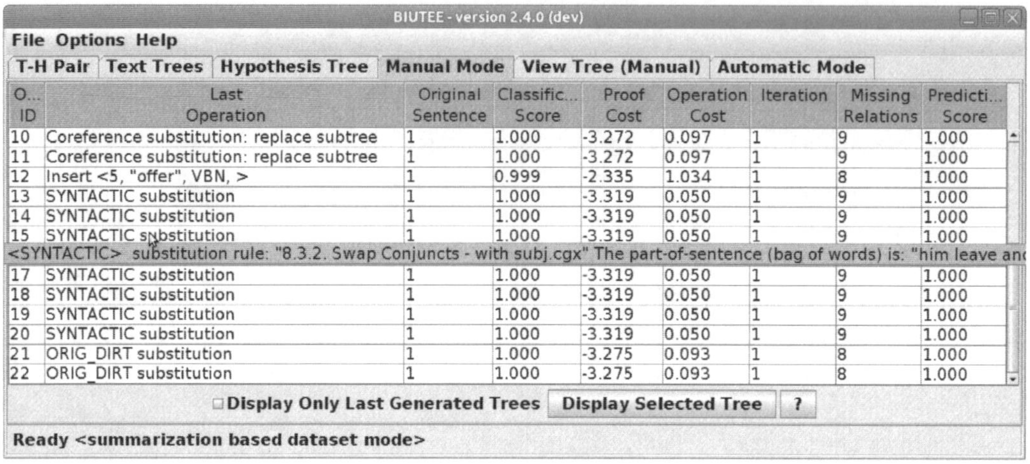

Figure 3: List of available transformations, provided by *Tracer* in the manual mode. The user can manually choose and apply each of these transformations, and observe their impact on the parse-tree.

2 Network of Excellence of the European Community FP7-ICT-2007-1-216886, and the European Community's Seventh Framework Programme (FP7/2007-2013) under grant agreement no. 287923 (EXCITEMENT).

References

Roy Bar-Haim, Ido Dagan, Iddo Greental, and Eyal Shnarch. 2007. Semantic inference at the lexical-syntactic level. In *Proceedings of AAAI*.

Luisa Bentivogli, Peter Clark, Ido Dagan, Hoa Dang, and Danilo Giampiccolo. 2010. The sixth pascal recognizing textual entailment challenge. In *Proceedings of TAC*.

Luisa Bentivogli, Peter Clark, Ido Dagan, Hoa Dang, and Danilo Giampiccolo. 2011. The seventh pascal recognizing textual entailment challenge. In *Proceedings of TAC*.

Johan Bos and Katja Markert. 2005. Recognising textual entailment with logical inference. In *Proceedings of EMNLP*.

Peter Clark and Phil Harrison. 2010. Blue-lite: a knowledge-based lexical entailment system for rte6. In *Proceedings of TAC*.

Ido Dagan, Oren Glickman, and Bernardo Magnini. 2006. The pascal recognising textual entailment challenge. In *Quionero-Candela, J.; Dagan, I.; Magnini, B.; d'Alch-Buc, F. (Eds.) Machine Learning Challenges. Lecture Notes in Computer Science*.

Rodrigo de Salvo Braz, Roxana Girju, Vasin Punyakanok, Dan Roth, and Mark Sammons. 2005. An inference model for semantic entailment in natural language. In *Proceedings of AAAI*.

Christiane Fellbaum, editor. 1998. *WordNet An Electronic Lexical Database*. The MIT Press, May.

Jenny Rose Finkel, Trond Grenager, and Christopher Manning. 2005. Incorporating non-local information into information extraction systems by gibbs sampling. In *Proceedings of ACL*.

Yoav Goldberg and Michael Elhadad. 2010. An efficient algorithm for easy-first non-directional dependency parsing. In *Proceedings of NAACL*.

Aria Haghighi and Dan Klein. 2009. Simple coreference resolution with rich syntactic and semantic features. In *Proceedings of EMNLP*.

Adrian Iftene. 2008. Uaic participation at rte4. In *Proceedings of TAC*.

Philipp Koehn, Hieu Hoang, Alexandra Birch, Chris Callison-Burch, Marcello Federico, Nicola Bertoldi, Brooke Cowan, Wade Shen, Christine Moran, Richard Zens, Chris Dyer, Ondrej Bojar, Alexandra Constantin, and Evan Herbst. 2007. Moses: Open source toolkit for statistical machine translation. In *Proceedings of ACL*.

Milen Kouylekov and Matteo Negri. 2010. An open-source package for recognizing textual entailment. In *Proceedings of ACL Demo*.

Andrew MacKinlay and Timothy Baldwin. 2009. A baseline approach to the rte5 search pilot. In *Proceedings of TAC*.

Asher Stern and Ido Dagan. 2011. A confidence model for syntactically-motivated entailment proofs. In *Proceedings of RANLP*.

Asher Stern, Roni Stern, Ido Dagan, and Ariel Felner. 2012. Efficient search for transformation-based inference. In *Proceedings of ACL*.

Entailment-based Text Exploration with Application to the Health-care Domain

Meni Adler
Bar Ilan University
Ramat Gan, Israel
adlerm@cs.bgu.ac.il

Jonathan Berant
Tel Aviv University
Tel Aviv, Israel
jonatha6@post.tau.ac.il

Ido Dagan
Bar Ilan University
Ramat Gan, Israel
dagan@cs.biu.ac.il

Abstract

We present a novel text exploration model, which extends the scope of state-of-the-art technologies by moving from standard *concept*-based exploration to *statement*-based exploration. The proposed scheme utilizes the *textual entailment* relation between statements as the basis of the exploration process. A user of our system can explore the result space of a query by drilling down/up from one statement to another, according to entailment relations specified by an entailment graph and an optional concept taxonomy. As a prominent use case, we apply our exploration system and illustrate its benefit on the health-care domain. To the best of our knowledge this is the first implementation of an exploration system at the statement level that is based on the textual entailment relation.

1 Introduction

Finding information in a large body of text is becoming increasingly more difficult. Standard search engines output a set of documents for a given query, but do not allow any exploration of the thematic structure in the retrieved information. Thus, the need for tools that allow to effectively sift through a target set of documents is becoming ever more important.

Faceted search (Stoica and Hearst, 2007; Käki, 2005) supports a better understanding of a target domain, by allowing exploration of data according to multiple views or *facets*. For example, given a set of documents on Nobel Prize laureates we might have different facets corresponding to the laureate's nationality, the year when the prize was awarded, the field in which it was awarded, etc. However, this type of exploration is still severely limited insofar that it only allows exploration by *topic* rather than *content*. Put differently, we can only explore according to *what a document is about* rather than *what a document actually says*. For instance, the facets for the query *'asthma'* in the faceted search engine Yippy include the concepts *allergy* and *children*, but do not specify what are the exact *relations* between these concepts and the query (*e.g.*, allergy *causes* asthma, and children *suffer from* asthma).

Berant et al. (2010) proposed an exploration scheme that focuses on relations between concepts, which are derived from a graph describing textual entailment relations between *propositions*. In their setting a proposition consists of a predicate with two arguments that are possibly replaced by variables, such as *'X control asthma'*. A graph that specifies an entailment relation *'X control asthma* $\rightarrow$ *X affect asthma'* can help a user, who is browsing documents dealing with substances that affect asthma, drill down and explore only substances that control asthma. This type of exploration can be viewed as an extension of faceted search, where the new facet concentrates on the actual statements expressed in the texts.

In this paper we follow Berant et al.'s proposal, and present a novel entailment-based text exploration system, which we applied to the health-care domain. A user of this system can explore the result space of her query, by drilling down/up from one proposition to another, according to a set of entailment relations described by an *entailment graph*. In Figure 1, for example, the user looks for 'things'

Proceedings of the 50th Annual Meeting of the Association for Computational Linguistics, pages 79–84,
Jeju, Republic of Korea, 8-14 July 2012.

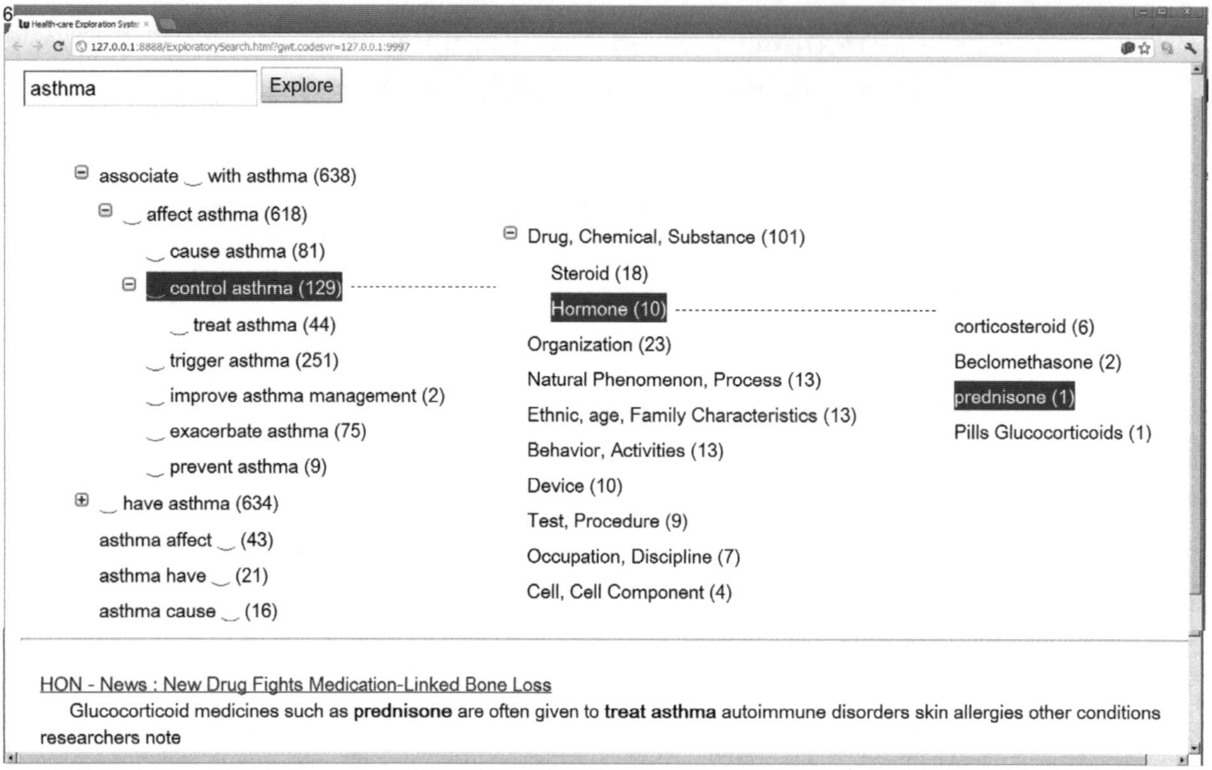

Figure 1: Exploring *asthma* results.

that affect asthma. She invokes an *'asthma'* query and starts drilling down the entailment graph to *'X control asthma'* (left column). In order to examine the arguments of a selected proposition, the user may drill down/up a concept taxonomy that classifies *terms* that occur as arguments. The user in Figure 1, for instance, drills down the concept taxonomy (middle column), in order to focus on *Hormones* that control asthma, such as *'prednisone'* (right column). Each drill down/up induces a subset of the documents that correspond to the aforementioned selections. The retrieved document in Figure 1 (bottom) is highlighted by the relevant proposition, which clearly states that prednisone is often given to treat asthma (and indeed in the entailment graph *'X treat asthma'* entails *'X control asthma'*).

Our system is built over a corpus of documents, a set of propositions extracted from the documents, an entailment graph describing entailment relations between propositions, and, optionally, a concept hierarchy. The system implementation for the health-care domain, for instance, is based on a web-crawled health-care corpus, the propositions automatically extracted from the corpus, entailment graphs borrowed from Berant et al. (2010), and the UMLS[1] taxonomy. To the best of our knowledge this is the first implementation of an exploration system, at the proposition level, based on the textual entailment relation.

2 Background

2.1 Exploratory Search

Exploratory search addresses the need of users to quickly identify the important pieces of information in a target set of documents. In exploratory search, users are presented with a result set and a set of exploratory facets, which are proposals for refinements of the query that can lead to more focused sets of documents. Each facet corresponds to a clustering of the current result set, focused on a more specific topic than the current query. The user proceeds in the exploration of the document set by selecting specific documents (to read them) or by selecting specific facets, to refine the result set.

[1] `http://www.nlm.nih.gov/research/umls/`

Early exploration technologies were based on a single hierarchical conceptual clustering of information (Hofmann, 1999), enabling the user to drill up and down the concept hierarchies. Hierarchical faceted meta-data (Stoica and Hearst, 2007), or *faceted search*, proposed more sophisticated exploration possibilities by providing multiple facets and a hierarchy per facet or dimension of the domain. These types of exploration techniques were found to be useful for effective access of information (Käki, 2005).

In this work, we suggest proposition-based exploration as an extension to concept-based exploration. Our intuition is that text exploration can profit greatly from representing information not only at the level of individual concepts, but also at the propositional level, where the relations that link concepts to one another are represented effectively in a hierarchical entailment graph.

2.2 Entailment Graph

Recognizing Textual Entailment (RTE) is the task of deciding, given two text fragments, whether the meaning of one text can be inferred from another (Dagan et al., 2009). For example, *'Levalbuterol is used to control various kinds of asthma' entails 'Levalbuterol affects asthma'*. In this paper, we use the notion of *proposition* to denote a specific type of text fragments, composed of a predicate with two arguments (*e.g., Levalbuterol control asthma*).

Textual entailment systems are often based on *entailment rules* which specify a directional inference relation between two fragments. In this work, we focus on leveraging a common type of entailment rules, in which the left-hand-side of the rule (LHS) and the right-hand-side of the rule (RHS) are *propositional templates* - a proposition, where one or both of the arguments are replaced by a variable, *e.g., 'X control asthma → X affect asthma'*.

The entailment relation between propositional templates of a given corpus can be represented by an *entailment graph* (Berant et al., 2010) (see Figure 2, top). The nodes of an entailment graph correspond to propositional templates, and its edges correspond to entailment relations (rules) between them. Entailment graph representation is somewhat analogous to the formation of ontological relations between concepts of a given domain, where in our case the nodes correspond to propositional templates rather than to concepts.

3 Exploration Model

In this section we extend the scope of state-of-the-art exploration technologies by moving from standard concept-based exploration to proposition-based exploration, or equivalently, statement-based exploration. In our model, it is the entailment relation between propositional templates which determines the granularity of the viewed information space. We first describe the inputs to the system and then detail our proposed exploration scheme.

3.1 System Inputs

Corpus A collection of *documents*, which form the search space of the system.

Extracted Propositions A set of propositions, extracted from the corpus document. The propositions are usually produced by an *extraction method*, such as TextRunner (Banko et al., 2007) or ReVerb (Fader et al., 2011). In order to support the exploration process, the documents are indexed by the propositional templates and argument terms of the extracted propositions.

Entailment graph for predicates The nodes of the entailment graph are propositional templates, where edges indicate entailment relations between templates (Section 2.2). In order to avoid circularity in the exploration process, the graph is transformed into a DAG, by merging 'equivalent' nodes that are in the same strong connectivity component (as suggested by Berant et al. (2010)). In addition, for clarity and simplicity, edges that can be inferred by transitivity are omitted from the DAG. Figure 2 illustrates the result of applying this procedure to a fragment of the entailment graph for *'asthma'* (*i.e.,* for propositional templates with *'asthma'* as one of the arguments).

Taxonomy for arguments The optional concept taxonomy maps *terms* to one or more pre-defined concepts, arranged in a hierarchical structure. These terms may appear in the corpus as arguments of predicates. Figure 3, for instance, illustrates a simple medical taxonomy, composed of three concepts (medical, diseases, drugs) and four terms (cancer, asthma, aspirin, flexeril).

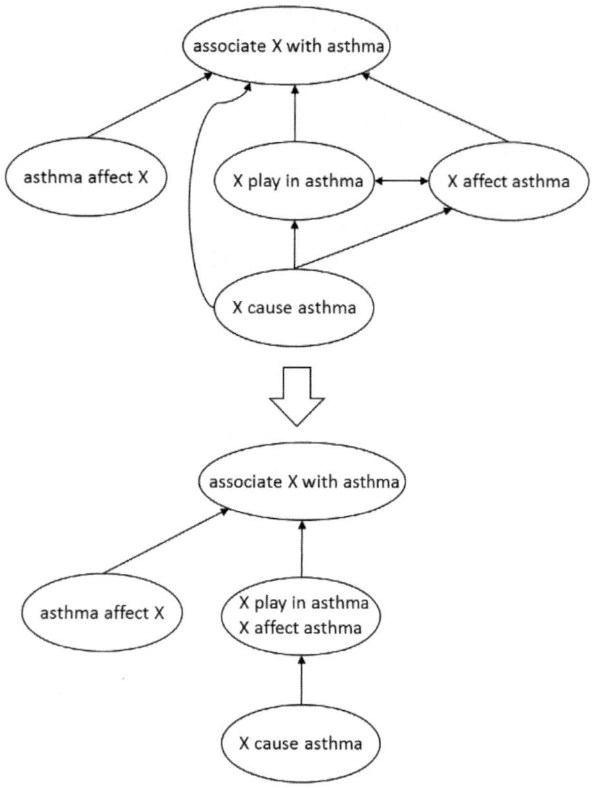

Figure 2: Fragment of the entailment graph for *'asthma'* (top), and its conversion to a DAG (bottom).

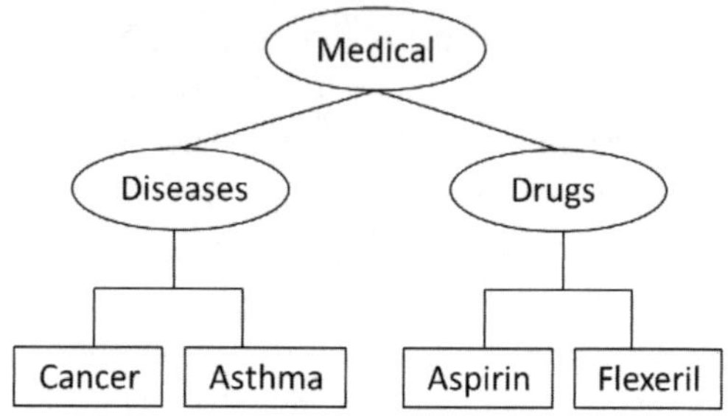

Figure 3: Partial medical taxonomy. Ellipses denote *concepts*, while rectangles denote *terms*.

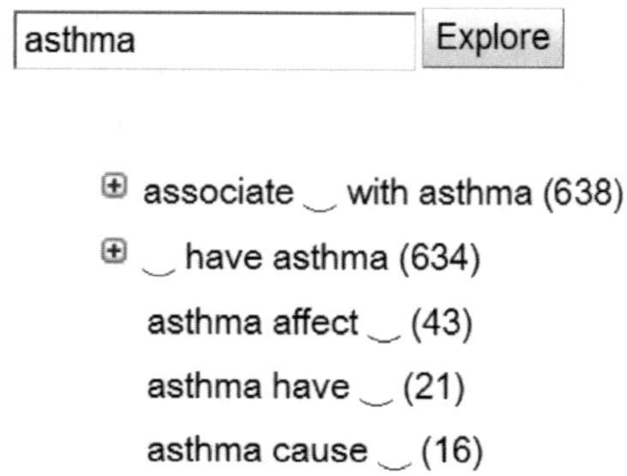

Figure 4: The roots of the entailment graph for the *'asthma'* query.

3.2 Exploration Scheme

The objective of the exploration scheme is to support querying and offer facets for result exploration, in a visual manner. The following components cover the various aspects of this objective, given the above system inputs:

Querying The user enters a search term as a query, *e.g.*, *'asthma'*. The given term induces a subgraph of the entailment graph that contains all propositional templates (graph nodes) with which this term appears as an argument in the extracted propositions (see Figure 2). This subgraph is represented as a DAG, as explained in Section 3.1, where all nodes that have no parent are defined as the *roots* of the DAG. As a starting point, only the roots of the DAG are displayed to the user. Figure 4 shows the five roots for the *'asthma'* query.

Exploration process The user selects one of the entailment graph nodes (*e.g.*, *'associate X with asthma'*). At each exploration step, the user can drill down to a more specific template or drill up to a more general template, by moving along the entailment hierarchy. For example, the user in Figure 5, expands the root *'associate X with asthma'*, in order to drill down through *'X affect asthma'* to *'X control Asthma'*.

Selecting a propositional template (Figure 1, left column) displays a concept taxonomy for the arguments that correspond to the variable in the selected template (Figure 1, middle column). The user can explore these argument concepts by drilling up and down the concept taxonomy. For example, in Figure 1 the user, who selected *'X control Asthma'*, explores the arguments of this template by drilling down the taxonomy to the concept *'Hormone'*.

Selecting a concept opens a third column, which lists the terms mapped to this concept that occurred as arguments of the selected template. For example, in Figure 1, the user is examining the list of arguments for the template *'X control Asthma'*, which are mapped to the concept *'Hormone'*, focusing on the argument *'prednisone'*.

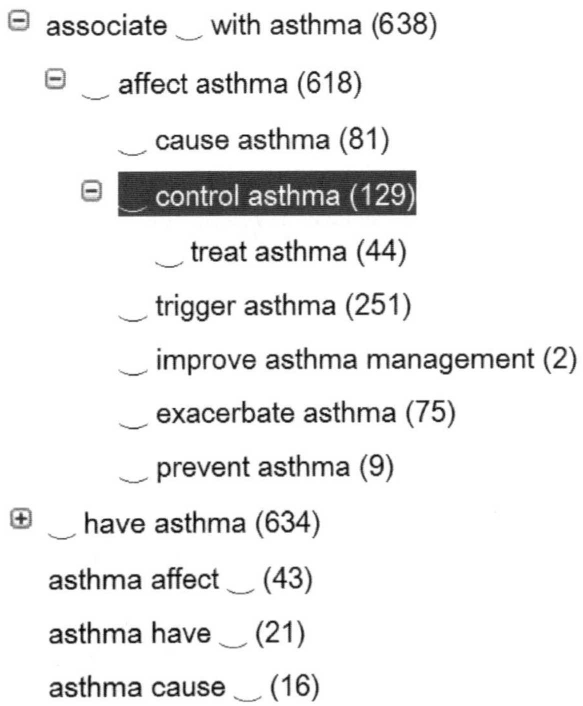

Figure 5: Part of the entailment graph for the *'asthma'* query, after two exploration steps. This corresponds to the left column in Figure 1.

Document retrieval At any stage, the list of documents induced by the current selected template, concept and argument is presented to the user, where in each document snippet the relevant proposition components are highlighted. Figure 1 (bottom) shows such a retrieved document. The highlighted extraction in the snippet, *'prednisone treat asthma'*, entails the proposition selected during exploration, *'prednisone control asthma'*.

4 System Architecture

In this section we briefly describe system components, as illustrated in the block diagram (Figure 6).

The *search service* implements full-text and faceted search, and document indexing. The *data service* handles data (*e.g.*, documents) replication for clients. The *entailment service* handles the logic of the entailment relations (for both the entailment graph and the taxonomy).

The *index server* applies periodic indexing of new texts, and the *exploration server* serves the exploration application on querying, exploration, and data

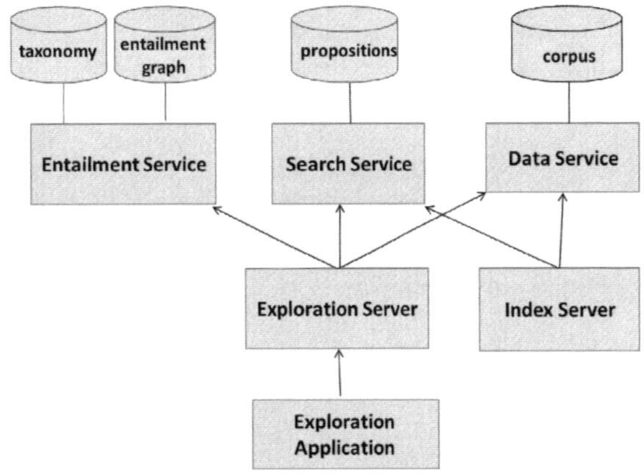

Figure 6: Block diagram of the exploration system.

access. The *exploration application* is the front-end user application for the whole exploration process described above (Section 3.2).

5 Application to the Health-care Domain

As a prominent use case, we applied our exploration system to the health-care domain. With the advent of the internet and social media, patients now have access to new sources of medical information: consumer health articles, forums, and social networks (Boulos and Wheeler, 2007). A typical non-expert health information searcher is uncertain about her exact questions and is unfamiliar with medical terminology (Trivedi, 2009). Exploring relevant information about a given medical issue can be essential and time-critical.

System implementation For the search service, we used SolR servlet, where the data service is built over FTP. The exploration application is implemented as a web application.

Input resources We collected a health-care corpus from the web, which contains more than 2M sentences and about 50M word tokens. The texts deal with various aspects of the health care domain: answers to questions, surveys on diseases, articles on life-style, etc. We extracted propositions from the health-care corpus, by applying the method described by Berant et al. (2010). The corpus was parsed, and propositions were extracted from dependency trees according to the method suggested by Lin and Pantel (2001), where propositions are dependency paths between two arguments of a predicate. We filtered out any proposition where one of the arguments is not a term mapped to a medical concept in the UMLS taxonomy.

For the entailment graph we used the 23 entailment graphs published by Berant et al.[2]. For the argument taxonomy we employed UMLS – a database that maps natural language phrases to over one million unique concept identifiers (CUIs) in the health-care domain. The CUIs are also mapped in UMLS to a concept taxonomy for the health-care domain.

The web application of our system is available at: `http://132.70.6.148:8080/exploration`

6 Conclusion and Future Work

We presented a novel exploration model, which extends the scope of state-of-the-art exploration technologies by moving from standard concept-based exploration to proposition-based exploration. Our model combines the textual entailment paradigm within the exploration process, with application to the health-care domain. According to our model, it is the entailment relation between propositions, encoded by the entailment graph and the taxonomy, which leads the user between more specific and more general statements throughout the search result space. We believe that employing the entailment relation between propositions, which focuses on the statements expressed in the documents, can contribute to the exploration field and improve information access.

Our current application to the health-care domain relies on a small set of entailment graphs for 23 medical concepts. Our ongoing research focuses on the challenging task of learning a larger entailment graph for the health-care domain. We are also investigating methods for evaluating the exploration process (Borlund and Ingwersen, 1997). As noted by Qu and Furnas (2008), the success of an exploratory search system does not depend simply on how many relevant documents will be retrieved for a given query, but more broadly on how well the system helps the user with the exploratory process.

[2] `http://www.cs.tau.ac.il/~jonatha6/homepage_files/resources/HealthcareGraphs.rar`

Acknowledgments

This work was partially supported by the Israel Ministry of Science and Technology, the PASCAL-2 Network of Excellence of the European Community FP7-ICT-2007-1-216886, and the European Communitys Seventh Framework Programme (FP7/2007-2013) under grant agreement no. 287923 (EXCITEMENT).

References

Michele Banko, Michael J Cafarella, Stephen Soderl, Matt Broadhead, and Oren Etzioni. 2007. Open information extraction from the web. In *Proceedings of IJCAI*, pages 2670–2676.

Jonathan Berant, Ido Dagan, and Jacob Goldberger. 2010. Global learning of focused entailment graphs. In *Proceedings of ACL*, Uppsala, Sweden.

Pia Borlund and Peter Ingwersen. 1997. The development of a method for the evaluation of interactive information retrieval systems. *Journal of Documentation*, 53:225–250.

Maged N. Kamel Boulos and Steve Wheeler. 2007. The emerging web 2.0 social software: an enabling suite of sociable technologies in health and health care education. *Health Information & Libraries*, 24:2–23.

Ido Dagan, Bill Dolan, Bernardo Magnini, and Dan Roth. 2009. Recognizing textual entailment: Rational, evaluation and approaches. *Natural Language Engineering*, 15(Special Issue 04):i–xvii.

Anthony Fader, Stephen Soderland, and Oren Etzioni. 2011. Identifying relations for open information extraction. In *EMNLP*, pages 1535–1545. ACL.

Thomas Hofmann. 1999. The cluster-abstraction model: Unsupervised learning of topic hierarchies from text data. In *Proceedings of IJCAI*, pages 682–687.

Mika Käki. 2005. Findex: search result categories help users when document ranking fails. In *Proceedings of SIGCHI*, CHI '05, pages 131–140, New York, NY, USA. ACM.

Dekang Lin and Patrick Pantel. 2001. Discovery of inference rules for question answering. *Natural Language Engineering*, 7:343–360.

Yan Qu and George W. Furnas. 2008. Model-driven formative evaluation of exploratory search: A study under a sensemaking framework. *Inf. Process. Manage.*, 44:534–555.

Emilia Stoica and Marti A. Hearst. 2007. Automating creation of hierarchical faceted metadata structures. In *Proceedings of NAACL HLT*.

Mayank Trivedi. 2009. A study of search engines for health sciences. *International Journal of Library and Information Science*, 1(5):69–73.

CSNIPER
Annotation-by-query for non-canonical constructions in large corpora

Richard Eckart de Castilho, Iryna Gurevych
Ubiquitous Knowledge Processing Lab (UKP-TUDA)
Department of Computer Science
Technische Universität Darmstadt
http://www.ukp.tu-darmstadt.de

Sabine Bartsch
English linguistics
Department of Linguistics and Literary Studies
Technische Universität Darmstadt
http://www.linglit.tu-darmstadt.de

Abstract

We present CSNIPER (Corpus Sniper), a tool that implements (i) a web-based multi-user scenario for identifying and annotating non-canonical grammatical constructions in large corpora based on linguistic queries and (ii) evaluation of annotation quality by measuring inter-rater agreement. This annotation-by-query approach efficiently harnesses expert knowledge to identify instances of linguistic phenomena that are hard to identify by means of existing automatic annotation tools.

1 Introduction

Linguistic annotation by means of automatic procedures, such as part-of-speech (POS) tagging, is a backbone of modern corpus linguistics; POS tagged corpora enhance the possibilities of corpus query. However, many linguistic phenomena are not amenable to automatic annotation and are not readily identifiable on the basis of surface features. Non-canonical constructions (NCCs), which are the use-case of the tool presented in this paper, are a case in point. NCCs, of which *cleft-sentences* are a well-known example, raise a number of issues that prevent their reliable automatic identification in corpora. Yet, they warrant corpus study due to the relatively low frequency of individual instances, their deviation from canonical construction patterns and frequent ambiguity. This makes them hard to distinguish from other, seemingly similar constructions. Expert knowledge is thus required to reliably identify and annotate such phenomena in sufficiently large corpora like the 100 mil. word British National Corpus (BNC Consortium, 2007). This necessitates manual annotation which is time-consuming and error-prone when carried out by individual linguists.

To overcome these issues, CSNIPER implements a web-based multi-user annotation scenario in which linguists formulate and refine queries that identify a given linguistic construction in a corpus and assess the query results to distinguish instances of the phenomenon under study (*true positives*) from such examples that are wrongly identified by the query (*false positives*). Each expert linguist thus acts as a rater rather than an annotator. The tool records assessments made by each rater. A subsequent evaluation step measures the inter-rater agreement. The actual annotation step is deferred until after this evaluation in order to achieve high annotation confidence.

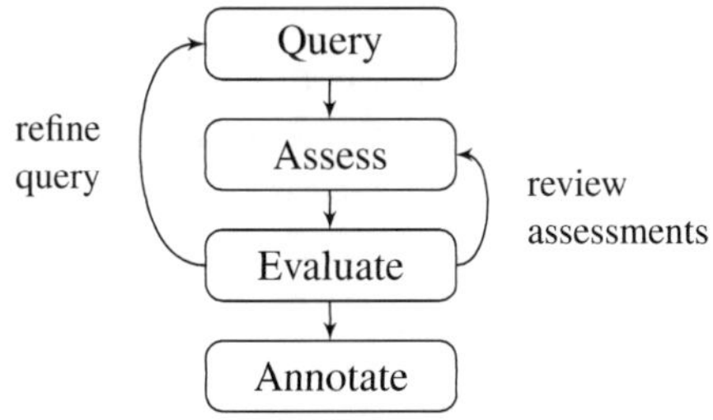

Figure 1: *Annotation-by-query* workflow

CSNIPER implements an *annotation-by-query* approach which entails the following interlinking functionalities (see fig. 1):

Query development: Corpus queries can be developed and refined within the tool. Based on query results which are assessed and labeled by the user, queries can be systematically evaluated and refined for precision. This transfers some of the ideas of

Proceedings of the 50th Annual Meeting of the Association for Computational Linguistics, pages 85–90,
Jeju, Republic of Korea, 8-14 July 2012.

relevance feedback, which is a common method of improving search results in information retrieval, to a linguistic corpus query system.

Assessment: Query results are presented to the user as a list of sentences with optional additional context; the user assesses and labels each sentence as representing or not representing an instance of the linguistic phenomenon under study. The tool implements a function that allows the user to comment on decisions and to temporarily mark sentences with uncertain assessments for later review.

Evaluation: Evaluation is a central functionality of CSNIPER serving three purposes. 1) It integrates with the query development by providing feedback to refine queries and improve query precision. 2) It provides information on sentences not labeled consistently by all users, which can be used to review the assessments. 3) It calculates the inter-rater agreement which is used in the corpus annotation step to ensure high annotation confidence.

Corpus annotation: By assessing and labeling query results as *correct* or *wrong*, raters provide the tool with their annotation decisions. CSNIPER annotates the corpus with those annotation decisions that exceed a certain inter-rater agreement threshold.

This *annotation-by-query* approach of querying, assessing, evaluating and annotating allows multiple distributed raters to incrementally improve query results and achieve high quality annotations. In this paper, we show how such an approach is well-suited for annotation tasks that require manual analysis over large corpora. The approach is generalizable to any kind of linguistic phenomena that can be located in corpora on the basis of queries and require manual assessment by multiple expert raters.

In the next two sections, we are providing a more detailed description of the use-case driving the development of CSNIPER (sect. 2) and discuss why existing tools do not provide viable solutions (sect. 3). Sect. 4 discusses CSNIPER and sect. 5 draws some conclusions and offers an outlook on the next steps.

2 Non-canonical grammatical constructions

The initial purpose of CSNIPER is the corpus-based study of so-called *non-canonical grammatical constructions* (NCC) (examples (2) - (5) below):

1. *The media was now calling Reagan the frontrunner. (canonical)*
2. *It was Reagan whom the media was now calling the frontrunner. (it-cleft)*
3. *It was the media who was now calling Reagan the frontrunner. (it-cleft)*
4. *It was now that the media were calling Reagan the frontrunner. (it-cleft)*
5. *Reagan the media was not calling the frontrunner. (inversion)*

NCCs are linguistic constructions that deviate in characteristic ways from the unmarked lexicogrammatical patterning and informational ordering in the sentence. This is exemplified by the constructions of sentences (2) - (5) above. While expressing the same propositional content, the order of information units available through the permissible grammatical constructions offers interesting insights into the constructional inventory of a language. It also opens up the possibility of comparing seemingly closely related languages in terms of the sets of available related constructions as well as the relations between instances of canonical and non-canonical constructions.

In linguistics, a *cleft* sentence is defined as a complex sentence that expresses a single proposition where the clefted element is co-referential with the following clause. E.g., *it-clefts* are comprised of the following constituents:

dummy subject *it*	main verb *to be*	clefted element	clause

The NCCs under study pose interesting challenges both from a linguistic and a natural language processing perspective. Due to their deviation from the canonical constructions, they come in a variety of potential construction patterns as exemplified above. Non-canonical constructions can be expected to be individually rarer in any given corpus than their canonical counterparts. Their patterns of usage and their discourse functions have not yet been described exhaustively, especially not in representative corpus studies because they are notoriously hard to identify without suitable software. Their empirical distribution in corpora is thus largely unknown.

A major task in recognizing NCCs is distinguishing them from structurally similar constructions with default logical and propositional content. An example of a particular difficulty from the domain of *it-clefts* are anaphoric uses of *it* as in (6) below that do not refer forward to the following clause, but are the antecedents of entities previously introduced in the context of preceding sentences. Other issues arise in cases of true relative clauses as exemplified in (7) below:

6. *London will be the only capital city in Europe where rail services are expected to make a profit,' he added. It is a policy that could lead to economic and environmental chaos. [BNC: A9N-s400]*
7. *It is a legal manoeuvre that declined in currency in the '80s. [BNC: B1L-s576]*

Further examples of NCCs apart from the *it-clefts* addressed in this paper are *wh-clefts* and their subtypes, *all-clefts*, *there-clefts*, *if-because-clefts* and demonstrative clefts as well as inversions. All of these are as hard to identify in a corpus as *it-clefts*.

The linguistic aim of our research is a comparison of non-canonical constructions in English and German. Research on these requires very large corpora due to the relatively low frequency of the individual instances. Due to the ambiguous nature of many NCC candidates, automatically finding them in corpora is difficult. Therefore, multiple experts have to manually assess candidates in corpora.

Our approach does not aim at the exhaustive annotation of all NCCs. The major goal is to improve the understanding of the linguistic properties and usage of NCCs. Furthermore, we define a gold standard to evaluate algorithms for automatic NCC identification. In our task, the total number of NCCs in any given corpus is unknown. Thus, while we can measure the precision of queries, we cannot measure their recall. To address this, we exhaustively annotate a small part of the corpus and extrapolate the estimated number of total NCC candidates.

In summary, the requirements for a tool to support multi-user annotation of NCCs are as follows:

1. **querying** large linguistically pre-processed corpora and query refinement
2. **assessment** of sentences that are true instances of NCCs in a multi-user setting
3. **evaluation** of inter-rater agreement and query precision

In the following section, we review previous work to support linguistic annotation tasks.

3 Related work

We differentiate three categories of linguistic tools which all partially fulfill our requirements: *querying tools*, *annotation tools*, and *transformation tools*.

Linguistic query tools: Such tools allow to query a corpus using linguistic features, e.g. part-of-speech tags. Examples are *ANNIS2* (Zeldes et al., 2009) and the *IMS Open Corpus Workbench* (CWB) (Christ, 1994). Both tools provide powerful query engines designed for large linguistically annotated corpora. Both are server-based tools that can be used concurrently by multiple users. However, they do not allow to assess the query results.

Linguistic annotation tools: Such tools allow the user to add linguistic annotations to a corpus. Examples are *MMAX2* (Müller and Strube, 2006) and the *UIMA CAS Editor*[1]. These tools typically display a full document for the user to annotate. As NCCs appear only occasionally in a text, such tools cannot be effectively applied to our task, as they offer no linguistic query capabilities to quickly locate potential NCCs in a large corpus.

Linguistic transformation tools: Such tools allow the creation of annotations using transformation rules. Examples are *TextMarker* (Kluegl et al., 2009) and the *UAM CorpusTool* (O'Donnell, 2008). A rule has the form *category := pattern* and creates new annotation of the type *category* on any part of a text matching *pattern*. A rule for the annotation of passive clauses in the *UAM CorpusTool* could be *passive-clause := clause + containing be% participle*. These tools do not support the assessment of the results, though. In contrast to the querying tools, transformation tools are not specifically designed to operate efficiently on large corpora. Thus, they are hardly productive for our task, which requires the analysis of large corpora.

4 CSniper

We present CSniper, an annotation tool for non-canonical constructions. Its main features are:

[1] `http://uima.apache.org/`

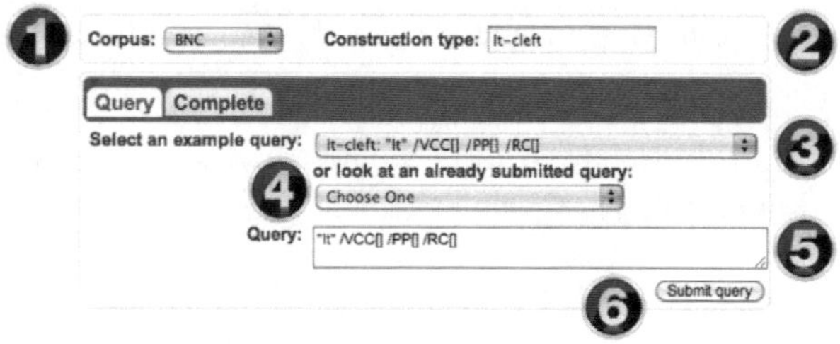

Figure 2: Search form

Annotation-by-query – Sentences potentially containing a particular type of NCC are retrieved using a query. If the sentence contains the NCC of interest, the user manually labels it as *correct* and otherwise *wrong*. Annotations are generated based on the users' assessments.

Distributed multi-user setting – Our web-based tool supports multiple users concurrently assessing query results. Each user can only see and edit their own assessments and has a personal query history.

Evaluation – The evaluation module provides information on assessments, number of annotated instances, query precision and inter-rater agreement.

4.1 Implementation and data

CSNIPER is implemented in Java and uses the CWB as its linguistic search engine (cf. sect. 3). Assessments are stored in a MySQL database. Currently, the British National Corpus (BNC) is used in our study. *Apache UIMA* and *DKPro Core*[2] are used for linguistic pre-processing, format conversion, and to drive the indexing of the corpora. In particular, *DKPro Core* includes a reader for the BNC and a writer for the CWB. As the BNC does not carry lemma annotations, we add them using the DKPro *TreeTagger* (Schmid, 1994) module.

4.2 Query (Figure 2)

The user begins by selecting a ① *corpus* and a ② *construction type* (e.g. *It-Cleft*). A query can be chosen from a ③ list of examples, from the ④ personal query history, or a new ⑤ query can be entered. The query is applied to find instances of that construction (e.g. *"It" /VCC[] /PP[] /RC[]*). After pressing the ⑥ *Submit query* button, the tool presents the user with a KWIC view of the query results (fig. 3). At this point, the user may choose to refine and re-run the query.

As each user may use different queries, they will typically assess different sets of query results. This can yield a set of sentences labeled by a single user only. Therefore, the tool can display those sentences for assessment that other users have assessed, but the current user has not. This allows getting labels from all users for every NCC candidate.

4.3 Assessment (Figure 3)

If the query results match the expectation, the user can switch to the assessment mode by clicking the ⑦ *Begin assessment* button. At this point, an *AnnotationCandidate* record is created in the database for each sentence unless a record is already present. These records contain the offsets of the sentence in the original text, the sentence text and the construction type. In addition, an *AnnotationCandidateLabel* record is created for each sentence to hold the assessment to be provided by the user.

In the assessment mode, an additional ⑧ *Label* column appears in the KWIC view. Clicking in this column cycles through the labels *correct*, *wrong*, *check* and *nothing*. When the user is uncertain, the label *check* can be used to mark candidates for later review. The view can be ⑨ *filtered* for those sentences that need to be assessed, those that have been assessed, or those that have been labeled with *check*. A ⑩ *comment* can be left to further describe difficult cases or to justify decisions. All changes are immediately saved to the database, so the user can stop assessing at any time and resume the process later.

The proper assessment of a sentence as an instance of a particular construction type sometimes depends on the context found in the preceding and following sentences. For this purpose, clicking on the ⑪ *book* icon in the KWIC view displays the sentence in its larger context (fig. 4). POS tags are shown in the sentence to facilitate query refinement.

4.4 Evaluation (Figure 5)

The evaluation function provides an overview of the current assessment state (fig. 5). We support two evaluation views: *by construction type* and *by query*.

By construction type: In this view, one or more ⑫ *corpora*, ⑬ *types*, and ⑭ *users* can be selected for evaluation. For these, all annotation candidates and the respective statistics are displayed. It is pos-

[2] http://www.ukp.tu-darmstadt.de/research/current-projects/dkpro/

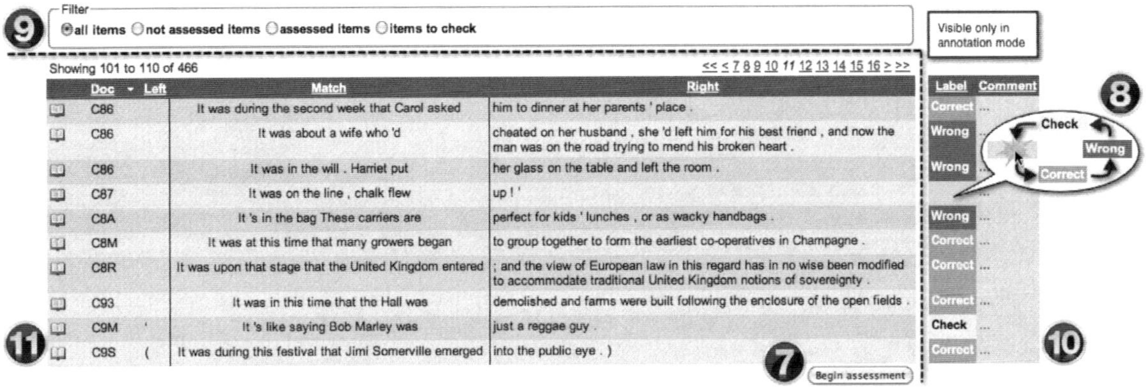

Figure 3: KWIC view of query results and assessments

sible to (15) *filter* for *correct*, *wrong*, *disputed*, *incompletely assessed*, and *unassessed* candidates. A candidate is *disputed* if it is not labeled consistently by all selected users. A candidate is *incompletely assessed* if at least one of the selected users labeled it and at least one other did not. Investigating disputed cases and (16) *inter-rater agreement* per type using Fleiss' Kappa (Fleiss, 1971) are the main uses of this view. The inter-rater agreement is calculated using only candidates labeled by all selected users.

By query: In this view, query precision and assessment completeness are calculated for a set of (17) *queries* and (18) *users*. The query precision is calculated from the labeled candidates as:

$$precision = \frac{|TP|}{|TP| + |FP|}$$

We treat a candidate as a *true positive* (*TP*) if: 1) the number of *correct* labels is larger than the number of *wrong* labels; 2) the ratio of *correct* labels compared to the number of raters exceeds a given (19) *threshold*. Candidates are conversely treated as *false positives* (*FPs*) if the number of *wrong* labels is larger and the *threshold* is exceeded. The threshold controls the confidence of the *TP* and, thus, of the annotations generated from them (cf. sect. 4.5).

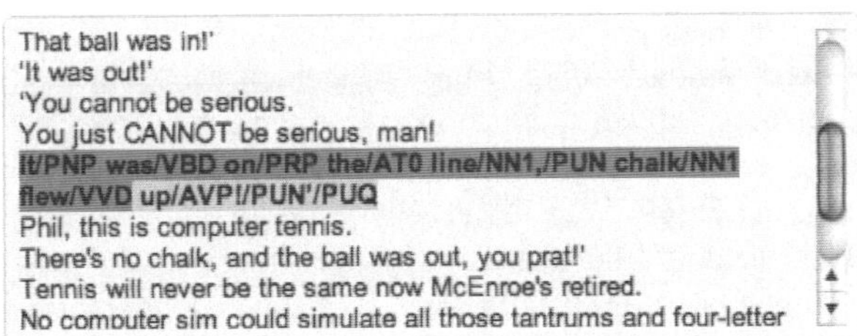

Figure 4: Sentence context view with POS tags

If a candidate is neither *TP* nor *FP*, it is *unknown* (*UNK*). When calculating *precision*, *UNK* candidates are counted as *FP*. The *estimated precision* is the precision to be expected if *TP* and *FP* are equally distributed over the set of candidates. It takes into account only the currently known *TP* and *FP* and ignores the *UNK* candidates. Both values are the same once all candidates have been labeled by all users.

4.5 Annotation

When the assessment process is complete, corpus annotations can be generated from the assessed candidates. Here, we employ the thresholded majority vote approach that we also use to determine the *TP*/*FP* in sect. 4.4. Annotations for the respective NCC type are added directly to the corpus. The augmented corpus can be used in further exploratory work. Alternatively, a file with all assessed candidates can be generated to serve as training data for identification methods based on machine learning.

5 Conclusions

We have presented CSNIPER, a tool for the annotation of linguistic phenomena whose investigation requires the analysis of large corpora due to a relatively low frequency of instances and whose identification requires expert knowledge to distinguish them from other similar constructions. Our tool integrates the complete functionality needed for the *annotation-by-query* workflow. It provides distributed multi-user annotation and evaluation. The feedback provided by the integrated evaluation module can be used to systematically refine queries and improve assessments. Finally, high-confidence annotations can be generated from the assessments.

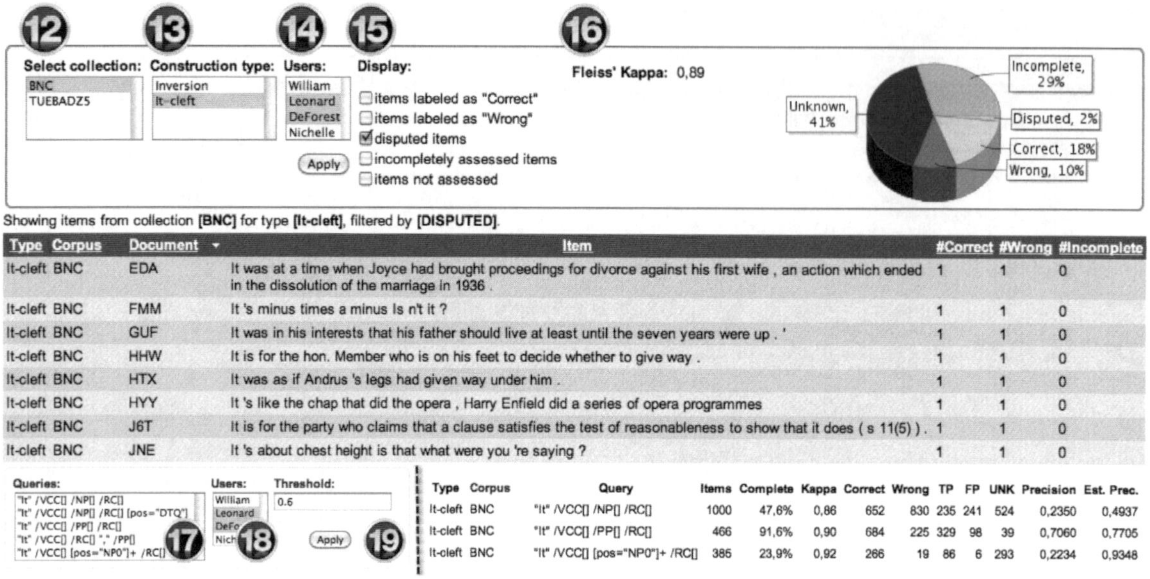

Figure 5: Evaluation by query and by NCC type

The *annotation-by-query* approach can be generalized beyond non-canonical constructions to other linguistic phenomena with similar properties. An example could be metaphors, which typically also appear with comparatively low frequency and require expert knowledge to be annotated. We plan to integrate further automatic annotations and query possibilities to support such further use-cases.

Acknowledgments

We would like to thank Erik-Lân Do Dinh, who assisted in implementing CSNIPER as well as Gert Webelhuth and Janina Rado for testing and providing valuable feedback.

This work has been supported by the Hessian research excellence program "Landes-Offensive zur Entwicklung Wissenschaftlich-ökonomischer Exzellenz" (LOEWE) as part of the research center "Digital Humanities" and by the Volkswagen Foundation as part of the Lichtenberg-Professorship Program under grant No. I/82806.

Data cited herein have been extracted from the British National Corpus, distributed by Oxford University Computing Services on behalf of the BNC Consortium. All rights in the texts cited are reserved.

References

BNC Consortium. 2007. The British National Corpus, version 3 (BNC XML Edition). Distributed by Oxford University Computing Services p.p. the BNC Consortium, `http://www.natcorp.ox.ac.uk/`.

Oliver Christ. 1994. A modular and flexible architecture for an integrated corpus query system. In *Proc. of the 3rd Conference on Computational Lexicography and Text Research (COMPLEX'94)*, pages 23–32, Budapest, Hungary, Jul.

Joseph L. Fleiss. 1971. Measuring nominal scale agreement among many raters. In *Psychological Bulletin*, volume 76 (5), pages 378–381. American Psychological Association, Washington, DC.

Peter Kluegl, Martin Atzmueller, and Frank Puppe. 2009. TextMarker: A tool for rule-based information extraction. In Christian Chiarcos, Richard Eckart de Castilho, and Manfred Stede, editors, *Proc. of the Biennial GSCL Conference 2009, 2nd UIMA@GSCL Workshop*, pages 233–240. Gunter Narr Verlag, Sep.

Christoph Müller and Michael Strube. 2006. Multi-level annotation of linguistic data with MMAX2. In Sabine Braun, Kurt Kohn, and Joybrato Mukherjee, editors, *Corpus Technology and Language Pedagogy: New Resources, New Tools, New Methods*, pages 197–214. Peter Lang, Frankfurt am Main, Germany, Aug.

Mick O'Donnell. 2008. The UAM CorpusTool: Software for corpus annotation and exploration. In Carmen M. et al. Bretones Callejas, editor, *Applied Linguistics Now: Understanding Language and Mind / La Lingüística Aplicada Hoy: Comprendiendo el Lenguaje y la Mente*, pages 1433–1447. Almería: Universidad de Almería.

Helmut Schmid. 1994. Improvements in part-of-speech tagging with an application to German. In *Proc. of Int. Conference on New Methods in Language Processing*, pages 44–49, Manchester, UK, Sep.

Amir Zeldes, Julia Ritz, Anke Lüdeling, and Christian Chiarcos. 2009. ANNIS: A search tool for multi-layer annotated corpora. In *Proc. of Corpus Linguistics 2009*, Liverpool, UK, Jul.

ACCURAT Toolkit for Multi-Level Alignment and Information Extraction from Comparable Corpora

Mārcis Pinnis[1], Radu Ion[2], Dan Ştefănescu[2], Fangzhong Su[3], Inguna Skadiņa[1], Andrejs Vasiļjevs[1], Bogdan Babych[3]

[1]Tilde, Vienības gatve 75a, Riga, Latvia
{marcis.pinnis,inguna.skadina,andrejs}@tilde.lv

[2]Research Institute for Artificial Intelligence, Romanian Academy
{radu,danstef}@racai.ro

[3]Centre for Translation Studies, University of Leeds
{f.su,b.babych}@leeds.ac.uk

Abstract

The lack of parallel corpora and linguistic resources for many languages and domains is one of the major obstacles for the further advancement of automated translation. A possible solution is to exploit comparable corpora (non-parallel bi- or multi-lingual text resources) which are much more widely available than parallel translation data. Our presented toolkit deals with parallel content extraction from comparable corpora. It consists of tools bundled in two workflows: (1) alignment of comparable documents and extraction of parallel sentences and (2) extraction and bilingual mapping of terms and named entities. The toolkit pairs similar bilingual comparable documents and extracts parallel sentences and bilingual terminological and named entity dictionaries from comparable corpora. This demonstration focuses on the English, Latvian, Lithuanian, and Romanian languages.

Introduction

In recent decades, data-driven approaches have significantly advanced the development of machine translation (MT). However, lack of sufficient bilingual linguistic resources for many languages and domains is still one of the major obstacles for further advancement of automated translation. At the same time, comparable corpora, i.e., non-parallel bi- or multilingual text resources such as daily news articles and large knowledge bases like Wikipedia, are much more widely available than parallel translation data.

While methods for the use of parallel corpora in machine translation are well studied (Koehn, 2010), similar techniques for comparable corpora have not been thoroughly worked out. Only the latest research has shown that language pairs and domains with little parallel data can benefit from the exploitation of comparable corpora (Munteanu and Marcu, 2005; Lu et al., 2010; Smith et al., 2010; Abdul-Rauf and Schwenk, 2009 and 2011).

In this paper we present the ACCURAT toolkit[1] - a collection of tools that are capable of analysing comparable corpora and extracting parallel data which can be used to improve the performance of statistical and rule/example-based MT systems.

Although the toolkit may be used for parallel data acquisition for open (broad) domain systems, it will be most beneficial for under-resourced languages or specific domains which are not covered by available parallel resources.

The ACCURAT toolkit produces:

- **comparable document pairs** with comparability scores, allowing to estimate the overall comparability of corpora;
- **parallel sentences** which can be used as additional parallel data sources for statistical translation model learning;

[1] http://www.accurat-project.eu/

Proceedings of the 50th Annual Meeting of the Association for Computational Linguistics, pages 91–96,
Jeju, Republic of Korea, 8-14 July 2012.

- **terminology dictionaries** — this type of data is expected to improve domain-dependent translation;
- **named entity dictionaries**.

The demonstration showcases two general use case scenarios defined in the toolkit: "parallel data mining from comparable corpora" and "named entity/terminology extraction and mapping from comparable corpora".

The next section provides a general overview of workflows followed by descriptions of methods and tools integrated in the workflows.

1 Overview of the Workflows

The toolkit's tools are integrated within two workflows (visualised in Figure 1).

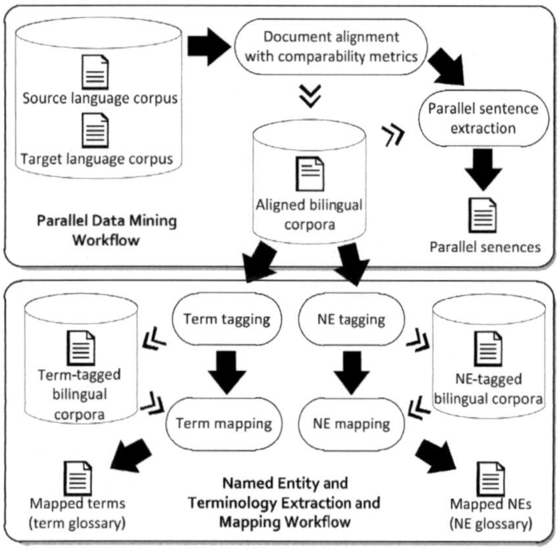

Figure 1. Workflows of the ACCURAT toolkit.

The **workflow for parallel data mining from comparable corpora** aligns comparable corpora in the document level (section 2.1). This step is crucial as the further steps are computationally intensive. To minimise search space, documents are aligned with possible candidates that are likely to contain parallel data. Then parallel sentence pairs are extracted from the aligned comparable corpora (section 2.2).

The **workflow for named entity** (NE) **and terminology extraction and mapping** from comparable corpora extracts data in a dictionary-like format. Providing a list of document pairs, the workflow tags NEs or terms in all documents using language specific taggers (named entity recognisers (NER) or term extractors) and performs multi-lingual NE (section 2.3) or term mapping (section 2.4), thereby producing bilingual NE or term dictionaries. The workflow also accepts pre-processed documents, thus skipping the tagging process.

Since all tools use command line interfaces, task automation and workflow specification can be done with simple console/terminal scripts. All tools can be run on the Windows operating system (some are also platform independent).

2 Tools and Methods

This section provides an overview of the main tools and methods in the toolkit. A full list of tools is described in ACCURAT D2.6. (2011).

2.1 Comparability Metrics

We define comparability by how useful a pair of documents is for parallel data extraction. The higher the comparability score, the more likely two documents contain more overlapping parallel data. The methods are developed to perform lightweight comparability estimation that minimises search space of relatively large corpora (e.g., 10,000 documents in each language). There are two comparability metric tools in the toolkit: a translation based and a dictionary based metric.

The **Translation based metric** (Su and Babych, 2012a) uses MT APIs for document translation into English. Then four independent similarity feature functions are applied to a document pair:

- Lexical feature — both documents are pre-processed (tokenised, lemmatised, and stop-words are filtered) and then vectorised. The lexical overlap score is calculated as a cosine similarity function over the vectors of two documents.
- Structural feature — the difference of sentence counts and content word counts (equally interpolated).
- Keyword feature — the cosine similarity of top 20 keywords.
- NE feature — the cosine similarity of NEs (extracted using Stanford NER).

These similarity measures are linearly combined in a final comparability score. This is implemented by a simple weighted average strategy, in which each type of feature is associated with a weight indicating its relative confidence or importance. The comparability scores are normalised on a scale of 0 to 1, where a higher comparability score indicates a higher comparability level.

The reliability of the proposed metric has been evaluated on a gold standard of comparable corpora for 11 language pairs (Skadiņa et al., 2010). The gold standard consists of news articles, legal documents, knowledge-base articles, user manuals, and medical documents. Document pairs in the gold standard were rated by human judges as being parallel, strongly comparable, or weakly comparable. The evaluation results suggest that the comparability scores reliably reflect comparability levels. In addition, there is a strong correlation between human defined comparability levels and the confidence scores derived from the comparability metric, as the Pearson R correlation scores vary between 0.966 and 0.999, depending on the language pair.

The **Dictionary based metric** (Su and Babych, 2012b) is a lightweight approach, which uses bilingual dictionaries to lexically map documents from one language to another. The dictionaries are automatically generated via word alignment using GIZA++ (Och and Ney, 2000) on parallel corpora. For each word in the source language, the top two translation candidates (based on the word alignment probability in GIZA++) are retrieved as possible translations into the target language. This metric provides a much faster lexical translation process, although word-for-word lexical mapping produces less reliable translations than MT based translations. Moreover, the lower quality of text translation in the dictionary based metric does not necessarily degrade its performance in predicting comparability levels of comparable document pairs. The evaluation on the gold standard shows a strong correlation (between 0.883 and 0.999) between human defined comparability levels and the confidence scores of the metric.

2.2 Parallel Sentence Extractor from Comparable Corpora

Phrase-based statistical translation models are among the most successful translation models that currently exist (Callison-Burch et al., 2010). Usually, phrases are extracted from parallel corpora by means of symmetrical word alignment and/or by phrase generation (Koehn et al., 2003). Our toolkit exploits comparable corpora in order to find and extract comparable sentences for SMT training using a tool named *LEXACC* (Ştefănescu et al., 2012).

LEXACC requires aligned document pairs (also *m* to *n* alignments) for sentence extraction. It also allows extraction from comparable corpora as a whole; however, precision may decrease due to larger search space.

LEXACC scores sentence pairs according to five lexical overlap and structural matching feature functions. These functions are combined using linear interpolation with weights trained for each language pair and direction using logistic regression. The feature functions are:

- a lexical (translation) overlap score for content words (nouns, verbs, adjectives, and adverbs) using GIZA++ (Gao and Vogel, 2008) format dictionaries;
- a lexical (translation) overlap score for functional words (all except content words) constrained by the content word alignment from the previous feature;
- the alignment obliqueness score, a measure that quantifies the degree to which the relative positions of source and target aligned words differ;
- a score indicating whether strong content word translations are found at the beginning and the end of each sentence in the given pair;
- a punctuation score which indicates whether the sentences have identical sentence ending punctuation.

For different language pairs, the relevance of the individual feature functions differ. For instance, the locality feature is more important for the English-Romanian pair than for the English-Greek pair. Therefore, the weights are trained on parallel corpora (in our case - 10,000 pairs).

LEXACC does not score every sentence pair in the Cartesian product between source and target document sentences. It reduces the search space using two filtering steps (Ştefănescu et al., 2012). The first step makes use of the Cross-Language Information Retrieval framework and uses a search engine to find sentences in the target corpus that are the most probable translations of a given sentence. In the second step (which is optional), the resulting candidates are further filtered, and those that do not meet minimum requirements are eliminated.

To work for a certain language pair, *LEXACC* needs additional resources: (i) a GIZA++-like translation dictionary, (ii) lists of stop-words in both languages, and (iii) lists of word suffixes in both languages (used for stemming).

The performance of *LEXACC*, regarding precision and recall, can be controlled by a threshold applied to the overall interpolated parallelism score. The tool has been evaluated on news article comparable corpora. Table 1 shows results achieved by *LEXACC* with different parallelism thresholds on automatically crawled English-Latvian corpora, consisting of 41,914 unique English sentences and 10,058 unique Latvian sentences.

Threshold	Aligned pairs	Precision	Useful pairs
0.25	1036	39.19%	406
0.3	813	48.22%	392
0.4	553	63.47%	351
0.5	395	76.96%	304
0.6	272	84.19%	229
0.7	151	88.74%	134
0.8	27	88.89%	24
0.9	0	-	0

Table 1. English-Latvian parallel sentence extraction results on a comparable news corpus.

Threshold	Aligned pairs	Precision	Useful pairs
0.2	2324	10.32%	240
0.3	1105	28.50%	315
0.4	722	53.46%	386
0.5	532	89.28%	475
0.6	389	100%	389
0.7	532	100%	532
0.8	386	100%	386
0.9	20	100%	20

Table 2. English-Romanian parallel sentence extraction results on a comparable news corpus.

Table 2 shows results for English-Romanian on corpora consisting of 310,740 unique English and 81,433 unique Romanian sentences.

Useful pairs denote the total number of parallel and strongly comparable sentence pairs (at least 80% of the source sentence is a translation in the target sentence). The corpora size is given only as an indicative figure, as the amount of extracted parallel data greatly depends on the comparability of the corpora.

2.3 Named Entity Extraction and Mapping

The second workflow of the toolkit allows NE and terminology extraction and mapping. Starting with named entity recognition, the toolkit features the first NER systems for Latvian and Lithuanian (Pinnis, 2012). It also contains NER systems for English (through an *OpenNLP NER*[2] wrapper) and Romanian (*NERA*). In order to map named entities, documents have to be tagged with NER systems that support MUC-7 format NE SGML tags.

The toolkit contains the mapping tool *NERA2*. The mapper requires comparable corpora aligned in the document level as input. *NERA2* compares each NE from the source language to each NE from the target language using cognate based methods. It also uses a GIZA++ format statistical dictionary to map NEs containing common nouns that are frequent in location names. This approach allows frequent NE mapping if the cognate based method fails, therefore, allowing increasing the recall of the mapper. Precision and recall can be tuned with a confidence score threshold.

2.4 Terminology Mapping

During recent years, automatic bilingual term mapping in comparable corpora has received greater attention in light of the scarcity of parallel data for under-resourced languages. Several methods have been applied to this task, e.g., contextual analysis (Rapp, 1995; Fung and McKeown, 1997) and compositional analysis (Daille and Morin, 2008). Symbolic, statistical, and hybrid techniques have been implemented for bilingual lexicon extraction (Morin and Prochasson, 2011).

Our terminology mapper is designed to map terms extracted from comparable or parallel

[2] Open NLP - http://incubator.apache.org/opennlp/.

documents. The method is language independent and can be applied if a translation equivalents table exists for a language pair. As input, the application requires term-tagged bilingual corpora aligned in the document level.

The toolkit includes term-tagging tools for English, Latvian, Lithuanian, and Romanian, but can be easily extended for other languages if a POS-tagger, a phrase pattern list, a stop-word list, and an inverse document frequency list (calculated on balanced corpora) are available.

The aligner maps terms based on two criteria (Pinnis et al., 2012; Ştefănescu, 2012): (i) a GIZA++-like translation equivalents table and (ii) string similarity in terms of *Levenshtein* distance between term candidates. For evaluation, Eurovoc (Steinberger et al., 2002) was used. Tables 4 and 5 show the performance figures of the mapper for English-Romanian and English-Latvian.

Threshold	P	R	F-measure
0.3	0.562	0.194	0.288
0.4	0.759	0.295	0.425
0.5	**0.904**	**0.357**	**0.511**
0.6	0.964	0.298	0.456
0.7	0.986	0.216	0.359
0.8	0.996	0.151	0.263
0.9	0.995	0.084	0.154

Table 3. Term mapping performance for English-Romanian.

Threshold	P	R	F-measure
0.3	0.636	0.210	0.316
0.4	0.833	0.285	0.425
0.5	**0.947**	**0.306**	**0.463**
0.6	0.981	0.235	0.379
0.7	0.996	0.160	0.275
0.8	0.996	0.099	0.181
0.9	0.997	0.057	0.107

Table 4. Term mapping performance for English-Latvian.

3 Conclusions and Related Information

This demonstration paper describes the ACCURAT toolkit containing tools for multi-level alignment and information extraction from comparable corpora. These tools are integrated in predefined workflows that are ready for immediate use. The workflows provide functionality for the extraction of parallel sentences, bilingual NE dictionaries, and bilingual term dictionaries from comparable corpora.

The methods, including comparability metrics, parallel sentence extraction and named entity/term mapping, are language independent. However, they may require language dependent resources, for instance, POS-taggers, Giza++ translation dictionaries, NERs, term taggers, etc.[3]

The ACCURAT toolkit is released under the Apache 2.0 licence and is freely available for download after completing a registration form[4].

Acknowledgements

The research within the project ACCURAT leading to these results has received funding from the European Union Seventh Framework Programme (FP7/2007-2013), grant agreement no 248347.

References

Sadaf Abdul-Rauf and Holger Schwenk. On the use of comparable corpora to improve SMT performance. EACL 2009: Proceedings of the 12th conference of the European Chapter of the Association for Computational Linguistics, Athens, Greece, 16-23.

Sadaf Abdul-Rauf and Holger Schwenk. 2011. Parallel sentence generation from comparable corpora for improved SMT. Machine Translation, 25(4): 341-375.

ACCURAT D2.6 2011. Toolkit for multi-level alignment and information extraction from comparable corpora (http://www.accurat-project.eu).

Dan Gusfield. 1997. Algorithms on strings, trees and sequences. Cambridge University Press.

Chris Callison-Burch, Philipp Koehn, Christof Monz, Kay Peterson, Mark Przybocki and Omar Zaidan. 2010. Findings of the 2010 Joint Workshop on Statistical Machine Translation and Metrics for Machine Translation. Proceedings of the Joint Fifth Workshop on Statistical Machine Translation and MetricsMATR, 17-53.

Béatrice Daille and Emmanuel Morin. 2008. Effective compositional model for lexical alignment. Proceedings of the 3rd International Joint Conference

[3] Full requirements are defined in the documentation of each tool (ACCURAT D2.6, 2011).

[4] http://www.accurat-project.eu/index.php?p=toolkit

on Natural Language Processing, Hyderabad, India, 95-102.

Franz Josef Och and Hermann Ney. 2000. Improved statistical alignment models. Proceedings of the 38th Annual Meeting of the Association for Computational Linguistics, 440-447.

Pascale Fung and Kathleen Mckeown. 1997. Finding terminology translations from non-parallel corpora. Proceedings of the 5th Annual Workshop on Very Large Corpora, 192-202.

Qin Gao and Stephan Vogel. 2008. Parallel implementations of a word alignment tool. Proceedings of ACL-08 HLT: Software Engineering, Testing, and Quality Assurance for Natural Language Processing, June 20, 2008. The Ohio State University, Columbus, Ohio, USA, 49-57.

Philipp Koehn, Franz Josef Och, and Daniel Marcu. 2003. Statistical phrase-based translation. Proceedings of the Human Language Technology and North American Association for Computational Linguistics Conference (HLT/NAACL), May 27-June 1, Edmonton, Canada.

Philip Koehn. 2010. Statistical machine translation, Cambridge University Press.

Bin Lu, Tao Jiang, Kapo Chow and Benjamin K. Tsou. 2010. Building a large English-Chinese parallel corpus from comparable patents and its experimental application to SMT. Proceedings of the 3rd workshop on building and using comparable corpora: from parallel to non-parallel corpora, Valletta, Malta, 42-48.

Dragoş Ştefan Munteanu and Daniel Marcu. 2006. Extracting parallel sub-sentential fragments from nonparallel corpora. ACL-44: Proceedings of the 21st International Conference on Computational Linguistics and the 44th annual meeting of the Association for Computational Linguistics, Morristown, NJ, USA, 81-88.

Emmanuel Morin and Emmanuel Prochasson. 2011. Bilingual lexicon extraction from comparable corpora enhanced with parallel corpora. ACL HLT 2011, 27-34.

Mārcis Pinnis. 2012. Latvian and Lithuanian named entity recognition with TildeNER. Proceedings of the 8th international conference on Language Resources and Evaluation (LREC 2012), Istanbul, Turkey.

Mārcis Pinnis, Nikola Ljubešić, Dan Ştefănescu, Inguna Skadiņa, Marko Tadić, Tatiana Gornostay. 2012. Term extraction, tagging, and mapping tools for under-resourced languages. Proceedings of the 10th Conference on Terminology and Knowledge Engineering (TKE 2012), June 20-21, Madrid, Spain.

Reinhard Rapp. 1995. Identifying word translations in non-parallel texts. Proceedings of the 33rd annual meeting on Association for Computational Linguistics, 320-322.

Jason R. Smith, Chris Quirk, and Kristina Toutanova. 2010. Extracting parallel sentences from comparable corpora using document level alignment. Proceedings of NAACL 2010, Los Angeles, USA.

Dan Ştefănescu. 2012. Mining for term translations in comparable corpora. Proceedings of the 5th Workshop on Building and Using Comparable Corpora (BUCC 2012) to be held at the 8th edition of Language Resources and Evaluation Conference (LREC 2012), Istanbul, Turkey, May 23-25, 2012.

Ralf Steinberger, Bruno Pouliquen and Johan Hagman. 2002. Cross-lingual document similarity calculation using the multilingual thesaurus Eurovoc. Proceedings of the 3rd International Conference on Computational Linguistics and Intelligent Text Processing (CICLing '02), Springer-Verlag London, UK, ISBN:3-540-43219-1.

Inguna Skadiņa, Ahmet Aker, Voula Giouli, Dan Tufis, Rob Gaizauskas, Madara Mieriņa and Nikos Mastropavlos. 2010. Collection of comparable corpora for under-resourced languages. In *Proceedings of the Fourth International Conference Baltic HLT 2010*, IOS Press, Frontiers in Artificial Intelligence and Applications, Vol. 219, pp. 161-168.

Fangzhong Su and Bogdan Babych. 2012a. Development and application of a cross-language document comparability metric. Proceedings of the 8th international conference on Language Resources and Evaluation (LREC 2012), Istanbul, Turkey.

Fangzhong Su and Bogdan Babych. 2012b. Measuring comparability of documents in non-parallel corpora for efficient extraction of (semi-) parallel translation equivalents. Proceedings of EACL'12 joint workshop on Exploiting Synergies between Information Retrieval and Machine Translation (ESIRMT) and Hybrid Approaches to Machine Translation (HyTra), Avignon, France.

Dan Ştefănescu, Radu Ion and Sabine Hunsicker. 2012. Hybrid parallel sentence mining from comparable corpora. Proceedings of the 16th Conference of the European Association for Machine Translation (EAMT 2012), Trento, Italy.

Demonstration of IlluMe: Creating Ambient According to Instant Message Logs

Lun-Wei Ku **Cheng-Wei Sun** **Ya-Hsin Hsueh**
National Yunlin University of Science and Technology
123 University Road, Section 3
Douliou, Yunlin 64002, Taiwan
lwku@yuntech.edu.tw;chengwei.kenny.sun@gmail.com;hsuehyh@yuntech.edu.tw

Abstract

We present IlluMe, a software tool pack which creates a personalized ambient using the music and lighting. IlluMe includes an emotion analysis software, the small space ambient lighting, and a multimedia controller. The software analyzes emotional changes from instant message logs and corresponds the detected emotion to the best sound and light settings. The ambient lighting can sparkle with different forms of light and the smart phone can broadcast music respectively according to different atmosphere. All settings can be modified by the multimedia controller at any time and the new settings will be feedback to the emotion analysis software. The IlluMe system, equipped with the learning function, provides a link between residential situation and personal emotion. It works in a Chinese chatting environment to illustrate the language technology in life.

1 Introduction

Emotion analysis as well as recommendation technology has drawn a lot attention in the natural language processing research community. The development of fundamental approaches as well as applications has been proposed (Das, 2011; Sarwar *et al.*, 2001; Zheng *et al.*, 2010). However, most of them were Internet applications, and to the best knowledge of the authors, these technologies have not yet been involved in the ambient creation. To create an intelligent living space, some researchers utilized the facial expression and speech recognizer to detect emotions (Busso *et al.*, 2004), but then the accompanied cameras and microphones were necessary. Some researchers tried to use sensors to watch the heart beat and the body temperature of residents to know their current emotion for further applications, but the problem was that users had to wear sensors and it was inconvenient. Instead of watching body signals, we postulate that the communications among people is one of the important factors to influence their emotions. Therefore, we tried to find clues from the textual conversations of the residents in order to detect their psychological state.

There are many ways to categorize emotions. Different emotion states were used for experiments in previous research (Bellegarda, 2010). To find suitable categories of emotions, we adopted the three-layered emotion hierarchy proposed by Parrott (2001)[1]. Six emotions are in the first layer, including love, joy, surprise, anger, sadness and fear. The second layer includes 25 emotions, and the third layer includes 135 emotions. Using this hierarchical classification benefits the system. We can categorize emotions from rough to fine granularities and degrade to the upper level when the experimental materials are insufficient. How to map categories in other researches to ours becomes clearer, and annotators have more information when marking their current emotion.

As to the music, most researchers looked for the emotions in songs or rhythms (Yang and Chen, 2011; Zbikowski, 2011). They classified music into different emotional categories and developed the system to tell what emotion a song might bring to a listener. However, if the aim is to create a

[1] http://changingminds.org/explanations/emotions/basic%20emotions.htm

Proceedings of the 50th Annual Meeting of the Association for Computational Linguistics, pages 97–102,
Jeju, Republic of Korea, 8-14 July 2012. ©2012 Association for Computational Linguistics

comfortable ambient, what songs a person in a certain emotional state wants to listen to becomes the question. A happy user does not always enjoy happy songs, and vice versa. In this case, the technology developed in the previous work did not meet the new requirement.

IlluMe was designed for a small space personal environment. We expect that users would like to use it because this system could interactively respond to their personal status to provide a feeling of the companion. We view the IlluMe system as a realization of detecting emotions from users' textual conversations and then recommending the best ambient accordingly. There are three major contributions in the development of the system. First, a corpus for ambient creation according to emotions was constructed. Second, IlluMe demonstrates a way to apply the state of the art technology of emotion analysis and recommendation to create an intelligent living space. Third, along with the developed technology, several further applications utilizing the components of IlluMe become feasible.

2 System Description

The potential working area for IlluMe is home or a small space. The system was designed to fit in with the modern people's life style: programs are installed in users' personal computer and smart phone. The smart phone functions as the remote control and the music player, while all setting signals are sent out from the personal computer. The smart phone and the personal computer communicate through the wireless network. The only additional hardware requirement is the lighting set.

2.1 System Features

Emotion Detection Switch: The system detects users' current emotion according to messenger logs once a preset time period. It is ON/OFF switchable if users do not want the conversations to be recorded or utilized when determining the ambient.

Auto Ambient Setting: The system sets the current ambient by a specific combination of a song and a light group which corresponds to the emotion or represents a special atmosphere.

Manual Ambient Adjustment: IlluMe provides a friendly user interface to change the settings of music and lighting at any time.

Personal Preference Learning: When users change the settings, the new ones are recorded. IlluMe learns the preference and then performs the user adaptation. After a period of time users will have their unique ambient creating system.

Unlimited Melodies and Rich Light Colors: Users can add their songs in the smart phone for selection at any time. The learning process will help propose the new songs to create ambient later.

Instant State Update: IlluMe watches the user input from messenger when the software is on. Therefore, it is able to change the music and lighting according to the detected emotion within a preset time period and users will feel like the environment is interacting with them.

2.2 System Framework

Figure 1 demonstrates the system framework of IlluMe. The system automatically watches the *User Messages* from messenger logs. The *Emotion Analysis* component detects the emotion of users, while the *Ambient Learning Model* determines the music and lighting accordingly, considering also the *Personal Information* of users.

After the lights are on and the music is played, the user can change the settings they are not satisfying. A smart phone (*Mobile Device*) is used to change the settings, with two controllers on it: the *Preference Controller* and the *Ambient Controller*. The former takes the *User Input* for new settings, and then the music and lighting are changed by the latter. At the same time, the *Preference Controller* also sends the new settings to *Ambient Learning Model* to be recorded for user adaptation when creating the next ambient.

The *Emotion Analysis Component* and *Ambient Learning Model* are two programs in a personal computer, and the *Personal Info* is saved in the personal computer, too. *ANT* wireless personal network protocol (Dynastream) is adopted to send the control signals to the *Lighting*. The LED lighting board is utilized to implement the *Lighting* of 65,536 colors.

2.3 Operation Flowchart of User Interface

The IlluMe system provides a user interface to change the settings by a smart phone (*Mobile Device*), functioning as a remote control. Users can select the location of music or the lighting, e.g. the living room or the bedroom, and the control mode, i.e. manual or automatic. In the manual mode, users can set the color of a specific light; in the automatic mode, users select an emotional color set or a desired atmosphere for the lighting. Figure 2 shows the operational flow of the user interface.

2.4 Ambient Lighting and Music Playing

To design the ambient lighting, one has to take LED array board, controlling mode and the light-mixing effect of the lampshade into consideration. The LED lamp should sprinkle the LED components of red, cyan, green, white and orange lights equally onto the LED array board, so as to achieve uniform distribution. The controlling module distinguishes each lamp by its own code to modify the brightness of different colored LEDs within.

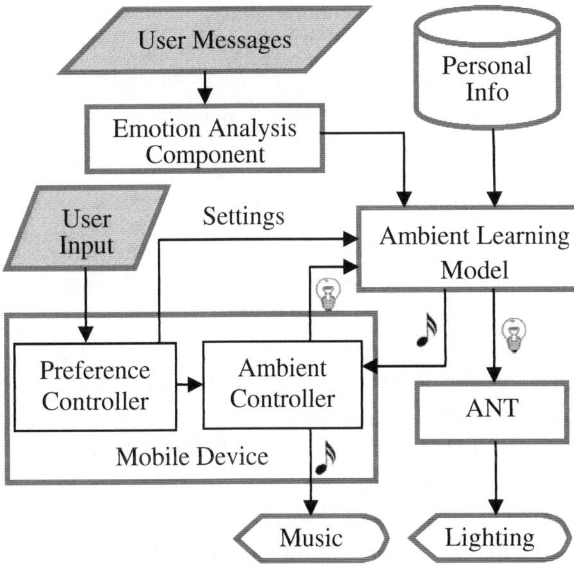

Figure 1. System Framework of IlluMe

As the LED lighting changes its color according to the controlling signals from the remote controller, the system transfer appropriate RF signals from the user's personal computer to the *ANT* board, and then the *ANT* board controls the LED lighting board to change the color of lights.

Music is broadcasted according to the detected emotional state. The broadcasting function and the controlling function are both realized by the software in the smart phone. Music is broadcasted directly through the phone, which conforms to the habits of modern people. Figure 3 shows the illustration of the usage of IlluMe.

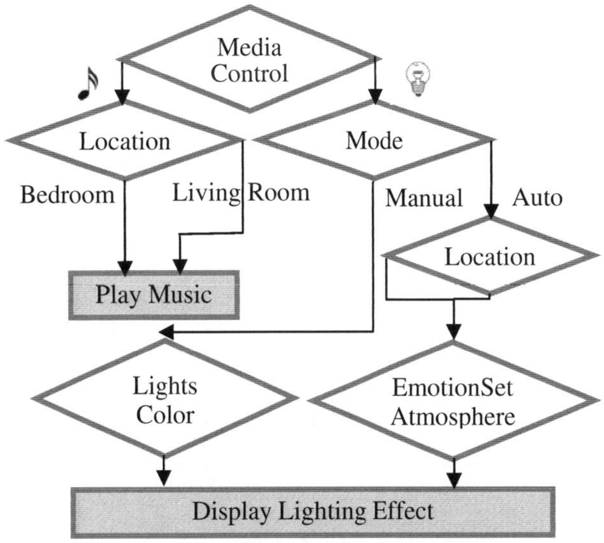

Figure 2. Operation Flowchart

Figure 3. Usage Illustration

3 Emotion Analysis

The emotion analysis that IlluMe performed is to find the emotions that texts in messenger logs bear in order to create a comfort ambient by sound and lighting accordingly. To achieve this, the system needs to understand the Internet language first, and then detect emotions and categorize them. The system works on the Chinese chatting environment and analyzes Chinese texts to detect emotions. The materials, approaches, and preliminary results in the development phase are described in this section.

3.1 Experimental Materials

Two dictionaries, the Chinese sentiment dictionary NTUSD (Ku and Chen, 2007) and the Chinese emotion dictionary (Lin *et al.*, 2008), were adopted for detecting emotions. The former categorized sentiment words into positive and negative, while the latter into eight emotion types: awesome, heartwarming, surprising, sad, useful, happy, boring, and angry. Notice that these eight emotion types appeared in Yahoo! News Taiwan in the year 2008 and not all of them were general emotion states. Therefore, we tried to find Lin's emotion categories in Parrott's emotion hierarchy before using this dictionary. Those could not be found were categorized in the *Other* class.

Messenger logs were used as the source to detect emotions. We collected texts from Yahoo! Messenger and MSN Messenger logs of 8 annotators. When the installed collecting program in their computers was on, it ran as a service and continuously logged their messages. Whenever there was at least one new message, once an hour the collecting program would pop up the menu and ask them to annotate the current emotion together with the preferred settings of the music and lighting. There were 3,290 songs, 15 emotional lighting colors and 6 atmospheres for selection. When selecting the settings of lighting, a full-screen colored photo would be displayed to help annotators make their decisions. A total of 150 records are annotated for experiments and statistics are shown in Table 1.

Emo	1	2	3	4	5	6	
	11	80	1	15	39	4	
Color	1	2	3	4	5	6	7
14	6	5	25	9	5	11	14
8	9	10	11	12	13	14	15
11	7	4	13	7	15	5	13
Atm	1	2	3	4	5	6	
	28	40	16	33	17	16	

Table 1. Statistics of Annotated Materials
(Emo: Emotions, 1=Love, 2=Joy, 3=Surprise, 4=Angry, 5=Sad, 6=Fear; Color:15 color sets; Atm:6 atmospheres)

3.2 Interpretation of Zhuyin Wen

When processing Internet Chinese texts, IlluMe transformed messenger logs and sentiment dictionaries into zhuyin (Su, 2003) before looking for emotions[2]. There were many reasons to do this. Zhuyin Wen (注音文) is one of many creative uses of writing systems in the Internet language. As Blakeman (2004) found in his study of English, Internet language is fraught with initializations. However, as to the traditional Chinese, both Wikipedia and Zhang and Dai (2006) indicated that stylized initials and stylized numbers are rarely used in Taiwan. Su reported that the most popular type of creative use of writing systems is "Zhuyin Wen" (注音文). In "Zhuyin Wen" the complete phonetic representation of a character is reduced to a consonant, or sometimes a vowel. This creative use appeared commonly in the collected conversations. Generally we had to figure out the missing vowels to understand the word, but in our system a reversed approach (dropping vowels) was adopted to make sure the system did not miss any possible match of dictionary terms observed in the conversations.

When messenger users typed characters by their phonetics (consonants and vowels), very often they selected the wrong one from candidates of the same pronunciation, or they were just too lazy to select so the writing system chose the default candidate for them. In these cases, the system could not find a match because of wrong composite characters. Transforming characters in both dictionaries and conversations into their zhuyin representations before detecting emotions also help recover this kind of errors.

3.3 Emotion Detection from Texts

Section 3.2 shows how the system dealt with the error prone Internet texts and found the dictionaries terms. Ku and Chen's (2007) approach for calculating sentiment scores was then adopted to give scores to these terms. The scores of terms of different emotional categories were summed up and the emotion category of the highest score was selected as the detected emotion. The *Ambient Learning Model* takes the detected emotion and selects the corresponding music and lighting by the Naïve Bayes classifier trained by the annotated materials.

3.4 Experiment and Preliminary Results

Table 2 shows that using enhanced NTUSD (an augmented version of NTUSD) together with zhuyin transformation achieves the best results for emotion classification (positive/negative).

Ku (2008) reported the set precision of their approach was 0.489 when texts were categorized into positive, neutral and negative. Though they had one additional neutral category, our system achieved the precision of 0.620 when processing the noisy Internet texts without word segmentation and part of speech tagging, which was satisfactory.

[2] Lookup Table: http://cclookup.cctserver.com/

Because IlluMe would always recommend a new or unchanged ambient setting, it would always find the closest emotion category of the user's current emotion. In other words, the chatting content would always be connected to one of six emotion categories, so precision is the best metric to evaluate the performance of the system. The micro-average precision of the emotion detection was 0.207, while the macro-average precision was 0.338. Bellegarda reported that his best f-measure was 0.340 also for 6 categories. Notice that the categories in Lin's Chinese emotional dictionary were not identical to ours and hence we could not find terms for some categories in it. Therefore, though Bellegarda's and our results were done on different datasets and evaluated by different metrics, considering our system suffered for the lack of terms in some categories and the ambiguous texts from the creative writing, the performance was considered acceptable.

For the ambient recommendation, the micro-average precision of selecting the settings of lighting according to the detected emotion was 0.441 for 15 color sets and 0.461 for 6 atmospheres.

	Positive	Negative	Total
A	0.489	0.534	0.507
B	0.902	0.155	0.613
A+C	0.902	0.172	0.620

Table 2. Precision of Emotion Detection (A: NTUSD; B: Enhanced NTUSD; C:Zhuyin transformation)

3.5 Ambient Learning Function

Because bringing up the settings to users is like a behavior of recommendation, we adopted the concept of collaborative filtering to design the function of the *Ambient Learning Model*. In the early stage of using IlluMe, it proposes the most frequently selected settings, that is, the choice of a group of people in the specific emotional state. If the user is connected to the Internet, the user experience will be transferred back to the servers to help recommend a better ambient to other users.

The user experience optimization was feasible in this system because of the use of the smart phone, and this function was also implemented. As the users update the settings, the system knows their preference. In the later stage of using IlluMe, the *Ambient Learning Model* considers the preference of both the individual and the group to create a unique ambient for each user.

4 Conclusion and Future Work

Through the work we aim to apply the language technology to redefine the concept of a small house or working space. They should be a family-like existence which possesses the intellectual capacity to observe human behavior and emotion, and create consoling spaces according to the residents' different status. Therefore we implemented emotion analysis technique to equip a space with the ability to observe the status of its residents and interact with them accordingly. The instant interior lightings and music change can be viewed as a new form of "conversation". Residents can not only take the ambient provided by IlluMe, but can also give feedbacks. The concept of collaborative filtering was also implemented as we viewed the proposing of ambient as a kind of recommendation.

Through the demonstration of the IlluMe system, we hope to show another way to apply language technology in life and retrieve the positive and relaxing atmosphere to rebuild our sense of trust and safety toward space, and finally recollect the long-lost attachment toward it.

We will continue collecting annotated materials and user feedbacks for learning, and make the materials a corpus for the research community. Facebook will be a source of text collection to gather more complete personal conversations for emotion detection. Making the IlluMe components real products like the home lighting system, the intelligent table lamp, or the music album promoter is also a future plan.

5 Demonstration

As demonstrating the IlluMe system by our original model house may be difficult in transportation and it may need a large space for demonstration, we will demonstrate the lightings by several table lamps, in which the LED lighting board resides. Other software will be performed on the smart phone and the personal computer.

5.1 Demonstration Outline

There are three purposes of the demonstration: first, to show how we apply the emotion analysis and recommendation technique in an ambient creating system; second, to illustrate actual and live operation of the system to the potential users; third, to show the annotation process of the experiment materials and the underlying algorithms for those interested in the technical details.

Potential users might be interested in how the system will work if they have it in their personal computers and smart phones. Therefore, we demonstrate the whole IlluMe system with the actual music and lighting. Users can type Chinese words in messengers from the personal computer, and then the IlluMe system will change the music and lighting according to the proposed settings in a short time. The user can also control the music and lighting from the interface by the smart phone.

In addition to demonstrating the functionality of the system, we will also provide accompanying visual aids that illustrate the underlying algorithms and the technical details. For example, zhuyin, terms found in the dictionaries, emotion scores, the detected emotion and the suggested settings.

Acknowledgements

Research of this paper was partially supported by National Science Council, Taiwan, under the contract NSC100-2218-E-224-013-.

References

Bellegarda, Jerome R. 2010. Emotion Analysis Using Latent Affective Folding and Embedding. Proceedings of the NAACL HLT 2010 Workshop on Computational Approaches to Analysis and Generation of Emotion in Text, Los Angeles, 1-9.

Blakeman, Adam. 2004. An Investigation of the Language of Internet Chat Rooms. http://www.lancs.ac.uk/fss/courses/ling/ling201/res/dissertations.html.

Busso, Carlos, Deng, Zhigang, Yildirim, Serdar, Bulut, Murtaza, Lee, Chul Min, Kazemzadeh, Abe, Lee, Sungbok, Neumann, Ulrich and Narayanan, Shrikanth. 2004. Analysis of Emotion Recognition using Facial Expressions, Speech and Multimodal Information. Proceedings of ACM 6th International Conference on Mutlmodal Interfaces (ICMI 2004), State College, PA, Oct 2004

Das, Dipankar, 2011. Analysis and Tracking of Emotions in English and Bengali Texts: A Computational Approach. Proceedings of the International World Wide Web Conference (WWW 2011), Ph. D. Symposium. 343-347.

Dynastream Innovations Inc., ANT AT3 RF Transceiver Chipset_Datasheet_Rev1.2, http://www.thisisant.com/.

Ku, Lun-Wei and Chen, Hsin-Hsi. 2007. Mining Opinions from the Web: Beyond Relevance Retrieval. Journal of American Society for Information Science and Technology, Special Issue on Mining Web Resources for Enhancing Information Retrieval, 58(12), 1838-1850.

Ku, Lun-Wei, Liu, I-Chien, Lee, Chia-Ying, Chen, Kuan-hua. and Chen, Hsin-His. 2008. Sentence-Level Opinion Analysis by CopeOpi in NTCIR-7. Proceedings of the 7th NTCIR Workshop Meeting, Tokyo, Japan. 260-267.

Lin, Kevin Hsin-Yih, Yang, Changhua, and Chen, Hsin-His. 2008. Emotion Classification of Online News Articles from the Reader's Perspective. Proceedings of the 2008 IEEE/WIC/ACM International Conference on Web Intelligence. 220-226.

Ortony, A. and Turner, T. J. 1990. What's basic about basic emotions? Psychological Review, 97, 315-331.

Parrott, W. 2001. Emotions in Social Psychology, Psychology Press, Philadelphia.

Sarwar, Badrul, Karypis, George, Konstan, Joseph, and Riedl, John. 2001. ItemBased Collaborative Filtering Recommendation Algorithms. Proceedings of the International World Wide Web Conference (WWW 2001), 285-295.

Su, Hsi-Yao. 2003. The Multilingual and Multi-Orthographic Taiwan-Based Internet: Creative Uses of Writing Systems on College-Affiliated BBSs. Journal of Computer-Mediated Communication 9(1). http://jcmc.indiana.edu/vol9/issue1/su.html.

Yang, Yi-Hsuan and Chen, Homer H., Fellow, IEEE. 2011. Ranking-Based Emotion Recognition for Music Organization and Retrieval. IEEE Transactions on audio, speech, and language processing, 19(4).

Zbikowski, Lawrence M., 2011. Music, Emotion, Analysis. Music Analysis, Blackwell Publishing Ltd, Oxford, UK.

Zhang, Jiawei and Dai, Jiaxing. 2006. Qiantan shixia qingnian wangluo yongyu – huoxing wen 浅探时下下 青 年 网 路 用 语 — 火 星 文 http://www.shs.edu.tw/works/essay/2006/03/2006032816043532.pdf

Zheng, Vincent W., Cao, Bin, Zheng, Yu, Xie, Xing and Yang, Qiang. 2010. Collaborative Filtering Meets Mobile Recommendation: A User-centered Approach Proceedings of Twenty-Fourth National Conference on Artificial Intelligence (AAAI-10).

INPRO_iSS: A Component for Just-In-Time Incremental Speech Synthesis

Timo Baumann
University of Hamburg
Department for Informatics
Germany
baumann@informatik.uni-hamburg.de

David Schlangen
University of Bielefeld
Faculty of Linguistics and Literary Studies
Germany
david.schlangen@uni-bielefeld.de

Abstract

We present a component for incremental speech synthesis (iSS) and a set of applications that demonstrate its capabilities. This component can be used to increase the responsivity and naturalness of spoken interactive systems. While iSS can show its full strength in systems that generate output incrementally, we also discuss how even otherwise unchanged systems may profit from its capabilities.

1 Introduction

Current state of the art in speech synthesis for spoken dialogue systems (SDSs) is for the synthesis component to expect full utterances (in textual form) as input and to deliver an audio stream verbalising this full utterance. At best, timing information is returned as well so that a control component can determine in case of an interruption / barge-in by the user where in the utterance this happened (Edlund, 2008; Matsuyama et al., 2010).

We want to argue here that providing capabilities to speech synthesis components for dealing with units smaller than full utterances can be beneficial for a whole range of interactive speech-based systems. In the easiest case, incremental synthesis simply reduces the utterance-initial delay before speech output starts, as output already starts when its beginning has been produced. In an otherwise conventional dialogue system, the synthesis module could make it possible to interrupt the output speech stream (e. g., when a noise event is detected that makes it likely that the user will not be able to hear what is being said), and continue production when the interruption is over. If other SDS components are adapted more to take advantage of incremental speech synthesis, even more flexible behaviours can be realised, such as providing utterances in *installments* (Clark, 1996) that prompt for backchannel signals, which in turn can prompt different utterance continuations, or starting an utterance before all information required in the utterance is available ("so, uhm, there are flights to Seoul on uh ..."), signaling that the turn is being held. Another, less conventional type of speech-based system that could profit from iSS is "babelfish-like" simultaneous speech-to-speech translation.

Research on architectures, higher-level processing modules and lower-level processing modules that would enable such behaviour is currently underway (Skantze and Schlangen, 2009; Skantze and Hjalmarsson, 2010; Baumann and Schlangen, 2011), but a synthesis component that would unlock the full potential of such strategies is so far missing. In this paper, we present such a component, which is capable of

(a) starting to speak before utterance processing has finished;
(b) handling edits made to (as-yet unspoken) parts of the utterance even while a prefix is already being spoken;
(c) enabling adaptations of delivery parameters such as speaking rate or pitch;
(d) autonomously making appropriate delivery-related decisions;
(e) providing information about progress in delivery; and, last but not least,
(f) running in real time.

Our iSS component is built on top of an existing non-incremental synthesis component, MaryTTS (Schröder and Trouvain, 2003), and on an existing architecture for incremental processing, INPROTK (Baumann and Schlangen, 2012).

Proceedings of the 50th Annual Meeting of the Association for Computational Linguistics, pages 103–108,
Jeju, Republic of Korea, 8-14 July 2012.

After a discussion of related work (Section 2), we describe the basic elements of our iSS component (Section 3) and some demonstrator applications that we created which showcase certain abilities.[1]

2 Related Work

Typically, in current SDSs utterances are generated (either by lookup/template-based generation, or, less commonly, by concept-to-utterance natural language generation (NLG)) and then synthesised in full (McTear, 2002). There is very little work on incremental synthesis (i.e., one that would work with units smaller than full utterances). Edlund (2008) outlines some requirements for incremental speech synthesis: to *give constant feedback* to the dialogue system about what has been delivered, to *be interruptible* (and possibly continue from that position), and to *run in real time*. Edlund (2008) also presents a prototype that meets these requirements, but is limited to diphone synthesis that is performed non-incrementally before utterance delivery starts. We go beyond this in processing just-in-time, and also enabling changes during delivery.

Skantze and Hjalmarsson (2010) describe a system that generates utterances incrementally (albeit in a WOz-enviroment), allowing earlier components to incrementally produce and revise their hypothesis about the user's utterance. The system can automatically play hesitations if by the time it has the turn it does not know what to produce yet. They show that users prefer such a system over a non-incremental one, even though it produced longer dialogues. Our approach is complementary to this work, as it targets a lower layer, the realisation or synthesis layer. Where their system relies on 'regular' speech synthesis which is called on relatively short utterance fragments (and thus pays for the increase in responsiveness with a reduction in synthesis quality, esp. regarding prosody), we aim to incrementalize the speech synthesis component itself.

Dutoit et al. (2011) have presented an incremental formulation for HMM-based speech synthesis. However, their system works offline and is fed by non-incrementally produced phoneme target sequences. We aim for a fully incremental speech synthesis component that can be integrated into dialogue systems.

There is some work on incremental NLG (Kilger and Finkler, 1995; Finkler, 1997; Guhe, 2007); however, that work does not concern itself with the actual synthesis of speech and hence describes only what would generate the input to our component.

3 Incremental Speech Synthesis

3.1 Background on Speech Synthesis

Text-to-speech (TTS) synthesis normally proceeds in a top-down fashion, starting on the utterance level (for stress patterns and sentence-level intonation) and descending to words and phonemes (for pronunciation details), in order to make globally optimised decisions (Taylor, 2009). In that way, target phoneme sequences annotated with durations and pitch contours are generated, in what is called the linguistic pre-processing step.

The then following synthesis step proper can be executed in one of several ways, with HMM-based and unit-selection synthesis currently being seen as producing the perceptually best results (Taylor, 2009). The former works by first turning the target sequence into a sequence of HMM states; a global optimization then computes a stream of vocoding features that optimize both HMM emission probabilities and continuity constraints (Tokuda et al., 2000). Finally, the parameter frames are fed to a vocoder which generates the speech audio signal. Unit-selection, in contrast, searches for the best sequence of (variably sized) units of speech in a large, annotated corpus of recordings, aiming to find a sequence that closely matches the target sequence.

As mentioned above, Dutoit et al. (2011) have presented an online formulation of the optimization step in HMM-based synthesis. Beyond this, two other factors influenced our decision to follow the HMM-based approach: (a) HMM-based synthesis nicely separates the production of vocoding parameter frames from the production of the speech audio signal, which allows for more fine-grained concurrent processing (see next subsection); (b) parameters are partially independent in the vocoding frames, which makes it possible to manipulate e. g. pitch independently (and outside of the HMM framework) without altering other parameters or deteriorating speech quality.

[1]The code of the toolkit and its iSS component and the demo applications discussed below have been released as open-source at `http://inprotk.sourceforge.net`.

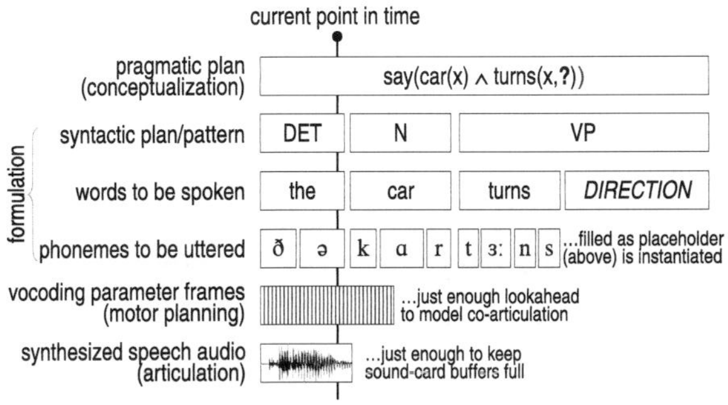

Figure 1: Hierarchic structure of incremental units describing an example utterance as it is being produced during utterance delivery.

3.2 System Architecture

Our component works by reducing the aforementioned top-down requirements. We found that it is not necessary to work out all details at one level of processing before starting to process at the next lower level. For example, not all *words* of the utterance need to be known to produce the sentence-level intonation (which itself however is necessary to determine pitch contours) as long as a structural outline of the utterance is available. Likewise, post-lexical phonological processes can be computed as long as a local context of one word is available; vocoding parameter computation (which must model co-articulation effects) in turn can be satisfied with just one phoneme of context; vocoding itself does not need any lookahead at all (aside from audio buffering considerations).

Thus, our component generates its data structures incrementally in a top-down-and-left-to-right fashion with different amounts of pre-planning, using several processing modules that work concurrently. This results in a 'triangular' structure (illustrated in Figure 1) where only the absolutely required minimum has to be specified at each level, allowing for later adaptations with few or no recomputations required.

As an aside, we observe that our component's architecture happens to correspond rather closely to Levelt's (1989) model of human speech production. Levelt distinguishes several, partially independent processing modules (conceptualization, formulation, articulation, see Figure 1) that function incrementally and "in a highly automatic, reflex-like way" (Levelt, 1989, p. 2).

3.3 Technical Overview of Our System

As a basis, we use MaryTTS (Schröder and Trouvain, 2003), but we replace Mary's internal data structures with structures that support incremental specifications; these we take from an extant incremental spoken dialogue system architecture and toolkit, INPROTK (Schlangen et al., 2010; Baumann and Schlangen, 2012). In this architecture, incremental processing as the processing of *incremental units* (IUs), which are the smallest 'chunks' of information at a specific level (such as words, or phonemes, as can be seen in Figure 1). IUs are interconnected to form a network (e. g. words keep links to their associated phonemes, and vice-versa) which stores the system's complete information state.

The iSS component takes an IU sequence of chunks of words as input (from an NLG component). Crucially, this sequence can then still be modified, through: (a) *continuations*, which simply link further words to the end of the sequence; or (b) *replacements*, where elements in the sequence are "unlinked" and other elements are spliced in. Additionally, a chunk can be marked as *open*; this has the effect of linking to a special *hesitation word*, which is produced only if it is not replaced (by the NLG) in time with other material.

Technically, the representation levels below the chunk level are generated in our component by MaryTTS's linguistic preprocessing and converting the output to IU structures. Our component provides for two modes of operation: Either using MaryTTS' HMM optimization routines which non-incrementally solve a large matrix operation and subsequently iteratively optimize the global variance constraint (Toda and Tokuda, 2007). Or, using the incremental algorithm as proposed by Dutoit et al. (2011). In our implementation of this algorithm, HMM emissions are computed with one phoneme of context in both directions; Dutoit et al. (2011) have found this setting to only slightly degrade synthesis quality. While the former mode incurs some utterance-initial delay, switching between alternatives and prosodic alteration can be performed at virtually no lookahead, while requiring just little lookahead for the truly incremental mode. The resulting vocoding frames then are attached to their corresponding phoneme units. Phoneme units then contain all the information

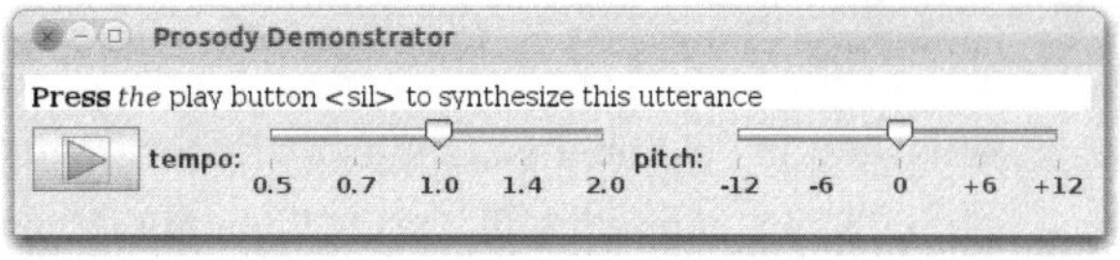

Figure 2: Example application that showcases just-in-time manipulation of prosodic aspects (tempo and pitch) of the ongoing utterance.

needed for the final vocoding step, in an accessible form, which makes possible various manipulations before the final synthesis step.

The lowest level module of our component is what may be called a *crawling vocoder*, which actively moves along the phoneme IU layer, querying each phoneme for its parameter frames one-by-one and producing the corresponding audio via vocoding. The vocoding algorithm is entirely incremental, making it possible to vocode "just-in-time": only when audio is needed to keep the sound card buffer full does the vocoder query for a next parameter frame. This is what gives the higher levels the maximal amount of time for re-planning, i. e., to be incremental.

3.4 Quality of Results

As these descriptions should have made clear, there are some elements in the processing steps in our iSS component that aren't yet fully incremental, such as assigning a sentence-level prosody. The best results are thus achieved if a full utterance is presented to the component initially, which is used for computation of prosody, and of which then elements may be changed (e. g., adjectives are replaced by different ones) on the fly. It is unavoidable, though, that there can be some "breaks" at the seams where elements are replaced. Moreover, the way feature frames can be modified (as described below) and the incremental HMM optimization method may lead to deviations from the global optimum. Finally, our system still relies on Mary's non-incremental HMM state selection technique which uses decision trees with non-incremental features.

However, preliminary evaluation of the component's prosody given varying amounts of lookahead indicate that degradations are reasonably small. Also, the benefits in naturalness of behaviour enabled by iSS may outweigh the drawback in prosodic quality.

4 Interface Demonstrations

We will describe the features of iSS, their implementation, their programming interface, and corresponding demo applications in the following subsections.

4.1 Low-Latency Changes to Prosody

Pitch and tempo can be adapted on the phoneme IU layer (see Figure 1). Figure 2 shows a demo interface to this functionality. Pitch is determined by a single parameter in the vocoding frames and can be adapted independently of other parameters in the HMM approach. We have implemented capabilities of adjusting all pitch values in a phoneme by an offset, or to change the values gradually for all frames in the phoneme. (The first feature is show-cased in the application in Figure 2, the latter is used to cancel utterance-final pitch changes when a continuation is appended to an ongoing utterance.) Tempo can be adapted by changing the phoneme units' durations which will then repeat (or skip) parameter frames (for lengthened or shortened phonemes, respectively) when passing them to the *crawling vocoder*. Adaptations are conducted with virtually no lookahead, that is, they can be executed even on a phoneme that is currently being output.

4.2 Feedback on Delivery

We implemented a fine-grained, hierarchical mechanism to give detailed feedback on delivery. A new *progress* field on IUs marks whether the IU's production is upcoming, ongoing, or completed. Listeners may subscribe to be notified about such progress changes using an update interface on IUs. The applications in Figures 2 and 4 make use of this interface to mark the words of the utterance in bold for completed, and in italic for ongoing words (incidentally, the screenshot in Figure 4 was taken exactly at the boundary between "delete" and "the").

4.3 Low-Latency Switching of Alternatives

A major goal of iSS is to change what is being said while the utterance is ongoing. Forward-pointing same-level links (SLLs, (Schlangen and Skantze, 2009; Baumann and Schlangen, 2012)) as shown in Figure 3 allow to construct alternative utterance paths beforehand. Deciding on the actual utterance continuation is a simple re-ranking of the forward

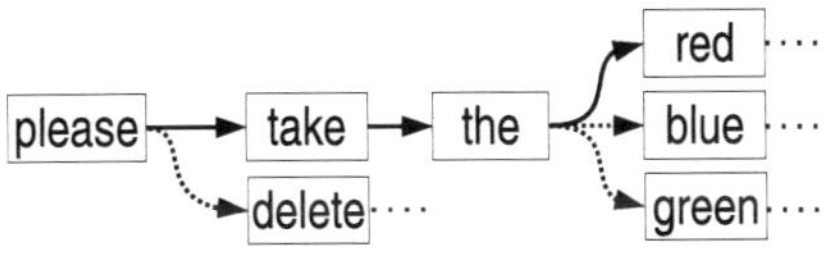

Figure 3: Incremental units chained together via forward-pointing same-level links to form an utterance tree.

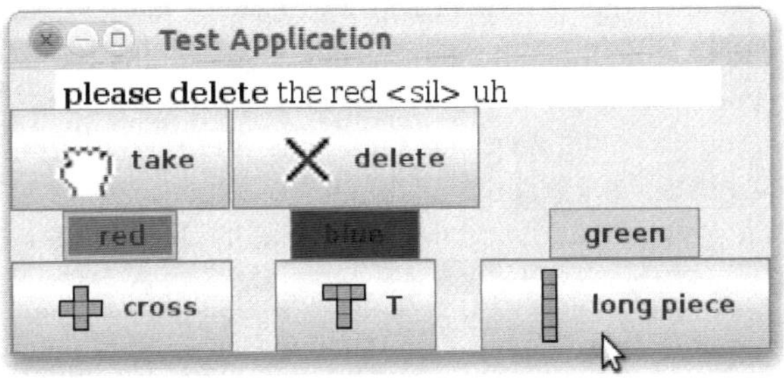

Figure 4: Example application to showcase just-in-time selection between different paths in a complex utterance.

SLLs which can be changed until immediately before the word (or phoneme) in question is being uttered.

The demo application shown in Figure 4 allows the user to select the path through a fairly complex utterance tree. The user has already decided on the color, but not on the type of piece to be deleted and hence the currently selected plan is to play a hesitation (see below).

4.4 Extension of the Ongoing Utterance

In the previous subsection we have shown how alternatives in utterances can be selected with very low latency. Adding continuations (or alternatives) to an ongoing utterance incurs some delay (some hundred milliseconds), as we ensure that an appropriate sentence-level prosody for the alternative (or continuation) is produced by re-running the linguistic pre-processing on the complete utterance; we then integrate only the new, changed parts into the IU structure (or, if there still is time, parts just before the change, to account for co-articulation).

Thus, practical applications which use incremental NLG must generate their next steps with some lookahead to avoid stalling the output. However, utterances can be marked as non-final, which results in a special hesitation word being inserted, as explained below.

4.5 Autonomously Performing Disfluencies

In a multi-threaded, real-time system, the *crawling vocoder* may reach the end of synthesis before the NLG component (in its own thread) has been able to add a continuation to the ongoing utterance. To avoid this case, special *hesitation word*s can be inserted at the end of a yet unfinished utterance. If the crawling vocoder nears such a word, a hesitation will be played, unless a continuation is available. In that case, the hesitation is skipped (or aborted if currently ongoing).[2]

4.6 Type-to-Speech

A final demo application show-cases truly incremental HMM synthesis taken to its most extreme: A text input window is presented, and each word that is typed is treated as a single-word chunk which is immediately sent to the incremental synthesizer. (For this demonstration, synthesis is slowed to half the regular speed, to account for slow typing speeds and to highlight the prosodic improvements when more right context becomes available to iSS.) A use case with a similar (but probably lower) level of incrementality could be simultaneous speech-to-speech translation, or type-to-speech for people with speech disabilities.

5 Conclusions

We have presented a component for incremental speech synthesis (iSS) and demonstrated its capabilities with a number of example applications. This component can be used to increase the responsivity and naturalness of spoken interactive systems. While iSS can show its full strengths in systems that also generate output incrementally (a strategy which is currently seeing some renewed attention), we discussed how even otherwise unchanged systems may profit from its capabilities, e. g., in the presence of intermittent noise. We provide this component in the hope that it will help spur research on incremental natural language generation and more interactive spoken dialogue systems, which so far had to made do with inadequate ways of realising its output.

[2]Thus, in contrast to (Skantze and Hjalmarsson, 2010), hesitations do not take up any additional time.

References

Timo Baumann and David Schlangen. 2011. Predicting the Micro-Timing of User Input for an Incremental Spoken Dialogue System that Completes a User's Ongoing Turn. In *Proceedings of SigDial 2011*, pages 120–129, Portland, USA, June.

Timo Baumann and David Schlangen. 2012. The INPROTK 2012 release. In *Proceedings of SDCTD*. to appear.

Herbert H. Clark. 1996. *Using Language*. Cambridge University Press.

Thierry Dutoit, Maria Astrinaki, Onur Babacan, Nicolas d'Alessandro, and Benjamin Picart. 2011. pHTS for Max/MSP: A Streaming Architecture for Statistical Parametric Speech Synthesis. Technical Report 1, numediart Research Program on Digital Art Technologies, March.

Jens Edlund. 2008. Incremental speech synthesis. In *Second Swedish Language Technology Conference*, pages 53–54, Stockholm, Sweden, November. System Demonstration.

Wolfgang Finkler. 1997. *Automatische Selbstkorrektur bei der inkrementellen Generierung gesprochener Sprache unter Realzeitbedingungen*. Dissertationen zur Künstlichen Intelligenz. infix Verlag.

Markus Guhe. 2007. *Incremental Conceptualization for Language Production*. Lawrence Erlbaum Asso., Inc., Mahwah, USA.

Anne Kilger and Wolfgang Finkler. 1995. Incremental Generation for Real-time Applications. Technical Report RR-95-11, DFKI, Saarbrücken, Germany.

William J.M. Levelt. 1989. *Speaking: From Intention to Articulation*. MIT Press.

Kyoko Matsuyama, Kazunori Komatani, Ryu Takeda, Toru Takahashi, Tetsuya Ogata, and Hiroshi G. Okuno. 2010. Analyzing User Utterances in Barge-in-able Spoken Dialogue System for Improving Identification Accuracy. In *Proceedings of Interspeech*, pages 3050–3053, Makuhari, Japan, September.

Michael McTear. 2002. *Spoken Dialogue Technology. Toward the Conversational User-Interface*. Springer, London, UK.

David Schlangen and Gabriel Skantze. 2009. A General, Abstract Model of Incremental Dialogue Processing. In *Proceedings of the EACL*, Athens, Greece.

David Schlangen, Timo Baumann, Hendrik Buschmeier, Okko Buß, Stefan Kopp, Gabriel Skantze, and Ramin Yaghoubzadeh. 2010. Middleware for Incremental Processing in Conversational Agents. In *Proceedings of SigDial 2010*, pages 51–54, Tokyo, Japan, September.

Marc Schröder and Jürgen Trouvain. 2003. The German Text-to-Speech Synthesis System MARY: A Tool for Research, Development and Teaching. *International Journal of Speech Technology*, 6(3):365–377, October.

Gabriel Skantze and Anna Hjalmarsson. 2010. Towards incremental speech generation in dialogue systems. In *Proceedings of SigDial 2010*, pages 1–8, Tokyo, Japan, September.

Gabriel Skantze and David Schlangen. 2009. Incremental dialogue processing in a micro-domain. In *Proceedings of EACL 2009*, Athens, Greece, April.

Paul Taylor. 2009. *Text-to-Speech Synthesis*. Cambridge Univ Press, Cambridge, UK.

Tomoki Toda and Keiichi Tokuda. 2007. A Speech Parameter Generation Algorithm Considering Global Variance for HMM-based Speech Synthesis. *IEICE Transactions on Information and Systems*, 90(5):816–824.

Keiichi Tokuda, Takayoshi Yoshimura, Takashi Masuko, Takao Kobayashi, and Tadashi Kitamura. 2000. Speech Parameter Generation Algorithms for HMM-based Speech Synthesis. In *Proceedings of ICASSP 2000*, pages 1315–1318, Istanbul, Turkey.

WizIE: A Best Practices Guided Development Environment for Information Extraction

Yunyao Li **Laura Chiticariu** **Huahai Yang** **Frederick R. Reiss** **Arnaldo Carreno-fuentes**
IBM Research - Almaden
650 Harry Road
San Jose, CA 95120
{yunyaoli,chiti,hyang,frreiss,acarren}@us.ibm.com

Abstract

Information extraction (IE) is becoming a critical building block in many enterprise applications. In order to satisfy the increasing text analytics demands of enterprise applications, it is crucial to enable developers with general computer science background to develop high quality IE extractors. In this demonstration, we present WizIE, an IE development environment intended to reduce the development life cycle and enable developers with little or no linguistic background to write high quality IE rules. WizIE provides an integrated wizard-like environment that guides IE developers step-by-step throughout the entire development process, based on best practices synthesized from the experience of expert developers. In addition, WizIE reduces the manual effort involved in performing key IE development tasks by offering automatic result explanation and rule discovery functionality. Preliminary results indicate that WizIE is a step forward towards enabling extractor development for novice IE developers.

1 Introduction

Information Extraction (IE) refers to the problem of extracting structured information from unstructured or semi-structured text. It has been well-studied by the Natural Language Processing research community for a long time. In recent years, IE has emerged as a critical building block in a wide range of enterprise applications, including financial risk analysis, social media analytics and regulatory compliance, among many others. An important practical challenge driven by the use of IE in these applications is usability (Chiticariu et al., 2010c): specifically, how to enable the ease of development and maintenance of high-quality information extraction rules, also known as *annotators*, or *extractors*.

Developing extractors is a notoriously labor-intensive and time-consuming process. In order to ensure highly accurate and reliable results, this task is traditionally performed by trained linguists with domain expertise. As a result, extractor development is regarded as a major bottleneck in satisfying the increasing text analytics demands of enterprise applications. Hence, reducing the extractor development life cycle is a critical requirement. Towards this goal, we have built WizIE, an IE development environment designed primarily to (1) enable developers with little or no linguistic background to write high quality extractors, and (2) reduce the overall manual effort involved in extractor development.

Previous work on improving the usability of IE systems has mainly focused on reducing the manual effort involved in extractor development (Brauer et al., 2011; Li et al., 2008; Li et al., 2011a; Soderland, 1999; Liu et al., 2010). In contrast, the focus of WizIE is on lowering the extractor development entry barrier by means of a wizard-like environment that guides extractor development based on best practices drawn from the experience of trained linguists and expert developers. In doing so, WizIE also provides natural entry points for different tools focused on reducing the effort required for performing common tasks during IE development.

Underlying our WizIE are a state-of-the-art IE rule language and corresponding runtime engine (Chiticariu et al., 2010a; Li et al., 2011b). The runtime engine and WizIE are commercially avail-

Proceedings of the 50th Annual Meeting of the Association for Computational Linguistics, pages 109–114,
Jeju, Republic of Korea, 8-14 July 2012. ©2012 Association for Computational Linguistics

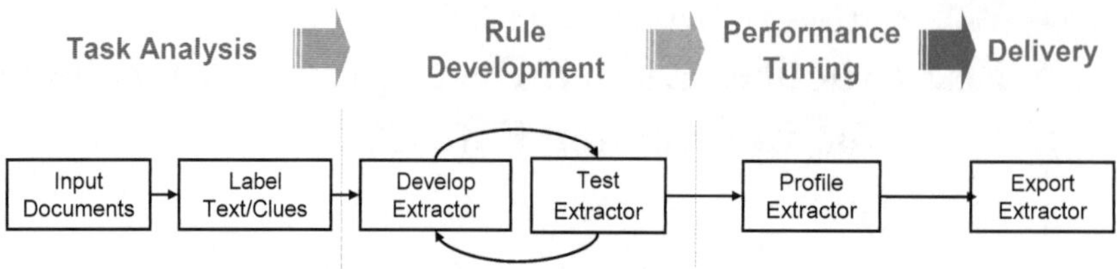

Figure 1: Best Practices for Extractor Development

able as part of IBM InfoSphere BigInsights (IBM, 2012).

2 System Overview

The development process for high-quality, high-performance extractors consists of four phases, as illustrated in Fig. 1. First, in the *Task Analysis* phase, concrete extraction tasks are defined based on high-level business requirements. For each extraction task, IE rules are developed during the *Rule Development* phase. The rules are profiled and further fine-tuned in the *Performance Tuning* phase, to ensure high runtime performance. Finally, in the *Delivery* phase, the rules are packaged so that they can be easily embedded in various applications.

WizIE is designed to assist and enable both novice and experienced developers by providing an intuitive wizard-like interface that is informed by the best practices in extractor development throughout each of these phases. By doing so, WizIE seeks to provide the key missing pieces in a conventional IE development environment (Cunningham et al., 2002; Li et al., 2011b; Soundrarajan et al., 2011), based on our experience as expert IE developers, as well as our interactions with novice developers with general computer science background, but little text analytics experience, during the development of several enterprise applications.

3 The Development Environment

In this section, we present the general functionality of WizIE in the context of extraction tasks driven by real business use cases from the media and entertainment domain. We describe WizIE in details and show how it guides and assists IE developers in a step-by-step fashion, based on best practices.

3.1 Task Analysis

The high-level business requirement of our running example is to identify *intention to purchase* for movies from online forums. Such information is of great interest to marketers as it helps predict future purchases (Howard and Sheth, 1969). During the first phrase of IE development (Fig. 2), WizIE guides the rule developer in turning such a high-level business requirement into concrete extraction tasks by explicitly asking her to select and manually examine a small number [1] of sample documents, identify and label snippets of interest in the sample documents, and capture clues that help to identify such snippets.

The definition and context of the concrete extraction tasks are captured by a tree structure called the *extraction plan* (e.g. right panel in Fig. 2). Each leaf node in an extraction plan corresponds to an atomic extraction task, while the non-leaf nodes denote higher-level tasks based on one or more atomic extraction tasks. For instance, in our running example, the business question of identifying intention of purchase for movies has been converted into the extraction task of identifying *MovieIntent* mentions, which involves two atomic extraction tasks: identifying *Movie* mentions and *Intent* mentions.

The extraction plan created, as we will describe later, plays a key role in the IE development process in WizIE. Such tight coupling of task analysis with actual extractor development is a key departure from conventional IE development environments.

3.2 Rule Development

Once concrete extraction tasks are defined, WizIE guides the IE developer to write actual rules based on best practices. Fig. 3(a) shows a screenshot of the second phase of building an extractor, the *Rule Development* phase. The *Extraction Task* panel on the left provides information and tips for rule development, whereas the *Extraction Plan* panel on the right guides the actual rule development for each extraction task. As shown in the figure, the types of rules associated with each label node fall into three categories: *Basic Features*, *Can-*

[1] The exact sample size varies by task type.

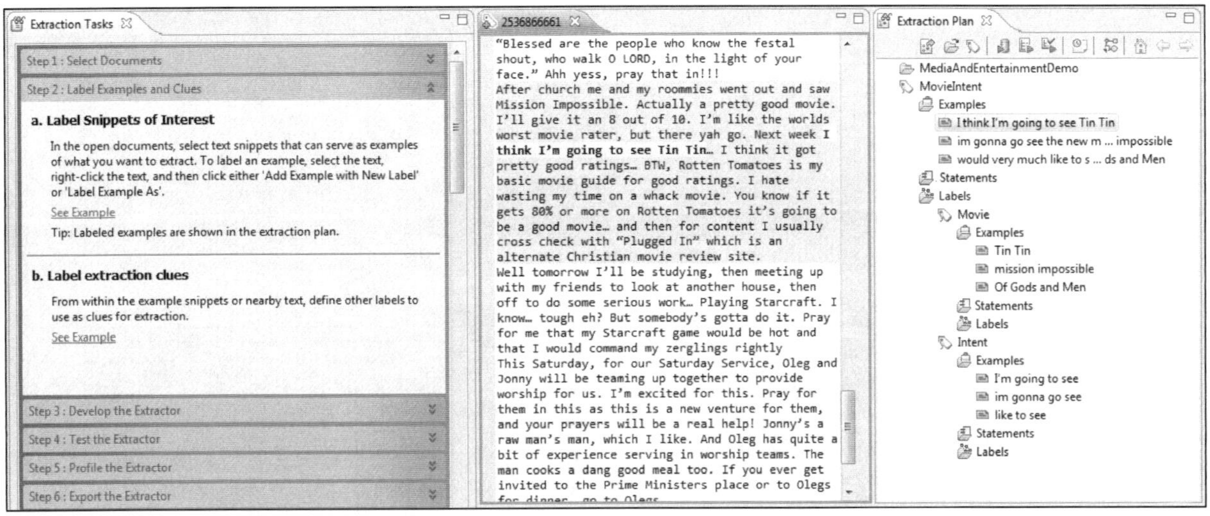

Figure 2: Labeling Snippets and Clues of Interest

didate Generation and *Filter&Consolidate*. This categorization is based on best practices for rule development (Chiticariu et al., 2010b). As such, the extraction plan groups together the high-level specification of extraction tasks via examples, and the actual implementation of those tasks via rules.

The developer creates rules directly in the Rule Editor, or via the *Create Statement* wizard, accessible from the *Statements* node of each label in the Extraction Plan panel:

The wizard allows the user to select a type for the new rule, from predefined sets for each of the three categories. The types of rules exposed in each category are informed by best practices. For example, the Basic Features category includes rules for defining basic features using regular expressions, dictionaries or part of speech information, whereas the Candidate Generation category includes rules for combining basic features into candidate mentions by means of operations such as sequence or alternation. Once the developer provides a name for the new rule (*view*) and selects its type, the appropriate rule template (such as the one illustrated below) is automatically generated in an appropriate file on disk and displayed in the editor, for further editing [2].

```
create dictionary MovieNameCandidateDict
from file '<path to your dictionary here>'
with language as 'en';

create view MovieNameCandidate as
extract dictionary 'MovieNameCandidateDict'
    on R.<input column> as match
from <input view> R;
```

Once the developer completes an iteration of rule development, WizIE guides her in testing and refining the extractor, as shown in Fig. 3(b). The *Annotation Explorer* at the bottom of the screen gives a global view of the extraction results, while other panels highlight individual results in the context of the original input documents. The Annotation Explorer enables filtering and searching results, and comparing results with those from a previous iteration. WizIE also provides a facility for manually labeling a document collection with "ground truth" annotations, then comparing the extraction results with the ground truth in order to formally evaluate the quality of the extractor and avoid regressions during the development process.

An important differentiator of WizIE compared with conventional IE development environments is a suite of sophisticated tools for automatic *result explanation* and *rule discovery*. We briefly describe them next.

Provenance Viewer. When the user clicks on an extracted result, the Provenance Viewer shows a complete explanation of how that result has been pro-

[2] Details on the rule syntax can be found in (IBM,)

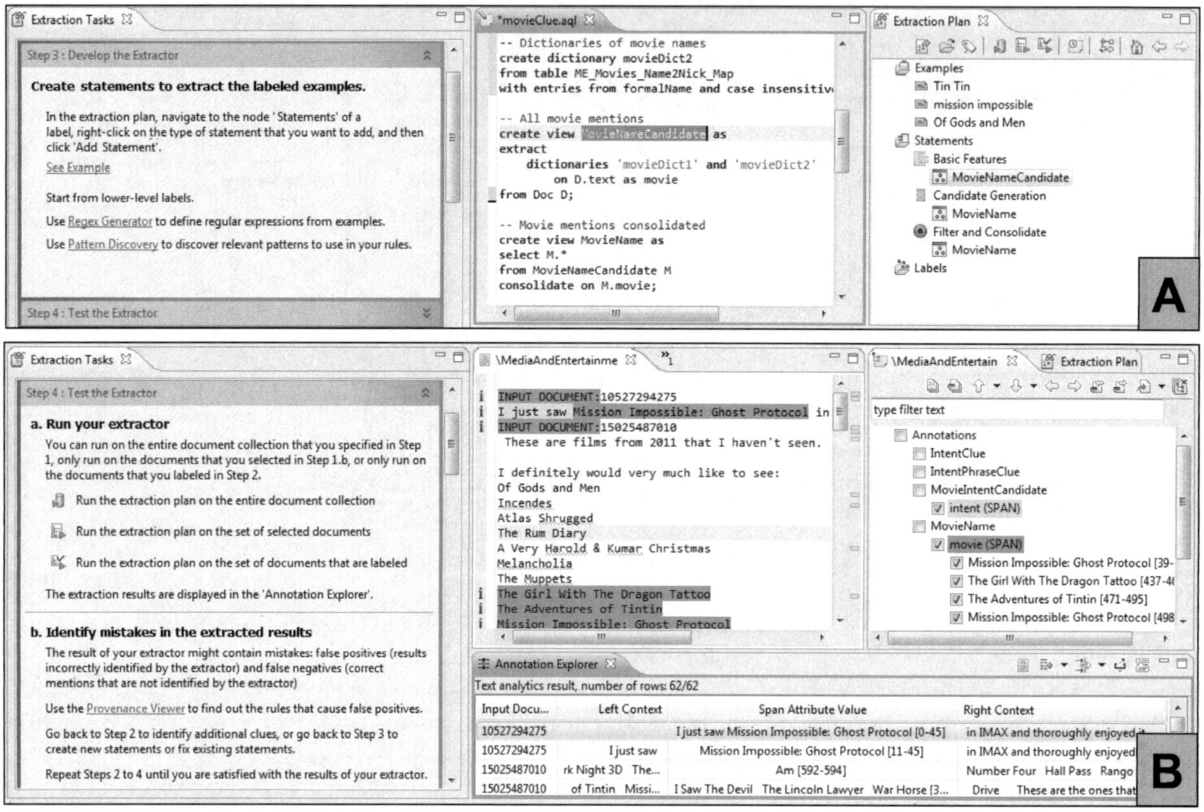

Figure 3: Extractor Development: (a) Developing, and (b) Testing.

duced by the extractor, in the form of a graph that demonstrates the sequence of rules and individual pieces of text responsible for that result. Such explanations are critical to enable the developer to understand why a false positive is generated by the system, and identify problematic rule(s) that could be refined in order to correct the mistake. An example explanation for an incorrect *MovieIntent* mention *"I just saw Mission Impossible"* is shown below.

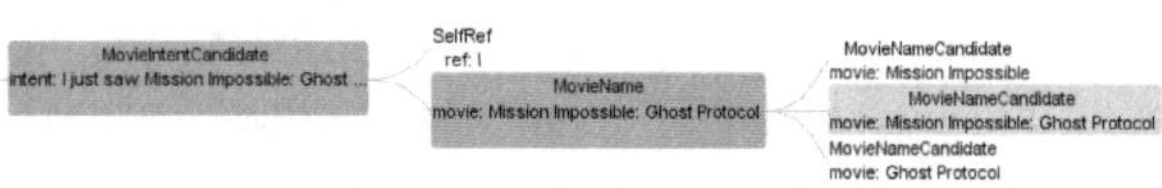

As can be seen, the *MovieIntent* mention is generated by combining a *SelfRef* (matching first person pronouns) with a *MovieName* mention, and in turn, the latter is obtained by combining several *MovieNameCandidate* mentions. With this information, the developer can quickly determine that the *SelfRef* and *MovieName* mentions are correct, but their combination in *MovieIntentCandidate* is problematic. She can then proceed to refine the *MovieIntentCandidate* rule, for example, by avoiding any *MovieIntentCandidate* mentions containing a past tense verb form such as *saw*, since past tense in not usually indicative of intent (Liu et al., 2010).

Pattern Discovery. Negative contextual clues such as the verb *"saw"* above are useful for creating rules that filter out false positives. Conversely, positive clues such as the phrase *"will see"* are useful for creating rules that separate ambiguous matches from high-precision matches. WizIE's *Pattern Discovery* component facilitates automatic discovery of such clues by mining available sample data for common patterns in specific contexts (Li et al., 2011a). For example, when instructed to analyze the context between *SelfRef* and *MovieName* mentions, Pattern Discovery finds a suite of common patterns as shown in Fig. 4. The developer can analyze these patterns and choose those suitable for refining the rules. For example, patterns such as *"have to see"* can be seen as positive clues for intent, whereas phrases such as *"took ... to see"* or *"went to see"* are negative clues, and can be used for filtering false positives.

Regular Expression Generator. WizIE also enables the discovery of regular expression patterns. The Regular Expression Generator takes as input a

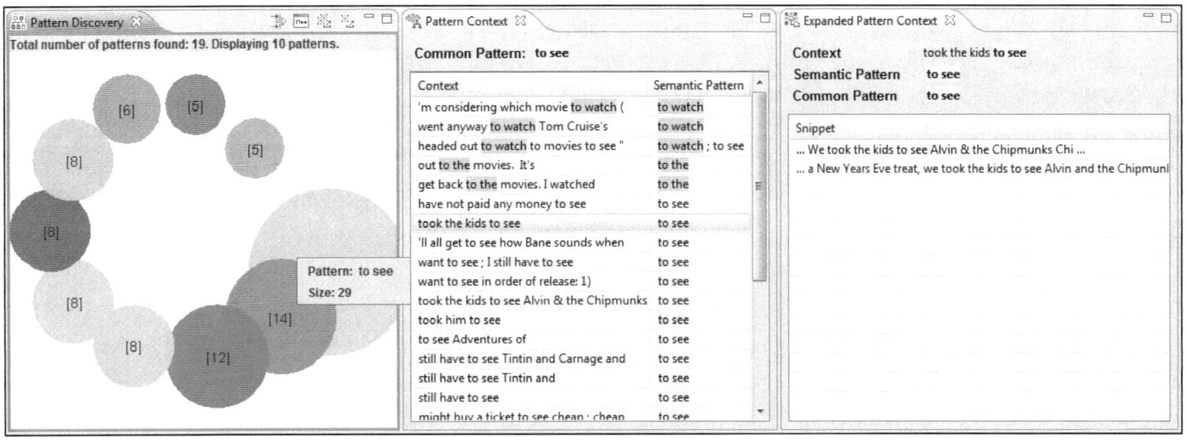

Figure 4: Pattern Discovery

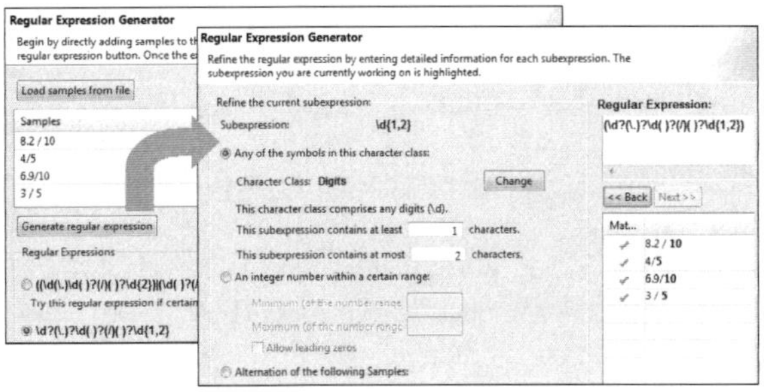

Figure 5: Regular Expression Generator

set of sample mentions and suggests regular expressions that capture the samples, ranging from more specific (higher accuracy) to more general expressions (higher coverage). Figure 5 shows two regular expressions automatically generated based on mentions of movie ratings, and how the developer is subsequently assisted in understanding and refining the generated expression. In our experience, regular expressions are complex concepts that are difficult to develop for both expert and novice developers. Therefore, such a facility to generate expressions based on examples is extremely useful.

3.3 Performance Tuning

Once the developer is satisfied with the quality of the extractor, WizIE guides her in measuring and tuning its runtime performance, in preparation for deploying the extractor in a production environment. The Profiler observes the execution of the extractor on a sample input collection over a period of time and records the percentage of time spent executing each rule, or performing certain runtime operations. After the profiling run completes, WizIE displays the top *25* most expensive rules and runtime operations, and the overall throughput (amount of input data processed per unit of time). Based on this information, the developer can hand-tune the critical parts of the extractor, rerun the Profiler, and validate an increase in throughput. She would repeat this process until satisfied with the extractor's runtime performance.

3.4 Delivery and Deployment

Once satisfied with both the result quality and runtime performance, the developer is guided by WizIE's Export wizard through the process of exporting the extractor in a compiled executable form. The generated executable can be embedded in an application using a Java API interface. WizIE can also wrap the executable plan in a pre-packaged application that can be run in a map-reduce environment, then deploy this application on a Hadoop cluster.

4 Evaluation

A preliminary user study was conducted to evaluate the effectiveness of WizIE in enabling novice IE developers. The study included 14 participants, all employed at a major technology company. In the pre-study survey, 10 of the participants reported no prior experience with IE tasks, two of them have seen demonstrations of IE systems, and two had brief involvement in IE development, but no experience with WizIE. For the question *"According to your understanding, how easy is it to build IE applications in general ?"*, the median rating was 5, on a scale of 1 (very easy) to 7 (very difficult).

The study was conducted during a 2-day training session. In Day 1, participants were given a thorough introduction to IE, shown example extractors, and instructed to develop extractors without WizIE. Towards the end of Day 1, participants were asked to solve an IE exercise: develop an extractor for the high-level requirement of identifying mentions of company revenue by division from the company's official press releases. WizIE was introduced to the participants in Day 2 of the training, and its features were demonstrated and explained with examples. Participants were then asked to complete the same exercise as in Day 1. Authors of this demonstration were present to help participants during the exercises in both days. At the end of each day, participants filled out a survey about their experience.

In Day 1, none of the participants were able to complete the exercise after 90 minutes. In the survey, one participant wrote *"I am in sales so it is all difficult"*; another participant indicated that *"I don't think I would be able to recreate the example on my own from scratch"*. In Day 2, most participants were able to complete the exercise in 90 minutes or less using WizIE. In fact, two participants created extractors with accuracy and coverage of over 90%, when measured against the ground truth. Overall, the participants were much more confident about creating extractors. One participant wrote *"My first impression is very good"*. On the other hand, another participant asserted that *"The nature of the task is still difficult"*. They also found that WizIE is useful and easy to use, and it is easier to build extractors with the help of WizIE.

In summary, our preliminary results indicate that WizIE is a step forward towards enabling extractor development for novice IE developers. In order to formally evaluate WizIE, we are currently conducting a formal study of using WizIE to create extractors for several real business applications.

5 Demonstration

In this demonstration we showcase WizIE's step-by-step approach to guide the developer in the iterative process of IE rule development, from task analysis to developing, tuning and deploying the extractor in a production environment. Our demonstration is centered around the high-level business requirement of identifying intent to purchase movies from blogs and forum posts as described in Section 3. We start by demonstrating the process of developing two relatively simple extractors for identifying *MovieIntent* and *MovieRating* mentions. We then showcase complex state-of-the-art extractors for identifying *buzz* and *sentiment* for the media and entertainment domain, to illustrate the quality and runtime performance of extractors built with WizIE.

References

F. Brauer, R. Rieger, A. Mocan, and W. M. Barczynski. 2011. Enabling information extraction by inference of regular expressions from sample entities. In *CIKM*.

L. Chiticariu, R. Krishnamurthy, Y. Li, S. Raghavan, F. Reiss, and S. Vaithyanathan. 2010a. SystemT: an algebraic approach to declarative information extraction. ACL.

L. Chiticariu, R. Krishnamurthy, Y. Li, F. Reiss, and S. Vaithyanathan. 2010b. Domain adaptation of rule-based annotators for named-entity recognition tasks. EMNLP.

L. Chiticariu, Y. Li, S. Raghavan, and F. Reiss. 2010c. Enterprise Information Extraction: Recent Developments and Open Challenges. In *SIGMOD (Tutorials)*.

H. Cunningham, D. Maynard, K. Bontcheva, and V. Tablan. 2002. Gate: an architecture for development of robust hlt applications. In *ACL*.

J.A. Howard and J.N. Sheth. 1969. *The Theory of Buyer Behavior*. Wiley.

IBM. InfoSphere BigInsights - Annotation Query Language (AQL) reference. http://ibm.co/kkzj1i.

IBM. 2012. InfoSphere BigInsights. http://ibm.co/jjbjfa.

Y. Li, R. Krishnamurthy, S. Raghavan, S. Vaithyanathan, and H. V. Jagadish. 2008. Regular expression learning for information extraction. In *EMNLP*.

Y. Li, V. Chu, S. Blohm, H. Zhu, and H. Ho. 2011a. Facilitating pattern discovery for relation extraction with semantic-signature-based clustering. In *CIKM*.

Y. Li, F. Reiss, and L. Chiticariu. 2011b. SystemT: A Declarative Information Extraction System. In *ACL (Demonstration)*.

B. Liu, L. Chiticariu, V. Chu, H. V. Jagadish, and F. Reiss. 2010. Automatic Rule Refinement for Information Extraction. *PVLDB*, 3(1):588–597.

S. Soderland. 1999. Learning information extraction rules for semi-structured and free text. *Machine Learning*, 34(1-3):233–272, February.

B. R. Soundrarajan, T. Ginter, and S. L. DuVall. 2011. An interface for rapid natural language processing development in UIMA. In *ACL (Demonstrations)*.

A System for Real-time Twitter Sentiment Analysis of 2012 U.S. Presidential Election Cycle

Hao Wang*, Dogan Can, Abe Kazemzadeh**,**
François Bar* and Shrikanth Narayanan**
Annenberg Innovation Laboratory (AIL)*
Signal Analysis and Interpretation Laboratory (SAIL)**
University of Southern California, Los Angeles, CA
{haowang@, dogancan@, kazemzad@, fbar@, shri@sipi}.usc.edu

Abstract

This paper describes a system for real-time analysis of public sentiment toward presidential candidates in the 2012 U.S. election as expressed on Twitter, a micro-blogging service. Twitter has become a central site where people express their opinions and views on political parties and candidates. Emerging events or news are often followed almost instantly by a burst in Twitter volume, providing a unique opportunity to gauge the relation between expressed public sentiment and electoral events. In addition, sentiment analysis can help explore how these events affect public opinion. While traditional content analysis takes days or weeks to complete, the system demonstrated here analyzes sentiment in the entire Twitter traffic about the election, delivering results instantly and continuously. It offers the public, the media, politicians and scholars a new and timely perspective on the dynamics of the electoral process and public opinion.

1 Introduction

Social media platforms have become an important site for political conversations throughout the world. In the year leading up to the November 2012 presidential election in the United States, we have developed a tool for real-time analysis of sentiment expressed through Twitter, a micro-blogging service, toward the incumbent President, Barack Obama, and the nine republican challengers - four of whom remain in the running as of this writing. With this analysis, we seek to explore whether Twitter provides insights into the unfolding of the campaigns and indications of shifts in public opinion.

Twitter allows users to post tweets, messages of up to 140 characters, on its social network. Twitter usage is growing rapidly. The company reports over 100 million active users worldwide, together sending over 250 million tweets each day (Twitter, 2012). It was actively used by 13% of on-line American adults as of May 2011, up from 8% a year prior (Pew Research Center, 2011). More than two thirds of U.S. congress members have created a Twitter account and many are actively using Twitter to reach their constituents (Lassen & Brown, 2010; TweetCongress, 2012). Since October 12, 2012, we have gathered over 36 million tweets about the 2012 U.S. presidential candidates, a quarter million per day on average. During one of the key political events, the Dec 15, 2011 primary debate in Iowa, we collected more than half a million relevant tweets in just a few hours. This kind of 'big data' vastly outpaces the capacity of traditional content analysis approaches, calling for novel computational approaches.

Most work to date has focused on post-facto analysis of tweets, with results coming days or even months after the collection time. However,

Proceedings of the 50th Annual Meeting of the Association for Computational Linguistics, pages 115–120,
Jeju, Republic of Korea, 8-14 July 2012.

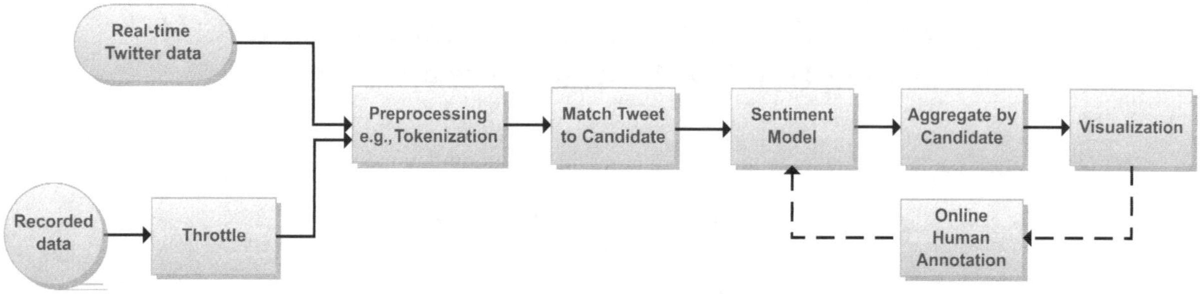

Figure 1. The system architecture for real-time processing Twitter data

because tweets are short and easy to send, they lend themselves to quick and dynamic expression of instant reactions to current events. We expect automated real-time sentiment analysis of this user-generated data can provide fast indications of changes in opinion, showing for example how an audience reacts to particular candidate's statements during a political debate. The system we present here, along with the dashboards displaying analysis results with drill-down ability, is precisely aimed at generating real-time insights as events unfold.

Beyond the sheer scale of the task and the need to keep up with a rapid flow of tweets, we had to address two additional issues. First, the vernacular used on Twitter differs significantly from common language and we have trained our sentiment model on its idiosyncrasies. Second, tweets in general, and political tweets in particular, tend to be quite sarcastic, presenting significant challenges for computer models (González-Ibáñez et al., 2011). We will present our approaches to these issues in a separate publication. Here, we focus on presenting the overall system and the visualization dashboards we have built. In section 2, we begin with a review of related work; we then turn in section 3 to a description of our system's architecture and its components (input, preprocessing, sentiment model, result aggregation, and visualization); in sections 4 and 5 we evaluate our early experience with this system and discuss next steps.

2 Related Work

In the last decade, interest in mining sentiment and opinions in text has grown rapidly, due in part to the large increase of the availability of documents and messages expressing personal opinions (Pang & Lee, 2008). In particular, sentiment in Twitter data has been used for prediction or measurement in a variety of domains, such as stock market, politics and social movements (Bollen et al., 2011; Choy et al., 2011; Tumasjan et al., 2010; Zeitzoff, 2011). For example, Tumasjan (2010) found tweet volume about the political parties to be a good predictor for the outcome of the 2009 German election, while Choy et al. (2011) failed to predict with Twitter sentiment the ranking of the four candidates in Singapore's 2011 presidential election.

Past studies of political sentiment on social networks have been either post-hoc and/or carried out on small and static samples. To address these issues, we built a unique infrastructure and sentiment model to analyze in real-time public sentiment on Twitter toward the 2012 U.S. presidential candidates. Our effort to gauge political sentiment is based on bringing together social science scholarship with advanced computational methodology: our approach combines real-time data processing and statistical sentiment modeling informed by, and contributing to, an understanding of the cultural and political practices at work through the use of Twitter.

3 The System

For accuracy and speed, we built our real-time data processing infrastructure on the IBM's InfoSphere Streams platform (IBM, 2012), which enables us to write our own analysis and visualization modules and assemble them into a real-time processing pipeline. Streams applications are highly scalable so we can adjust our system to handle higher volume of data by adding more servers and by distributing processing tasks. Twitter traffic often balloons during big events (e.g. televised debates or primary election days) and stays low between events, making high scalability strongly desirable. Figure 1 shows our system's architecture and its modules. Next, we introduce our data source and each individual module.

3.1 Input/Data Source

We chose the micro-blogging service Twitter as our data source because it is a major source of online political commentary and discussion in the U.S. People comment on and discuss politics by posting messages and 're-tweeting' others' messages. It played a significant role in political events worldwide, such as the Arab Spring Movement and the Moldovian protests in 2009. In response to events, Twitter volume goes up sharply and significantly. For example, during a republican debate, we receive several hundred thousand to a million tweets in just a few hours for all the candidates combined.

Twitter's public API provides only 1% or less of its entire traffic (the "firehose"), without control over the sampling procedure, which is likely insufficient for accurate analysis of public sentiment. Instead, we collect all relevant tweets in real-time from the entire Twitter traffic via Gnip Power Track, a commercial Twitter data provider. To cope with this challenge during the later stages of the campaign, when larger Twitter traffic is expected, our system can handle huge traffic bursts over short time periods by distributing the processing to more servers, even though most of the times its processing load is minimal.

Since our application targets the political domain (specifically the current Presidential election cycle), we manually construct rules that are simple logical keyword combinations to retrieve relevant tweets – those about candidates and events (including common typos in candidate names). For example, our rules for Mitt Romney include *Romney, @MittRomney, @PlanetRomney, @MittNews, @believeinromney, #romney, #mitt, #mittromney, and #mitt2012*. Our system is tracking the tweets for nine Republican candidates (some of whom have suspended their campaign) and Barack Obama using about 200 rules in total.

3.2 Preprocessing

The text of tweets differs from the text in articles, books, or even spoken language. It includes many idiosyncratic uses, such as emoticons, URLs, *RT* for re-tweet, @ for user mentions, # for hashtags, and repetitions. It is necessary to preprocess and normalize the text.

As standard in NLP practices, the text is tokenized for later processing. We use certain rules to handle the special cases in tweets. We compared several Twitter-specific tokenizers, such as TweetMotif (O'Connor et al., 2010) and found Christopher Potts' basic Twitter tokenizer best suited as our base. In summary, our tokenizer correctly handles URLs, common emoticons, phone numbers, HTML tags, twitter mentions and hashtags, numbers with fractions and decimals, repetition of symbols and Unicode characters (see Figure 2 for an example).

3.3 Sentiment Model

The design of the sentiment model used in our system was based on the assumption that the opinions expressed would be highly subjective and contextualized. Therefore, for generating data for model training and testing, we used a crowd-sourcing approach to do sentiment annotation on in-domain political data.

To create a baseline sentiment model, we used Amazon Mechanical Turk (AMT) to get as varied a population of annotators as possible. We designed an interface that allowed annotators to perform the annotations outside of AMT so that they could participate anonymously. The Turkers were asked their age, gender, and to describe their political orientation. Then they were shown a series of tweets and asked to annotate the tweets' sentiment (positive, negative, neutral, or unsure), whether the tweet was sarcastic or humorous, the sentiment on a scale from positive to negative, and the tweet author's political orientation on a slider scale from conservative to liberal. Our sentiment model is based on the sentiment label and the sarcasm and humor labels. Our training data consists of nearly 17000 tweets (16% positive, 56% negative, 18% neutral, 10% unsure), including nearly 2000 that were multiply annotated

Tweet	`WAAAAAH!!! RT @politico: Romney: Santorum's 'dirty tricks' could steal Michigan: http://t.co/qEns1Pmi #MIprimary #tcot #teaparty #GOP`
Tokens	`WAAAAAH !!! RT @politico : Romney : Santorum's ' dirty tricks ' could steal Michigan : http://politi.co/wYUz7m #MIprimary #tcot #teaparty #GOP`

Figure 2. The output tokens of a sample tweet from our tokenizer

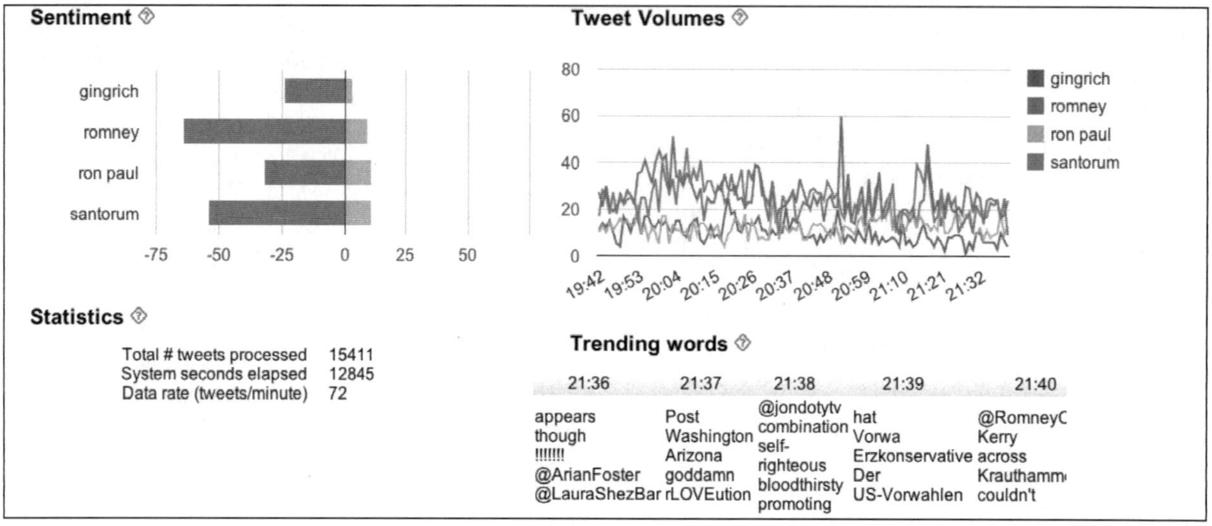

Figure 3. Dashboard for volume, sentiment and trending words

to calculate inter-annotator agreement. About 800 Turkers contributed to our annotation.

The statistical classifier we use for sentiment analysis is a naïve Bayes model on unigram features. Our features are calculated from tokenization of the tweets that attempts to preserve punctuation that may signify sentiment (e.g., emoticons and exclamation points) as well as twitter specific phenomena (e.g., extracting intact URLs). Based on the data we collected our classifier performs at 59% accuracy on the four category classification of negative, positive, neutral, or unsure. These results exceed the baseline of classifying all the data as negative, the most prevalent sentiment category (56%). The choice of our model was not strictly motivated by global accuracy, but took into account class-wise performance so that the model performed well on each sentiment category.

3.4 Aggregation

Because our system receives tweets continuously and uses multiple rules to track each candidate's tweets, our display must aggregate sentiment and tweet volume within each time period for each candidate. For volume, the system outputs the number of tweets every minute for each candidate. For sentiment, the system outputs the number of *positive*, *negative*, *neutral* and *unsure* tweets in a sliding five-minute window.

3.5 Display and Visualization

We designed an Ajax-based HTML dashboard (Figure 3) to display volume and sentiment by candidate as well as trending words and system statistics. The dashboard pulls updated data from a web server and refreshes its display every 30 seconds. In Figure 3, the top-left bar graph shows the number of positive and negative tweets about each candidate (right and left bars, respectively) in the last five minutes as an indicator of sentiment towards the candidates. We chose to display both positive and negative sentiment, instead of the difference between these two, because events typically trigger sharp variations in both positive and negative tweet volume. The top-right chart displays the number of tweets for each candidate every minute in the last two hours. We chose this time window because a live-broadcast primary debate usually lasts about two hours. The bottom-left shows system statistics, including the total number of tweets, the number of seconds since system start and the average data rate. The bottom-right table shows trending words of the last five minutes, computed using TF-IDF measure as follows: tweets about all candidates in a minute are treated as a single "document"; trending words are the tokens from the current minute with the highest TF-IDF weights when using the last two hours as a corpus (i.e., 120 "documents"). Qualitative examination suggests that the simple TF-IDF metric effectively identifies the most prominent words when an event occurs.

The dashboard gives a synthetic overview of volume and sentiment for the candidates, but it is often desirable to view selected tweets and their sentiments. The dashboard includes another page

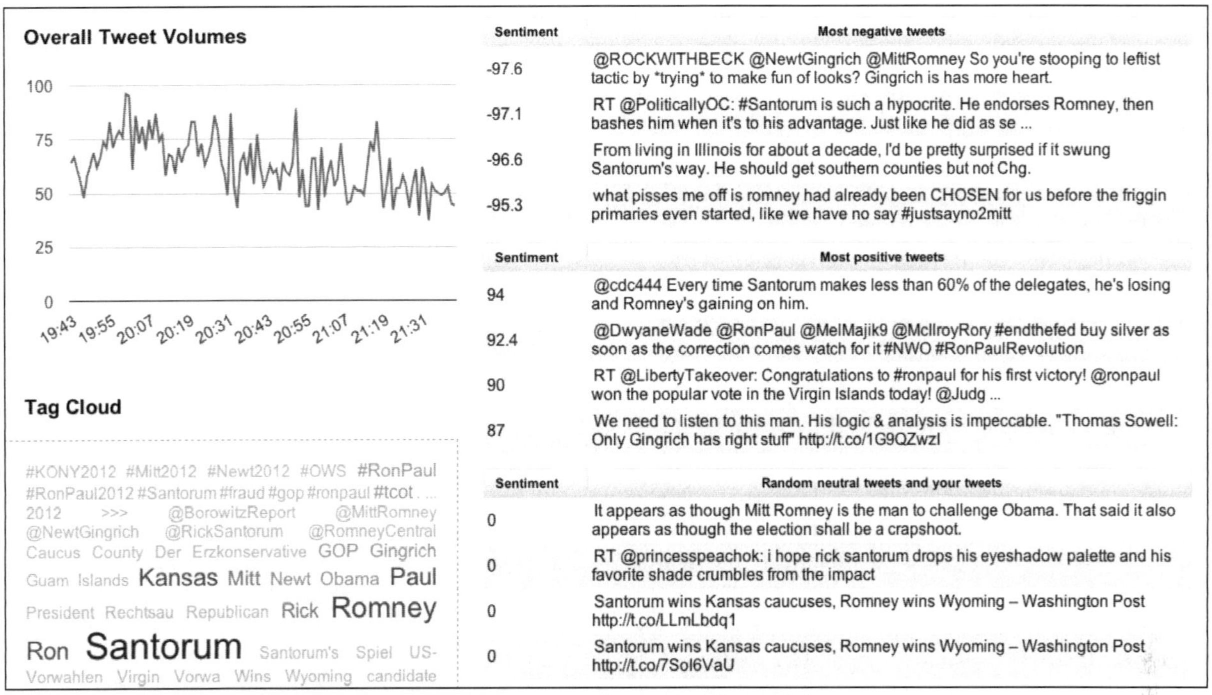

Figure 5. Dashboard for most positive, negative and frequent tweets

(Figure 4) that displays the most positive, negative and frequent tweets, as well as some random neutral tweets. It also shows the total volume over time and a tag cloud of the most frequent words in the last five minutes across all candidates. Another crucial feature of this page is that clicking on one of the tweets brings up an annotation interface, so the user can provide his/her own assessment of the sentiment expressed in the tweet. The next section describes the annotation interface.

3.6 Annotation Interface

The online annotation interface shown in Figure 5 lets dashboard (Figure 4) users provide their own judgment of a tweet. The tweet's text is displayed at the top, and users can rate the sentiment toward the candidate mentioned in the tweet as *positive*, *negative* or *neutral* or mark it as *unsure*. There are also two options to specify whether a tweet is *sarcastic* and/or *funny*. This interface is a simplified version of the one we used to collect annotations from Amazon Mechanical Turk so that annotation can be performed quickly on a single tweet. The online interface is designed to be used while watching a campaign event and can be displayed on a tablet or smart phone.

The feedback from users allows annotation of recent data as well as the ability to correct misclassifications. As a future step, we plan to establish an online feedback loop between users and the sentiment model, so users' judgment serves to train the model actively and iteratively.

4 System Evaluation

In Section 3.3, we described our preliminary sentiment model that automatically classifies tweets into four categories: positive, negative, neutral or unsure. It copes well with the negative bias in political tweets. In addition to evaluating

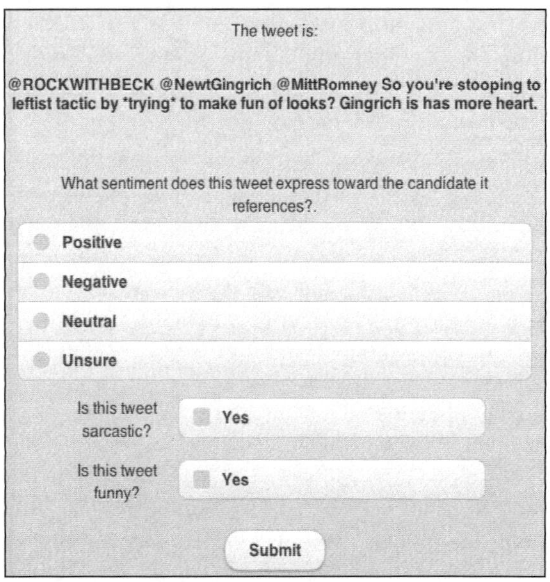

Figure 4. Online sentiment annotation interface

the model using annotated data, we have also begun conducting correlational analysis of aggregated sentiment with political events and news, as well as indicators such as poll and election results. We are exploring whether variations in twitter sentiment and tweet volume are predictive or reflective of real-world events and news. While this quantitative analysis is part of ongoing work, we present below some quantitative and qualitative expert observations indicative of promising research directions.

One finding is that tweet volume is largely driven by campaign events. Of the 50 top hourly intervals between Oct 12, 2011 and Feb 29, 2012, ranked by tweet volume, all but two correspond either to President Obama's State of the Union address, televised primary debates or moments when caucus or primary election results were released. Out of the 100 top hourly intervals, all but 18 correspond to such events. The 2012 State of the Union address on Jan 24 is another good example. It caused the biggest volume we have seen in a single day since last October, 1.37 million tweets in total for that day. Both positive and negative tweets for President Obama increased three to four times comparing to an average day.

During the Republican Primary debate on Jan 19, 2012 in Charleston, NC one of the Republican candidates, Newt Gingrich, was asked about his ex-wife at the beginning of the debate. Within minutes, our dashboard showed his negative sentiment increase rapidly – it became three times more negative in just two minutes. This illustrates how tweet volume and sentiment are extremely responsive to emerging events in the real world (Vergeer et al., 2011).

These examples confirm our assessment that it is especially relevant to offer a system that can provide real-time analysis during key moments in the election cycle. As the election continues and culminates with the presidential vote this November, we hope that our system will provide rich insights into the evolution of public sentiment toward the contenders.

5 Conclusion

We presented a system for real-time Twitter sentiment analysis of the ongoing 2012 U.S. presidential election. We use the Twitter "firehose" and expert-curated rules and keywords to get a full and accurate picture of the online political landscape. Our real-time data processing infrastructure and statistical sentiment model evaluates public sentiment changes in response to emerging political events and news as they unfold. The architecture and method are generic, and can be easily adopted and extended to other domains (for instance, we used the system for gauging sentiments about films and actors surrounding Oscar nomination and selection).

References

Bollen, J., Mao, H., & Zeng, X. (2011). Twitter mood predicts the stock market. *Journal of Computational Science, 2*(1), 1-8. doi: 10.1016/j.jocs.2010.12.007

Choy, M., Cheong, L. F. M., Ma, N. L., & Koo, P. S. (2011). A sentiment analysis of Singapore Presidential Election 2011 using Twitter data with census correction.

González-Ibáñez, R., Muresan, S., & Wacholder, N. (2011). *Identifying Sarcasm in Twitter: A Closer Look.* In Proceedings of the 49th Annual Meeting of the Association for Computational Linguistics.

IBM. (2012). InfoSphere Streams, from http://www-01.ibm.com/software/data/infosphere/streams/

Lassen, D. S., & Brown, A. R. (2010). Twitter: The Electoral Connection? *Social Science Computer Review.*

O'Connor, B., Krieger, M., & Ahn, D. (2010). *TweetMotif: Exploratory Search and Topic Summarization for Twitter.* In Proceedings of the the Fourth International AAAI Conference on Weblogs and Social Media, Washington, DC.

Pang, B., & Lee, L. (2008). Opinion Mining and Sentiment Analysis. *Foundations and Trends in Information Retrieval, 2*(1-2), 1-135. doi: 10.1561/1500000011

Pew Research Center. (2011). 13% of online adults use Twitter. Retrieved from http://www.pewinternet.org/~/media//Files/Reports/2011/Twitter%20Update%202011.pdf

Tumasjan, A., Sprenger, T. O., Sandner, P. G., & Welpe, I. M. (2010). *Predicting Elections with Twitter: What 140 Characters Reveal about Political Sentiment.*

TweetCongress. (2012). Congress Members on Twitter Retrieved Mar 18, 2012, from http://tweetcongress.org/members/

Twitter. (2012). What is Twitter Retrieved Mar 18, 2012, from https://business.twitter.com/en/basics/what-is-twitter/

Vergeer, M., Hermans, L., & Sams, S. (2011). Is the voter only a tweet away? Micro blogging during the 2009 European Parliament election campaign in the Netherlands. *First Monday [Online], 16*(8).

Zeitzoff, T. (2011). Using Social Media to Measure Conflict Dynamics. *Journal of Conflict Resolution, 55*(6), 938-969. doi: 10.1177/0022002711408014

Building trainable taggers in a web-based, UIMA-supported NLP workbench

Rafal Rak, BalaKrishna Kolluru and Sophia Ananiadou
National Centre for Text Mining
School of Computer Science, University of Manchester
Manchester Interdisciplinary Biocentre
131 Princess St, M1 7DN, Manchester, UK
{rafal.rak,balakrishna.kolluru,sophia.ananiadou}@manchester.ac.uk

Abstract

Argo is a web-based NLP and text mining workbench with a convenient graphical user interface for designing and executing processing workflows of various complexity. The workbench is intended for specialists and non-technical audiences alike, and provides the ever expanding library of analytics compliant with the Unstructured Information Management Architecture, a widely adopted interoperability framework. We explore the flexibility of this framework by demonstrating workflows involving three processing components capable of performing self-contained machine learning-based tagging. The three components are responsible for the three distinct tasks of 1) generating observations or features, 2) training a statistical model based on the generated features, and 3) tagging unlabelled data with the model. The learning and tagging components are based on an implementation of conditional random fields (CRF); whereas the feature generation component is an analytic capable of extending basic token information to a comprehensive set of features. Users define the features of their choice directly from Argo's graphical interface, without resorting to programming (a commonly used approach to feature engineering). The experimental results performed on two tagging tasks, chunking and named entity recognition, showed that a tagger with a generic set of features built in Argo is capable of competing with task-specific solutions.

1 Introduction

The applications of automatic recognition of categories, or tagging, in natural language processing (NLP), range from part of speech tagging to chunking to named entity recognition and complex scientific discourse analyses. Currently, there is a variety of tools capable of performing these tasks. A commonly used approach involves the use of machine learning to first build a statistical model based on a manually or semi-automatically tagged sample data and then to tag new data using this model. Since the machine learning algorithms for building models are well established, the challenge shifted to *feature engineering*, i.e., developing task-specific features that form the basis of these statistical models. This task is usually accomplished programmatically which pose an obstacle to a non-technically inclined audience. We alleviate this problem by demonstrating Argo[1], a web-based platform that allows the user to build NLP and other text analysis workflows via a graphical user interface (GUI) available in a web browser. The system is equipped with an ever growing library of text processing components ranging from low-level syntactic analysers to semantic annotators. It also allows for including user-interactive components, such as an annotation editor, into otherwise fully automatic workflows. The interoperability of processing components is ensured in Argo by adopting Unstructured Information Management Architecture (UIMA) (Ferrucci and Lally, 2004) as the system's framework. In this work we explore the capabilities of this framework to support machine

[1] http://nactem.ac.uk/Argo

Proceedings of the 50th Annual Meeting of the Association for Computational Linguistics, pages 121–126,
Jeju, Republic of Korea, 8-14 July 2012. ©2012 Association for Computational Linguistics

learning components for tagging textual content.

In the following section we present related work. Section 3 provides background information on Argo and its relationship to UIMA. The details of the three machine learning components are discussed in Section 4. Section 5 provides evaluation, whereas Section 6 concludes the paper.

2 Related work

Language processing tools with machine learning capabilities for tagging textual content have been distributed by various groups in form of either standalone applications or application programming interfaces (API). Packages such as Lingpipe[2], Mallet[3], Stanford NLP tools[4] and OpenNLP[5] have been extensively used by the NLP and text mining communities (Kolluru et al., 2011; Corbett and Murray-Rust, 2006). However, such tools inherently impose inconveniences on users, such as a lack of GUI, often arduous manual installation procedures, proficiency in programming or familiarity with the details of machine learning algorithms.

These limitations are overcome by GUI-equipped, workflow-supporting platforms that often directly use the solutions provided by the former tools. The notable examples of such platforms designed specifically for NLP and text mining tasks are GATE (Cunningham et al., 2002), a suite of text processing and annotation tools, and U-Compare (Kano et al., 2010), a standalone application supporting the UIMA framework that formed the inspiration for Argo.

Although the GUI platforms provide machine learning solutions, these are usually limited to using pre-trained models and providing a rich set of features for training requires resorting to programming. Argo, on the other hand, allows the users to train their own models with either a generic set of features or customisable features without having to write a single line of code. This capability is provided in Argo entirely through its GUI.

[2]http://alias-i.com/lingpipe

[3]http://mallet.cs.umass.edu

[4]http://nlp.stanford.edu/software/index.shtml

[5]http://opennlp.apache.org

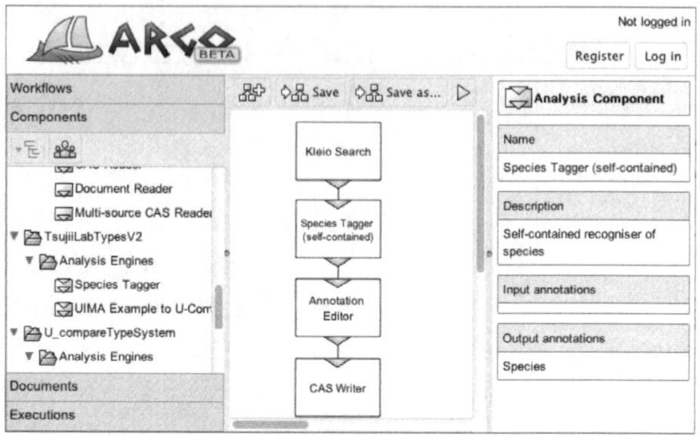

Figure 1: Screen capture of Argo's web-based interface.

3 Argo and UIMA

Argo's main user interface consists of three panels as shown in Figure 1. The left-hand panel includes user-owned or shared storable objects; the middle panel is a drawing space for constructing workflows and the right-hand panel displays context-dependent information. The storable objects are categorised into *workflows*, represented as block diagrams of interconnected processing components, *documents* that represent the user's space intended for uploading resources and saving processing results, and *executions* that provide past and live workflow execution details and access points to user-interactive components should such be present in a workflow.

Component interoperability in Argo is ensured by UIMA which defines common structures and interfaces. A typical UIMA processing pipeline consists of a *collection reader*, a set of *analysis engines* and a *consumer*. The role of a collection reader is to fetch a resource (e.g., a text document) and deposit it in a *common annotation structure*, or *CAS*, as the subject of annotation. Analysis engines then process the subject of annotation stored in the CAS and populate the CAS with their respective annotations. The consumer's role is to transform some or all of the annotations and/or the subject of annotation from the CAS and serialise it into some storable format.

Readers, analysers and consumers are represented graphically in Argo as blocks with incoming only, incoming and outgoing, and outgoing only ports, respectively, visible in the middle of Figure 1.

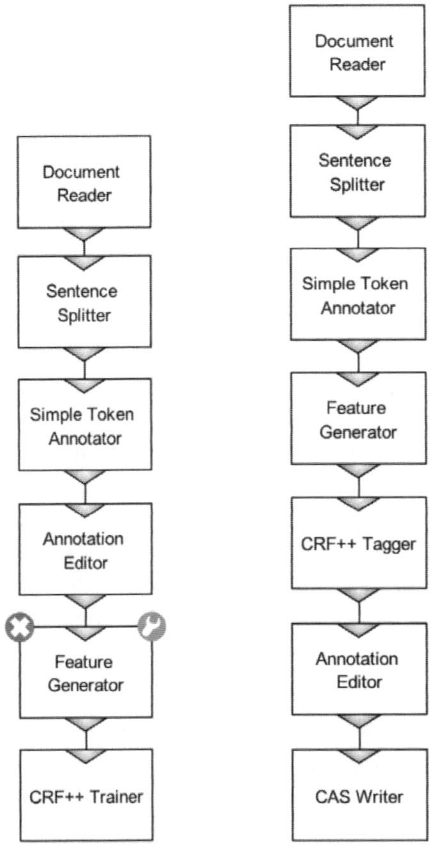

(a) Training (b) Tagging

Figure 2: Two generic workflows demonstrating the use of the Feature Generator component for (a) training and (b) tagging.

4 Machine learning components in Argo

In order to ensure flexibility in building workflows, we split the machine learning capability into three distinct processing components, namely feature generator, model trainer and tagger. The trainer and the tagger are intrinsic machine learning components, whereas the feature generator is a convenient and customisable processing component capable of building a feature space for a user-defined domain.

From UIMA's perspective, the feature generator and the tagger are both analysis engines whose purpose is to analyse the incoming CASes and enrich them with additional annotations; whereas the trainer is a consumer that transforms the information stored in CASes into a statistical model.

A typical use of the three components is shown in Figure 2. The three components are represented as the Feature Generator, CRF++ Trainer and CRF++ Tagger blocks. Figure 2a shows a process of building a statistical model supported by a document reader, common, well-established preprocessing components (in this case, to establish boundaries of sentences and tokens), and the previously mentioned editor for manually creating annotations[6]. The manual annotations serve to generate tags/labels which are used in the training process together with the features produced by Feature Generator. The trained model is then used in the workflow shown in Figure 2b to tag new resources. Although the tagging workflow automatically recognises the labels of interest (based on the model supplied in CRF++ Tagger), in practice, the labels need further correction, hence the use of Annotation Editor after the tagger.

4.1 Training and tagging

At present, our implementation of the training and tagging components is based on the conditional random fields (CRF) (Lafferty et al., 2001). Our choice is dictated by the fact that CRF models are currently one of the best models for tagging and efficient algorithms to compute marginal probabilities and n-best sequences are freely available.

We used the CRF++ implementation[7] and wrapped it into two UIMA-compatible components, CRF++ Trainer and CRF++ Tagger. The trainer deals with the optimisation of feature parameters, whereas word observations are produced by Feature Generator, as described in the following section.

4.2 From annotations to features

The Feature Generator component is an intermediary between annotations stored in CASes and the training component. This component is customisable via the component's settings panel, parts of which are shown in Figure 3. The panel allows the user to 1) identify the stream of tokens[8] (Figure 3a), 2) identify the stream of token sequences (usually

[6]The preprocessing and manual annotation components could be replaced with CAS Reader, a component capable of supplying the workflow with a previously annotated set of documents.

[7]http://code.google.com/p/crfpp/

[8]The definition of *token* depends on the selected UIMA annotation type. It may range from a simple span of text to a complex lexical or semantic structure.

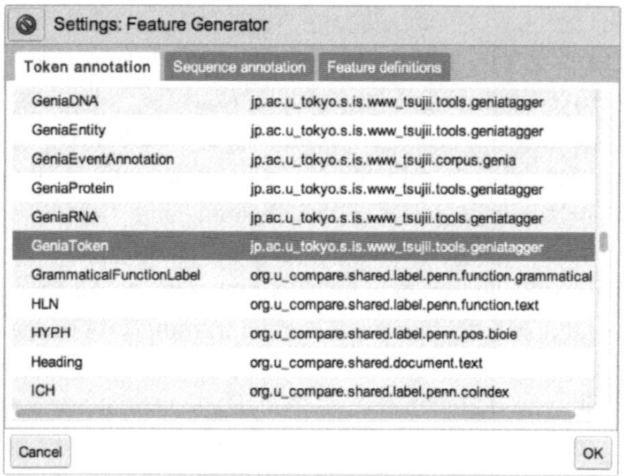

(a) Selecting a token annotation type

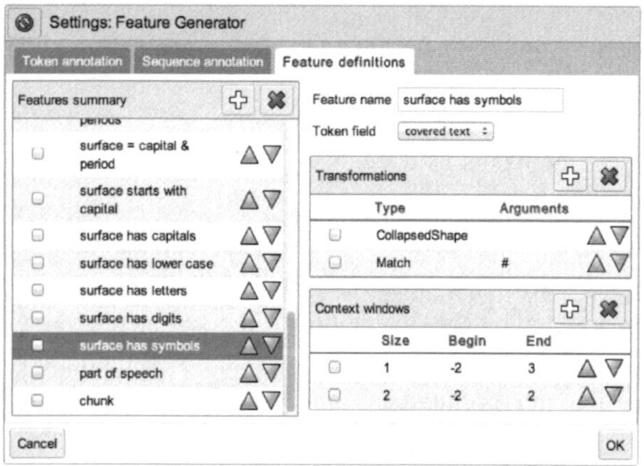

(b) Defining features

Figure 3: Feature Generator settings panel allows the user to (a) select labels for machine learning and (b) define features.

sentences), and 3) define features or token observations (Figure 3b).

Each feature definition consists of a name, a token field, an optional list of token field transformations, and an optional set of context windows. The name is only for the user's convenience of identifying individual feature definitions. The token field is the primary subject of transformations (if any) and it is one of the data fields of the selected token annotation type. For instance, the token annotation type may define data fields such as part of speech, chunk, or lemma. By default, the system selects "covered text", i.e., the span of text covered by an annotation, since this data field is available for any annotation.

If no transformation is declared, the string representation of the token field's value ultimately becomes the value of the generated feature. If the user declares one or more transformations then these are applied on the token field's value in sequence, i.e., an outcome of the preceding transformation becomes an input of the following one. Figure 4 shows the various transformations currently available in the system.

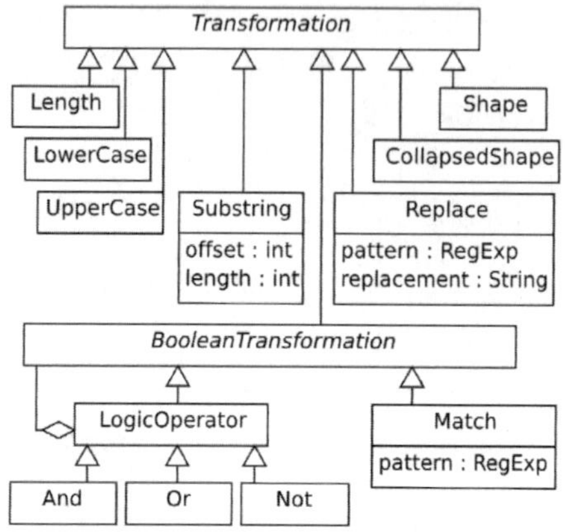

Figure 4: UML diagram of transformation types

Context windows allow for enriching the current token's feature set by introducing observations from surrounding tokens as n-grams. For example, the selected feature definition in Figure 3b, "surface has symbols", declares the covered text as the feature's basis and defines two transformations and two context windows. The two transformations will first transform the covered text to a collapsed shape (e.g., "NF-kappa" will become "A#a") and then produce "Y" or "N" depending on whether the collapsed shape matches the simple regular expression "#" (e.g., "A#a" will become "Y"). The two context windows define six unigrams and four bigrams, which will ultimately result in this single feature definition's producing ten observations for training.

5 Evaluation

We show the performance of taggers trained with two distinct sets of features, basic and extended. The basic set of features uses token fields such as the covered text and the part of speech *without* any transformations or context n-grams. The extended set makes the full use of Feature Generator's settings and enriches the basic set with various transformations and context n-grams. The transformations in-

Dataset	Setup	P	R	F
CoNLL	Best	94.29	94.01	94.13
	L2 IOBES	92.20	93.43	92.81
	L2 IOB	92.14	93.27	92.70
	L1 IOBES	91.95	93.17	92.55
	L1 IOB	91.83	93.11	92.46
	Baseline	72.58	82.14	77.07
BioNLP/ NLPBA	Best	76.00	69.40	72.6
	L1 IOBES	66.22	65.06	65.63
	L2 IOB	66.06	64.87	65.46
	L1 IOB	66.05	64.61	65.32
	L2 IOBES	65.77	64.79	65.28
	Baseline	52.60	43.60	47.70

Table 1: Performance of various setups (L1 vs L2, and IOB vs IOBES) on the chunking and NER tasks. The setups are ordered by F-score.

Dataset	Setup	P	R	F
CoNLL	Basic	73.80	84.50	78.78
	Extended	92.20	93.43	92.81
BioNLP/ NLPBA	Basic	37.06	48.13	41.88
	Extended	66.22	65.06	65.63

Table 2: Comparison of setups with basic and extended features for the chunking and NER tasks.

clude surface shape, length, prefixes, suffixes, and the presence of various combinations of letters, digits and symbols. The context n-grams include unigrams for all feature definitions and bigrams for selected ones. Figure 3b shows a sample of the actual extended set.

We use two datasets, one prepared for the CoNLL 2000 shared task (Tjong et al., 2000) and another prepared for the BioNLP/NLPBA 2004 shared task (Kim et al., 2004). They represent two different tagging tasks, chunking and named entity recognition, respectively. The CoNLL 2000 chunking dataset involves 10 labels and comes pre-tokenised with 211,727 tokens in the training set and 47,377 tokens in the test set. The dataset also provides part-of-speech tags for each token. The BioNLP/NLPBA 2004 named entity recognition dataset involves five biology-related labels and consists of 472,006 and 96,780 tokens in the training and testing sets, respectively. Contrary to the former dataset, there is no other information supporting the tokens in the BioNLP/NLPBA dataset. To compensate for it we automatically generated part of speech and chunk labels for each token.

The chosen datasets/tasks are by no means an exhaustive set of representative comparative-setup datasets available. Our goal is *not* to claim the superiority of our approach over the solutions reported in the respective shared tasks. Instead, we aim to show that our generic setup is comparable to those task-tuned solutions.

We further explore the options of both Feature Generator and CRF++ Trainer by manipulating labelling formats (IOB vs IOBES (Kudo and Matsumoto, 2001)) for the former and parameter estimation algorithms (L_2- vs L_1-norm regularisation) for the latter. Ultimately, there are 32 setups as the result of the combinations of the two feature sets, the two datasets, the two labelling formats and the two estimation algorithms.

5.1 Results

Table 1 shows the precision, recall and f-scores of our extended-feature setups against each other as well as with reference to the best and baseline solutions as reported in the respective shared tasks. The gap to the best performing solution for the chunking task is about 1.3% points in F-score, ahead of the baseline by 15.7% points. Respectively for the NER task, our best setup stands behind the best reported solution by about 7% points, ahead of the baseline by about 18% points. In both instances our solution would be placed in the middle of the reported rankings, which is a promising result, especially that our setups are based solely on the tokens' surface form, part of speech, and (in the case of the NER task) chunk. In contrast, the best solutions for the NER task involve the use of dictionaries and advanced analyses such as acronym resolution.

The tested combinations of the labelling formats and parameter estimation algorithms showed to be inconclusive, with a difference between the best and worst setups of only 0.35% points for both tasks.

The advantage of using the extended set of features over the basic set is clearly illustrated in Table 2. The performance of the basic set on the chunking dataset is only at the level of the baseline, whereas for the NER task it falls nearly 6% points behind the

Dataset	Setup	L2	L1
CoNLL	Extended IOB	555	187
	Basic IOB	134	70
	Extended IOBES	528	209
	Basic IOBES	139	72
BioNLP/ NLPBA	Extended IOB	865	179
	Basic IOB	226	72
	Extended IOBES	860	201
	Basic IOBES	217	79

Table 3: Number of iterations needed for the optimisation algorithm to converge.

baseline (which comes as no surprise given that the baseline system is a string match of entities found in the training set).

Table 3 shows the number of iterations[9] needed for the optimisation algorithm of the trainer to converge. The advantage of the L1 regularisation is apparent with nearly two to five times less iterations needed when compared to the L2 regularisation. Given the close F-scores achieved by the two family of setups, the L1 regularisation becomes a clear winner in our experimentation setup.

6 Conclusions

Argo's strength is manifested by its online availability, an intuitive graphical user interface available from a web browser, convenience in building even most complex text processing workflows, and the availability of trainable machine learning components. The Feature Generator component, customisable entirely through a GUI, provides the flexibility needed to extend the basic set of features without resorting to programming. The experiment results showed that an extended, yet generic, set of features can be taken to competitive levels in terms of effectiveness.

7 Acknowledgements

This work was partially supported by Biotechnology and Biological Sciences Research Council (BBSRC BB/G53025X/1 From Text to Pathways) and Korea Institute of Science and Technology Information (KISTI Text Mining and Pathways).

[9]We do not report detailed CPU times due to experimenting on resource-shared machines. Such a setup makes direct side-by-side comparisons largely skewed. As a reference we note that the workflows completed in 15 minutes to about 11 hours depending on a feature space size and machine load.

References

P. Corbett and P. Murray-Rust. 2006. High-throughput identification of chemistry in life science texts. *Comp Life*, pages 107–118. LNBI 4216.

H. Cunningham, D. Maynard, K. Bontcheva, and V. Tablan. 2002. GATE: A framework and graphical development environment for robust NLP tools and applications. In *Proc. of the 40th Anniversary Meeting of the Association for Computational Linguistics*.

D. Ferrucci and A. Lally. 2004. UIMA: An Architectural Approach to Unstructured Information Processing in the Corporate Research Environment. *Natural Language Engineering*, 10(3-4):327–348.

Y. Kano, R. Dorado, L. McCrochon, S. Ananiadou, and J. Tsujii. 2010. U-Compare: An integrated language resource evaluation platform including a comprehensive UIMA resource library. In *Proc. of the Seventh International Conference on Language Resources and Evaluation (LREC 2010)*, pages 428–434.

J.-D. Kim, T. Ohta, Y. Tsuruoka, Y. Tateisi, and N. Collier. 2004. Introduction to the bio-entity recognition task at jnlpba. In *Proc. of the International Joint Workshop on Natural Language Processing in Biomedicine and its Applications*, JNLPBA '04, pages 70–75, Geneva, Switzerland. Association for Computational Linguistics.

B. Kolluru, S. Nakjang, R. P. Hirt, A. Wipat, and S. Ananiadou. 2011. Automatic extraction of microorganisms and their habitats from free text using text mining workflows. *Journal of Integrative Bioinformatics*, 8(2):184.

T. Kudo and Y. Matsumoto. 2001. Chunking with support vector machines. In *Proc. of the second meeting of the North American Chapter of the Association for Computational Linguistics on Language technologies*, NAACL '01, pages 1–8, Stroudsburg, PA, USA. Association for Computational Linguistics.

J. Lafferty, A. Mccallum, and F. Pereira. 2001. Conditional Random Fields: Probabilistic Models for Segmenting and Labeling Sequence Data. In *Proc. 18th International Conf. on Machine Learning*, pages 282–289. Morgan Kaufmann, San Francisco, CA.

K. S. Tjong, F. Erik, and S. Buchholz. 2000. Introduction to the CoNLL-2000 shared task: chunking. In *Proc. of the 2nd workshop on Learning language in logic and the 4th Conference on Computational natural language learning*, pages 127–132, Morristown, NJ, USA. Association for Computational Linguistics.

Akamon: An Open Source Toolkit for Tree/Forest-Based Statistical Machine Translation*

Xianchao Wu[†], **Takuya Matsuzaki**[*], **Jun'ichi Tsujii**[‡]
[†] Baidu Inc.
[*] National Institute of Informatics
[‡] Microsoft Research Asia
wuxianchao@gmail.com, takuya-matsuzaki@nii.ac.jp, jtsujii@microsoft.com

Abstract

We describe **Akamon**, an open source toolkit for tree and forest-based statistical machine translation (Liu et al., 2006; Mi et al., 2008; Mi and Huang, 2008). Akamon implements all of the algorithms required for tree/forest-to-string decoding using tree-to-string translation rules: *multiple-thread* forest-based decoding, n-gram language model integration, beam- and cube-pruning, k-best hypotheses extraction, and minimum error rate training. In terms of tree-to-string translation rule extraction, the toolkit implements the traditional maximum likelihood algorithm using PCFG trees (Galley et al., 2004) and HPSG trees/forests (Wu et al., 2010).

1 Introduction

Syntax-based statistical machine translation (SMT) systems have achieved promising improvements in recent years. Depending on the type of input, the systems are divided into two categories: *string-based* systems whose input is a string to be simultaneously parsed and translated by a synchronous grammar (Wu, 1997; Chiang, 2005; Galley et al., 2006; Shen et al., 2008), and *tree/forest-based* systems whose input is already a parse tree or a packed forest to be directly converted into a target tree or string (Ding and Palmer, 2005; Quirk et al., 2005; Liu et al., 2006; Huang et al., 2006; Mi et al., 2008; Mi and Huang, 2008; Zhang et al., 2009; Wu et al., 2010; Wu et al., 2011a).

Depending on whether or not parsers are explicitly used for obtaining linguistically annotated data during training, the systems are also divided into two categories: *formally syntax-based* systems that do not use additional parsers (Wu, 1997; Chiang, 2005; Xiong et al., 2006), and *linguistically syntax-based* systems that use PCFG parsers (Liu et al., 2006; Huang et al., 2006; Galley et al., 2006; Mi et al., 2008; Mi and Huang, 2008; Zhang et al., 2009), HPSG parsers (Wu et al., 2010; Wu et al., 2011a), or dependency parsers (Ding and Palmer, 2005; Quirk et al., 2005; Shen et al., 2008). A classification[1] of syntax-based SMT systems is shown in Table 1.

Translation rules can be extracted from aligned string-string (Chiang, 2005), tree-tree (Ding and Palmer, 2005) and tree/forest-string (Galley et al., 2004; Mi and Huang, 2008; Wu et al., 2011a) data structures. Leveraging structural and linguistic information from parse trees/forests, the latter two structures are believed to be better than their string-string counterparts in handling non-local reordering, and have achieved promising translation results. Moreover, the tree/forest-string structure is more widely used than the tree-tree structure, presumably because using two parsers on the source and target languages is subject to more problems than making use of a parser on one language, such as the shortage of high precision/recall parsers for languages other than English, compound parse error rates, and inconsistency of errors. In Table 1, note that tree-to-string rules are generic and applicable to many syntax-based models such as tree/forest-to-

*Work done when all the authors were in The University of Tokyo.

[1] This classification is inspired by and extends the Table 1 in (Mi and Huang, 2008).

Proceedings of the 50th Annual Meeting of the Association for Computational Linguistics, pages 127–132,
Jeju, Republic of Korea, 8-14 July 2012.

Source-to-target	Examples (partial)	Decoding	Rules	Parser
tree-to-tree	(Ding and Palmer, 2005)	$\downarrow$	dep.-to-dep.	DG
forest-to-tree	(Liu et al., 2009a)	$\downarrow \uparrow\downarrow$	tree-to-tree	PCFG
tree-to-string	(Liu et al., 2006)	$\uparrow$	*tree-to-string*	PCFG
	(Quirk et al., 2005)	$\uparrow$	dep.-to-string	DG
forest-to-string	(Mi et al., 2008)	$\downarrow \uparrow\downarrow$	*tree-to-string*	PCFG
	(Wu et al., 2011a)	$\downarrow \uparrow\downarrow$	*tree-to-string*	HPSG
string-to-tree	(Galley et al., 2006)	CKY	*tree-to-string*	PCFG
	(Shen et al., 2008)	CKY	string-to-dep.	DG
string-to-string	(Chiang, 2005)	CKY	string-to-string	none
	(Xiong et al., 2006)	CKY	string-to-string	none

Table 1: A classification of syntax-based SMT systems. Tree/forest-based and string-based systems are split by a line. All the systems listed here are linguistically syntax-based except the last two (Chiang, 2005) and (Xiong et al., 2006), which are formally syntax-based. DG stands for dependency (abbreviated as dep.) grammar. $\downarrow$ and $\uparrow$ denote top-down and bottom-up traversals of a source tree/forest.

string models and string-to-tree model.

However, few tree/forest-to-string systems have been made open source and this makes it difficult and time-consuming to testify and follow existing proposals involved in recently published papers. The Akamon system[2], written in Java and following the tree/forest-to-string research direction, implements all of the algorithms for both tree-to-string translation rule extraction (Galley et al., 2004; Mi and Huang, 2008; Wu et al., 2010; Wu et al., 2011a) and tree/forest-based decoding (Liu et al., 2006; Mi et al., 2008). We hope this system will help related researchers to catch up with the achievements of tree/forest-based translations in the past several years without re-implementing the systems or general algorithms from scratch.

2 Akamon Toolkit Features

Limited by the successful parsing rate and coverage of linguistic phrases, Akamon currently achieves comparable translation accuracies compared with the most frequently used SMT baseline system, Moses (Koehn et al., 2007). Table 2 shows the automatic translation accuracies (case-sensitive) of Akamon and Moses. Besides BLEU and NIST score, we further list RIBES score[3], , i.e., the software implementation of Normalized Kendall's τ as proposed by (Isozaki et al., 2010a) to automatically evaluate the translation between distant language pairs based on rank correlation coefficients and significantly penalizes word order mistakes.

In this table, Akamon-Forest differs from Akamon-Comb by using different configurations: Akamon-Forest used only 2/3 of the total training data (limited by the experiment environments and time). Akamon-Comb represents the system combination result by combining Akamon-Forest and other phrase-based SMT systems, which made use of pre-ordering methods of head finalization as described in (Isozaki et al., 2010b) and used the total 3 million training data. The detail of the pre-ordering approach and the combination method can be found in (Sudoh et al., 2011) and (Duh et al., 2011).

Also, Moses (hierarchical) stands for the hierarchical phrase-based SMT system and Moses (phrase) stands for the flat phrase-based SMT system. For intuitive comparison (note that the result achieved by Google is only for reference and not a comparison, since it uses a different and unknown training data) and following (Goto et al., 2011), the scores achieved by using the Google online translation system[4] are also listed in this table.

Here is a brief description of Akamon's main features:

- *multiple-thread* forest-based decoding: Akamon first loads the development (with source and reference sentences) or test (with source sentences only) file into memory and then perform parameter tuning or decoding in a parallel way. The forest-based decoding algorithm is alike that described in (Mi et al., 2008),

[2]Code available at https://sites.google.com/site/xianchaowu2012

[3]Code available at http://www.kecl.ntt.co.jp/icl/lirg/ribes

[4]http://translate.google.com/

Systems	BLEU	NIST	RIBES
Google online	0.2546	6.830	0.6991
Moses (hierarchical)	0.3166	7.795	0.7200
Moses (phrase)	0.3190	7.881	0.7068
Moses (phrase)*	0.2773	6.905	0.6619
Akamon-Forest*	0.2799	7.258	0.6861
Akamon-Comb	0.3948	8.713	0.7813

Table 2: Translation accuracies of Akamon and the baseline systems on the NTCIR-9 English-to-Japanese translation task (Wu et al., 2011b). * stands for only using 2 million parallel sentences of the total 3 million data. Here, HPSG forests were used in Akamon.

i.e., first construct a *translation forest* by applying the tree-to-string translation rules to the original parsing forest of the source sentence, and then collect k-best hypotheses for the root node(s) of the translation forest using Algorithm 2 or Algorithm 3 as described in (Huang and Chiang, 2005). Later, the k-best hypotheses are used both for parameter tuning on additional development set(s) and for final optimal translation result extracting.

- language models: Akamon can make use of one or many n-gram language models trained by using SRILM[5] (Stolcke, 2002) or the Berkeley language model toolkit, berkeleylm-1.0b3[6] (Pauls and Klein, 2011). The weights of multiple language models are tuned under minimum error rate training (MERT) (Och, 2003).

- pruning: traditional beam-pruning and cube-pruning (Chiang, 2007) techniques are incorporated in Akamon to make decoding feasible for large-scale rule sets. Before decoding, we also perform the marginal probability-based inside-outside algorithm based pruning (Mi et al., 2008) on the original parsing forest to control the decoding time.

- MERT: Akamon has its own MERT module which optimizes weights of the features so as to maximize some automatic evaluation metric, such as BLEU (Papineni et al., 2002), on a development set.

[5]http://www.speech.sri.com/projects/srilm/

[6]http://code.google.com/p/berkeleylm/

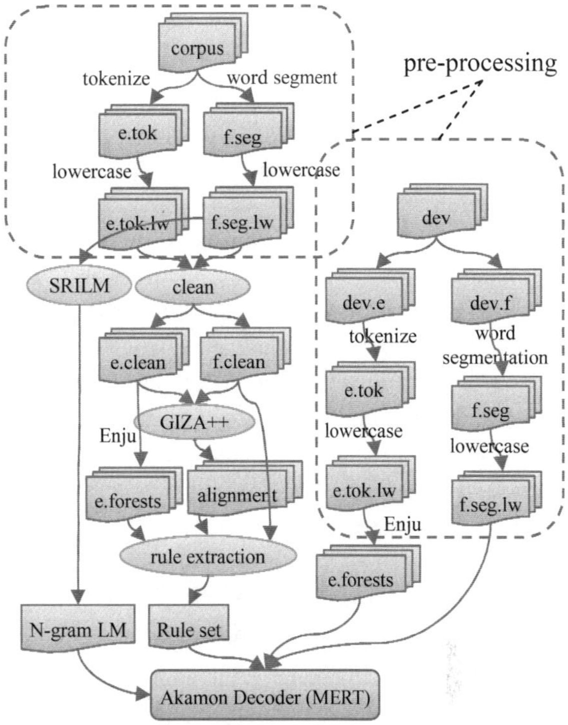

Figure 1: Training and tuning process of the Akamon system. Here, e = source English language, f = target foreign language.

- translation rule extraction: as former mentioned, we extract tree-to-string translation rules for Akamon. In particular, we implemented the GHKM algorithm as proposed by Galley et al. (2004) from word-aligned tree-string pairs. In addition, we also implemented the algorithms proposed by Mi and Huang (2008) and Wu et al. (2010) for extracting rules from word-aligned PCFG/HPSG forest-string pairs.

3 Training and Decoding Frameworks

Figure 1 shows the training and tuning progress of the Akamon system. Given original bilingual parallel corpora, we first tokenize and lowercase the source and target sentences (e.g., word segmentation of Chinese and Japanese, punctuation segmentation of English).

The pre-processed monolingual sentences will be used by SRILM (Stolcke, 2002) or BerkeleyLM (Pauls and Klein, 2011) to train a n-gram language model. In addition, we filter out too long sentences here, i.e., only relatively short sentence pairs will be used to train word alignments. Then, we can use GIZA++ (Och and Ney, 2003) and symmetric strategies, such as *grow-diag-final* (Koehn et al., 2007), on the tokenized parallel corpus to obtain a word-aligned parallel corpus.

The source sentence and its packed forest, the target sentence, and the word alignment are used for tree-to-string translation rule extraction. Since a 1-best tree is a special case of a packed forest, we will focus on using the term 'forest' in the continuing discussion. Then, taking the target language model, the rule set, and the preprocessed development set as inputs, we perform MERT on the decoder to tune the weights of the features.

The Akamon forest-to-string system includes the decoding algorithm and the rule extraction algorithm described in (Mi et al., 2008; Mi and Huang, 2008).

Feature	Description
CAT	phrasal category
XCAT	fine-grained phrasal category
SCHEMA	name of the schema applied in the node
HEAD	*pointer* to the head daughter
SEM_HEAD	*pointer* to the semantic head daughter
CAT	syntactic category
POS	Penn Treebank-style part-of-speech tag
BASE	base form
TENSE	tense of a verb (past, present, untensed)
ASPECT	aspect of a verb (none, perfect, progressive, perfect-progressive)
VOICE	voice of a verb (passive, active)
AUX	auxiliary verb or not (minus, modal, have, be, do, to, copular)
LEXENTRY	lexical entry, with supertags embedded
PRED	type of a predicate
ARG$\langle x \rangle$	*pointer* to semantic arguments, $x = 1..4$

Table 3: Syntactic/semantic features extracted from HPSG signs that are included in the output of Enju. Features in phrasal nodes (top) and lexical nodes (bottom) are listed separately.

4 Using Deep Syntactic Structures

In Akamon, we support the usage of *deep syntactic structures* for obtaining fine-grained translation rules as described in our former work (Wu et al., 2010)[7]. Similarly, Enju[8], a state-of-the-art and freely available HPSG parser for English, can be used to generate packed parse forests for source sentences[9]. Deep syntactic structures are included in the HPSG trees/forests, which includes a fine-grained description of the syntactic property and a semantic representation of the sentence. We extract fine-grained rules from aligned HPSG forest-string pairs and use them in the forest-to-string decoder. The detailed algorithms can be found in (Wu et al., 2010; Wu et al., 2011a). Note that, in Akamon, we also provide the codes for generating HPSG forests from Enju.

Head-driven phrase structure grammar (HPSG) is a lexicalist grammar framework. In HPSG, linguistic entities such as words and phrases are represented by a data structure called a *sign*. A sign gives a factored representation of the syntactic features of a word/phrase, as well as a representation of their semantic content. Phrases and words represented by signs are composed into larger phrases by applications of *schemata*. The semantic representation of the new phrase is calculated at the same time. As such, an HPSG parse tree/forest can be considered as a tree/forest of signs (c.f. the HPSG forest in Figure 2 in (Wu et al., 2010)).

An HPSG parse tree/forest has two attractive properties as a representation of a source sentence in syntax-based SMT. First, we can carefully control the condition of the application of a translation rule by exploiting the fine-grained syntactic description in the source parse tree/forest, as well as those in the translation rules. Second, we can identify sub-trees in a parse tree/forest that correspond to basic units of the semantics, namely sub-trees covering a predicate and its arguments, by using the semantic representation given in the signs. Extraction of translation rules based on such *semantically-connected* sub-trees is expected to give a compact and effective set of translation rules.

A sign in the HPSG tree/forest is represented by a typed feature structure (TFS) (Carpenter, 1992). A TFS is a directed-acyclic graph (DAG) wherein the edges are labeled with feature names and the nodes

[7] However, Akamon still support PCFG tree/forest based translation. A special case is to yield PCFG style trees/forests by ignoring the rich features included in the nodes of HPSG trees/forests and only keep the POS tag and the phrasal categories.

[8] http://www-tsujii.is.s.u-tokyo.ac.jp/enju/index.html

[9] Until the date this paper was submitted, Enju supports generating English and Chinese forests.

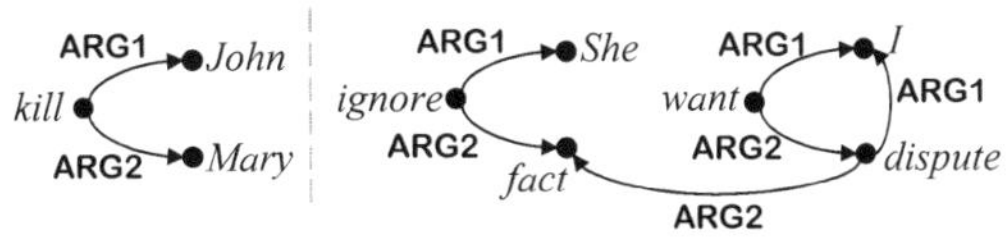

Figure 2: Predicate argument structures for the sentences of "*John killed Mary*" and "*She ignored the fact that I wanted to dispute*".

(feature values) are typed. In the original HPSG formalism, the types are defined in a hierarchy and the DAG can have arbitrary shape (e.g., it can be of any depth). We however use a simplified form of TFS, for simplicity of the algorithms. In the simplified form, a TFS is converted to a (flat) set of pairs of feature names and their values. Table 3 lists the features used in our system, which are a subset of those in the original output from Enju.

In the Enju English HPSG grammar (Miyao et al., 2003) used in our system, the semantic content of a sentence/phrase is represented by a predicate-argument structure (PAS). Figure 2 shows the PAS of a simple sentence, "*John killed Mary*", and a more complex PAS for another sentence, "*She ignored the fact that I wanted to dispute*", which is adopted from (Miyao et al., 2003). In an HPSG tree/forest, each leaf node generally introduces a predicate, which is represented by the pair of LEXENTRY (lexical entry) feature and PRED (predicate type) feature. The arguments of a predicate are designated by the pointers from the ARG$\langle x \rangle$ features in a leaf node to non-terminal nodes. Consequently, Akamon includes the algorithm for extracting compact composed rules from these PASs which further lead to a significant fast tree-to-string decoder. This is because it is not necessary to exhaustively generate the subtrees for all the tree nodes for rule matching any more. Limited by space, we suggest the readers to refer to our former work (Wu et al., 2010; Wu et al., 2011a) for the experimental results, including the training and decoding time using standard English-to-Japanese corpora, by using deep syntactic structures.

5 Content of the Demonstration

In the demonstration, we would like to provide a brief tutorial on:

- describing the format of the packed forest for a source sentence,
- the training script on translation rule extraction,
- the MERT script on feature weight tuning on a development set, and,
- the decoding script on a test set.

Based on Akamon, there are a lot of interesting directions left to be updated in a relatively fast way in the near future, such as:

- integrate target dependency structures, especially target dependency language models, as proposed by Mi and Liu (2010),
- better pruning strategies for the input packed forest before decoding,
- derivation-based combination of using other types of translation rules in one decoder, as proposed by Liu et al. (2009b), and
- taking other evaluation metrics as the optimal objective for MERT, such as NIST score, RIBES score (Isozaki et al., 2010a).

Acknowledgments

We thank Yusuke Miyao and Naoaki Okazaki for their invaluable help and the anonymous reviewers for their comments and suggestions.

References

Bob Carpenter. 1992. *The Logic of Typed Feature Structures*. Cambridge University Press.

David Chiang. 2005. A hierarchical phrase-based model for statistical machine translation. In *Proceedings of ACL*, pages 263–270, Ann Arbor, MI.

David Chiang. 2007. Hierarchical phrase-based translation. *Computational Lingustics*, 33(2):201–228.

Yuan Ding and Martha Palmer. 2005. Machine translation using probabilistic synchronous dependency insertion grammers. In *Proceedings of ACL*, pages 541–548, Ann Arbor.

Kevin Duh, Katsuhito Sudoh, Xianchao Wu, Hajime Tsukada, and Masaaki Nagata. 2011. Generalized minimum bayes risk system combination. In *Proceedings of IJCNLP*, pages 1356–1360, November.

Michel Galley, Mark Hopkins, Kevin Knight, and Daniel Marcu. 2004. What's in a translation rule? In *Proceedings of HLT-NAACL*.

Michel Galley, Jonathan Graehl, Kevin Knight, Daniel Marcu, Steve DeNeefe, Wei Wang, and Ignacio Thayer. 2006. Scalable inference and training of context-rich syntactic translation models. In *Proceedings of COLING-ACL*, pages 961–968, Sydney.

Isao Goto, Bin Lu, Ka Po Chow, Eiichiro Sumita, and Benjamin K. Tsou. 2011. Overview of the patent machine translation task at the ntcir-9 workshop. In *Proceedings of NTCIR-9*, pages 559–578.

Liang Huang and David Chiang. 2005. Better k-best parsing. In *Proceedings of IWPT*.

Liang Huang, Kevin Knight, and Aravind Joshi. 2006. Statistical syntax-directed translation with extended domain of locality. In *Proceedings of 7th AMTA*.

Hideki Isozaki, Tsutomu Hirao, Kevin Duh, Katsuhito Sudoh, and Hajime Tsukada. 2010a. Automatic evaluation of translation quality for distant language pairs. In *Proc.of EMNLP*, pages 944–952.

Hideki Isozaki, Katsuhito Sudoh, Hajime Tsukada, and Kevin Duh. 2010b. Head finalization: A simple reordering rule for sov languages. In *Proceedings of WMT-MetricsMATR*, pages 244–251, July.

Philipp Koehn, Hieu Hoang, Alexandra Birch, Chris Callison-Burch, Marcello Federico, Nicola Bertoldi, Brooke Cowan, Wade Shen, Christine Moran, Richard Zens, Chris Dyer, Ondřej Bojar, Alexandra Constantin, and Evan Herbst. 2007. Moses: Open source toolkit for statistical machine translation. In *Proceedings of the ACL 2007 Demo and Poster Sessions*, pages 177–180.

Yang Liu, Qun Liu, and Shouxun Lin. 2006. Tree-to-string alignment templates for statistical machine transaltion. In *Proceedings of COLING-ACL*, pages 609–616, Sydney, Australia.

Yang Liu, Yajuan Lü, and Qun Liu. 2009a. Improving tree-to-tree translation with packed forests. In *Proceedings of ACL-IJCNLP*, pages 558–566, August.

Yang Liu, Haitao Mi, Yang Feng, and Qun Liu. 2009b. Joint decoding with multiple translation models. In *Proceedings of ACL-IJCNLP*, pages 576–584, August.

Haitao Mi and Liang Huang. 2008. Forest-based translation rule extraction. In *Proceedings of EMNLP*, pages 206–214, October.

Haitao Mi and Qun Liu. 2010. Constituency to dependency translation with forests. In *Proceedings of ACL*, pages 1433–1442, July.

Haitao Mi, Liang Huang, and Qun Liu. 2008. Forest-based translation. In *Proceedings of ACL-08:HLT*, pages 192–199, Columbus, Ohio.

Yusuke Miyao, Takashi Ninomiya, and Jun'ichi Tsujii. 2003. Probabilistic modeling of argument structures including non-local dependencies. In *Proceedings of RANLP*, pages 285–291, Borovets.

Franz Josef Och and Hermann Ney. 2003. A systematic comparison of various statistical alignment models. *Computational Linguistics*, 29(1):19–51.

Franz Josef Och. 2003. Minimum error rate training in statistical machine translation. In *Proceedings of ACL*, pages 160–167.

Kishore Papineni, Salim Roukos, Todd Ward, and Wei-Jing Zhu. 2002. Bleu: a method for automatic evaluation of machine translation. In *Proceedings of ACL*, pages 311–318.

Adam Pauls and Dan Klein. 2011. Faster and smaller n-gram language models. In *Proceedings of ACL-HLT*, pages 258–267, June.

Chris Quirk, Arul Menezes, and Colin Cherry. 2005. Dependency treelet translation: Syntactically informed phrasal smt. In *Proceedings of ACL*, pages 271–279.

Libin Shen, Jinxi Xu, and Ralph Weischedel. 2008. A new string-to-dependency machine translation algorithm with a target dependency language model. In *Proceedings of ACL-08:HLT*, pages 577–585.

Andreas Stolcke. 2002. Srilm-an extensible language modeling toolkit. In *Proceedings of International Conference on Spoken Language Processing*, pages 901–904.

Katsuhito Sudoh, Kevin Duh, Hajime Tsukada, Masaaki Nagata, Xianchao Wu, Takuya Matsuzaki, and Jun'ichi Tsujii. 2011. Ntt-ut statistical machine translation in ntcir-9 patentmt. In *Proceedings of NTCIR-9 Workshop Meeting*, pages 585–592, December.

Xianchao Wu, Takuya Matsuzaki, and Jun'ichi Tsujii. 2010. Fine-grained tree-to-string translation rule extraction. In *Proceedings of ACL*, pages 325–334, July.

Xianchao Wu, Takuya Matsuzaki, and Jun'ichi Tsujii. 2011a. Effective use of function words for rule generalization in forest-based translation. In *Proceedings of ACL-HLT*, pages 22–31, June.

Xianchao Wu, Takuya Matsuzaki, and Jun'ichi Tsujii. 2011b. Smt systems in the university of tokyo for ntcir-9 patentmt. In *Proceedings of NTCIR-9 Workshop Meeting*, pages 666–672, December.

Dekai Wu. 1997. Stochastic inversion transduction grammars and bilingual parsing of parallel corpora. *Computational Linguistics*, 23(3):377–403.

Deyi Xiong, Qun Liu, and Shouxun Lin. 2006. Maximum entropy based phrase reordering model for statistical machine translation. In *Proceedings of COLING-ACL*, pages 521–528, July.

Hui Zhang, Min Zhang, Haizhou Li, Aiti Aw, and Chew Lim Tan. 2009. Forest-based tree sequence to string translation model. In *Proceedings of ACL-IJCNLP*, pages 172–180, Suntec, Singapore, August.

Subgroup Detector: A System for Detecting Subgroups in Online Discussions

Amjad Abu-Jbara
EECS Department
University of Michigan
Ann Arbor, MI, USA
amjbara@umich.edu

Dragomir Radev
EECS Department
University of Michigan
Ann Arbor, MI, USA
radev@umich.edu

Abstract

We present Subgroup Detector, a system for analyzing threaded discussions and identifying the attitude of discussants towards one another and towards the discussion topic. The system uses attitude predictions to detect the split of discussants into subgroups of opposing views. The system uses an unsupervised approach based on rule-based opinion target detecting and unsupervised clustering techniques. The system is open source and is freely available for download. An online demo of the system is available at: http://clair.eecs.umich.edu/SubgroupDetector/

1 Introduction

Online forums discussing ideological and political topics are common[1]. When people discuss a controversial topic, it is normal to see situations of both agreement and disagreement among the discussants. It is even not uncommon that the big group of discussants split into two or more smaller subgroups. The members of each subgroup have the same opinion toward the discission topic. The member of a subgroup is more likely to show positive attitude to the members of the same subgroup, and negative attitude to the members of opposing subgroups. For example, consider the following snippet taken from a debate about school uniform

(1) Discussant 1: I believe that school uniform is a good idea because it improves student attendance.

(2) Discussant 2: I disagree with you. School uniform is a bad idea because people cannot show their personality.

In (1), the writer is expressing positive attitude regarding school uniform. The writer of (2) is expressing negative attitude (disagreement) towards the writer of (1) and negative attitude with respect to the idea of school uniform. It is clear from this short dialog that the writer of (1) and the writer of (2) are members of two opposing subgroups. Discussant 1 supports school uniform, while Discussant 2 is against it.

In this demo, we present an unsupervised system for determining the subgroup membership of each participant in a discussion. We use linguistic techniques to identify attitude expressions, their polarities, and their targets. We use sentiment analysis techniques to identify opinion expressions. We use named entity recognition, noun phrase chunking and coreference resolution to identify opinion targets. Opinion targets could be other discussants or subtopics of the discussion topic. Opinion-target pairs are identified using a number of hand-crafted rules. The functionality of this system is based on our previous work on attitude mining and subgroup detection in online discussions.

This work is related to previous work in the areas of sentiment analysis and online discussion mining. Many previous systems studied the problem of iden-

[1] www.politicalforum.com, www.createdebate.com, www.forandagainst.com, etc

Proceedings of the 50th Annual Meeting of the Association for Computational Linguistics, pages 133–138,
Jeju, Republic of Korea, 8-14 July 2012.

tifying the polarity of individual words (Hatzivassiloglou and McKeown, 1997; Turney and Littman, 2003). Opinionfinder (Wilson et al., 2005) is a system for mining opinions from text. SENTIWORDNET (Esuli and Sebastiani, 2006) is a lexical resource in which each WordNet synset is associated to three numerical scores Obj(s), Pos(s) and Neg(s), describing how objective, positive, and negative the terms contained in the synset are. Dr Sentiment (Das and Bandyopadhyay, 2011) is an online interactive gaming technology used to crowd source human knowledge to build an extension of SentiWordNet.

Another research line focused on analyzing online discussions. For example, Lin et al. (2009) proposed a sparse coding-based model that simultaneously models the semantics and the structure of threaded discussions. Shen et al. (2006) proposed a method for exploiting the temporal and lexical similarity information in discussion streams to identify the reply structure of the dialog. Many systems addressed the problem of extracting social networks from discussions (Elson et al., 2010; McCallum et al., 2007). Other related sentiment analysis systems include MemeTube (Li et al., 2011), a sentiment-based system for analyzing and displaying microblog messages; and C-Feel-It (Joshi et al., 2011), a sentiment analyzer for micro-blogs.

In the rest of this paper, we describe the system architecture, implementation, usage, and its evaluation.

2 System Overview

Figure 1 shows a block diagram of the system components and the processing pipeline. The first component is the *thread parsing* component which takes as input a discussion thread and parses it to identify posts, participants, and the reply structure of the thread. The second component in the pipeline processes the text of posts to identify polarized words and tag them with their polarity. The list of polarity words that we use in this component has been taken from the OpinionFinder system (Wilson et al., 2005).

The polarity of a word is usually affected by the context in which it appears. For example, the word *fine* is positive when used as an adjective and negative when used as a noun. For another example, a positive word that appears in a negated context becomes negative. To address this, we take the part-of-speech (POS) tag of the word into consideration when we assign word polarities. We require that the POS tag of a word matches the POS tag provided in the list of polarized words that we use. The negation issue is handled in the opinion-target pairing step as we will explain later.

The next step in the pipeline is to identify the candidate targets of opinion in the discussion. The target of attitude could be another discussant, an entity mentioned in the discussion, or an aspect of the discussion topic. When the target of opinion is another discussant, either the discussant name is mentioned explicitly or a second person pronoun (e.g you, your, yourself) is used to indicate that the opinion is targeting the recipient of the post.

The target of opinion could also be a subtopic or an entity mentioned in the discussion. We use two methods to identify such targets. The first method depends on identifying noun groups (NG). We consider as an entity any noun group that is mentioned by at least two different discussants. We only consider as entities noun groups that contain two words or more. We impose this requirement because individual nouns are very common and considering all of them as candidate targets will introduce significant noise. In addition to this shallow parsing method, we also use named entity recognition (NER) to identify more targets. The named entity tool that we use recognizes three types of entities: person, location, and organization. We impose no restrictions on the entities identified using this method.

A challenge that always arises when performing text mining tasks at this level of granularity is that entities are usually expressed by anaphorical pronouns. Jakob and Gurevych (2010) showed experimentally that resolving the anaphoric links

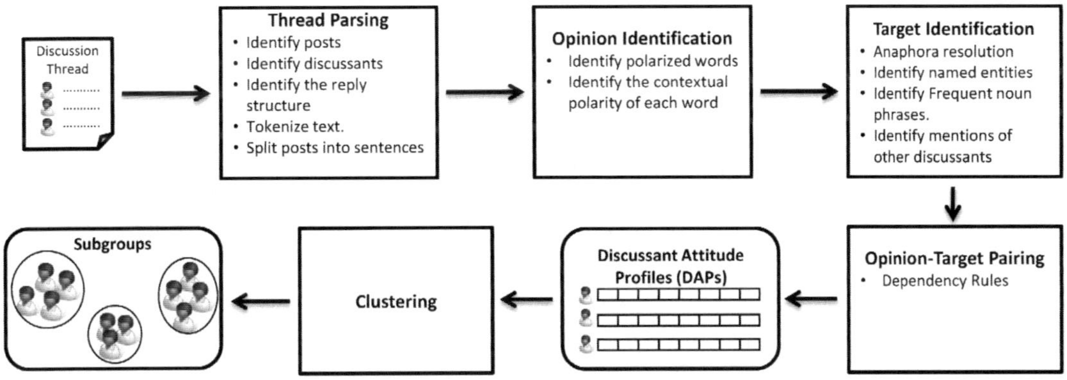

Figure 1: A block diagram illustrating the processing pipeline of the subgroup detection system

in text significantly improves opinion target extraction. Therefore, we use co-reference resolution techniques to resolve all the anaphoric links in the discussion thread.

At this point, we have all the opinion words and the potential targets identified separately. The next step is to determine which opinion word is targeting which target. We propose a rule based approach for opinion-target pairing. Our rules are based on the dependency relations that connect the words in a sentence. An opinion word and a target form a pair if the dependency path between them satisfies at least one of our dependency rules. Table 1 illustrates some of these rules. The rules basically examine the types of dependency relations on the shortest path that connect the opinion word and the target in the dependency parse tree. It has been shown in previous work on relation extraction that the shortest dependency path between any two entities captures the information required to assert a relationship between them (Bunescu and Mooney, 2005). If a sentence S in a post written by participant P_i contains an opinion word OP_j and a target TR_k, and if the opinion-target pair satisfies one of our dependency rules, we say that P_i expresses an attitude towards TR_k. The polarity of the attitude is determined by the polarity of OP_j. We represent this as $P_i \xrightarrow{+} TR_k$ if OP_j is positive and $P_i \xrightarrow{-} TR_k$ if OP_j is negative. Negation is handled in this step by reversing the polarity if the polarized expression is part of a *neg* dependency relation.

It is likely that the same participant P_i expresses sentiment towards the same target TR_k multiple times in different sentences in different posts. We keep track of the counts of all the instances of positive/negative attitude P_i expresses toward TR_k. We represent this as $P_i \xrightarrow[n-]{m+} TR_k$ where m (n) is the number of times P_i expressed positive (negative) attitude toward TR_k.

Now, we have information about each discussant attitude. We propose a representation of discussantsáttitudes towards the identified targets in the discussion thread. As stated above, a target could be another discussant or an entity mentioned in the discussion. Our representation is a vector containing numerical values. The values correspond to the counts of positive/negative attitudes expressed by the discussant toward each of the targets. We call this vector the *discussant attitude profile (DAP)*. We construct a DAP for every discussant. Given a discussion thread with d discussants and e entity targets, each attitude profile vector has $n = (d + e) * 3$ dimensions. In other words, each target (discussant or entity) has three corresponding values in the DAP: 1) the number of times the discussant expressed positive attitude toward the target, 2) the number of times the discussant expressed a negative attitude towards the target, and 3) the number of times the the discussant interacted with or mentioned the target. It has to be noted that these values are not symmet-

ID	Rule	In Words
R1	$OP \rightarrow nsubj \rightarrow TR$	The target *TR* is the nominal subject of the opinion word *OP*
R2	$OP \rightarrow dobj \rightarrow TR$	The target *T* is a direct object of the opinion *OP*
R3	$OP \rightarrow prep\_* \rightarrow TR$	The target *TR* is the object of a preposition that modifies the opinion word *OP*
R4	$TR \rightarrow amod \rightarrow OP$	The opinion is an adjectival modifier of the target
R5	$OP \rightarrow nsubjpass \rightarrow TR$	The target *TR* is the nominal subject of the passive opinion word *OP*
R6	$OP \rightarrow prep\_* \rightarrow poss \rightarrow TR$	The opinion word *OP* connected through a $prep\_*$ relation as in $R2$ to something possessed by the target *TR*
R7	$OP \rightarrow dobj \rightarrow poss \rightarrow TR$	The target *TR* possesses something that is the direct object of the opinion word *OP*
R8	$OP \rightarrow csubj \rightarrow nsubj \rightarrow TR$	The opinon word *OP* is a causal subject of a phrase that has the target *TR* as its nominal subject.

Table 1: Examples of the dependency rules used for opinion-target pairing.

ric since the discussions explicitly denote the source and the target of each post.

At this point, we have an attitude profile (or vector) constructed for each discussant. Our goal is to use these attitude profiles to determine the subgroup membership of each discussant. We can achieve this goal by noticing that the attitude profiles of discussants who share the same opinion are more likely to be similar to each other than to the attitude profiles of discussants with opposing opinions. This suggests that clustering the attitude vector space will achieve the goal and split the discussants into subgroups based on their opinion.

3 Implementation

The system is fully implemented in Java. Part-of-speech tagging, noun group identification, named entity recognition, co-reference resolution, and dependency parsing are all computed using the Stanford Core NLP API.[2] The clustering component uses the JavaML library[3] which provides implementations to several clustering algorithms such as k-means, EM, FarthestFirst, and OPTICS.

The system requires no installation. It, however, requires that the Java Runtime Environment (JRE) be installed. All the dependencies of the system come bundled with the system in the same package. The system works on all the standard platforms.

The system has a command-line interface that provides full access to the system functionality. It can be used to run the whole pipeline to detect subgroups or any portion of the pipeline. For example, it can be used to tag an input text with polarity or to identify candidate targets of opinion in a given input. The system behavior can be controlled by passing arguments through the command line interface. For example, the user can specify which clustering algorithm should be used.

To facilitate using the system for research purposes, the system comes with a clustering evaluation component that uses the ClusterEvaluator package.[4]. If the input to the system contains subgroup labels, it can be run in the evaluation mode in which case the system will output the scores of several different clustering evaluation metrics such as purity, entropy, f-measure, Jaccard, and RandIndex. The system also has a Java API that can be used by researchers to develop other systems using our code.

The system can process any discussion thread that is input to it in a specific format. The format of the input and output is described in the accompanying documentation. It is the user responsibility to write a parser that converts an online discussion thread to the expected format. However, the system package comes with two such parsers for two different discussion sites: www.politicalforum.com and www.createdebate.com.

The distribution also comes with three datasets

[2]http://nlp.stanford.edu/software/corenlp.shtml
[3]http://java-ml.sourceforge.net/
[4]http://eniac.cs.qc.cuny.edu/andrew/v-measure/javadoc/index.html

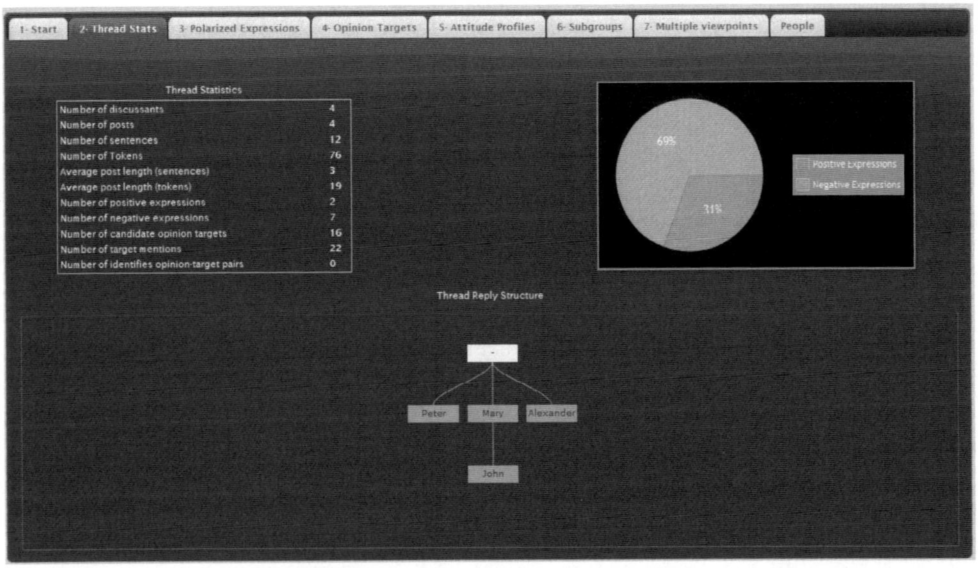

Figure 2: A screenshot of the online demo

(from three different sources) comprising a total of 300 discussion threads. The datasets are annotated with the subgroup labels of discussants.

Finally, we created a web interface to demonstrate the system functionality. The web interface is intended for demonstration purposes only. No web-service is provided. Figure 2 shows a screenshots of the web interface. The online demo can be accessed at http://clair.eecs.umich.edu/SubgroupDetector/

4 Evaluation

In this section, we give a brief summary of the system evaluation. We evaluated the system on discussions comprising more than 10,000 posts in more than 300 different topics. Our experiments show that the system detects subgroups with promising accuracy. The average clustering purity of the detected subgroups in the dataset is 0.65. The system significantly outperforms baseline systems based on text clustering and discussant interaction frequency. Our experiments also show that all the components in the system (such as co-reference resolution, noun phrase chunking, etc) contribute positively to the accuracy.

5 Conclusion

We presented a demonstration of a discussion mining system that uses linguistic analysis techniques to predict the attitude the participants in online discussions forums towards one another and towards the different aspects of the discussion topic. The system is capable of analyzing the text exchanged in discussions and identifying positive and negative attitudes towards different targets. Attitude predictions are used to assign a subgroup membership to each participant using clustering techniques. The system predicts attitudes and identifies subgroups with promising accuracy.

References

Razvan Bunescu and Raymond Mooney. 2005. A shortest path dependency kernel for relation extraction. In *Proceedings of Human Language Technology Conference and Conference on Empirical Methods in Natural Language Processing*, pages 724–731, Vancouver, British Columbia, Canada, October. Association for Computational Linguistics.

Amitava Das and Sivaji Bandyopadhyay. 2011. Dr sentiment knows everything! In *Proceedings of the ACL-HLT 2011 System Demonstrations*, pages 50–55, Portland, Oregon, June. Association for Computational Linguistics.

David Elson, Nicholas Dames, and Kathleen McKeown. 2010. Extracting social networks from literary fiction. In *Proceedings of the 48th Annual Meeting of the Association for Computational Linguistics*, pages 138–147, Uppsala, Sweden, July.

Andrea Esuli and Fabrizio Sebastiani. 2006. Sentiwordnet: A publicly available lexical resource for opinion mining. In *In Proceedings of the 5th Conference on Language Resources and Evaluation (LREC06*, pages 417–422.

Vasileios Hatzivassiloglou and Kathleen R. McKeown. 1997. Predicting the semantic orientation of adjectives. In *EACL'97*, pages 174–181.

Niklas Jakob and Iryna Gurevych. 2010. Using anaphora resolution to improve opinion target identification in movie reviews. In *Proceedings of the ACL 2010 Conference Short Papers*, pages 263–268, Uppsala, Sweden, July. Association for Computational Linguistics.

Aditya Joshi, Balamurali AR, Pushpak Bhattacharyya, and Rajat Mohanty. 2011. C-feel-it: A sentiment analyzer for micro-blogs. In *Proceedings of the ACL-HLT 2011 System Demonstrations*, pages 127–132, Portland, Oregon, June. Association for Computational Linguistics.

Cheng-Te Li, Chien-Yuan Wang, Chien-Lin Tseng, and Shou-De Lin. 2011. Memetube: A sentiment-based audiovisual system for analyzing and displaying microblog messages. In *Proceedings of the ACL-HLT 2011 System Demonstrations*, pages 32–37, Portland, Oregon, June. Association for Computational Linguistics.

Chen Lin, Jiang-Ming Yang, Rui Cai, Xin-Jing Wang, and Wei Wang. 2009. Simultaneously modeling semantics and structure of threaded discussions: a sparse coding approach and its applications. In *SIGIR '09*, pages 131–138.

Andrew McCallum, Xuerui Wang, and Andrés Corrada-Emmanuel. 2007. Topic and role discovery in social networks with experiments on enron and academic email. *J. Artif. Int. Res.*, 30:249–272, October.

Dou Shen, Qiang Yang, Jian-Tao Sun, and Zheng Chen. 2006. Thread detection in dynamic text message streams. In *SIGIR '06*, pages 35–42.

Peter Turney and Michael Littman. 2003. Measuring praise and criticism: Inference of semantic orientation from association. *ACM Transactions on Information Systems*, 21:315–346.

Theresa Wilson, Paul Hoffmann, Swapna Somasundaran, Jason Kessler, Janyce Wiebe, Yejin Choi, Claire Cardie, Ellen Riloff, and Siddharth Patwardhan. 2005. Opinionfinder: a system for subjectivity analysis. In *HLT/EMNLP - Demo*.

A Graphical Interface for MT Evaluation and Error Analysis

Meritxell Gonzàlez and **Jesús Giménez** and **Lluís Màrquez**
TALP Research Center
Universitat Politècnica de Catalunya
{mgonzalez,jgimenez,lluism}@lsi.upc.edu

Abstract

Error analysis in machine translation is a necessary step in order to investigate the strengths and weaknesses of the MT systems under development and allow fair comparisons among them. This work presents an application that shows how a set of heterogeneous automatic metrics can be used to evaluate a test bed of automatic translations. To do so, we have set up an online graphical interface for the ASIYA toolkit, a rich repository of evaluation measures working at different linguistic levels. The current implementation of the interface shows constituency and dependency trees as well as shallow syntactic and semantic annotations, and word alignments. The intelligent visualization of the linguistic structures used by the metrics, as well as a set of navigational functionalities, may lead towards advanced methods for automatic error analysis.

1 Introduction

Evaluation methods are a key ingredient in the development cycle of machine translation (MT) systems. As illustrated in Figure 1, they are used to identify and analyze the system weak points (error analysis), to introduce new improvements and adjust the internal system parameters (system refinement), and to measure the system performance in comparison to other systems or previous versions of the same system (evaluation).

We focus here on the processes involved in the error analysis stage in which MT developers need to understand the output of their systems and to assess the improvements introduced.

Automatic detection and classification of the errors produced by MT systems is a challenging problem. The cause of such errors may depend not only on the translation paradigm adopted, but also on the language pairs, the availability of enough linguistic resources and the performance of the linguistic processors, among others. Several past research works studied and defined fine-grained typologies of translation errors according to various criteria (Vilar et al., 2006; Popović et al., 2006; Kirchhoff et al., 2007), which helped manual annotation and human analysis of the systems during the MT development cycle. Recently, the task has received increasing attention towards the automatic detection, classification and analysis of these errors, and new tools have been made available to the community. Examples of such tools are AMEANA (Kholy and Habash, 2011), which focuses on morphologically rich languages, and Hjerson (Popović, 2011), which addresses automatic error classification at lexical level.

In this work we present an online graphical interface to access ASIYA, an existing software designed to evaluate automatic translations using an heterogeneous set of metrics and meta-metrics. The primary goal of the online interface is to allow MT developers to upload their test beds, obtain a large set of metric scores and then, detect and analyze the errors of their systems using just their Internet browsers. Additionally, the graphical interface of the toolkit may help developers to better understand the strengths and weaknesses of the existing evaluation measures and to support the development of further improvements or even totally new evaluation metrics. This information can be gathered both from the experi-

Proceedings of the 50th Annual Meeting of the Association for Computational Linguistics, pages 139–144,
Jeju, Republic of Korea, 8-14 July 2012.

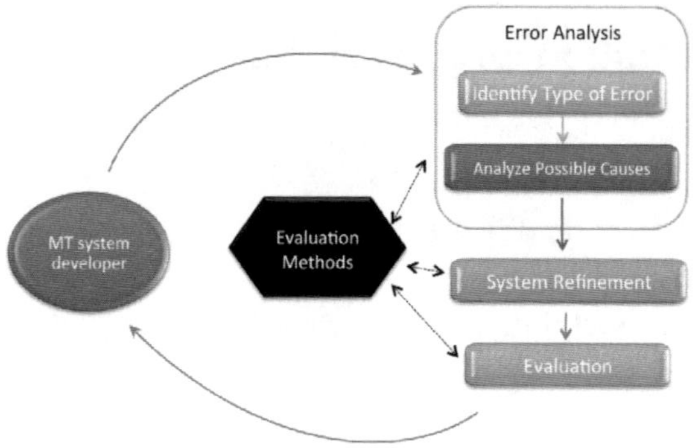

Figure 1: MT systems development cycle

ence of ASIYA's developers and also from the statistics given through the interface to the ASIYA's users.

In the following, Section 2 gives a general overview of the ASIYA toolkit. Section 3 describes the variety of information gathered during the evaluation process, and Section 4 provides details on the graphical interface developed to display this information. Finally, Section 5 overviews recent work related to MT error analysis, and Section 6 concludes and reports some ongoing and future work.

2 The ASIYA Toolkit

ASIYA is an open toolkit designed to assist developers of both MT systems and evaluation measures by offering a rich set of metrics and meta-metrics for assessing MT quality (Giménez and Màrquez, 2010a). Although automatic MT evaluation is still far from manual evaluation, it is indeed necessary to avoid the bottleneck introduced by a fully manual evaluation in the system development cycle. Recently, there has been empirical and theoretical justification that a combination of several metrics scoring different aspects of translation quality should correlate better with humans than just a single automatic metric (Amigó et al., 2011; Giménez and Màrquez, 2010b).

ASIYA offers more than 500 metric variants for MT evaluation, including the latest versions of the most popular measures. These metrics rely on different similarity principles (such as precision, recall and overlap) and operate at different linguistic layers (from lexical to syntactic and semantic). A general classification based on the similarity type is given below along with a brief summary of the information they use and the names of a few examples[1].

Lexical similarity: n-gram similarity and edit distance based on word forms (e.g., PER, TER, WER, BLEU, NIST, GTM, METEOR).

Syntactic similarity: based on part-of-speech tags, base phrase chunks, and dependency and constituency trees (e.g., SP-Overlap-POS, SP-Overlap-Chunk, DP-HWCM, CP-STM).

Semantic similarity: based on named entities, semantic roles and discourse representation (e.g., NE-Overlap, SR-Overlap, DRS-Overlap).

Such heterogeneous set of metrics allow the user to analyze diverse aspects of translation quality at *system*, *document* and *sentence* levels. As discussed in (Giménez and Màrquez, 2008), the widely used lexical-based measures should be considered carefully at sentence level, as they tend to penalize translations using different lexical selection. The combination with complex metrics, more focused on adequacy aspects of the translation (e.g., taking into account also semantic information), should help reducing this problem.

3 The Metric-dependent Information

ASIYA operates over a fixed set of translation test cases, i.e., a source text, a set of candidate translations and a set of manually produced reference translations. To run ASIYA the user must provide a test case and select the preferred set of metrics (it may depend on the evaluation purpose). Then, ASIYA outputs complete tables of score values for all the possible combination of metrics, systems, documents and segments. This kind of results is valuable for rapid evaluation and ranking of translations and systems. However, it is unfriendly for MT developers that need to manually analyze and compare specific aspects of their systems.

During the evaluation process, ASIYA generates a number of intermediate analysis containing partial work outs of the evaluation measures. These data constitute a priceless source for analysis purposes since a close examination of their content allows for analyzing the particular characteristics that

[1] A more detailed description of the metric set and its implementation can be found in (Giménez and Màrquez, 2010b).

		O_l score
Reference	The remote **control of** the Wii **helps** to diagnose **an infantile ocular** disease .	
Candidate 1	The Wii Remote to **help** diagnose **childhood eye** disease .	$\frac{7}{17} = 0.41$
Candidate 2	The control of the Wii helps to diagnose an ocular infantile disease .	$\frac{13}{14} = 0.93$

Table 1: The reference sentence, two candidate translation examples and the O_l scores calculation

differentiate the score values obtained by each candidate translation.

Next, we review the type of information used by each family of measures according to their classification, and how this information can be used for MT error analysis purposes.

Lexical information. There are several variants under this family. For instance, *lexical overlap* (O_l) is an F-measure based metric, which computes similarity roughly using the Jaccard coefficient. First, the sets of all lexical items that are found in the reference and the candidate sentences are considered. Then, O_l is computed as the cardinality of their intersection divided by the cardinality of their union. The example in Table 1 shows the counts used to calculate O_l between the reference and two candidate translations (boldface and underline indicate non-matched items in candidate 1 and 2, respectively). Similarly, metrics in another category measure the edit distance of a translation, i.e., the number of word insertions, deletions and substitutions that are needed to convert a candidate translation into a reference. From the algorithms used to calculate these metrics, these words can be identified in the set of sentences and marked for further processing. On another front, metrics as BLEU or NIST compute a weighted average of matching n-grams. An interesting information that can be obtained from these metrics are the weights assigned to each individual matching n-gram. Variations of all of these measures include looking at stems, synonyms and paraphrases, instead of the actual words in the sentences. This information can be obtained from the implementation of the metrics and presented to the user through the graphical interface.

Syntactic information. ASIYA considers three levels of syntactic information: shallow, constituent and dependency parsing. The shallow parsing annotations, that are obtained from the linguistic processors, consist of word level part-of-speech, lemmas and chunk Begin-Inside-Outside labels. Useful figures such as the matching rate of a given (sub)category of items are the base of a group of metrics (i.e., the ratio of prepositions between a reference and a candidate). In addition, dependency and constituency parse trees allow for capturing other aspects of the translations. For instance, DP-HCWM is a specific subset of the dependency measures that consists of retrieving and matching all the head-word chains (or the ones of a given length) from the dependency trees. Similarly, CP-STM, a subset of the constituency parsing family of measures, consists of computing the lexical overlap according to the phrase constituent of a given type. Then, for error analysis purposes, parse trees combine the grammatical relations and the grammatical categories of the words in the sentence and display the information they contain. Figure 2 and 3 show, respectively, several annotation levels of the sentences in the example and the constituency trees.

Semantic information. ASIYA distinguishes also three levels of semantic information: named entities, semantic roles and discourse representations. The former are post-processed similarly to the lexical annotations discussed above; and the semantic predicate-argument trees are post-processed and displayed in a similar manner to the syntactic trees. Instead, the purpose of the discourse representation analysis is to evaluate candidate translations at document level. In the nested discourse structures we could identify the lexical choices for each discourse sub-type. Presenting this information to the user remains as an important part of the future work.

4 The Graphical Interface

This section presents the web application that makes possible a graphical visualization and interactive access to ASIYA. The purpose of the interface is twofold. First, it has been designed to facilitate the use of the ASIYA toolkit for rapid evaluation of test beds. And second, we aim at aiding the analysis of the errors produced by the MT systems by creating

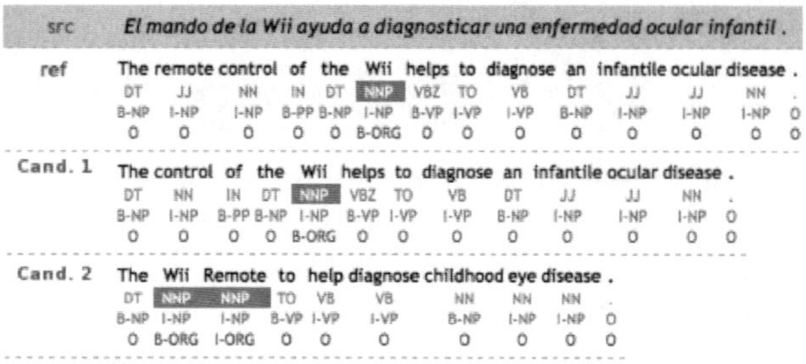

Figure 2: PoS, chunk and named entity annotations on the source, reference and two translation hypotheses

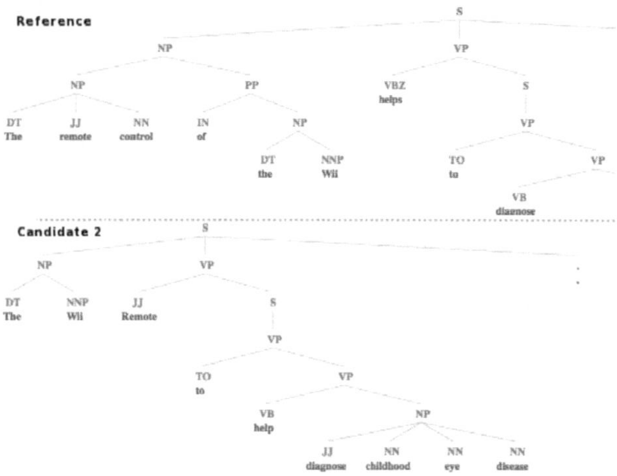

Figure 3: Constituency trees for the reference and second translation candidate

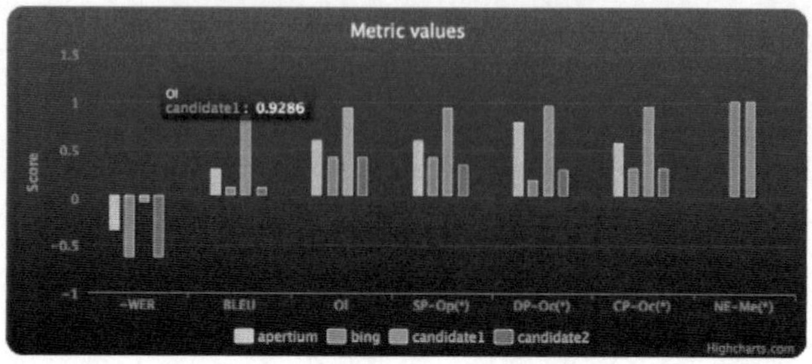

Figure 4: The bar charts plot to compare the metric scores for several systems

a significant visualization of the information related to the evaluation metrics.

The online interface consists of a simple web form to supply the data required to run ASIYA, and then, it offers several views that display the results in friendly and flexible ways such as interactive score tables, graphical parsing trees in SVG format and interactive sentences holding the linguistic annotations captured during the computation of the metrics, as described in Section 3.

4.1 Online MT evaluation

ASIYA allows to compute scores at three granularity levels: *system* (entire test corpus), *document* and *sentence* (or *segment*). The online application obtains the measures for all the metrics and levels and generates an interactive table of scores displaying the values for all the measures. Table organization can swap among the three levels of granularity, and it can also be transposed with respect to system and metric information (transposing rows and columns). When the metric basis table is shown, the user can select one or more metric columns in order to re-rank the rows accordingly. Moreover, the source, reference and candidate translation are displayed along with metric scores. The combination of all these functionalities makes it easy to know which are the highest/lowest-scored sentences in a test set.

We have also integrated a graphical library[2] to generate real-time interactive plots to show the metric scores graphically. The current version of the interface shows interactive bar charts, where different metrics and systems can be combined in the same plot. An example is shown in Figure 4.

4.2 Graphically-aided Error Analysis and Diagnosis

Human analysis is crucial in the development cycle because humans have the capability to spot errors and analyze them subjectively, in relation to the underlying system that is being examined and the scores obtained. Our purpose, as mentioned previously, is to generate a graphical representation of the information related to the source and the translations, enabling a visual analysis of the errors. We have focused on the linguistic measures at the syntactic and semantic level, since they are more robust than lexical metrics when comparing systems based on different paradigms. On the one hand, one of the views of the interface allows a user to navigate and inspect the segments of the test set. This view highlights the elements in the sentences that match a

[2]http://www.highcharts.com/

given criteria based on the various linguistic annotations aforementioned (e.g., PoS prepositions). The interface integrates also the mechanisms to upload word-by-word alignments between the source and any of the candidates. The alignments are also visualized along with the rest of the annotations, and they can be also used to calculate artificial annotations projected from the source in such test beds for which there is no linguistic processors available. On the other hand, the web application includes a library for SVG graph generation in order to create the dependency and the constituent trees dynamically (as shown in Figure 3).

4.3 Accessing the Demo

The online interface is fully functional and accessible at `http://nlp.lsi.upc.edu/asiya/`. Although the ASIYA toolkit is not difficult to install, some specific technical skills are still needed in order to set up all its capabilities (i.e., external components and resources such as linguistic processors and dictionaries). Instead, the online application requires only an up to date browser. The website includes a tarball with sample input data and a video recording, which demonstrates the main functionalities of the interface and how to use it.

The current web-based interface allows the user to upload up to five candidate translation files, five reference files and one source file (maximum size of 200K each, which is enough for test bed of about 1K sentences). Alternatively, the command based version of ASIYA can be used to intensively evaluate a large set of data.

5 Related Work

In the literature, we can find detailed typologies of the errors produced by MT systems (Vilar et al., 2006; Farrús et al., 2011; Kirchhoff et al., 2007) and graphical interfaces for human classification and annotation of these errors, such as BLAST (Stymne, 2011). They represent a framework to study the performance of MT systems and develop further refinements. However, they are defined for a specific pair of languages or domain and they are difficult to generalize. For instance, the study described in (Kirchhoff et al., 2007) focus on measures relying on the characterization of the input documents (source, genre, style, dialect). In contrast, Farrús et al. (2011) classify the errors that arise during Spanish-Catalan translation at several levels: orthographic, morphological, lexical, semantic and syntactic errors.

Works towards the automatic identification and classification of errors have been conducted very recently. Examples of these are (Fishel et al., 2011), which focus on the detection and classification of common lexical errors and misplaced words using a specialized alignment algorithm; and (Popović and Ney, 2011), which addresses the classification of inflectional errors, word reordering, missing words, extra words and incorrect lexical choices using a combination of WER, PER, RPER and HPER scores. The AMEANA tool (Kholy and Habash, 2011) uses alignments to produce detailed morphological error diagnosis and generates statistics at different linguistic levels. To the best of our knowledge, the existing approaches to automatic error classification are centered on the lexical, morphological and shallow syntactic aspects of the translation, i.e., word deletion, insertion and substitution, wrong inflections, wrong lexical choice and part-of-speech. In contrast, we introduce additional linguistic information, such as dependency and constituent parsing trees, discourse structures and semantic roles. Also, there exist very few tools devoted to visualize the errors produced by the MT systems. Here, instead of dealing with the automatic classification of errors, we deal with the automatic selection and visualization of the information used by the evaluation measures.

6 Conclusions and Future Work

The main goal of the ASIYA toolkit is to cover the evaluation needs of researchers during the development cycle of their systems. ASIYA generates a number of linguistic analyses over both the candidate and the reference translations. However, the current command-line interface returns the results only in text mode and does not allow for fully exploiting this linguistic information. We present a graphical interface showing a visual representation of such data for monitoring the MT development cycle. We believe that it would be very helpful for carrying out tasks such as error analysis, system comparison and graphical representations.

The application described here is the first release of a web interface to access ASIYA online. So far, it includes the mechanisms to analyze 4 out of 10 categories of metrics: shallow parsing, dependency parsing, constituent parsing and named entities. Nonetheless, we aim at developing the system until we cover all the metric categories currently available in ASIYA.

Regarding the analysis of the sentences, we have conducted a small experiment to show the ability of the interface to use word level alignments between the source and the target sentences. In the near future, we will include the mechanisms to upload also phrase level alignments. This functionality will also give the chance to develop a new family of evaluation metrics based on these alignments.

Regarding the interactive aspects of the interface, the grammatical graphs are dynamically generated in SVG format, which proffers a wide range of interactive functionalities. However their interactivity is still limited. Further development towards improved interaction would provide a more advanced manipulation of the content, e.g., selection, expansion and collapse of branches.

Concerning the usability of the interface, we will add an alternative form for text input, which will require users to input the source, reference and candidate translation directly without formatting them in files, saving a lot of effort when users need to analyze the translation results of one single sentence.

Finally, in order to improve error analysis capabilities, we will endow the application with a search engine able to filter the results according to varied user defined criteria. The main goal is to provide the mechanisms to select a case set where, for instance, all the sentences are scored above (or below) a threshold for a given metric (or a subset of them).

Acknowledgments

This research has been partially funded by the Spanish Ministry of Education and Science (OpenMT-2, TIN2009-14675-C03) and the European Community's Seventh Framework Programme under grant agreement numbers 247762 (FAUST project, FP7-ICT-2009- 4-247762) and 247914 (MOLTO project, FP7-ICT-2009-4- 247914).

References

Enrique Amigó, Julio Gonzalo, Jesús Giménez, and Felisa Verdejo. 2011. Corroborating text evaluation results with heterogeneous measures. In *Proc. of the EMNLP, Edinburgh, UK*, pages 455–466.

Mireia Farrús, Marta R. Costa-Jussà, José B. Mariño, Marc Poch, Adolfo Hernández, Carlos Henríquez, and José A. Fonollosa. 2011. Overcoming Statistical Machine Translation Limitations: Error Analysis and Proposed Solutions for the Catalan—Spanish Language Pair. *LREC*, 45(2):181–208.

Mark Fishel, Ondřej Bojar, Daniel Zeman, and Jan Berka. 2011. Automatic Translation Error Analysis. In *Proc. of the 14th TSD*, volume LNAI 3658. Springer Verlag.

Jesús Giménez and Lluís Màrquez. 2008. Towards Heterogeneous Automatic MT Error Analysis. In *Proc. of LREC, Marrakech, Morocco*.

Jesús Giménez and Lluís Màrquez. 2010a. Asiya: An Open Toolkit for Automatic Machine Translation (Meta-)Evaluation. *The Prague Bulletin of Mathematical Linguistics*, (94):77–86.

Jesús Giménez and Lluís Màrquez. 2010b. Linguistic Measures for Automatic Machine Translation Evaluation. *Machine Translation*, 24(3–4):77–86.

Ahmed El Kholy and Nizar Habash. 2011. Automatic Error Analysis for Morphologically Rich Languages. In *Proc. of the MT Summit XIII, Xiamen, China*, pages 225–232.

Katrin Kirchhoff, Owen Rambow, Nizar Habash, and Mona Diab. 2007. Semi-Automatic Error Analysis for Large-Scale Statistical Machine Translation Systems. In *Proc. of the MT Summit XI*, Copenhagen, Denmark.

Maja Popović and Hermann Ney. 2011. Towards Automatic Error Analysis of Machine Translation Output. *Computational Linguistics*, 37(4):657–688.

Maja Popović, Hermann Ney, Adrià de Gispert, José B. Mariño, Deepa Gupta, Marcello Federico, Patrik Lambert, and Rafael Banchs. 2006. Morpho-Syntactic Information for Automatic Error Analysis of Statistical Machine Translation Output. In *Proc. of the SMT Workshop*, pages 1–6, New York City, USA. ACL.

Maja Popović. 2011. Hjerson: An Open Source Tool for Automatic Error Classification of Machine Translation Output. *The Prague Bulletin of Mathematical Linguistics*, 96:59–68.

Sara Stymne. 2011. Blast: a Tool for Error Analysis of Machine Translation Output. In *Proc. of the 49th ACL, HLT, Systems Demonstrations*, pages 56–61.

David Vilar, Jia Xu, Luis Fernando D'Haro, and Hermann Ney. 2006. Error Analysis of Machine Translation Output. In *Proc. of the LREC*, pages 697–702, Genoa, Italy.

Online Plagiarism Detection Through Exploiting Lexical, Syntactic, and Semantic Information

Wan-Yu Lin	Nanyun Peng	Chun-Chao Yen	Shou-de Lin
Graduate Institute of Networking and Multimedia, National Taiwan University	Institute of Computational Linguistic, Peking University	Graduate Institute of Networking and Multimedia, National Taiwan University	Graduate Institute of Networking and Multimedia, National Taiwan University
r99944016@csie.ntu.edu.tw	pengnanyun@pku.edu.cn	r96944016@csie.ntu.edu.tw	sdlin@csie.ntu.edu.tw

Abstract

In this paper, we introduce a framework that identifies online plagiarism by exploiting lexical, syntactic and semantic features that includes duplication-gram, reordering and alignment of words, POS and phrase tags, and semantic similarity of sentences. We establish an ensemble framework to combine the predictions of each model. Results demonstrate that our system can not only find considerable amount of real-world online plagiarism cases but also outperforms several state-of-the-art algorithms and commercial software.

Keywords

Plagiarism Detection, Lexical, Syntactic, Semantic

1. Introduction

Online plagiarism, the action of trying to create a new piece of writing by copying, reorganizing or rewriting others' work identified through search engines, is one of the most commonly seen misusage of the highly matured web technologies. As implied by the experiment conducted by (Braumoeller and Gaines, 2001), a powerful plagiarism detection system can effectively discourage people from plagiarizing others' work. A common strategy people adopt for online-plagiarism detection is as follows. First they identify several suspicious sentences from the write-up and feed them one by one as a query to a search engine to obtain a set of documents. Then human reviewers can manually examine whether these documents are truly the sources of the suspicious sentences. While it is quite straightforward and effective, the limitation of this strategy is obvious. First, since the length of search query is limited, suspicious sentences are usually queried and examined independently. Therefore, it is harder to identify document level plagiarism than sentence level plagiarism. Second, manually checking whether a query sentence plagiarizes certain websites requires specific domain and language knowledge as well as considerable amount of energy and time. To overcome the above shortcomings, we introduce an online plagiarism detection system using natural language processing techniques to simulate the above reverse-engineering approach. We develop an ensemble framework that integrates lexical, syntactic and semantic features to achieve this goal. Our system is language independent and we have implemented both Chinese and English versions for evaluation.

2. Related Work

Plagiarism detection has been widely discussed in the past decades (Zou et al., 2010). Table 1. summarizes some of them:

Author	Comparison Unit	Similarity Function
Brin et al., 1995	Word + Sentence	Percentage of matching sentences.
White and Joy, 2004	Sentence	Average overlap ratio of the sentence pairs using 2 pre-defined thresholds.
Niezgoda and Way, 2006	A human defined sliding window	Sliding windows ranked by the average length per word.
Cedeno and Rosso, 2009	Sentence + n-gram	Overlap percentage of n-gram in the sentence pairs.

Proceedings of the 50th Annual Meeting of the Association for Computational Linguistics, pages 145–150,
Jeju, Republic of Korea, 8-14 July 2012. ©2012 Association for Computational Linguistics

Pera and Ng, 2010	Sentence	A pre-defined resemblance function based on word correlation factor.
Stamatatos, 2011	Passage	Overlap percentage of stopword n-grams.
Grman and Ravas, 2011	Passage	Matching percentage of words with given thresholds on both ratio and absolute number of words in passage.

Table 1. Summary of related works

Comparing to those systems, our system exploits more sophisticated syntactic and semantic information to simulate what plagiarists are trying to do.

There are several online or charged/free downloadable plagiarism detection systems such as Turnitin, EVE2, Docol©c, and CATPPDS which detect mainly verbatim copy. Others such as Microsoft Plagiarism Detector (MPD), Safeassign, Copyscape and VeriGuide, claim to be capable of detecting obfuscations. Unfortunately those commercial systems do not reveal the detail strategies used, therefore it is hard to judge and reproduce their results for comparison.

3. Methodology

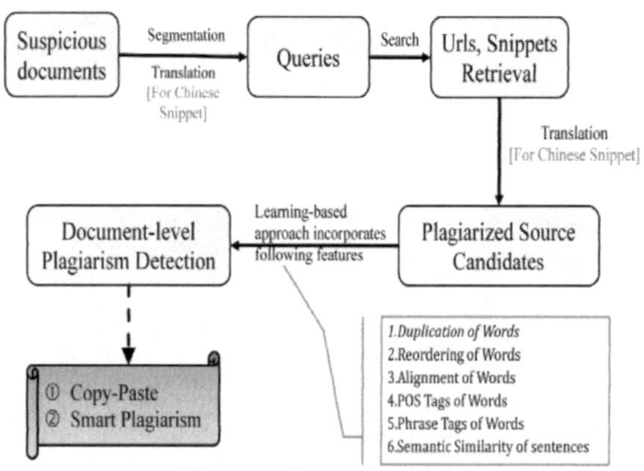

Figure 1. Detection Flow

The data flow is shown above in Figure 1.

3.1 Query a Search Engine

We first break down each article into a series of queries to query a search engine. Several systems such as (Liu at al., 2007) have proposed a similar idea. The main difference between our method and theirs is that we send *unquoted* queries rather than quoted ones. We do not require the search results to completely match to the query sentence. This strategy allows us to not only identify the copy/paste type of plagiarism but also re-write/edit type of plagiarism.

3.2 Sentence-based Plagiarism Detection

Since not all outputs of a search engine contain an exact copy of the query, we need a model to quantify how likely each of them is the source of plagiarism. For better efficiency, our experiment exploits the snippet of a search output to represent the whole document. That is, we want to measure how likely a snippet is the plagiarized source of the query. We designed several models which utilized rich lexical, syntactic and semantic features to pursue this goal, and the details are discussed below.

3.2.1 Ngram Matching (NM)

One straightforward measure is to exploit the n-gram similarity between source and target texts. We first enumerate all n-grams in source, and then calculate the overlap percentage with the n-grams in the target. The larger n is, the harder for this feature to detect plagiarism with insertion, replacement, and deletion. In the experiment, we choose n=2.

3.2.2 Reordering of Words (RW)

Plagiarism can come from the reordering of words. We argue that the permutation distance between S_1 and S_2 is an important indicator for reordered plagiarism. The permutation distance is defined as the minimum number of pair-wise exchanging of matched words needed to transform a sentence, S_2, to contain the same order of matched words as another sentence, S_1. As mentioned in (Sörensena and Sevaux, 2005), the permutation distance can be calculated by the following expression $d(S_1,S_2) = \sum_{i=1}^{n-1}\sum_{j=i+1}^{n} z_{ij}$
where

$$z_{ij} = \begin{cases} 1, & if\ S_1(j) > S_1(i) and\ S_2(j) < S_2(i) \\ 0, & otherwise \end{cases}$$

$S_1(i)$ and $S_2(i)$ are indices of the ith matched word in sentences S_1 and S_2 respectively and n is the number of matched words between the sentences S_1 and S_2. Let $\mu = \frac{n^2-n}{2}$ be the normalized term, which is the maximum possible distance between S_1 and S_2, then the reordering score of the two sentences, expressed as $s(S_1, S_2)$, will be $s(S_1, S_2) = 1 - \frac{d(S_1, S_2)}{\mu}$

3.2.3 *Alignment of Words (AW)*

Besides reordering, plagiarists often insert or delete words in a sentence. We try to model such behavior by finding the alignment of two word sequences. We perform the alignment using a dynamic programming method as mentioned in (Wagner and Fischer, 1975).

However, such alignment score does not reflect the continuity of the matched words, which can be an important cue to identify plagiarism. To overcome such drawback, we modify the score as below.

$$New\ Alignment\ Score = \frac{\sum_{i=1}^{|M|-1} G_i}{|M|-1}$$

where $G_i = \frac{1}{\#\ of\ words\ between\ (M_i, M_{i+1})+1}$

M is the list of matched words, and M_i is the ith matched word in M. This implies we prefer fewer unmatched words in between two matched ones.

3.2.4 *POS and Phrase Tags of Words (PT, PP)*

Exploiting only lexical features can sometimes result in some false positive cases because two sets of matched words can play different roles in the sentences. See S_1 and S_2 in Table 2. as a possible false positive case.

S_1: The man likes the woman				
S_2: The woman is like the man				
Word	S_1: Tag	S_2: Tag	S_1: Phrase	S_2: Phrase
man	NN	NN	NP	PP
like	VBZ	IN	VP	PP
woman	NN	NN	VP	NP

Table 2. An example of matched words with different tags and phrases

Therefore, we further explore syntactic features for plagiarism detection. To achieve this goal, we utilize a parser to obtain POS and phrase tags of the words. Then we design an equation to measure the tag/phrase similarity.

$$Sim = \frac{num\ (matched\ words\ with\ identical\ tag)}{num\ (matched\ words)}$$

We paid special attention to the case that transforms a sentence from an active form to a passive-form or vice versa. A subject originally in a Noun Phrase can become a Preposition Phrase, i.e. "by …", in the passive form while the object in a Verb Phrase can become a new subject in a Noun Phrase. Here we utilize the Stanford Dependency provided by Stanford Parser to match the tag/phrase between active and passive sentences.

3.2.5 *Semantic Similarity (LDA)*

Plagiarists, sometimes, change words or phrases to those with similar meanings. While previous works (Y. Lin et al., 2006) often explore semantic similarity using lexical databases such as WordNet to find synonyms, we exploit a topic model, specifically latent Dirichlet allocation (LDA, D. M. Blei et al., 2003), to extract the semantic features of sentences. Given a set of documents represented by their word sequences, and a topic number n, LDA learns the word distribution for each topic and the topic distribution for each document which maximize the likelihood of the word co-occurrence in a document. The topic distribution is often taken as semantics of a document. We use LDA to obtain the topic distribution of a query and a candidate snippet, and compare the cosine similarity of them as a measure of their semantic similarity.

3.3 Ensemble Similarity Scores

Up to this point, for each snippet the system generates six similarity scores to measure the degree of plagiarism in different aspects. In this stage, we propose two strategies to linearly combine the scores to make better prediction. The first strategy utilizes each model's predictability (e.g. accuracy) as the weight to linearly combine the scores. In other words, the models that perform better individually will obtain higher weights. In the second strategy we exploit a learning model (in the experiment section we use Liblinear) to learn the weights directly.

3.4 Document Level Plagiarism Detection

For each query from the input article, our system assigns a degree-of-plagiarism score to some plausible source URLs. Then, for each URL, the system sums up all the scores it obtains as the final score for document-level degree-of-plagiarism. We set up a cutoff threshold to obtain the most plausible URLs. At the end, our system highlights the suspicious areas of plagiarism for display.

4. Evaluation

We evaluate our system from two different angles. We first evalaute the *sentence level plagirism detection* using the PAN corpus in English. We then evaluate the capability of the full system to detect on-line plagiarism cases using annotated results in Chinese.

4.1 Sentence-based Evaluations

We want to compare our model with the state-of-the-art methods, in particular the winning entries in plagiarism detection competition in PAN [1]. However, the competition in PAN is designed for off-line plagiarism detection; the entries did not exploit an IR system to search the Web like we do. Nevertheless, we can still compare the core component of our system, the *sentence-based measuring* model with that of other systems. To achieve such goal, we first randomly sampled 370 documents from PAN-2011 external plagiarism corpus (M. Potthast et al., 2010) containing 2882 labeled plagiarism cases.

To obtain high-quality negative examples for evaluation, we built a full-text index on the corpus using Lucene package. Then we use the suspicious passages as queries to search the whole dataset using Lucene. Since there is length limitation in Lucene (as well as in the real search engines), we further break the 2882 plagiarism cases into 6477 queries. We then extract the top 30 snippets returned by the search engine as the potential negative candidates for each plagiarism case. Note that for each suspicious passage, there is only one target passage (given by the ground truth) that is considered as a positive plagiarism case in this data, and it can be either among these 30 cases or not. However, we union these 30 cases with the ground truth as a set, and use our (as well as the competitors') models to rank the degree-of-plagiarism for all the candidates. We then evaluate the rank by the area-under-PR-curve (AUC) score. We compared our system with the winning entry of PAN 2011 (Grman and Ravas, 2011) and the stopword ngram model that claims to perform better than this winning entry by Stamatatos (2011). The results of each individual model and ensemble using 5-fold cross validation are listed in Table 3. It shows that NM is the best individual model, and an ensemble of three features outperforms the state-of-the-art by 26%.

NM	*RW*	*AW*	*PT*	*PP*	*LDA*
0.876	0.596	0.537	0.551	0.521	0.596

(a)

	Ours ensemble	*Pan-11 Champion*	*Stopword Ngram*
AUC	0.882 (NM+RW+PP)	0.620	0.596

(b)

Table 3. (a) AUC for each individual model (b) AUC of our ensemble and other state-of-the-art algorithms

4.2 Evaluating the Full System

To evaluate the overall system, we manually collect 60 real-world review articles from the Internet for books (20), movies (20), and music albums (20). Unfortunately for an online system like ours, there is no ground truth available for recall measure. We conduct two differement evalautions. First we use the 60 articles as inputs to our system, ask 5 human annotators to check whether the articles returned by our system can be considered as plagiarism. Among all 60 review articles, our system identifies a considerablely high number of copy/paste articles, 231 in total. However, identifying this type of plagiarism is trivial, and has been done by many similar tools. Instead we focus on the so-called *smart-plagiarism* which cannot be found through quoting a query in a search engine. Table 4. shows the precision of the smart-plagiarism articles returned by our system. The precision is very high and outperforms a commertial tool Microsoft Plagiarism Detector.

	Book	*Movie*	*Music*
Ours	280/288 (97%)	88/110 (80%)	979/1033 (95%)
MPD	44/53 (83%)	123/172 (72%)	120/161 (75%)

Table 4. Precision of Smart Plagiarism

In the second evaluation, we first choose 30 reviews randomly. Then we use each of them as queries into Google and retrieve a total of 5636 pieces of snippet candidates. We then ask 63 human beings to annotate whether those snippets represent plagiarism cases of the original review article. Eventually we have obtained an annotated

[1] The website of PAN-2011 is http://pan.webis.de/

dataset and found a total of 502 plagiarized candidates with 4966 innocent ones for evalaution. Table 5. shows the average AUC of 5-fold cross validation. The results show that our method outperforms the Pan-11 winner slightly, and much better than the Stopword Ngram.

NM	*RW*	*AW*	*PT*	*PP*	*LDA*
0.904	0.778	0.874	0.734	0.622	0.581

(a)

	Ours ensemble	***Pan-11 Champion***	***Stopword Ngram***
AUC	0.919 (NM+RW+AW +PT+PP+LDA)	0.893	0.568

(b)

Table 5. (a) AUC for each individual model (b) AUC of our ensemble and other state-of-the-art algorithms

4.3 Discussion

There is some inconsistency of the performance of single features in these two experiments. The main reason we believe is that the plagiarism cases were created in very different manners. Plagiarism cases in PAN external source are created artificially through word insertions, deletions, reordering and synonym substitutions. As a result, features such as word alignment and reordering do not perform well because they did not consider the existence of synonym word replacement. On the other hand, real-world plagiarism cases returned by Google are those with matching-words, and we can find better performance for *AW*.

The performances of syntactic and semantic features, namely *PT, PP and LDA*, are consistently inferior than other features. It is because they often introduce false-positives as there are some non-plagiarism cases that might have highly overlapped syntactic or semantic tags. Nevertheless, experiments also show that these features can improve the overall accuracy in ensemble.

We also found that the *stopword Ngram* model is not applicable universally. For one thing, it is less suitable for on-line plagiarism detection, as the length limitation for queries diminishes the usability of stopword n-grams. For another, Chinese seems to be a language that does not rely as much on stopwords as the latin languages do to maintain its syntax structure.

Samples of our system's finding can be found here, http://tinyurl.com/6pnhurz

5. Online Demo System

We developed an online demos system using JAVA (JDK 1.7). The system currently supports the detection of documents in both English and Chinese. Users can either upload the plain text file of a suspicious document, or copy/paste the content onto the text area, as shown below in Figure 2.

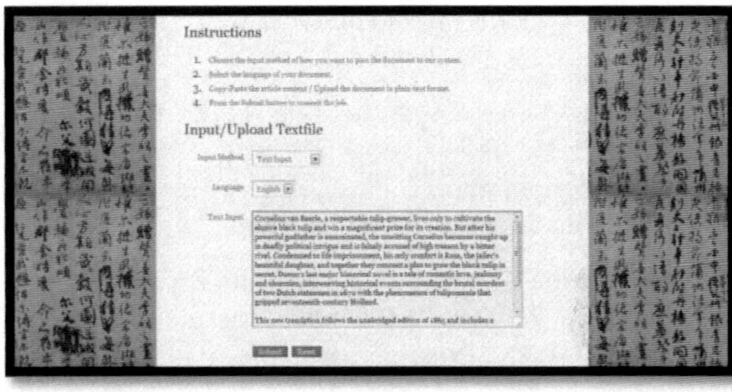

Figure 2. Input Screen-Shot

Then the system will output some URLs and snippets as the potential source of plagiarism. (see Figure 3.)

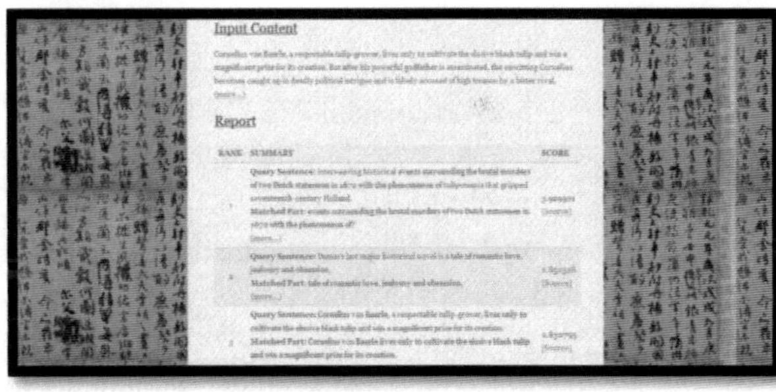

Figure 3. Output Screen-Shot

6. Conclusion

Comparing with other online plagiarism detection systems, ours exploit more sophisticated features by modeling how human beings plagiarize online sources. We have exploited sentence-level plagiarism detection on lexical, syntactic and semantic levels. Another noticeable fact is that our approach is almost language independent. Given a parser and a POS tagger of a language, our framework can be extended to support plagiarism detection for that language.

7. References

Salha Alzahrani, Naomie Salim, and Ajith Abraham, "Understanding Plagiarism Linguistic Patterns, Textual Features and Detection Methods " in IEEE Transactions on systems , man and cyberneticsPart C: Applications and reviews, 2011

D. M. Blei, A. Y. Ng, M. I. Jordan, and J. Lafferty. Latent dirichlet allocation. Journal of Machine Learning Research, 3:2003, 2003.

Bear F. Braumoeller and Brian J. Gaines. 2001. Actions Do Speak Louder Than Words: Deterring Plagiarism with the Use of Plagiarism-Detection Software. In Political Science & Politics, 34(4):835-839.

Sergey Brin, James Davis, and Hector Garcia-molina. 1995. Copy Detection Mechanisms for Digital Documents. In Proceedings of the ACM SIGMOD Annual Conference, 24(2):398-409.

Alberto Barrón Cedeño and Paolo Rosso. 2009. On Automatic Plagiarism Detection based on n-grams Comparison. In Proceedings of the 31th European Conference on IR Research on Advances in Information Retrieval, ECIR 2009, LNCS 5478:696-700, Springer-Verlag, and Berlin Heidelberg,

Jan Grman and Rudolf Ravas. 2011. Improved implementation for finding text similarities in large collections of data.In Proceedings of PAN 2011.

NamOh Kang, Alexander Gelbukh, and SangYong Han. 2006. PPChecker: Plagiarism Pattern Checker in Document Copy Detection. In Proceedings of TSD-2006, LNCS, 4188:661-667.

Yuhua Li, David McLean, Zuhair A. Bandar, James D. O' Shea, and Keeley Crockett. 2006. Sentence Similarity Based on Semantic Nets and Corpus Statistics. In Proceedings of the IEEE Transactions on Knowledge and Data Engineering, 18(8):1138-1150.

Yi-Ting Liu, Heng-Rui Zhang, Tai-Wei Chen, and Wei-Guang Teng. 2007. Extending Web Search for Online Plagiarism Detection. In Proceedings of the IEEE International Conference on Information Reuse and Integration, IRI 2007.

Caroline Lyon, Ruth Barrett, and James Malcolm. 2004. A Theoretical Basis to the Automated Detection of Copying Between Texts, and its Practical Implementation in the Ferret Plagiarism and Collusion Detector. In Proceedings of Plagiarism: Prevention, Practice and Policies 2004 Conference.

Sebastian Niezgoda and Thomas P. Way. 2006. SNITCH: A Software Tool for Detecting Cut and Paste Plagiarism. In Proceedings of the 37th SIGCSE Technical Symposium on Computer Science Education, p.51-55.

Maria Soledad Pera and Yiu-kai Ng. 2010. IOS Press SimPaD: A Word-Similarity Sentence-Based Plagiarism Detection Tool on Web Documents. In Journal on Web Intelligence and Agent Systems, 9(1).

Xuan-Hieu Phan and Cam-Tu Nguyen. GibbsLDA++: A C/C++ implementation of latent Dirichlet allocation (LDA), 2007

Martin Potthast, Benno Stein, Alberto Barrón Cedeño, and Paolo Rosso. An Evaluation Framework for Plagiarism Detection. In 23rd International Conference on Computational Linguistics (COLING 10), August 2010. Association for Computational Linguistics.

Kenneth Sörensena and Marc Sevaux. 2005. Permutation Distance Measures for Memetic Algorithms with Population Management. In Proceedings of 6th Metaheuristics International Conference.

Efstathios Stamatatos, "Plagiarism Detection Based on Structural Information" in Proceedings of the 20th ACM international conference on Information and knowledge management, CIKM'11

Robert A. Wagner and Michael J. Fischer. 1975. The String-to-string correction problem. In Journal of the ACM, 21(1):168-173.

Daniel R. White and Mike S. Joy. 2004. Sentence-Based Natural Language Plagiarism Detection. In Journal on Educational Resources in Computing JERIC Homepage archive, 4(4).

Du Zou, Wei-jiang Long, and Zhang Ling. 2010. A Cluster-Based Plagiarism Detection Method. In Lab Report for PAN at CLEF 2010.

UWN: A Large Multilingual Lexical Knowledge Base

Gerard de Melo
ICSI Berkeley
demelo@icsi.berkeley.edu

Gerhard Weikum
Max Planck Institute for Informatics
weikum@mpi-inf.mpg.de

Abstract

We present UWN, a large multilingual lexical knowledge base that describes the meanings and relationships of words in over 200 languages. This paper explains how link prediction, information integration and taxonomy induction methods have been used to build UWN based on WordNet and extend it with millions of named entities from Wikipedia. We additionally introduce extensions to cover lexical relationships, frame-semantic knowledge, and language data. An online interface provides human access to the data, while a software API enables applications to look up over 16 million words and names.

1 Introduction

Semantic knowledge about words and named entities is a fundamental building block both in various forms of language technology as well as in end-user applications. Examples of the latter include word processor thesauri, online dictionaries, question answering, and mobile services. Finding semantically related words is vital for query expansion in information retrieval (Gong et al., 2005), database schema matching (Madhavan et al., 2001), sentiment analysis (Godbole et al., 2007), and ontology mapping (Jean-Mary and Kabuka, 2008). Further uses of lexical knowledge include data cleaning (Kedad and Métais, 2002), visual object recognition (Marszałek and Schmid, 2007), and biomedical data analysis (Rubin and others, 2006).

Many of these applications have used English-language resources like WordNet (Fellbaum, 1998). However, a more multilingual resource equipped with an easy-to-use API would not only enable us to perform all of the aforementioned tasks in additional languages, but also to explore cross-lingual applications like cross-lingual IR (Etzioni et al., 2007) and machine translation (Chatterjee et al., 2005).

This paper describes a new API that makes lexical knowledge about millions of items in over 200 languages available to applications, and a corresponding online user interface for users to explore the data. We first describe link prediction techniques used to create the multilingual core of the knowledge base with word sense information (Section 2). We then outline techniques used to incorporate named entities and specialized concepts (Section 3) and other types of knowledge (Section 4). Finally, we describe how the information is made accessible via a user interface (Section 5) and a software API (Section 6).

2 The UWN Core

UWN (de Melo and Weikum, 2009) is based on WordNet (Fellbaum, 1998), the most popular lexical knowledge base for the English language. WordNet enumerates the senses of a word, providing a short description text (gloss) and synonyms for each meaning. Additionally, it describes relationships between senses, e.g. via the hyponymy/hypernymy relation that holds when one term like '*publication*' is a generalization of another term like '*journal*'.

This model can be generalized by allowing words in multiple languages to be associated with a meaning (without, of course, demanding every meaning be lexicalized in every language). In order to accomplish this at a large scale, we automatically link

Proceedings of the 50th Annual Meeting of the Association for Computational Linguistics, pages 151–156,
Jeju, Republic of Korea, 8-14 July 2012.

terms in different languages to the meanings already defined in WordNet. This transforms WordNet into a multilingual lexical knowledge base that covers not only English terms but hundreds of thousands of terms from many different languages.

Unfortunately, a straightforward translation runs into major difficulties because of homonyms and synonyms. For example, a word like '*bat*' has 10 senses in the English WordNet, but a German translation like '*Fledermaus*' (the animal) only applies to a small subset of those senses (cf. Figure 1). This challenge can be approached by disambiguating using machine learning techniques.

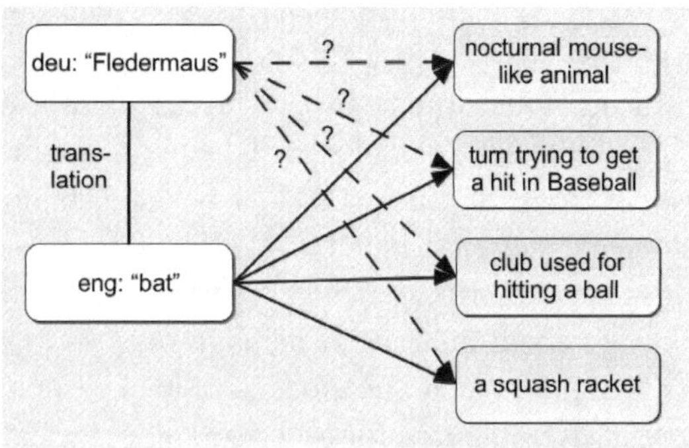

Figure 1: Word sense ambiguity

Knowledge Extraction An initial input knowledge base graph G_0 is constructed by extracting information from existing wordnets, translation dictionaries including Wiktionary (*http://www.wiktionary.org*), multilingual thesauri and ontologies, and parallel corpora. Additional heuristics are applied to increase the density of the graph and merge near-duplicate statements.

Link Prediction A sequence of knowledge graphs G_i are iteratively derived by assessing paths from a new term x to an existing WordNet sense z via some English translation y covered by WordNet. For instance, the German '*Fledermaus*' has '*bat*' as a translation and hence initially is tentatively linked to all senses of '*bat*' with a confidence of 0. In each iteration, the confidence values are then updated to reflect how likely it seems that those links are correct. The confidences are predicted using RBF-kernel SVM models that are learnt from a training set of labelled links between non-English words and senses. The feature space is constructed using a series of graph-based statistical scores that represent properties of the previous graph G_{i-1} and additionally make use of measures of semantic relatedness and corpus frequencies. The most salient features $x_i(x, z)$ are of the form:

$$\sum_{y \in \Gamma(x,G_{i-1})} \phi(x,y)\,\mathrm{sim}^*_x(y,z) \qquad (1)$$

$$\sum_{y \in \Gamma(x,G_{i-1})} \frac{\phi(x,y)\,\mathrm{sim}^*_x(y,z)}{\mathrm{sim}^*_x(y,z)\;+\mathrm{dissim}_x(y,z)} \qquad (2)$$

The formulae consider the out-neighbourhood $y \in \Gamma(x, G_{i-1})$ of x, i.e. its translations, and then observe how strongly each y is tied to z. The function sim^* computes the maximal similarity between any sense of y and the current sense z. The dissim function computes the sum of dissimilarities between senses of y and z, essentially quantifying how many alternatives there are to z. Additional weighting functions ϕ, γ are used to bias scores towards senses that have an acceptable part-of-speech and senses that are more frequent in the SemCor corpus.

Relying on multiple iterations allows us to draw on multilingual evidence for greater precision and recall. For instance, after linking the German '*Fledermaus*' to the animal sense of '*bat*', we may be able to infer the same for the Turkish translation '*yarasa*'.

Results We have successfully applied these techniques to automatically create UWN, a large-scale multilingual wordnet. Evaluating random samples of term-sense links, we find (with Wilson-score intervals at $\alpha = 0.05$) that for French the precision is $89.2\% \pm 3.4\%$ (311 samples), for German $85.9\% \pm 3.8\%$ (321 samples), and for Mandarin Chinese $90.5\% \pm 3.3\%$ (300 samples). The overall number of new term-sense links is 1,595,763, for 822,212 terms in over 200 languages. These figures can be grown further if the input is extended by tapping on additional sources of translations.

3 MENTA: Named Entities and Specialized Concepts

The UWN Core is extended by incorporating large amounts of named entities and language- and domain-specific concepts from Wikipedia (de Melo and Weikum, 2010a). In the process, we also obtain human-readable glosses in many languages, links to images, and other valuable information. These additions are not simply added as a separate knowledge base, but fully connected and integrated with the core. In particular, we create a mapping between Wikipedia and WordNet in order to merge equivalent entries and we use taxonomy construction methods in order to attach all new named entities to their most likely classes, e.g. '*Haight-Ashbury*' is linked to a WordNet sense of the word '*neighborhood*'.

Information Integration Supervised link prediction, similar to the method presented in Section 2, is used in order to attach Wikipedia articles to semantically equivalent WordNet entries, while also exploiting gloss similarity as an additional feature. Additionally, we connect articles from different multilingual Wikipedia editions via their cross-lingual interwiki links, as well as categories with equivalent articles and article redirects with redirect targets.

We then consider connected components of directly or transitively linked items. In the ideal case, such a connected component consists of a number of items all describing the same concept or entity, including articles from different versions of Wikipedia and perhaps also categories or WordNet senses.

Unfortunately, in many cases one obtains connected components that are unlikely to be correct, because multiple articles from the same Wikipedia edition or multiple incompatible WordNet senses are included in the same component. This can be due to incorrect links produced by the supervised link prediction, but often even the original links from Wikipedia are not consistent.

In order to obtain more consistent connected components, we use combinatorial optimization methods to delete certain links. In particular, for each connected component to be analysed, an Integer Linear Program formalizes the objective of minimizing the costs for deleted edges and the costs for ignoring soft constraints. The basic aim is that of deleting as few edges as possible while simultaneously ensuring that the graph becomes as consistent as possible. In some cases, there is overwhelming evidence indicating that two slightly different articles should be grouped together, while in other cases there might be little evidence for the correctness of an edge and so it can easily be deleted with low cost.

While obtaining an exact solution is NP-hard and APX-hard, we can solve the corresponding Linear Program using a fast LP solver like CPLEX and subsequently apply region growing techniques to obtain a solution with a logarithmic approximation guarantee (de Melo and Weikum, 2010b).

The clean connected components resulting from this process can then be merged to form aggregate entities. For instance, given WordNet's standard sense for '*fog*', water vapor, we can check which other items are in the connected component and transfer all information to the WordNet entry. By extracting snippets of text from the beginning of Wikipedia articles, we can add new gloss descriptions for fog in Arabic, Asturian, Bengali, and many other languages. We can also attach pictures showing fog to the WordNet word sense.

Taxonomy Induction The above process connects articles to their counterparts in WordNet. In the next step, we ensure that articles without any direct counterpart are linked to WordNet as well, by means of taxonomic hypernymy/instance links (de Melo and Weikum, 2010a).

We generate individual hypotheses about likely parents of entities. For instance, articles are connected to their Wikipedia categories (if these are not assessed to be mere topic descriptors) and categories are linked to parent categories, etc. In order to link categories to possible parent hypernyms in WordNet, we adapt the approach proposed for YAGO (Suchanek et al., 2007) of determining the headword of the category name and disambiguating it.

Since we are dealing with a multilingual scenario that draws on articles from different multilingual Wikipedia editions that all need to be connected to WordNet, we apply an algorithm that jointly looks at an entity and all of its parent candidates (not just from an individual article, but all articles in the same connected component) as well as superordinate parent candidates (parents of parents, etc.), as depicted in Figure 2. We then construct a Markov chain based on this graph of parents that also incorporates the possibility of random jumps from any parent back to the current entity under consideration. The stationary probability of this Markov chain, which can be obtained using random walk methods, provides us a ranking of the most likely parents.

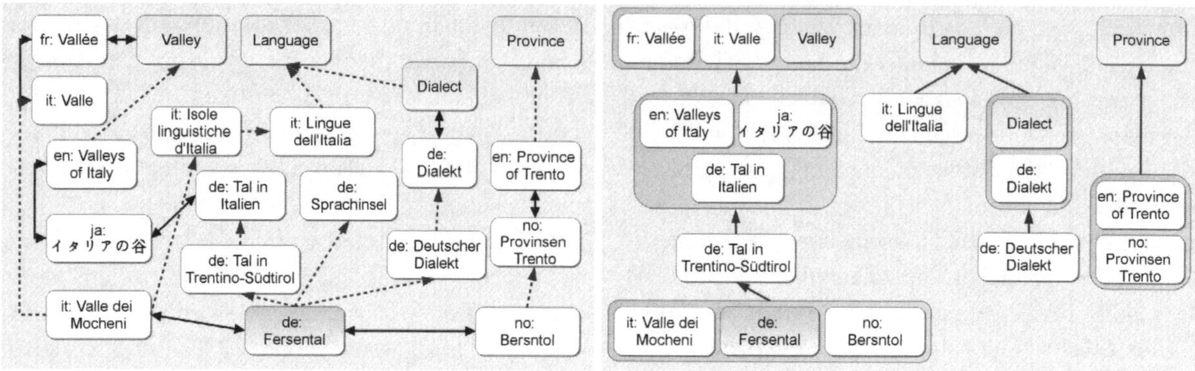

Figure 2: Noisy initial edges (left) and cleaned, integrated output (right), shown in a simplified form

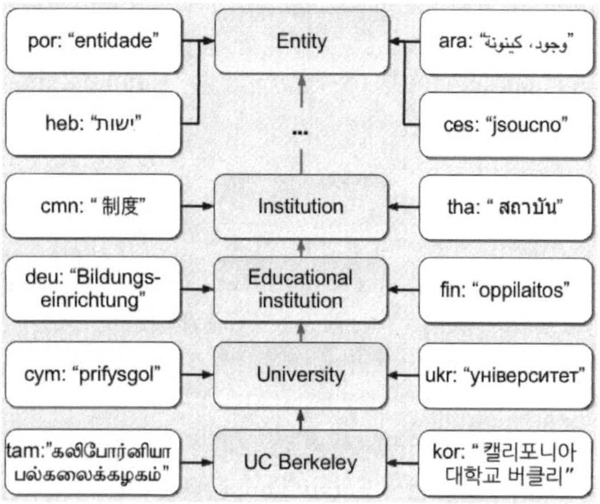

Figure 3: UWN with named entities

Results Overall, we obtain a knowledge base with 5.4 million concepts or entities and 16.7 million words or names associated with them from over 200 languages. Over 2 million named entities come only from non-English Wikipedia editions, but their taxonomic links to WordNet still have an accuracy around 90%. An example excerpt is shown in Figure 3, with named entities connected to higher-level classes in UWN, all with multilingual labels.

4 Other Extensions

Word Relationships Another plugin provides word relationships and properties mined from Wiktionary. These include derivational and etymological word relationships (e.g. that '*grotesque*' comes from the Italian '*grotta*': grotto, artificial cave), alternative spellings (e.g. '*encyclopædia*' for '*encyclopedia*'), common misspellings (e.g. '*miniscule*' for '*minuscule*'), pronunciation information (e.g. how to pronounce '*nuclear*'), and so on.

Frame-Semantic Knowledge Frame semantics is a cognitively motivated theory that describes words in terms of the cognitive frames or scenarios that they evoke and the corresponding participants involved in them. For a given frame, FrameNet provides definitions, involved participants, associated words, and relationships. For instance, the `Commerce_goods-transfer` frame normally involves a seller and a buyer, among other things, and different words like '*buy*' and '*sell*' can be chosen to describe the same event.

Such detailed knowledge about scenarios is largely complementary in nature to the sense relationships that WordNet provides. For instance, WordNet emphasizes the opposite meaning of the words '*happy*' and '*unhappy*', while frame semantics instead emphasizes the cognitive relatedness of words like '*happy*', '*unhappy*', '*astonished*', and '*amusement*', and explains that typical participants include an experiencer who experiences the emotions and external stimuli that evoke them. There have been individual systems that made use of both forms of knowledge (Shi and Mihalcea, 2005; Coppola and others, 2009), but due to their very different nature, there is currently no simple way to accomplish this feat. Our system addresses this by seamlessly integrating frame semantic knowledge into the system. We draw on FrameNet (Baker et al., 1998), the most well-known computational instantiation of frame semantics. While the FrameNet project is generally well-known, its use in practical applications has been limited due to the lack of easy-to-use APIs and because FrameNet alone does not cover as many words as WordNet. Our API simultaneously provides access to both sources.

Language information For a given language, this extension provides information such as relevant writing systems, geographical regions, identification codes, and names in many different languages. These are all integrated into WordNet's hypernym hierarchy, i.e. from language families like the Sinitic languages one may move down to macrolanguages like Chinese, and then to more specific forms like Mandarin Chinese, dialect groups like Ji-Lu Mandarin, or even dialects of particular cities.

The information is obtained from ISO standards, the Unicode CLDR as well as Wikipedia and then integrated with WordNet using the information integration strategies described above (de Melo and Weikum, 2008). Additionally, information about writing systems is taken from the Unicode CLDR and information about individual characters is obtained from the Unicode, Unihan, and Hanzi Data databases. For instance, the Chinese character '娴' is connected to its radical component '女' and to its pronunciation component '闲'.

5 Integrated Query Interface and Wiki

We have developed an online interface that provides access to our data to interested researchers (*yago-knowledge.org/uwn/*), as shown in Figure 4.

Interactive online interfaces offer new ways of interacting with lexical knowledge that are not possible with traditional print dictionaries. For example, a user wishing to find a Spanish word for the concept of persuading someone not to believe something might look up the word '*persuasion*' and then navigate to its antonym '*dissuasion*' to find the Spanish translation. A non-native speaker of English looking up the word '*tercel*' might find it helpful to see pictures available for the related terms '*hawk*' or '*falcon*' – a Google Image search for '*tercel*' merely delivers images of Toyota Tercel cars.

While there have been other multilingual interfaces to WordNet-style lexical knowledge in the past (Pianta et al., 2002; Atserias and others, 2004), these provide less than 10 languages as of 2012. The most similar resource is BabelNet (Navigli and Ponzetto, 2010), which contains multilingual synsets but does not connect named entities from Wikipedia to them in a multilingual taxonomy.

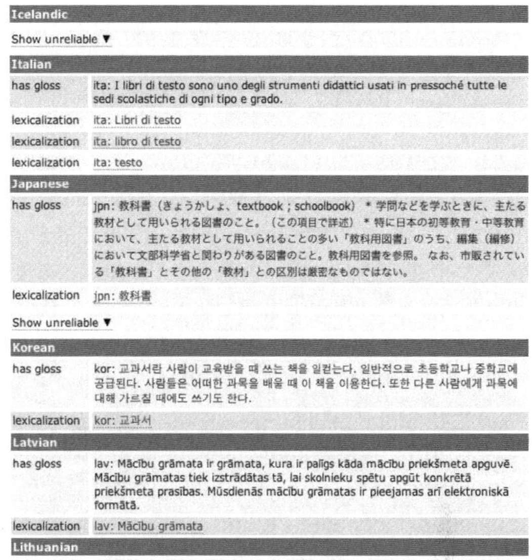

Figure 4: Part of Online Interface

6 Integrated API

Our goal is to make the knowledge that we have derived available for use in applications. To this end, we have developed a fully downloadable API that can easily be used in several different programming languages. While there are many existing APIs for WordNet and other lexical resources (e.g. (Judea et al., 2011; Gurevych and others, 2012)), these don't provide a comparable degree of integrated multilingual and taxonomic information.

Interface The API can be used by initializing an accessor object and possibly specifying the list of plugins to be loaded. Depending on the particular application, one may choose only Princeton WordNet and the UWN Core, or one may want to include named entities from Wikipedia and frame-semantic knowledge derived from FrameNet, for instance. The accessor provides a simple graph-based lookup API as well as some convenience methods for common types of queries.

An additional higher-level API module implements several measures of semantic relatedness. It also provides a simple word sense disambiguation method that, given a tokenized text with part-of-speech and lemma annotations, selects likely word senses by choosing the senses (with matching part-of-speech) that are most similar to words in the context. Note that these modules go beyond existing APIs because they operate on words in many different languages and semantic similarity can even be assessed across languages.

Data Structures Under the hood, each plugin relies on a disk-based associative array to store the knowledge base as a labelled multi-graph. The outgoing labelled edges of an entity are saved on disk in a serialized form, including relation names and relation weights. An index structure allows determining the position of such records on disk.

Internally, this index structure is implemented as a linearly-probed hash table that is also stored externally. Note that such a structure is very efficient in this scenario, because the index is used as a read-only data store by the API. Once an index has been created, write operations are no longer performed, so B+ trees and similar disk-based balanced tree indices commonly used in relational database management systems are not needed. The advantage is that this enables faster lookups, because retrieval operations normally require only two disk reads per plugin, one to access a block in the index table, and another to access a block of actual data.

7 Conclusion

UWN is an important new multilingual lexical resource that is now freely available to the community. It has been constructed using sophisticated knowledge extraction, link prediction, information integration, and taxonomy induction methods. Apart from an online querying and browsing interface, we have also implemented an API that facilitates the use of the knowledge base in applications.

References

Jordi Atserias et al. 2004. The MEANING multilingual central repository. In *Proc. GWC 2004*.

Collin F. Baker, Charles J. Fillmore, and John B. Lowe. 1998. The Berkeley FrameNet project. In *Proc. COLING-ACL 1998*.

Niladri Chatterjee, Shailly Goyal, and Anjali Naithani. 2005. Resolving pattern ambiguity for English to Hindi machine translation using WordNet. In *Proc. Workshop Translation Techn. at RANLP 2005*.

Bonaventura Coppola et al. 2009. Frame detection over the Semantic Web. In *Proc. ESWC*.

Gerard de Melo and Gerhard Weikum. 2008. Language as a foundation of the Semantic Web. In *Proc. ISWC*.

Gerard de Melo and Gerhard Weikum. 2009. Towards a universal wordnet by learning from combined evidence. In *Proc. CIKM 2009*.

Gerard de Melo and Gerhard Weikum. 2010a. MENTA: Inducing multilingual taxonomies from Wikipedia. In *Proc. CIKM 2010*.

Gerard de Melo and Gerhard Weikum. 2010b. Untangling the cross-lingual link structure of Wikipedia. In *Proc. ACL 2010*.

Oren Etzioni, Kobi Reiter, Stephen Soderland, and Marcus Sammer. 2007. Lexical translation with application to image search on the Web. In *Proc. MT Summit*.

Christiane Fellbaum, editor. 1998. *WordNet: An Electronic Lexical Database*. The MIT Press.

Namrata Godbole, Manjunath Srinivasaiah, and Steven Skiena. 2007. Large-scale sentiment analysis for news and blogs. In *Proc. ICWSM*.

Zhiguo Gong, Chan Wa Cheang, and Leong Hou U. 2005. Web query expansion by WordNet. In *Proc. DEXA 2005*.

Iryna Gurevych et al. 2012. Uby: A large-scale unified lexical-semantic resource based on LMF. In *Proc. EACL 2012*.

Yves R. Jean-Mary and Mansur R. Kabuka. 2008. ASMOV: Results for OAEI 2008. In *Proc. OM 2008*.

Alex Judea, Vivi Nastase, and Michael Strube. 2011. WikiNetTk – A tool kit for embedding world knowledge in NLP applications. In *Proc. IJCNLP 2011*.

Zoubida Kedad and Elisabeth Métais. 2002. Ontology-based data cleaning. In *Proc. NLDB 2002*.

Jayant Madhavan, P. Bernstein, and E. Rahm. 2001. Generic schema matching with Cupid. In *Proc. VLDB*.

Marcin Marszałek and C. Schmid. 2007. Semantic hierarchies for visual object recognition. In *Proc. CVPR*.

Roberto Navigli and Simone Paolo Ponzetto. 2010. BabelNet: Building a very large multilingual semantic network. In *Proc. ACL 2010*.

Emanuele Pianta, Luisa Bentivogli, and Christian Girardi. 2002. MultiWordNet: Developing an aligned multilingual database. In *Proc. GWC*.

Daniel L. Rubin et al. 2006. National Center for Biomedical Ontology. *OMICS*, 10(2):185–98.

Lei Shi and Rada Mihalcea. 2005. Putting the pieces together: Combining FrameNet, VerbNet, and WordNet for robust semantic parsing. In *Proc. CICLing*.

Fabian M. Suchanek, Gjergji Kasneci, and Gerhard Weikum. 2007. YAGO: A core of semantic knowledge. In *Proc. WWW 2007*.

FLOW: A First-Language-Oriented Writing Assistant System

Mei-Hua Chen[*], **Shih-Ting Huang**[+], **Hung-Ting Hsieh**[*], **Ting-Hui Kao**[+], **Jason S. Chang**[+]
[*]Institute of Information Systems and Applications
[+]Department of Computer Science
National Tsing Hua University
HsinChu, Taiwan, R.O.C. 30013
{chen.meihua,koromiko1104,vincent732,maxis1718,jason.jschang}@gmail.com

Abstract

Writing in English might be one of the most difficult tasks for EFL (English as a Foreign Language) learners. This paper presents FLOW, a writing assistance system. It is built based on first-language-oriented input function and context sensitive approach, aiming at providing immediate and appropriate suggestions including translations, paraphrases, and n-grams during composing and revising processes. FLOW is expected to help EFL writers achieve their writing flow without being interrupted by their insufficient lexical knowledge.

1. Introduction

Writing in a second language (L2) is a challenging and complex process for foreign language learners. Insufficient lexical knowledge and limited exposure to English might interrupt their writing flow (Silva, 1993). Numerous writing instructions have been proposed (Kroll, 1990) as well as writing handbooks have been available for learners. Studies have revealed that during the writing process, EFL learners show the inclination to rely on their native languages (Wolfersberger, 2003) to prevent a breakdown in the writing process (Arndt, 1987; Cumming, 1989). However, existing writing courses and instruction materials, almost second-language-oriented, seem unable to directly assist EFL writers while writing.

This paper presents FLOW[1] (Figure 1), an interactive system for assisting EFL writers in composing and revising writing. Different from existing tools, its context-sensitive and first-language-oriented features enable EFL writers to concentrate on their ideas and thoughts without being hampered by the limited lexical resources. Based on the studies that first language use can positively affect second language composing, FLOW attempts to meet such needs. Given any L1 input, FLOW displays appropriate suggestions including translation, paraphrases, and n-grams during composing and revising processes. We use the following example sentences to illustrate these two functionalities.

Consider the sentence "*We propose a method to*". During the composing stage, suppose a writer is unsure of the phrase "*solve the problem*", he could write "*解決問題*", a corresponding word in his native language, like "*We propose a method to 解決問題*". The writer's input in the writing area of FLOW actively triggers a set of translation suggestions such as "*solve the problem*" and "*tackle the problem*" for him/her to complete the sentence.

In the revising stage, the writer intends to improve or correct the content. He/She is likely to change the sentence illustrated above into "*We **try all means** to solve the problem.*" He would select the phrase "*propose a method*" in the original sentence and input a L1 phrase "*盡力*", which specifies the meaning he prefers. The L1 input triggers a set of context-aware suggestions corresponding to the translations such as "*try our best*" and "*do our best*" rather than "*try **your** best*" and "*do **your** best*". The system is able to do that mainly by taking a context-sensitive approach. FLOW then inserts the phrase the writer selects into the sentence.

[1] FLOW: http:// flowacldemo.appspot.com

Proceedings of the 50th Annual Meeting of the Association for Computational Linguistics, pages 157–162,
Jeju, Republic of Korea, 8-14 July 2012. ©2012 Association for Computational Linguistics

Figure 1. Screenshot of FLOW

In this paper, we propose a context-sensitive disambiguation model which aims to automatically choose the appropriate phrases in different contexts when performing n-gram prediction, paraphrase suggestion and translation tasks. As described in (Carpuat and Wu, 2007), the disambiguation model plays an important role in the machine translation task. Similar to their work, we further integrate the multi-word phrasal lexical disambiguation model to the n-gram prediction model, paraphrase model and translation model of our system. With the phrasal disambiguation model, the output of the system is sensitive to the context the writer is working on. The context-sensitive feature helps writers find the appropriate phrase while composing and revising.

This paper is organized as follows. We review the related work in the next section. In Section 3, we brief our system and method. Section 4 reports the evaluation results. We conclude this paper and point out future directions to research in Section 5.

2. Related Work

2.1 Sub-sentential paraphrases

A variety of data-driven paraphrase extraction techniques have been proposed in the literature. One of the most popular methods leveraging bilingual parallel corpora is proposed by Bannard and Callison-Burch (2005). They identify paraphrases using a phrase in another language as a pivot. Using bilingual parallel corpora for paraphrasing demonstrates the strength of semantic equivalence. Another line of research further considers context information to improve the performance. Instead of addressing the issue of local paraphrase acquisition, Max (2009) utilizes the source and target contexts to extract sub-sentential paraphrases by using pivot SMT systems.

2.2 N-gram suggestions

After a survey of several existing writing tools, we focus on reviewing two systems closely related to our study.

PENS (Liu et al, 2000), a machine-aided English writing system, provides translations of the corresponding English words or phrases for writers' reference. Different from PENS, FLOW further suggests paraphrases to help writers revise their writing tasks. While revising, writers would alter the use of language to express their thoughts. The suggestions of paraphrases could meet their need, and they can reproduce their thoughts more fluently.

Another tool, TransType (Foster, 2002), a text editor, provides translators with appropriate translation suggestions utilizing trigram language model. The differences between our system and TransType lie in the purpose and the input. FLOW aims to assist EFL writers whereas TransType is a tool for skilled translators. On the other hand, in TransType, the human translator types translation of a given source text, whereas in FLOW the input, either a word or a phrase, could be source or target languages.

2.3 Multi-word phrasal lexical disambiguation

In the study more closely related to our work, Carpuat and Wu (2007) propose a novel method to train a phrasal lexical disambiguation model to benefit translation candidates selection in machine translation. They find a way to integrate the state-of-the-art Word Sense Disambiguation (WSD) model into phrase-based statistical machine translation. Instead of using predefined senses drawn from manually constructed sense inventories, their model directly disambiguates between all phrasal translation candidates seen during SMT training. In this paper, we also use the phrasal lexical disambiguation model; however, apart from using disambiguation model to help machine translation, we extend the disambiguation model. With the help of the phrasal lexical disambiguation model, we build three models: a context-sensitive n-gram prediction model, a paraphrase suggestion model, and a translation model which are introduced in the following sections.

3. Overview of FLOW

The FLOW system helps language learners in two ways: predicting n-grams in the composing stage and suggesting paraphrases in the revising stage (Figure 2).

3.1 System architecture

Composing Stage

During the composing process, a user inputs *S*. FLOW first determines if the last few words of *S* is a L1 input. If not, FLOW takes the last *k* words to predict the best matching following n-grams. Otherwise, the system uses the last *k* words as the query to predict the corresponding n-gram translation. With a set of prediction (either translations or n-grams), the user could choose an appropriate suggestion to complete the sentence in the writing area.

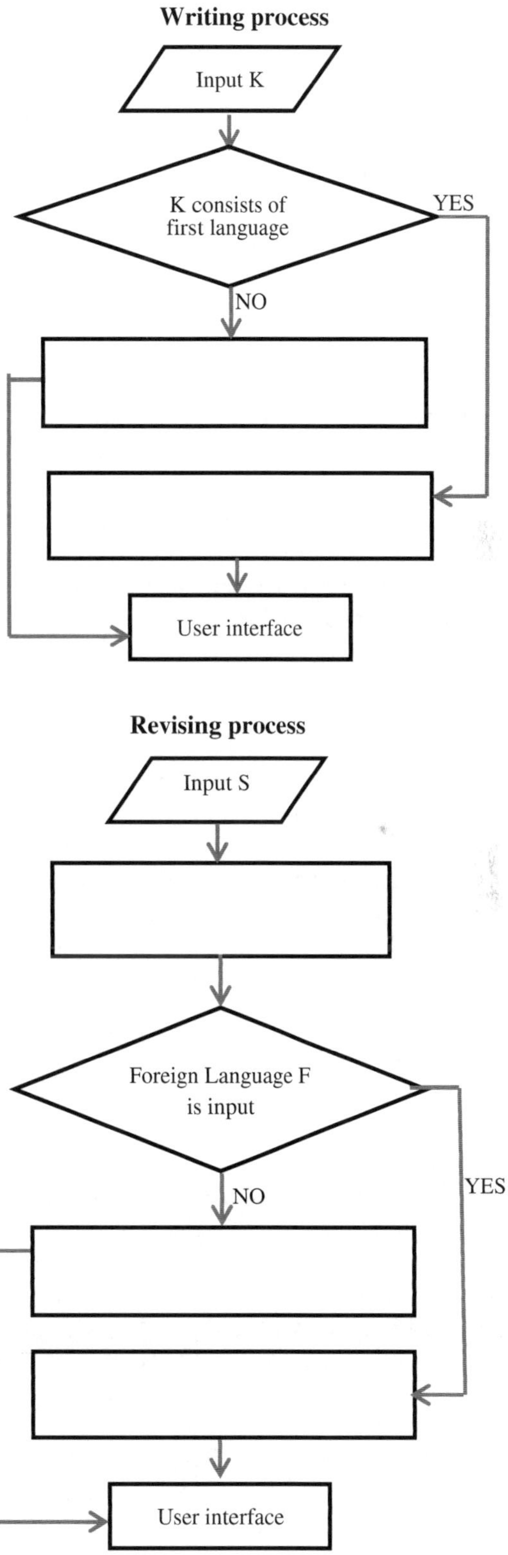

Figure 2. Overall Architecture of *FLOW* in writing and revising processes

Revising Stage

In the revising stage, given an input I and the user selected words K, FLOW obtains the word sequences L and R surrounding K as reference for prediction. Next, the system suggests sub-sentential paraphrases for K based on the information of L and R. The system then searches and ranks the translations.

3.2 N-gram prediction

In the n-gram prediction task, our model takes the last k words with m [2] English words and n foreign language words, $\{e_1, e_2, \ldots e_m, f_1, f_2 \ldots f_n\}$, of the source sentences S as the input. The output would be a set of n-gram predictions. These n-grams can be concatenated to the end of the user-composed sentence fluently.

Context-Sensitive N-gram Prediction (CS-NP)

The CS-NP model is triggered to predict a following n-gram when a user composes sentences consisted of only English words with no foreign language words, namely, n is equal to 0. The goal of the CS-NP model is to find the English phrase e that maximizes the language model probability of the word sequence, $\{e_1, e_2, \ldots e_m, e\}$:

$$e = \underset{e, \forall m \leq k}{\text{argmax}}\, P(e|e_1, e_2, \ldots e_m)$$

$$P(e|e_1, e_2, \ldots e_m) = \frac{P(e_1, e_2, \ldots e_m, e)}{P(e_1, e_2, \ldots e_m)}$$

Translation-based N-gram Prediction (TB-NP)

When a user types a set of L1 expression $f = \{ f_1, f_2 \ldots f_n \}$, following the English sentences S, the FLOW system will predict the possible translations of f. A simple way to predict the translations is to find the bilingual phrase alignments T(f) using the method proposed by (Och and Ney, 2003). However, the T(f) is ambiguous in different contexts. Thus, we use the context $\{e_1, e_2, \ldots e_m\}$ proceeding f to fix the prediction of the translation. Predicting the translation e can be treated as a sub-sentential translation task:

$$e = \text{argmax}_{e \in T(f)}\, P(e|\, e_1, e_2, \ldots e_m),$$

where we use the user-composed context $\{e_1, e_2, \ldots e_m\}$ to disambiguate the translation of f. Although there exist more sophisticated models which could make a better prediction, a simple naïve-Bayes model is shown to be accurate and efficient in the lexical disambiguation task according to (Yarowsky and Florian, 2002). Therefore, in this paper, a naïve-Bayes model is used to disambiguate the translation of f. In addition to the context-word feature, we also use the context-syntax feature, namely surrounding POS tag Pos, to constrain the syntactic structure of the prediction. The TB-NP model could be represented in the following equation:

$$e^* = \underset{e}{\text{argmax}}\, P(e|e_1, e_2, \ldots e_m, p_1, p_2, \ldots p_m),$$

$$Pos = \{p_1, p_2, \ldots p_m\}$$

According to the Bayes theorem,

$$P(e|e_1, e_2, \ldots e_m, p_1, p_2, \ldots p_m) = \prod_{e_i \in E} P(e_i|e) * \prod_{p_j \in P} P(p_j|e)$$

The probabilities can be estimated using a parallel corpus, which is also used to obtain bilingual phrase alignment.

3.3 Paraphrase Suggestion

Unlike the N-gram prediction, in the paraphrase suggestion task, the user selects k words, $\{e_1, e_2, \ldots e_k\}$, which he/she wants to paraphrase. The model takes the m words $\{r_1, r_2, \ldots r_m\}$ and n words $\{l_1, l_2, \ldots l_n\}$ in the right and left side of the user-selected k words respectively. The system also accepts an additional foreign language input, $\{f_1, f_2, \ldots f_l\}$, which helps limit the meaning of suggested paraphrases to what the user really wants. The output would be a set of paraphrase suggestions that the user-selected phrases can be replaced by those paraphrases precisely.

Context-Sensitive Paraphrase Suggestion (CS-PS)

The CS-PS model first finds a set of local paraphrases P of the input phrase K using the

[2] In this paper, m = 5.

pivot-based method proposed by Bannard and Callison-Burch (2005). Although the pivot-based method has been proved efficient and effective in finding local paraphrases, the local paraphrase suggestions may not fit different contexts. Similar to the previous n-gram prediction task, we use the naïve-Bayes approach to disambiguate these local paraphrases. The task is to find the best e such that e with the highest probability for the given context R and L. We further require paraphrases to have similar syntactic structures to the user-selected phrase in terms of POS tags, *Pos*.

$$e^* = \underset{e \epsilon P}{\operatorname{argmax}} P(e|l_1, l_2, \dots l_n, r_1, r_2, \dots r_m, Pos)$$

Translation-based Paraphrase Suggestion (TB-PS)

After the user selects a phrase for paraphrasing, with a L1 phrase F as an additional input, the suggestion problem will be:

$$e^* = \underset{e \epsilon T(F)}{\operatorname{argmax}} P(e|l_1, l_2, \dots l_n, r_1, r_2, \dots r_m, Pos)$$

The TB-PS model disambiguates paraphrases from the translations of F instead of paraphrases P.

4. Experimental Results

In this section, we describe the experimental setting and the preliminary results. Instead of training a whole machine translation using toolkits such as Moses (Koehn et. al, 2007), we used only bilingual phrase alignment as translations to prevent from the noise produced by the machine translation decoder. Word alignments were produced using Giza++ toolkit (Och and Ney, 2003), over a set of 2,220,570 Chinese-English sentence pairs in Hong Kong Parallel Text (LDC2004T08) with sentences segmented using the CKIP Chinese word segmentation system (Ma and Chen, 2003). In training the phrasal lexical disambiguation model, we used the English part of Hong Kong Parallel Text as our training data.

To assess the effectiveness of FLOW, we selected 10 Chinese sentences and asked two students to translate the Chinese sentences to English sentences using FLOW. We kept track of the sentences the two students entered. Table 1 shows the selected results.

Model	Results
TB-PS	**總而言之,** the price of rice...
	in short
	all in all
	in a nutshell
	in a word
	to sum up
CS-PS	She **looks forward to** coming
	look forward to
	looked forward to
	is looking forward to
	forward to
	expect
CS-PS	**there is no doubt** that …
	there is no question
	it is beyond doubt
	I have no doubt
	beyond doubt
	it is true
CS-NP	We put forward **…**
	the proposal
	additional
	our opinion
	the motion
	the bill
TB-NP	...on ways to identify tackle **洗錢**
	money laundering
	money
	his
	forum entitled
	money laundry

Table 1. The preliminary results of *FLOW*

Both of the paraphrase models CS-PS and TB-PS perform quite well in assisting the user in the writing task. However, there are still some problems such as the redundancy suggestions, e.g., "*look forward to*" and "*looked forward to*". Besides, although we used the POS tags as features, the syntactic structures of the suggestions are still not consistent to an input or selected phrases. The CS-NP and the TB-NP model also perform a good task. However, the suggested phrases are usually too short to be a semantic unit. The disambiguation model tends to produce shorter phrases because they have more common context features.

5. Conclusion and Future Work

In this paper, we presented FLOW, an interactive writing assistance system, aimed at helping EFL writers compose and revise without interrupting their writing flow. First-language-oriented and context-sensitive features are two main contributions in this work. Based on the studies on second language writing that EFL writers tend to use their native language to produce texts and then translate into English, the first-language-oriented function provides writers with appropriate translation suggestions. On the other hand, due to the fact that selection of words or phrases is sensitive to syntax and context, our system provides suggestions depending on the contexts. Both functions are expected to improve EFL writers' writing performance.

In future work, we will conduct experiments to gain a deeper understanding of EFL writers' writing improvement with the help of FLOW, such as integrating FLOW into the writing courses to observe the quality and quantity of students' writing performance. Many other avenues exist for future research and improvement of our system. For example, we are interested in integrating the error detection and correction functions into FLOW to actively help EFL writers achieve better writing success and further motivate EFL writers to write with confidence.

References

Valerie Arndt. 1987. Six writers in search of texts: A protocol based study of L1 and L2 writing. *ELT Journal*, 41, 257-267.

Colin Bannard and Chris Callison-Burch. 2005. Paraphrasing with bilingual parallel corpora. In *Proceedings of ACL*, pp. 597-604.

Marine Carpuat and Dekai Wu. 2007. Improving Statistical Machine Translation using Word Sense Disambiguation. In *Proceedings of EMNLP-CoNLL*, pp 61–72.

Alister Cumming. 1989. Writing expertise and second language proficiency. *Language Learning*, 39, 81-141.

George Foster, Philippe Langlais, and Guy Lapalme. 2002. Transtype: Text prediction for translators. In *Proceedings of ACL Demonstrations*, pp. 93-94.

Philipp Koehn, Hieu Hoang, Alexandra Birch, Chris Callison-Burch, Marcello Federico, Nicola Bertoldi, Brooke Cowan,Wade Shen, Christine Moran, Richard Zens, Chris Dyer, Ondrej Bojar, Alexandra Constrantin, and Evan Herbst. 2007. Moses: Open source toolkit for statistical machine translation. In *Proceedings of ACL Demonstration Session,* pp. 177–180.

Barbara Kroll. 1990. Second Language Writing: Research Insights for the Classroom. *Cambridge University Press, Cambridge.*

Aur´elien Max. 2009. Sub-sentential Paraphrasing by Contextual Pivot Translation. In *Proceedings of the 2009 Workshop on Applied Textual Inference, ACL-IJCNLP*, pp 18-26.

Tony Silva. 1993. Toward an Understanding of the Distinct Nature of L2 Writing: The ESL Research and Its Implications. *TESOL Quarterly 27*(4): 657–77.

Liu, Ting, Mingh Zhou, JianfengGao, Endong Xun, and Changning Huan. 2000. PENS: A Machine-Aided English Writing System for Chinese Users. In *Proceedings of ACL*, pp 529-536.

Mark Wolfersberger. 2003. L1 to L2 writing process and strategy transfer: a look at lower proficiency writers. *TESL-EJ: Teaching English as a Second or Foreign Language*, *7*(2), A6 1-15.

Social Event Radar: A Bilingual Context Mining and Sentiment Analysis Summarization System

Wen-Tai Hsieh
Department of IM,
National Taiwan University
wentai@iii.org.tw

Chen-Ming Wu
Institute for Information Industry
cmwu@iii.org.tw

Tsun Ku
Institute for Information Industry
cujing@iii.org.tw

Seng-cho T. Chou
Department of IM,
National Taiwan University
chou@im.ntu.edu.tw

Abstract

Social Event Radar is a new social networking-based service platform, that aim to alert as well as monitor any merchandise flaws, food-safety related issues, unexpected eruption of diseases or campaign issues towards to the Government, enterprises of any kind or election parties, through keyword expansion detection module, using bilingual sentiment opinion analysis tool kit to conclude the specific event social dashboard and deliver the outcome helping authorities to plan "risk control" strategy. With the rapid development of social network, people can now easily publish their opinions on the Internet. On the other hand, people can also obtain various opinions from others in a few seconds even though they do not know each other. A typical approach to obtain required information is to use a search engine with some relevant keywords. We thus take the social media and forum as our major data source and aim at collecting specific issues efficiently and effectively in this work.

1 Introduction

The primary function of S.E.R. technology is simple and clear: as a realtime risk control management technology to assist monitoring huge amount of new media related information and giving a warning for utility users' sake in efficiency way.

In general, S.E.R. technology constantly crawling all new media based information data relating to the client 24-hour a day so that the influential opinion/reports can be monitored, recorded, conveniently analyzed and more importantly is to send a warning signal before the issue outburst and ruining the authorities' reputation. These monitor and alert services are based on the socialnomics theory and provide two main sets of service functionalities to clients for access online: Monitor and alert of new media related information under the concept of cloud computing including two functionalities.

First functionality is the monitoring set. With the dramatic growth of Web's popularity, time becomes the most crucial factor. Monitoring functionalities of S.E.R. technology provides an access to the service platform realtime and online. All scalable mass social data coming from social network, forum, news portals, blogosphere of its login time, its social account and the content are monitored and recorded. In order to find key

Proceedings of the 50th Annual Meeting of the Association for Computational Linguistics, pages 163–168,
Jeju, Republic of Korea, 8-14 July 2012. ©2012 Association for Computational Linguistics

opinion leaders and influential, the S.E.R. technology used social network influence analysis to identify a node and base on the recorded data to sort and analyze opinion trends statistics for every customer's needs.

Second functionality is alert module. Alert functionalities of the S.E.R. technology automatically give a warning text-messages or an e-mail within 6 hours whenever the golden intersection happened, meaning the 1-day moving average is higher than the 7-days moving average line, in order to plan its reaction scheme in early stage.

In empirical studies, we present our application of a Social Event Radar. We also use a practical case to illustrate our system which is applied in industries and society. The rest of this paper is organized as follows. Preliminaries and related works are reviewed in Section 2. The primary functionality and academic theory are mentioned in Section 3. Practical example and influence are explored in Section 4. S.E.R. detail operations are shown in Section 5. Finally, this paper concludes with Section 6.

2 Preliminaries

For the purpose of identifying the opinions in the blogosphere, First of all, mining in blog entries from the perspective of content and sentiment is explored in Section 2.1. Second, sentiment analysis in blog entries is discussed in Section 2.2. Third, information diffusion is mentioned in Section 2.3.

2.1 Topic Detection in Blog Entries

Even within the communities of similar interests, there are various topics discussed among people. In order to extract these subjects, cluster-liked methods Viermetz (2007) and Yoon (2009)are proposed to explore the interesting subjects.

Topic-based events may have high impacts on the articles in blogosphere. However, it is impossible to view all the topics because of the large amount. By using the technique of topic detection and tracking (Wang, 2008), the related stories can be identified with a stream of media. It is convenient for users who intend to see what is going on through the blogosphere. The subjects are not only classified in the first step, but also rank their importance to help user read these articles.

After decomposing a topic into a keyword set, a concept space is appropriate for representing relations among people, article and keywords. A concept space is graph of terms occurring within objects linked to each other by the frequency with which they occur together. Hsieh (2009) explored the possibility of discovering relations between tags and bookmarks in a folksonomy system. By applying concept space, the relationship of topic can be measured by two keyword sets.

Some researches calculate the similarity to identify the characteristic. One of the indicators is used to define the opinion in blog entries which is "Blogs tend to have certain levels of topic consistency among their blog entries." The indicator uses the KL distance to identify the similarity of blog entries (Song, 2007). However, the opinion blog is easy to read and do not change their blog topics iteratively, this is the key factor that similarity comparison can be applied on this feature.

2.2 Opinion Discovery in Blog Entries

The numbers of online comments on products or subjects grow rapidly. Although many comments are long, there are only a few sentences containing distinctive opinion. Sentiment analysis is often used to extract the opinions in blog pages.

Opinion can be recognized from various aspects such as a word. The semantic relationship between opinion expression and topic terms is emphasized (Bo, 2004). It means that using the polarity of positive and negative terms in order to present the sentiment tendency from a document.

Within a given topic, similarity approach is often used to classify the sentences as opinions. Similarity approach measures sentence similarity based on shared words and synonym words with each sentence in documents and makes an average score. According to the highest score, the sentences can assign to the sentiment or opinion category (Varlamis, 2008).

Subjectivity in natural language refers to aspects of language used to express opinions and evaluation. Subjectivity classification can prevent the polarity classifier from considering irrelevant misleading text. Subjectivity detection can compress comments into much shorter sentences which still retain its polarity information comparable to the entire comments (Rosario, 2004; Yu, 2003).

2.3 Information Diffusion in Internet

The phenomenon of information diffusion is studied through the observation of evolving social relationship among bloggers (Gill, 2004; Wang, 2007). It is noted that a social network forms with bloggers and corresponding subscription relationship.

Information diffusion always concerns with temporal evolution. The blog topics are generated in proportion to what happened in real world. Media focus stands for how frequently and recently is the topic reported by new websites. User attention represents how much do bloggers like to read news stories about the topic. By utilizing these two factors, the news topics are ranked within a certain news story (Wang, 2008).

The phenomenon of information diffusion is driven by outside stimulation from real world (Gruhl, 2004). It focuses on the propagation of topics from blog to blog. The phenomenon can discuss from two directions. One is topic-oriented model which provides a robust structure to the whole interesting terms that bloggers care about. The other is individual-oriented model which helps users figure out which blogger has information impact to others.

3 BUILDING BLOCKS OF S.E.R TECHNOLOGY

The core technology building block of S.E.R. technology is the central data processing system that currently sits in III's project processing center. This core software system is now complete with a set of processing software that keeps analyzing the recorded data to produce reports and analytical information, all those monitoring functionalities provided to subscribers.

Two important technology building blocks for the success of the S.E.R. are the bilingual sentiment opinion analysis (BSOA) technique, and social network influence analysis (SNIA) technique. These techniques are keys to the successful collection and monitoring of new media information, which in turn is essential for identifying the key opinion web-leaders and influential intelligently. The following sections apply the academic theory combining with practical functionality into the S.E.R.

3.1 Bilingual Sentiment Opinion Analysis

BSOA technique under the S.E.R. technology is implemented along with lexicon based and domain knowledge. The research team starts with concept expansion technique for building up a measurable keyword network. By applying particularly Polysemy Processing Double negation Processing Adverb of Degree Processing sophisticated algorithm as shown in Figure 1, so that to rule out the irrelevant factors in an accurate and efficiency way.

Aim at the Chinese applications; we develop the system algorithm based on the specialty of Chinese language. The key approach crawl the hidden sentiment linking words, and then to build the association set. We can, therefore, identify feature-oriented sentiment orientation of opinion more conveniently and accurately by using this association set analysis.

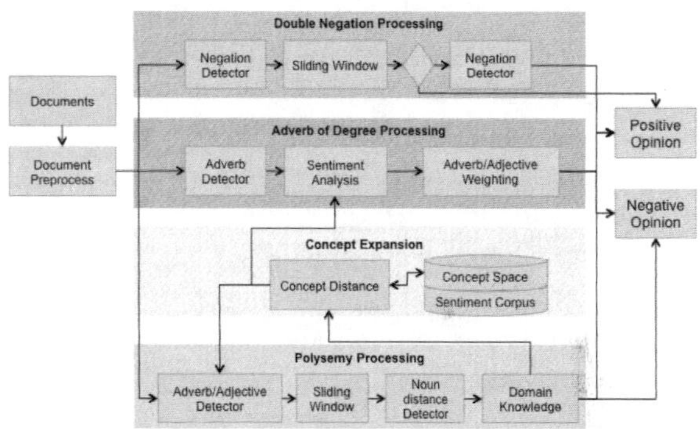

Figure 1. Bilingual Sentiment Opinion Analysis

3.2 Social Network Influence Analysis

Who are the key opinion leaders in the opinion world? How critical do the leaders diffusion power matters? Who do they influence? The more information we have, so as the social networking channels, the more obstacles of monitoring and finding the real influential we are facing right now.

Within a vast computer network, the individual computers are on what so-called the periphery of the network. Those nodes who have many links pointing to them is not always the most influential in the group. We use a more sophisticated algorithm that takes into account both the direct and indirect links in the network. This SNIA technique under the S.E.R. technology provides a more accurate evaluation and prediction of who really influences thought and affects the whole. Using the same algorithm, in reverse, we can quickly show the direct and indirect influence clusters of each key opinion leader.

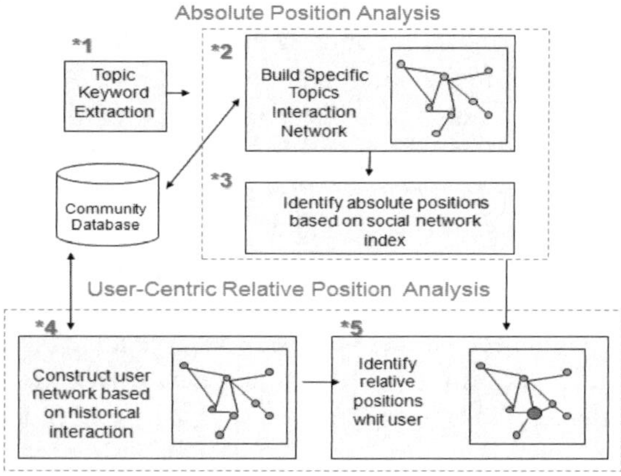

Figure 2. Social Network Influence Analysis

3.3 The monitoring methodology of agenda-tendency

In the web-society, the system architecture of monitoring and identifying on vast web reviews is one thing, being aware of when to start the risk control action plan is another story. We develop 3 different forms of analysis charts — long term average moving line, tendency line, 1-day, 7-day and monthly average moving line. For example, the moment when the 1-day moving average line is higher than the 7-day moving average line, it means the undiscovered issue is going to be outburst shortly, and it is the time the authority to take action dealing with the consequences. One news report reconfirmed that a wrong manipulated marketing promotion program using an "iPhone5" smart-phone as its complementary gift and was shown on the analysis chart 9 days before it revealed on the television news causing the company's reputation being damaged badly.

4 PRATICAL EXAMPLE

To make our proposed scheme into practice, corresponding systems are applying in the following example. S.E.R. plays an important role to support the enterprise, government and public society.

4.1 Food-safety Related Issues

S.E.R. research and development team built up the DEPH [di(2-ethylhexyl)phthalate] searching website within 2 days and made an officially announcement in June. 1st, 2011 under the pressure of the outbreak of Taiwan's food contamination storm, which in general estimated causing NT$10,000 million approximately profit lost in Taiwan's food industry. This DEPH website was to use the S.E.R. technology not only to collect 5 authorities' data (Food and Drug Administration of Health Department in Executive Yuan, Taipei City government) 24 hours a day but also gathering 3 news portals — Google, Yahoo, and UDN, 303 web online the latest news information approx., allowed every personal could instantly check whether their everyday food/drink has or failed passing the toxin examination by simply key-in any related words (jelly, orange juice, bubble tea). This website was highly recommended by the Ministry of Economic Affairs because of it fundamentally eased people's fear at the time.

4.2 Brand/Product Monitoring

A world leading smart phone company applying the S.E.R Technology service platform to set up its customer relationship management (CRM) platform for identifying the undiscovered product-defects issues, monitoring the web-opinion trends that targeting issues between its own and competitor's products/services mostly. This data processing and analyzing cost was accordingly estimated saving 70 % cost approximately.

4.3 Online to Offline Marketing

In order to develop new business in the word-of-mouth market, Lion Travel which is the biggest travel agency in Taiwan sat up a branch "Xinmedia". The first important thing for a new company to enter the word-of-mouth market is to own a sufficient number of experts who can affect most people's opinion to advertisers, however, this is a hard work right now. S.E.R. helps Xinmedia to easily find many traveling opinion leader, and those leaders can be products spokesperson to more accurately meet the business needs. More and more advertisers agree the importance of the word-of-mouth market, because Xinmedia do created better accomplishments for advertisers' sales by experts' opinion.

5 S.E.R. DETAIL OPERATIONS

In the following scenario, S.E.R. monitors more than twenty smartphone forums. In Figure 3, the cellphone "One X" is getting popular than others. From the news, we know this cellphone is upcoming release to the market and it becomes a topical subject.

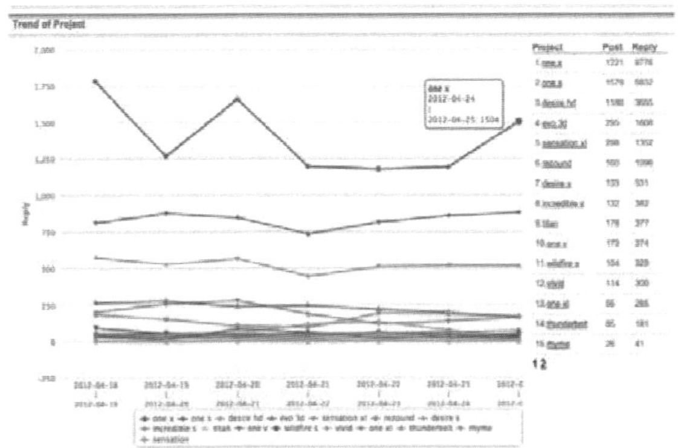

Figure 3: An example of Word-of-mouth of products

Beyond the products, some details are discussed with product in a topic. Thus, we use TF-IDF and fixed keyword to extract the important issue. These issues are coordinated with time slice and generated dynamically. It points out the most discussed issue with the product. In Figure 4, In this case, the "screen" issue is raising up after "ics" (ice cream sandwich, an android software version) may become the most concern issue that people care about.

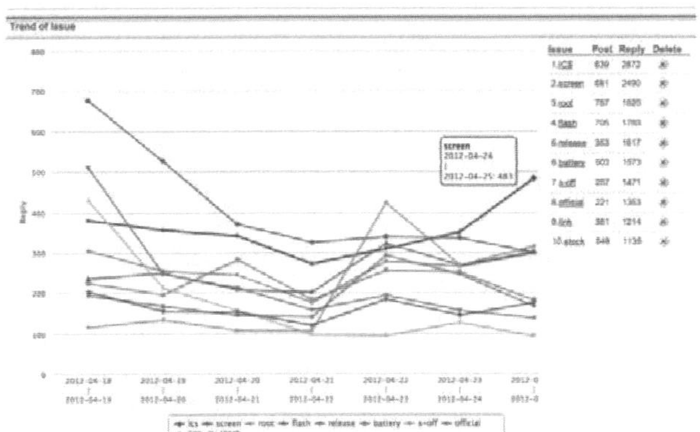

Figure 4. An example of hot topics

For different project, S.E.R. supports the training mode to assist user to train their specific domain knowledge. User can easily tag their important keyword to their customized category. With this benefit, we can accept different domain source and do not afraid data anomaly. We also apply training mechanism automatically if the tagging word arrive the training standard.

As shown in Figure 5, top side shows the analyzed information of whole topic thread. We just show the first post of this thread. As we can see, we provide three training mode, Category, Sentiment and Same Problem. The red word shows the positive sentiment and blue word shows the negative sentiment respectively. The special case is the "Same Problem". In forum, some author may just type "+1", "me2", "me too" to show they face the same problem. Therefore, we have to identify what they agreed or what they said. We solve this problem by using the relation between the same problem word and its name entity.

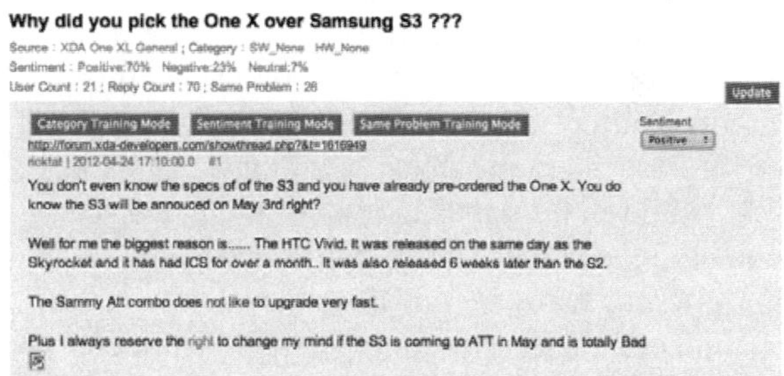

Figure 5: Training Mode – S.E.R. supports category training, sentiment training and same problem training

To senior manager, they may not spend times on detail issue. S.E.R. provides a quick summary of relevant issue into a cluster and shows a ratio to indicate which issue is important.

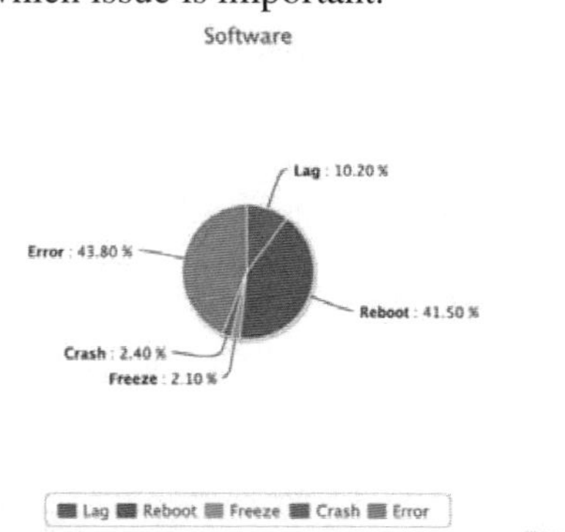

Figure 6. Quick Summary – Software relevant issues

6 Conclusions

In this networked era, known social issues get monitored and analyzed over the Net. Information gathering and analysis over Internet have become so important for efficient and effective responses to social events. S.E.R technology is an Internet mining technology that detects monitors and analyzes more than Net-related social incidents.

An impending event that's not yet attracted any attention, regardless of whether of known nature or of undetermined characteristic, gets lit up on the S.E.R radar screen – provided a relevant set of detection conditions are set in the S.E.R engine. S.E.R technology, like its related conventional counterparts, is certainly capable for monitoring and analyzing commercial and social, public events. It is the idea "to detect something uncertain out there" that distinguishes S.E.R from others.

It is also the same idea that is potentially capable of saving big financially for our society. It may seem to be – in fact it is – hindsight to talk about the DEPH food contamination incident of Taiwan in 2011, discussing how it would have been detected using this technology. But, the "morning-after case analysis" provides a good lesson to suggest that additional tests are worthwhile – thus the look into another issue of food additives: the curdlan gum.

Certainly there is – at this stage – not yet any example of successful uncovering of impending events of significant social impact by this technology, but with proper setting of an S.E.R engine by a set of adequate parameters, the team is confident that S.E.R will eventually reveal something astonishing – and helpful to our society.

7 Acknowledgments

This study is conducted under the "Social Intelligence Analysis Service Platform" project of the Institute for Information Industry which is subsidized by the Ministry of Economy Affairs of the Republic of China.

8 References

Hsieh, W.-T., Jay Stu, Chen, Y.-L., Seng-cho Timothy Chou. 2009. A collaborative desktop tagging system for group knowledge management based on concept space. Expert Syst. Appl., 36(5), 9513-9523

Wang, J.-C., Chiang, M.-J., Ho, J.-C., Hsieh, W.-T., Huang, I.-K.. 2007. Knowing Who to Know in Knowledge Sharing Communities: A Social Network Analysis Approach, In Proceeding of The Seventh International Conference on Electronic Business, 345-351.

Bo, P. and Lillian, L. 2004. A Sentimental Education: Sentiment Analysis Using Subjectivity Summarization Based on Minimum Cuts. In Proceedings of the 42nd Annual Meeting on Association for Computational Linguistics, 271-279.

Gill, K. E. 2004. How can We Measure the Influence of the Blogosphere, In Proceedings of the 2nd Workshop on the Weblogging Ecosystem, 17-22.

Gruhl, D., Guha, R., Liben-Nowell, D. and Tomkins, A. 2004. Information Diffusion through Blogspace, In Proceedings of the 13th International Conference on World Wide Web, 491-501.

Rosario, B. and Hearst, M. A. 2004. Classifying Semantic Relations in Bioscience Texts, In Proceedings of the 42nd Annual Meeting on Association for Computational Linguistics, 430.

Song, X., Chi, Y., Hino, K., and Tseng, B. Identifying Opinion Leaders in the Blogosphere. 2007. In Proceedings of the 16th ACM conference on Conference on Information and Knowledge Management, 971-974.

Varlamis, I., Vassalos, V., and Palaios, A. 2008. Monitoring the Evolution of Interests in the Blogosphere. In Proceedings of the 24th International Conference on Data Engineering Workshops.

Viermetz, M. and Skubacz, M. 2007. Using Topic Discovery to Segment Large Communication Graphs for Social Network Analysis, In Proceedings of the IEEE/WIC/ACM International Conference on Web Intelligence, 95-99.

Wang, C., Zhang, M., Ru, L., and Ma, S. 2008. Automatic Online News Topic Ranking Using Media Focus and User Attention based on Aging Theory, In Proceeding of the 17th ACM Conference on Information and Knowledge Management, 1033-1042.

Yoon, S.-H., Shin, J.-H., Kim, S.-W., and Park, S. 2009. Extraction of a Latent Blog Community based on Subject, In Proceeding of the 18th ACM Conference on Information and Knowledge Management, 1529-1532.

Yu, H and Hatzivassiloglou, V. 2003. Towards Answering Opinion Questions: Separating Facts from Opinions and Identifying the Polarity of Opinion Sentences, In Proceedings of the 2003 Conference on Empirical Methods in Natural Language Processing - Volume 10, 129-136.

Syntactic Annotations for the Google Books Ngram Corpus

Yuri Lin, Jean-Baptiste Michel, Erez Lieberman Aiden,
Jon Orwant, Will Brockman and Slav Petrov*
Google Inc.
{yurilin,jbmichel,drerez,orwant,brockman,slav}@google.com

Abstract

We present a new edition of the Google Books Ngram Corpus, which describes how often words and phrases were used over a period of five centuries, in eight languages; it reflects 6% of all books ever published. This new edition introduces syntactic annotations: words are tagged with their part-of-speech, and head-modifier relationships are recorded. The annotations are produced automatically with statistical models that are specifically adapted to historical text. The corpus will facilitate the study of linguistic trends, especially those related to the evolution of syntax.

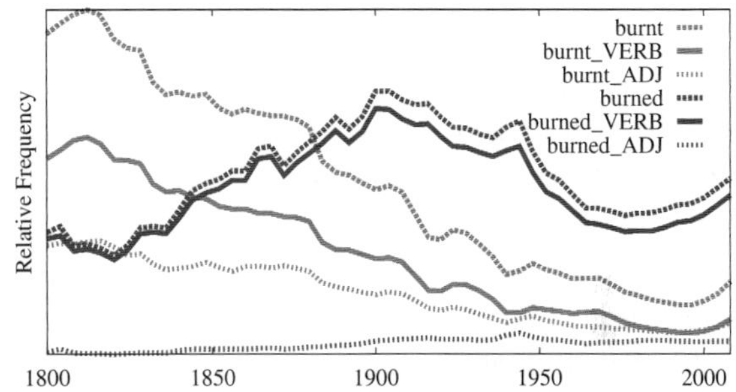

Figure 1: Usage frequencies of *burned* and *burnt* over time, showing that *burned* became the dominant spelling around 1880. Our new syntactic annotations enable a more refined analysis, suggesting that the crossing-point for the verb usage (*burned_VERB* vs. *burnt_VERB*) was decades earlier.

1 Introduction

The Google Books Ngram Corpus (Michel et al., 2011) has enabled the quantitative analysis of linguistic and cultural trends as reflected in millions of books written over the past five centuries. The corpus consists of words and phrases (i.e., ngrams) and their usage frequency over time. The data is available for download, and can also be viewed through the interactive Google Books Ngram Viewer at `http://books.google.com/ngrams`.

The sheer quantity of and broad historical scope of the data has enabled a wide range of analyses (Michel et al., 2011; Ravallion, 2011). Of course, examining raw ngram frequencies is of limited utility when studying many aspects of linguistic change, particularly the ones related to syntax. For instance, most English verbs are regular (their past tense is formed by adding -ed), and the few exceptions, known as irregular verbs, tend to regularize over the centuries (Lieberman et al., 2007). Figure 1 illustrates how *burned* gradually overtook *burnt*, becoming more frequent around 1880. Unfortunately, as a study of verb regularization, this analysis is skewed by a significant confound: both words can serve as either verbs (e.g., *the house burnt*) or adjectives (e.g., *the burnt toast*). Because many words have multiple syntactic interpretations, such confounds often limit the utility of raw ngram frequency data.

In this work we provide a new edition of the Google Books Ngram Corpus that contains over 8 million books, or 6% of all books ever published (cf. Section 3). Moreover, we include syntactic analysis in order to facilitate a fine-grained analysis of the evolution of syntax. Ngrams are annotated with part-of-speech tags (e.g., in the phrase *he burnt the toast*, *burnt* is a verb; in *the burnt toast*, *burnt* is an adjective) and head-modifier dependencies (e.g., in the phrase *the little black book*, *little* modifies *book*).

The annotated ngrams are far more useful for ex-

* Corresponding author.

Proceedings of the 50th Annual Meeting of the Association for Computational Linguistics, pages 169–174,
Jeju, Republic of Korea, 8-14 July 2012. ©2012 Association for Computational Linguistics

amining the evolution of grammar and syntax. For our study of the regularization of the verb *burn*, the availability of syntactic annotations resolves the verb vs. adjective ambiguity in the original data, allowing us to only examine instances where *burnt* and *burned* appear as verbs. This more refined analysis suggests a crossover date for the frequency of the verb forms that is several decades earlier than the overall (verbs and adjectives) crossover.

We use state-of-the-art statistical part-of-speech taggers and dependency parsers to produce syntactic annotations for eight languages in the Google Books collection. The annotations consist of 12 language universal part-of-speech tags and unlabeled head-modifier dependencies. Section 4 describes the models that we used and the format of the annotations in detail. We assess the expected annotation accuracies experimentally and discuss how we adapt the taggers and parsers to historical text in Section 5. The annotated ngrams are available as a new edition of the Google Books Ngram Corpus; we provide some examples from the new corpus in Figure 3.

2 Related Work

Michel et al. (2011) described the construction of the first edition of the Google Books Ngram Corpus and used it to quantitatively analyze a variety of topics ranging from language growth to public health. The related Ngram Viewer has become a popular tool for examining language trends by experts and non-experts alike.

In addition to studying frequency patterns in the data, researchers have also attempted to analyze the grammatical function of the ngrams (Davies, 2011). Such endeavors are hampered by the fact that the Ngram Corpus provides only aggregate statistics in the form of ngram counts and not the full sentences. Furthermore, only ngrams that pass certain occurrence thresholds are publicly available, making any further aggregation attempt futile: in heavy tail distributions like the ones common in natural languages, the counts of rare events (that do not pass the frequency threshold) can have a large cumulative mass.

In contrast, because we have access to the full text, we can annotate ngrams to reflect the particular grammatical functions they take in the sentences they were extracted from, and can also account for the contribution of rare ngrams to otherwise frequent grammatical functions.

Language	#Volumes	#Tokens
English	4,541,627	468,491,999,592
Spanish	854,649	83,967,471,303
French	792,118	102,174,681,393
German	657,991	64,784,628,286
Russian	591,310	67,137,666,353
Italian	305,763	40,288,810,817
Chinese	302,652	26,859,461,025
Hebrew	70,636	8,172,543,728

Table 1: Number of volumes and tokens for each language in our corpus. The total collection contains more than 6% of all books ever published.

3 Ngram Corpus

The Google Books Ngram Corpus has been available at `http://books.google.com/ngrams` since 2010. This work presents new corpora that have been extracted from an even larger book collection, adds a new language (Italian), and introduces syntactically annotated ngrams. The new corpora are available in addition to the already existing ones.

3.1 Books Data

The new edition of the Ngram Corpus supports the eight languages shown in Table 1. The book volumes were selected from the larger collection of all books digitized at Google following exactly the procedure described in Michel et al. (2011). The new edition contains data from 8,116,746 books, or over 6% of all books ever published. The English corpus alone comprises close to half a trillion words. This collection of books is much larger than any other digitized collection; its generation required a substantial effort involving obtaining and manually scanning millions of books.

3.2 Raw Ngrams

We extract ngrams in a similar way to the first edition of the corpus (Michel et al., 2011), but with some notable differences. Previously, tokenization was done on whitespace characters and all ngrams occurring on a given page were extracted, including ones that span sentence boundaries, but omitting

Tag	English	Spanish	French	German	Russian[1]	Italian	Chinese	Hebrew
ADJ	other, such	mayor, gran	tous, même	anderen, ersten	все,этой	stesso, grande	大, 新	גדול, אחר
ADP	of, in	de, en	de, à	in, von	в, на	di, in	在, 对	ל, ב
ADV	not, when	no, más	ne, plus	auch, so	так, более	non, piú	不, 也	לא, כל
CONJ	and, or	y, que	et, que	und, daß	и, что	che, ed	和, 与	כי, ו
DET	the, a	la, el	la, les	der, die	-	la, il	这, 各	ה
NOUN	time, people	parte, años	temps, partie	Zeit, Jahre	его, он	parte, tempo	年, 人	ישראל, בית
PRON	it, I	que, se	qui, il	sich, die	-	che, si	他, 我	זה, הוא
VERB	is, was	es, ha	est, sont	ist, werden	было, был	é, sono	是, 有	היה, אין

Table 2: The two most common words for some POS tags in the new Google Books NGram Corpus for all languages.

ngrams that span page boundaries.

Instead, we perform tokenization and sentence boundary detection by applying a set of manually devised rules (except for Chinese, where a statistical system is used for segmentation). We capture sentences that span across page boundaries, and then extract ngrams only within sentences. As is typically done in language model estimation, we add sentence beginning (*_START_*) and end tokens (*_END_*) that are included in the ngram extraction. This allows us to distinguish ngrams that appear in sentence-medial positions from ngrams that occur at sentence boundaries (e.g., *_START_ John*).

3.3 Differences to the First Edition

The differences between this edition and the first edition of the Ngram Corpus are as follows: (i) the underlying book collection has grown substantially in the meantime; (ii) OCR technology and metadata extraction have improved, resulting in higher quality digitalization; (iii) ngrams spanning sentence boundaries are omitted, and ngrams spanning page boundaries are included. As a result, this new edition is not a superset of the first edition.

4 Syntactic Annotations

In addition to extracting raw ngrams, we part-of-speech tag and parse the entire corpus and extract syntactically annotated ngrams (see Figure 2). We use manually annotated treebanks of modern text (often newswire) as training data for the POS tagger and parser models. We discuss our approach to adapting the models to historical text in Section 5.

4.1 Part-of-Speech Tagging

Part-of-speech tagging is one of the most fundamental disambiguation steps in any natural language processing system. Over the years, POS tagging accuracies have steadily improved, appearing to plateau at an accuracy level that approaches human inter-annotator agreement (Manning, 2011). As we demonstrate in the next section, these numbers are misleading since they are computed on test data that is very close to the training domain. We therefore need to specifically adapt our models to handle noisy and historical text.

We perform POS tagging with a state-of-the-art[2] Conditional Random Field (CRF) based tagger (Lafferty et al., 2001) trained on manually annotated treebank data. We use the following fairly standard features in our tagger: current word, suffixes and prefixes of length 1, 2 and 3; additionally we use word cluster features (Uszkoreit and Brants, 2008) for the current word, and transition features of the cluster of the current and previous word.

To provide a language-independent interface, we use the universal POS tagset described in detail in Petrov et al. (2012). This universal POS tagset defines the following twelve POS tags, which exist in similar form in most languages: NOUN (nouns), VERB (verbs), ADJ (adjectives), ADV (adverbs), PRON (pronouns), DET (determiners and articles), ADP (prepositions and postpositions), NUM (numerals), CONJ (conjunctions), PRT (particles), '.' (punctuation marks) and X (a catch-all for other categories such as abbreviations or foreign words).

Table 2 shows the two most common words for

[1]Pronouns and determiners are not explicitly annotated in the Russian treebank. As a result, the most common Russian nouns in the table are pronouns.

[2]On a standard benchmark (training on sections 1-18 of the Penn Treebank (Marcus et al., 1993) and testing on sections 22-24) our tagger achieves a state-of-the-art accuracy of 97.22%.

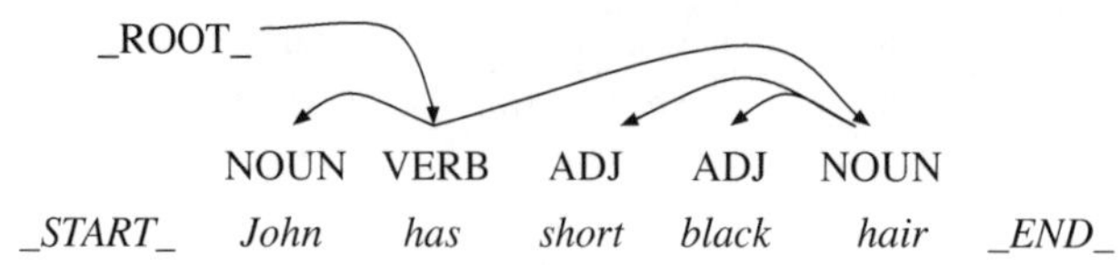

Raw Ngrams		Annotated Ngrams			
John	*short*	*_START_ John*	*John_NOUN*	*hair=>short*	*hair=>short_ADJ*
John has	...	...	*John has_VERB*	*hair=>black*	...
...	*short black hair*	*hair _END_*	*John _VERB_ short*	*_NOUN_<=has*	*_ROOT_=>has*

Figure 2: An English sentence and its part-of-speech tags and dependency parse tree. Below are some of the raw ngrams available in the first release of the Ngram Corpus, as well as some of the new, syntactically annotated ngrams.

some POS tag categories. It is interesting to see that there is overlap between the most frequent content words across language boundaries. In general, function words are more frequent than content words, resulting in somewhat less interesting examples for some POS tags. More typical examples might be *big* for adjectives, *quickly* for adverbs or *read* for verbs.

As suggested in Petrov et al. (2012), we train on the language-specific treebank POS tags, and then map the predicted tags to the universal tags. Table 3 shows POS tagging accuracies on the treebank evaluation sets using the 12 universal POS tags.

4.2 Syntactic Parsing

We use a dependency syntax representation, since it is intuitive to work with and can be predicted effectively. Additionally, dependency parse tree corpora exist for several languages, making the representation desirable from a practical standpoint. Dependency parse trees specify pairwise relationships between words in the same sentence. Directed arcs specify which words modify a given word (if any), or alternatively, which head word governs a given word (there can only be one). For example, in Figure 2, *hair* is the head of the modifier *short*.

We use a deterministic transition-based dependency parsing model (Nivre, 2008) with an arc-eager transition strategy. A linear kernel SVM with the following features is used for prediction: the part-of-speech tags of the first four words on the buffer and of the top two words on the stack; the word identities of the first two words on the buffer and of the top word on the stack; the word identity of the syntactic head of the top word on the stack (if available). All non-lexical feature conjunctions are included. For treebanks with non-projective trees we use the pseudo-projective parsing technique to transform the treebank into projective structures (Nivre and Nilsson, 2005). To standardize and simplify the dependency relations across languages we use unlabeled directed dependency arcs. Table 3 shows unlabeled attachment scores on the treebank evaluation sets with automatically predicted POS tags.

4.3 Syntactic Ngrams

As described above, we extract raw ngrams ($n \leq 5$) from the book text. Additionally, we provide ngrams annotated with POS tags and dependency relations.

The syntactic ngrams comprise words (e.g., *burnt*), POS-annotated words (e.g. *burnt_VERB*), and POS tags (e.g., *_VERB_*). All of these forms can be mixed freely in 1-, 2- and 3-grams (e.g., *the _ADJ_ toast_NOUN*). To limit the combinatorial explosion, we restrict the forms that can be mixed in 4- and 5-grams. Words and POS tags cab be mixed freely (e.g., *the house is _ADJ_*) and we also allow every word to be annotated (e.g., *the_DET house_NOUN is_VERB red_ADJ*). However, we do not allow annotated words to be mixed with other forms (e.g., both *the house_NOUN is _ADJ_* and *the house_NOUN is red* are not allowed). Head-modifier dependencies between pairs of words can be expressed similarly (we do not record chains of dependencies). Both the head and the modifier can take any of the forms described above. We use an arrow that points from the head word to the modifier word (e.g., *head=>modifier* or *modifier<=head*) to indicate a dependency relation. We use the designated *_ROOT_* for the root of the parse tree (e.g., *_ROOT_=>has*).

Language	POS Tags	Dependencies
English	97.9	90.1
Spanish	96.9	74.5
German	98.8	83.1
French	97.3	84.7
Italian	95.6	80.0
Russian	96.8	86.2
Chinese	92.6	73.2
Hebrew	91.3	76.2

Table 3: Part-of-speech and unlabeled dependency arc prediction accuracies on in-domain data. Accuracies on the out-of-domain book data are likely lower.

Figure 2 shows an English sentence, its POS tags and dependency parse tree, and some concrete examples of ngrams that are extracted. Note the flexibility and additional possibilities that the dependency relations provide. Using the raw ngrams it is not possible to accurately estimate how frequently *hair* is described as *short*, as there are often intervening words between the head and the modifier. Because dependency relations are independent of word order, we are able to calculate the frequency of both *hair=>black* and *hair=>short*.

Similarly, there are many ways to express that somebody is reading a book. The first plot in Figure 3 shows multiple related queries. The 3-gram *read _DET_ book* aggregates several more specific 3-grams like *read a book*, *read the book*, etc. The dependency representation *read=>book* is even more general, enforcing the requirement that the two words obey a specific syntactic configuration, but ignoring the number of words that appear in between.

5 Domain Adaptation

The results on the treebank evaluation sets need to be taken with caution, since performance often suffers when generalized to other domains. To get a better estimate of the POS tagging and parsing accuracies we conducted a detailed study for English. We chose English since it is the largest language in our corpus and because labeled treebank data for multiple domains is available. In addition to the WSJ (newswire) treebank (Marcus et al., 1993), we use: the Brown corpus (Francis and Kucera, 1979), which provides a balanced sample of text from the early 1960s; the QuestionBank (Judge et al., 2006), which consists entirely of questions; and the PPCMBE corpus (Kroch et al., 2010), which contains modern British English from 1700 to 1914 and is perhaps most close to our application domain.

	POS Tags		Dependencies	
Domain	base	adapted	base	adapted
Newswire	97.9	97.9	90.1	90.1
Brown	96.8	97.5	84.7	87.1
Questions	94.2	97.5	85.3	91.2
Historical	91.6	93.3	-	-

Table 4: English tagging and parsing accuracies on various domains for baseline and adapted models.

Since the English treebanks are in constituency format, we used the StanfordConverter (de Marneffe et al., 2006) to convert the parse trees to dependencies and ignored the arc labels. The dependency conversion was unfortunately not possible for the PPCMBE corpus since it uses a different set of constituency labels. The tagset of PPCMBE is also unique and cannot be mapped deterministically to the universal tagset. For example the string "one" has its own POS tag in PPCMBE, but is ambiguous in general – it can be used either as a number (NUM), noun (NOUN) or pronoun (PRON). We did our best to convert the tags as closely as possible, leaving tags that cannot be mapped untouched. Consequently, our evaluation results underestimate the accuracy of our tagger since it might correctly disambiguate certain words that are not disambiguated in the PPCMBE evaluation data.

Table 4 shows the accuracies on the different domains for our baseline and adapted models. The baseline model is trained only on newswire text and hence performs best on the newswire evaluation set. Our final model is adapted in two ways. First, we add the the Brown corpus and QuestionBank to the training data. Second, and more importantly, we estimate word cluster features on the books data and use them as features in the POS tagger.

The word cluster features group words deterministically into clusters that have similar distributional properties. When the model encounters a word that was never seen during training, the clusters allow the model to relate it to other, potentially known words. This approach improves the accuracy on rare words, and also makes our models robust to scanning er-

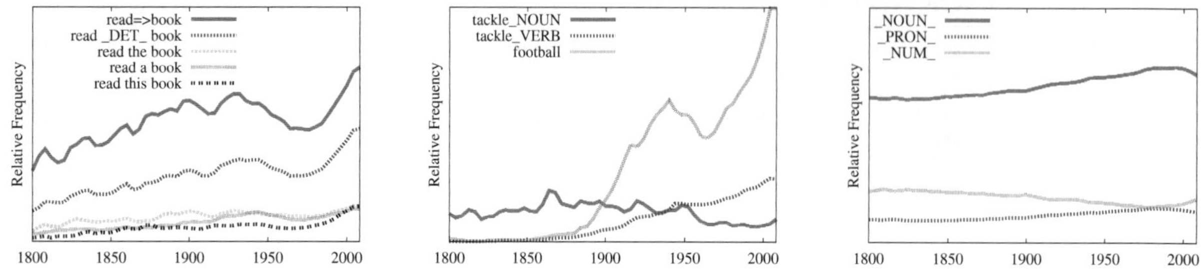

Figure 3: Several queries expressing that somebody is reading a book (left). Frequencies of *tackle* used as noun vs. verb compared to the frequency of *football* (middle). Relative frequencies of all nouns, pronouns and numbers (right).

rors. For example, in older books the medial-s (ſ) is often incorrectly recognized as an 'f' by the OCR software (e.g., "beft" instead of "best"). Such systematic scanning errors will produce spurious words that have very similar co-occurrence patterns as the correct spelling of the word. In fact, a manual examination reveals that words with systematic scanning errors tend to be in the same cluster as their correctly spelled versions. The cluster feature thus provides a strong signal for determining the correct POS tag.

While the final annotations are by no means perfect, we expect that in aggregate they are accurate enough to be useful when analyzing broad trends in the evolution of grammar.

6 Conclusions

We described a new edition of the Google Books Ngram Corpus that provides syntactically annotated ngrams for eight languages. The data is available for download and viewable through an interactive web application at `http://books.google.com/ngrams`. We discussed the statistical models used to produce the syntactic annotations and how they were adapted to handle historical text more robustly, resulting in significantly improved annotation quality. Analyzing the resulting data is beyond the scope of this paper, but we show some example plots in Figure 3.

References

M. Davies. 2011. Google Books (American English) Corpus (155 billion words, 1810-2009). In *http://googlebooks.byu.edu/*.

M.-C. de Marneffe, B. MacCartney, and C. Manning. 2006. Generating typed dependency parses from phrase structure parses. In *Proc. of LREC*.

W. N. Francis and H. Kucera. 1979. Manual of information to accompany a standard corpus of present-day edited American English. Technical report, Brown University.

J. Judge, A. Cahill, and J. van Genabith. 2006. Questionbank: Creating a corpus of parse-annotated questions. In *Proc. of ACL*.

A. Kroch, B. Santorini, and A. Diertani. 2010. Penn parsed corpus of modern british english. Technical report, LDC.

J. Lafferty, A. McCallum, and F. Pereira. 2001. Conditional random fields: Probabilistic models for segmenting and labeling sequence data. In *Proc. of ICML*.

E. Lieberman, J.-B. Michel, J. Jackson, T. Tang, and M. A. Nowak. 2007. Quantifying the evolutionary dynamics of language. *Nature*.

C. Manning. 2011. Part-of-speech tagging from 97% to 100%: is it time for some linguistics? *Proc. of CICLing*.

M. P. Marcus, M. A. Marcinkiewicz, and B. Santorini. 1993. Building a large annotated corpus of English: the Penn treebank. *Computational Linguistics*, 19.

J.-B. Michel, Y. K. Shen, A. P. Aiden, A. Veres, M. K. Gray, The Google Books Team, J. P. Pickett, D. Hoiberg, D. Clancy, P. Norvig, J. Orwant, S. Pinker, M. A. Nowak, and E. Lieberman Aiden. 2011. Quantitative analysis of culture using millions of digitized books. *Science*.

J. Nivre and J. Nilsson. 2005. Pseudo-projective dependency parsing. In *Proc. of ACL*.

J. Nivre. 2008. Algorithms for deterministic incremental dependency parsing. *Computational Linguistics*, 34(4):513–553.

S. Petrov, D. Das, and R. McDonald. 2012. A universal part-of-speech tagset. In *Proc. of LREC*.

M. Ravallion. 2011. The two poverty enlightenments: Historical insights from digitized books spanning three centuries. *Poverty And Public Policy*.

J. Uszkoreit and T. Brants. 2008. Distributed word clustering for large scale class-based language modeling in machine translation. In *Proc. of ACL*.

Author Index